HC
151
.T75
2009

A WORLD BANK COUNTRY STUDY

Accelerating Trade and Integration in the Caribbean

Policy Options for Sustained Growth, Job Creation, and Poverty Reduction

Yvonne Tsikata
Emmanuel Pinto Moreira
Pamela Coke Hamilton

Document of the World Bank and the Organization of American States, co-produced with the Governments of CARIFORUM Countries

THE WORLD BANK
Washington, D.C.

ORGANIZATION OF AMERICAN STATES
Washington, D.C.

Copyright © 2009
The International Bank for Reconstruction and Development/The World Bank
1818 H Street, N.W.
Washington, D.C. 20433, U.S.A.
All rights reserved
Manufactured in the United States of America
First Printing: June 2009

 printed on recycled paper

1 2 3 4 5 12 11 10 09
World Bank Country Studies are among the many reports originally prepared for internal use as part of the continuing analysis by the Bank of the economic and related conditions of its developing member countries and to facilitate its dialogs with the governments. Some of the reports are published in this series with the least possible delay for the use of governments, and the academic, business, financial, and development communities. The manuscript of this paper therefore has not been prepared in accordance with the procedures appropriate to formally-edited texts. Some sources cited in this paper may be informal documents that are not readily available.

The findings, interpretations, and conclusions expressed herein are those of the author(s) and do not necessarily reflect the views of the International Bank for Reconstruction and Development/The World Bank and its affiliated organizations, or those of the Executive Directors of The World Bank or the governments they represent.

The World Bank does not guarantee the accuracy of the data included in this work. The boundaries, colors, denominations, and other information shown on any map in this work do not imply any judgment on the part of The World Bank of the legal status of any territory or the endorsement or acceptance of such boundaries.

The material in this publication is copyrighted. Copying and/or transmitting portions or all of this work without permission may be a violation of applicable law. The International Bank for Reconstruction and Development/The World Bank encourages dissemination of its work and will normally grant permission promptly to reproduce portions of the work.

For permission to photocopy or reprint any part of this work, please send a request with complete information to the Copyright Clearance Center, Inc., 222 Rosewood Drive, Danvers, MA 01923, USA, Tel: 978-750-8400, Fax: 978-750-4470, www.copyright.com.

All other queries on rights and licenses, including subsidiary rights, should be addressed to the Office of the Publisher, The World Bank, 1818 H Street NW, Washington, DC 20433, USA, Fax: 202-522-2422, email: pubrights@worldbank.org.

ISBN-13: 978-0-8213-8017-8
eISBN: 978-0-8213-8019-2
ISSN: 0253-2123   DOI: 10.1596/978-0-8213-8017-8

Cover photos: Early evening over St. George's harbour by Lawrence Worcester/ Lonely Planet Images. St. George's Market Square courtesy Grenada Board of Tourism.

Library of Congress Cataloging-in-Publication Data
Accelerating trade and integration in the Caribbean : policy options for sustained growth, job creation, and poverty reduction.
    p. cm. -- (A World Bank country study)
  "Document of the World Bank and the Organization of American States, co-produced with the Governments of CARIFORUM Countries."
  Includes bibliographical references.
  ISBN 978-0-8213-8017-8 -- ISBN 978-0-8213-8019-2 (electronic)
  1. Caribbean Area--Economic integration. 2. Free trade--Caribbean Area. 3. Caribbean Area--Economic policy. I. World Bank. II. Organization of American States. III. Caribbean Forum.
  HC151.A53 2009
  337.1'7729--dc22
                                                                    2009015959

Contents

LIST OF FIGURES

LIST OF BOXS

Foreword

Almost five years ago the World Bank issued a flagship report entitled *A Time to Choose: Caribbean Development in the 21st Century* with the observation that "the Caribbean region is at a development crossroads and its member nations must take significant and concrete steps to improve productivity and competitiveness and face up to more global competition. . . . By [doing so], they will reposition themselves strategically as an emerging trading bloc for goods and services; without such action, they risk growing economic marginalization and erosion of many of the social gains of the last three decades." Notably, this report was issued long before the conclusion of the Economic Partnership Agreement (EPA), signed by CARICOM member states in October 2008, before the advent of the global economic crisis that has severely undermined the economic stability of the small vulnerable economies of the Caribbean and before the reintroduction of the tax haven laws in the US Congress which have the potential to decimate the foreign exchange earnings and tax base of many of these economies.

The Caribbean therefore is no longer at a development crossroads. The time to choose is now long past and, in a sense, the choices have already been made. Time is no longer on the region's side and the requirement at this juncture is to significantly accelerate the pace of regional integration if the Caribbean is to survive and achieve growth in the face of the economic challenges it faces. Despite enormous internal pressures, Caribbean countries must steadfastly resist the temptation to surrender to insularity as, while it may appear to resolve short-term challenges, it will only serve to destroy the fabric of regional integration which remains the only viable course for sustained development and competitiveness for these small states.

This volume builds on the foundation laid by the 2005 Report by focusing on the factors affecting the region's competitiveness and the critical role that the Caribbean Single Market and Economy (CSME) has to play as a driver of integration and economic development. In addition it highlights the potential of the EPA, if properly implemented, to significantly increase the region's competitiveness and to help it attain long-term sustained development. This potential, however, will only be realized if precise trade and competitiveness strategies are crafted to focus primarily on removing the constraints to competitiveness endemic in the region. In addition, and this is a critical element of any newly-devised strategy, is the necessity to revise regional institutional mechanisms and mandates to promote implementation and to take advantage of the market access opportunities presented by successive trade agreements such as the EPA.

This report, while highlighting the need for immediate and concrete actions on the part of the CARICOM member states, also recognizes the responsibility of the donor community in helping to play a catalytic role in supporting trade reform and macroeconomic stability. The Aid for Trade agenda must seek to address the weaknesses inherent in the formulation and application of international aid policies and implement new frameworks aimed at enhancing the ability of these small nation states to meet and overcome the challenges of global competitiveness.

Finally, this report has benefitted from the input of many of the region's best minds and intensive consultations with all stakeholders across the public sector, private sector, and civil society. We are indebted to these individuals and institutions and we hope that we have accurately and adequately reflected their ideas, observations and expert knowledge. In the final analysis, however, the full responsibility for the conclusions presented in this publication rests with our two organizations.

Yvonne Tsikata
Director
Latin American and Caribbean Region
World Bank

Pamela Coke Hamilton
Director
Department of Trade and Tourism
Organization of American States

Acknowledgments

This report is a joint report of the World Bank, the Organization of American States (OAS) and the Governments of the CARIFORUM countries. The report is a product of a year of teamwork and dialogue between World Bank/OAS staff and many people and institutions in Caribbean countries: the Caribbean Regional Negotiating Machinery (CRNM), the CARICOM Secretariat, the private sector, Non-Government Organizations (NGOs), academia, and bilateral and multilateral donors.

Two key events were organized to launch this trade report. In October 2007, the World Bank and OAS staffs organized a brainstorming session with the Head of the CRNM. This was followed two months later by another brainstorming session between Bank/OAS staff and the staff of the CARICOM Secretariat. The proposed scope and issues covered in this trade report reflect the outcomes of the discussions during those sessions. The report also benefitted largely from the outcomes of the conference on "Aid for Trade" organized by the staff of OAS in June 2008 in Kingston (Jamaica). The outcomes of these three important events help to lay the foundations and the strategic directions of the report.

The team would like to thank the following for their excellent collaboration throughout the preparation of the report: His Excellency Ambassador Richard Bernal (former Head of the CRNM); Ambassador Henry Gill (Head of the CRNM); Ambassador Irwin LaRocque (Assistant Secretary-General, Trade and Economic Integration, CARICOM Secretariat); David Hales (Program Manager, External Economic and Trade Relations, CARICOM Secretariat); Philomen Harrison (Project Director, Regional Statistics, CARICOM Secretariat); Timothy Odle (Deputy Program Manager, Statistics, CARICOM Secretariat); Margaret Kalloo (Deputy Programme Manager, Agricultural Development, CARICOM Secretariat); Enid Bissember (Deputy Program Manager, Economic Intelligence, CARICOM Secretariat); David Lord (Deputy Program Manager, External Economic and Trade Relations, CARICOM Secretariat); Desmond Simon (Senior Project Officer, Economic and Development Policy and Research, CARICOM Secretariat); Bernard Black (Senior Project Officer, Customs and Trade Policy, CARICOM Secretariat).

The team benefitted from the advice, guidance, and support of Benu Bidani (Lead Economist, LCC3, World Bank), Rodrigo Chaves (Sector Manager, LCSPE, World Bank), and Errol Graham (Senior Economist, AFTP4, World Bank). The team is grateful to Bernard Hoekman (Sector Director, PRMTR, World Bank) for his guidance and suggestions, which helped to define the topics and issues covered in the report. The team is particularly grateful to Pierre-Richard Agénor (Hallsworth Professor of International Macroeconomics and Development Economics, University of Manchester, and co-Director, Center for Growth and Business Cycle Research, United Kingdom) for his technical guidance, invaluable inputs, and suggestions throughout the preparation of the report. The team would also like to thank Sherman Robinson and Michael Gasiorek of the Institute of Development Studies (IDS, Sussex University, UK) for their technical assistance. The team is grateful to Yvonne Tsikata (Country Director for the Caribbean Countries, LCC3C, World Bank) for her constant support throughout the preparation of the report.

The task team leader and author of the report is Emmanuel Pinto Moreira (Senior Economist, LCSPE, World Bank). The OAS team leader is Pamela Coke-Hamilton (Director, Trade and Tourism, OAS). The report core team led by Emmanuel Pinto Moreira includes

Pierre-Richard Agénor (University of Manchester, UK); Sherman Robinson and Michael Gasiorek (Institute of Development Studies, and University of Sussex, UK); Caroline Freund (Senior Economist, DECRG, World Bank); Yolanda Strachan (Research Analyst, PRMTR, World Bank); Annelle Bellony (Summer Intern, LCC3C, World Bank); Daniel Cooper (Junior Professional Associate, LCC3C, World Bank); and Martha Garcia (Assistant, LCSPE, World Bank).

Valuable contributions were also provided by Paul Brenton (Senior Economist, PRMTR, World Bank); Peter Walkenshorst (Senior Economist, PRMTR, World Bank); Mathurin Gbetibouo (Resident Representative, LCCHT, World Bank); Pamela Coke-Hamilton (Director, Trade and Tourism, OAS); Maryse Robert (Trade Section Chief, OAS); and Reshma Mahabir (Trade Specialist, OAS).

Peer reviewers were Bernard Hoekman (Sector Director, PRMTR, World Bank); Salomon Samen (Senior Economist, WBIPR, World Bank); and David Tarr (Former Lead Economist and Consultant, DECRG, World Bank).

	IDA
Vice President:	Pamela Cox
Country Director	Yvonne Tsikata
Sector Director	Marcelo Guigale
Sector Manager:	Rodrigo Chaves
Task Manager and Author of the report:	Emmanuel Pinto Moreira
	OAS
Director:	Pamela Coke-Hamilton
Section Chief:	Maryse Robert
Trade Specialist:	Reshma Mahabir

Abbreviations and Acronyms

AGOA	Africa Growth and Opportunity Act
CAFTA-DR	Dominican-Republic Central America Free Trade Agreement
CARICOM	Caribbean Community
CARIFORUM	Caribbean Forum of ACP States
CARICRIS	Caribbean Credit Ratings Services Company
CARIFTA	Caribbean Free Trade Association
CARTAC	Caribbean Regional Technical Assistance Center
CBERA	Caribbean Basin Economic Recovery Act
CBI	Caribbean Basin Initiative
CBTPA	Caribbean Basin Trade Partnership Act
CCJ	Caribbean Court of Justice
CCMF	Caribbean Centre for Money and Finance
CDB	Caribbean Development Bank
CDERA	Caribbean Disaster Emergency Response Agency
CEDA	Caribbean Export Development Agency
CET	Common External Tariff
CFD	Caribbean Forum for Development (formerly CGCED)
CGE	Computable General Equilibrium
CIC	CARICOM Investment Code
CIDA	Canadian International Development Agency
COFAP	CARICOM Ministerial Council for Finance and Planning
COHSOD	CARICOM Council for Human and Social Development
COTED	CARICOM Council for Trade and Economic Development
CREP	Caribbean Renewable Energy Development Programme
CRNM	Caribbean Regional Negotiating Machinery
CROSQ	Caribbean Regional Organization for Standards and Quality
CSME	CARICOM Single Market Economy
CXC	Caribbean Examination Council
DFID	Department for International Development (UK)
EC	European Community
ECCB	Eastern Caribbean Central Bank
ECLAC	Economic Commission for Latin America and the Caribbean
EDF	European Development Fund
EPA	Economic Partnership Agreement
ESI	Export Specialization Index
EU	European Union
FDI	Foreign Direct Investment
FSO	Fund Special Operations
FTAA	Free Trade Area of the Americas
FTZ	Free Trade Zone
GATS	General Agreement on Trade and Services
GDP	Gross Domestic Product
HDI	Human Development Index

HHI	Herfindahl and Hirschman Index
HOPE Act	Haitian Hemispheric Opportunity through Partnership Encouragement Act
ICT	Information and Communications Technology
IDS	Institute of Development Studies
IFMAS	Integrated Financial Management and Accounting System
IIRSA	Initiative for Integration of Regional Infrastructure in South America
IMF	International Monetary Fund
INT	Integration and Regional Programs Department
INTAL	Institute for the Integration of Latin America and the Caribbean
ITD	Integration, Trade and Hemispheric Issues Division
LAC	Latin America and Caribbean
LDC	Less Developed Country (in CARICOM)
MDC	More Developed Country (in CARICOM)
MDG	Millennium Development Goal
MDRI	Multilateral Debt Relief Initiative
MFN	Most Favored Nation
MIF	Multilateral Investment Fund
NAFTA	North America Free Trade Agreement
OAS	Organization of American States
OECD	Organization for Economic Co-operation and Development
OECS	Organisation of Eastern Caribbean States
PRSP	Poverty Reduction Strategy Paper
RDF	Regional Development Fund
RIM	Regional Implementation Mechanism
RPTF	Regional Preparation Task Force
SME	Small and Medium-Sized Enterprises
SPAHD	Strategy Paper for Human Development
UNDP	United Nations Development Program
USAID	United States Agency for International Development
UWI	University of the West Indies
VAT	Value Added Tax
WDI	World Development Indicator
WIC	West Indian Commission
WITS	World Integrated Trade Solution
WTO	World Trade Organization

Executive Summary

Summary of Main Messages and Key Findings of the Report

The Caribbean Has Improved Human Development Outcomes Significantly over the Past Two Decades. But its Integration into the World Economy is Now Declining.

Over the past two decades, the Caribbean[1] has experienced significant human development improvement in all countries except Haiti (World Bank 2005a). Life expectancy has improved significantly. The Human Development Index (HDI) has improved steadily since 1980 for all countries for which information is available. At present, with the exception of Haiti, all countries rank among the medium and high HDI categories. Progress towards meeting the Millennium Development Goals (MDGs) has been quite good. Most countries (except Haiti) are likely to achieve universal primary school enrollment. Similarly, the region scores very high in terms of eliminating gender disparity in primary and secondary schools.[2] The goal of reducing child mortality rates by two-thirds by 2015 is on track for all countries, with seven having already achieved the goal.

The region also experienced relatively good growth performance, aided by massive flows of foreign direct investment, trade preferences, and public investment. Real GDP grew by 3.6 percent over the 1997–2006 period, driven mainly by the strong performance of Trinidad and Tobago (8.6 percent), Belize (6.2 percent), and the Dominican Republic (6.0 percent). Growth in OECS countries was relatively strong as well, averaging 3.5 percent over 1997–2006. This outcome reflects mainly the good performace of Antigua and Barbuda (4.8 percent) and Grenada (4.3 percent) (see Chapter 1).

However, the Caribbean region has not grown as fast as some comparable high per-forming developing countries and the long-run growth record of the region does not com-pare favorably with the best performing African countries (see Figure 1). Average GDP per capita (PPP) for the Caribbean fell below that of Botswana and Mauritius, in the mid-1990s (see Figure 2). Growth performance has also varied widely across countries of the region and has been highly volatile (see Figure 1). Those that have had the highest trend growth in the long-run are: St Kitts and Nevis, St. Vincent and the Grenadines, Grenada, and Antigua and Barbuda. The slowest growing countries in the region over the last decade were Haiti, Jamaica, and Guyana. Moreover, growth performance has not translated into higher employment, and unemployment has been a dominant feature of the labor market in many Caribbean countries.

In the current context, economic growth in the Caribbean countries is expected to slow down relative to 2007 as these economies have been hit hard by recent shocks including a reces-sion in the U.S. economy, the global financial crisis, and a period of high food and fuel prices—although prices are currently declining. As for most Caribbean countries, the economy and

---

1. In this study, the Caribbean is defined as comprising the OECS group—Antigua and Barbuda, Dominica, Grenada, St. Kitts and Nevis, St. Lucia, and St. Vincent and the Grenadines—as well as The Bahamas, Belize, Barbados, Dominican Republic, Guyana, Haiti, Jamaica, Suriname, and Trinidad and Tobago.
2. It is worth mentioning that the indicators used to measure this goal are believed not to capture per-sistent gender inequality (UNDP 2003).

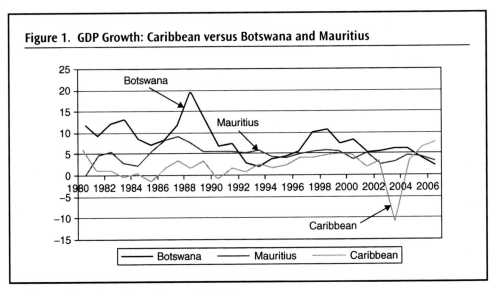

Figure 1. GDP Growth: Caribbean versus Botswana and Mauritius

Source: World Bank. World Development Indicators.

financial system are very dependent of the U.S. economy and financial markets conditions. Estimates of GDP growth in Jamaica have been revised down to between 0 and 1 percent for 2008, and 2 to 3 percent for 2007; in Haiti down to around 2 percent for 2008 from 3.7 percent in 2007; in the Dominican Republic to 5–6 percent in 2008 compared to 7–8 percent in 2007; and in the OECS 4.6 percent for 2007 compared to 7.2 percent in 2006. The main channels of transmission of the financial crisis to the economy are through (i) tourism, (ii) remittances, (iii) exports, (iv) reduced ability of highly indebted government to access financial market to fulfill their borrowing needs, (v) heightened cost of financing for the corporate sector,

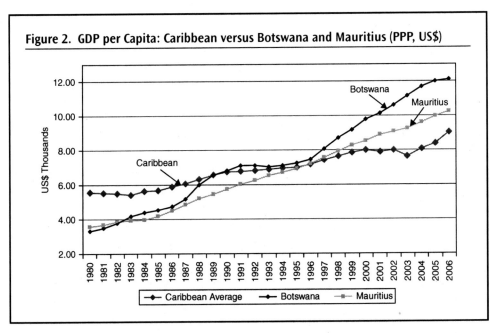

Figure 2. GDP per Capita: Caribbean versus Botswana and Mauritius (PPP, US$)

Source: World Bank. World Development Indicators.

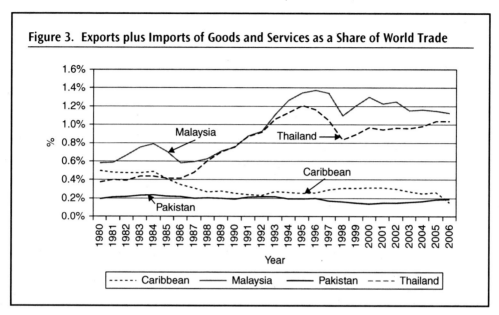

Figure 3. Exports plus Imports of Goods and Services as a Share of World Trade

Source: World Bank. World Development Indicators.

(vi) reduced FDI flows and capital flows affecting investment and most likely growth, and (vii) margin calls from foreign banks' parent company further drying up domestic liquidity.

For the past three decades the Caribbean has pursued an external trade policy anchored on unilateral preferential access to the European and North American markets. Under the Lomé and Cotonou agreements, Caribbean countries received unilateral preferential access to the EU for traditional agricultural exports. Similarly, the region has enjoyed 30 years of unilateral preferential access to the United States for certain products under the Caribbean Basin Initiative (CBI) and subsequently through the Caribbean Basin Trade Partnership Act (CBTPA)[3]. These preferential agreements have shaped the Caribbean external trade structure.

Caribbean countries are generally very open economies. Trade as a percentage of GDP averaged more than 110 percent for the region over the period. By this measure, Haiti is the least open country while Guyana is the most dependent on trade. On average, the OECS countries are more open than the rest of the region. The region nearly doubled its merchandise exports between 2000 and 2005, driven in large part by the surge in oil and natural gas exports from Trinidad and Tobago. In contrast, over the past 10 years, merchandise exports in Dominica, St. Lucia, and St. Vincent, measured in real US$ terms, declined by up to 40 percent due to preference erosion.

Although unilateral preferential trading arrangements were established as a development tool to stimulate and diversify Caribbean exports, the prevailing consensus is that ". . . trade preferences have not delivered expected results . . . they have not helped overall trade performance" (World Bank 2005a).

Despite trade preferences, the Caribbean's integration into the world economy has been slow and compares poorly with some Asian countries with similar levels of integration 30 years ago (see Figure 3). The Caribbean's share of world trade has also been declining

---

3. The Caribbean Basin Trade Partnership Act was extended in June 2008 and is in effect until September 30, 2010. It continues to provide preferential access for Caribbean Basin countries to the United States.

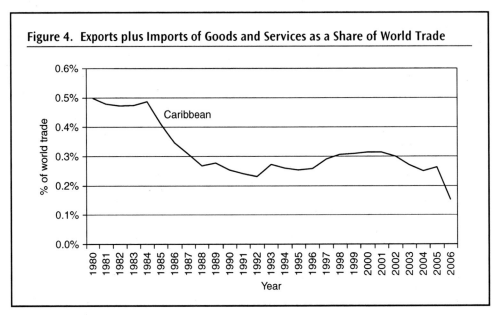

Figure 4. Exports plus Imports of Goods and Services as a Share of World Trade

Source: World Bank. World Development Indicators.

while countries such as Malaysia and Thailand have increased their share (see Figure 3 and 4). Weaknesses in access and low quality of infrastructure together with low labor productivity have resulted in relatively high production costs compared to competitor countries of Asia. Sugar exports and production in the Caribbean have declined by about half since 1970 owing to rising costs of production, resulting from rising wages, deteriorating field and factory performance and increasing inefficiencies associated with public sector control and management. Estimated costs of producing and exporting sugar in Guyana and Belize, the lowest cost producers in the Caribbean, are 50 to 60 percent higher than one of the higher cost free market exporters (see Figure 5). World sugar production costs have fallen by about 40 percent in real terms since 1980, while those in the Caribbean have been rising, and preferential quota prices have also been falling. Similarly, in bananas, the Caribbean countries are amongst the highest cost production in the world, rooted in low land productivity, and higher labor and transportation costs. For instance, St. Lucia, Jamaica and Dominica have yields that are 20–35 percent of Ecuador's (see Figure 6).

The Region's Competitiveness is Weak and Export Concentration is Relatively High

The region's competitiveness is low reflecting its high costs of doing business, labor market rigidities, tariff dispersion, and trade costs. Most of the Caribbean countries' overall performance of doing business ranks below that of comparable developing countries, including Mauritius, Hong Kong, Malaysia, and Singapore (see Table 1 below).

Time for and cost to export of most Caribbean countries, are relatively higher than those of comparable countries. For instance the cost to export of Trinidad and Tobago (best performer of the region) is higher to that of Vietnam (the second worst performer of the

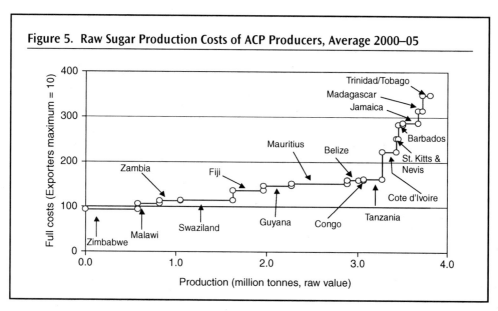

Figure 5. Raw Sugar Production Costs of ACP Producers, Average 2000–05

Source: World Bank (2005a).

selected comparable sample of countries). The same observation applies to time for and costs to import. Wages and non-wage costs are relatively high in the Caribbean, and have constrained competitiveness. In addition, the quality of Caribbean production and exports is relatively low as reflected in low technological intensity of exports. Available data suggest that for CARICOM, primary products accounted for 42 percent of exports in 1985 and 37 percent in 2000, while high technology manufactures declined from only 6 percent of exports in 1985 to 1.4 percent in 2000 (see Table 2). In East and South-East Asia, foreign

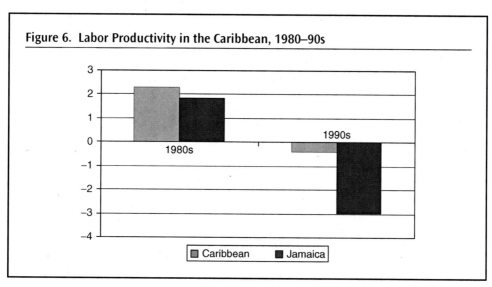

Figure 6. Labor Productivity in the Caribbean, 1980–90s

Source: World Bank (2005a).

Table 1. Doing Business: Selected Indicators Caribbean and Comparable
            Developing Countries

Country	Overall Doing Business Rank 2008	Overall Trading Across Borders Rank 2008	Time for Export (Days)		Cost to Export (US$ per Container)		Time for Export (Days)		Cost to Import (US$ per Container)	
			2007	2008	2007	2008	2007	2008	2007	2008
Caribbean										
Antigua and Barbuda	41	55	13	19	1,057	1,107	15	19	1,467	1,174
Belize	59	116	23	23	1,800	1,800	26	26	2,130	2,130
Dominica	77	80	11	16	1,478	1,197	17	18	1,512	1,107
Dominican Republic	99	35	17	12	770	815	17	13	990	1,015
Grenada	70	52	19	19	820	820	23	23	1,178	1,178
Guyana	104	101	30	30	850	850	35	35	856	856
Haiti	148	153	52	52	1,650	1,650	53	53	1,860	1,860
Jamaica	63	92	21	21	1,750	1,750	22	22	1,350	1,350
St. Kitts and Nevis	64	22	15	15	750	750	17	17	756	756
St. Lucia	34	88	18	18	1,375	1,375	21	21	1,420	1,420
St. Vincent and the Grenadines	54	75	15	15	1,770	1,770	16	16	1,769	1,769
Trinidad and Tobago	67	49	14	14	693	693	26	26	1,100	1,100
Comparators										
LAC Average	—	—	23	22	1080	1107	28	26	1,236	1,228
East Asia Average	—	—	26	24	778	775	28	25	945	917
Hong Kong, China	4	3	6	6	525	525	5	5	525	525
Malaysia	24	21	18	18	432	432	14	14	385	385
Mauritius	27	17	16	17	683	728	16	16	683	673
Singapore	1	1	5	5	416	416	3	3	367	367
Thailand	15	50	24	17	848	615	22	14	1,042	786
Vietnam	91	63	24	24	669	669	23	23	881	881

Source: Bank staff based on various Doing Business reports.

direct investment inflows helped to propel the diversification of the economies into high-quality, high value added manufacturing.

Recent analyses suggest that the Caribbean's exports may be moving down the value ladder. The average wage of exports declined in the Caribbean by about one percent, while it increased in LAC in the last ten years. Table 3 below shows the similarity of export structure between the Caribbean countries and their main trade partners.[4] It provides an indication

---

4. An index of 100 reflects identical structures and an index of 0 reflects very different structures.

Table 2. Exports Structure by Technological Intensity (percent of exports)

	Primary Products		Natural resource Based Manufactures		Low Technology Manufactures		Intermediate Technology Manufactures		High Technology Manufactures	
	1985	2000	1985	2000	1985	2000	1985	2000	1985	2000
CARICOM	41.7	37.4	39.3	34.9	5.4	10.2	5.7	11.6	6.0	1.4
Costa Rica	67.2	29.1	7.9	8.5	14.5	17.1	6.5	8.3	3.2	34.3
Taiwan Rep. of China	5.0	1.3	9.1	4.8	48.2	21.8	20.7	25.0	15.9	45.5

Source: Bank staff based on ECLAC data.

Note: The totals do not add up to 100% as the residual is accounted for by unclassified products.

of how much countries are likely to compete with one another. It shows that the Caribbean's export structure is very similar to Central America's, especially for Antigua and Barbuda, Jamaica, and Suriname. However, for the other trade partners competition is relatively weak. In the last column, the similarity with the rest of the Caribbean (i.e. the Caribbean total excluding the countries own exports) is shown for each exporter. Even among Caribbean countries, there is little similarity in export structure. Since 1997, export similarity has remained roughly constant. The Caribbean region countries look more different from China, that is, they are competing less with China now than in 1997, and have become more similar to Central America.

The analysis of the region's export structure shows increased concentration of products. In 1997, the top 20 products account for 51 percent of total exports; and this share increased to 70 percent in 2006.[5] The increase in concentration appears to be related to a decreasing dependence on bananas but increased dependence on fuels and metals as a source of foreign exchange, particularly in Trinidad and Tobago. A breakdown of the top 20 exports to the world during 2001–06 shows that four are agricultural and food products, six are minerals and ores, four are manufactures and six are a fuel-related product. The export concentration of individual CARICOM member states varies significantly. Export structures are most concentrated in The Bahamas (90 percent), St. Kitts and Nevis (85 percent), Suriname (94 percent), and Trinidad and Tobago (87 percent).[6]

Binding constraints to competitiveness include labor market rigidities, tariff dispersion, and trade costs (see Chapter 3). Labor markets in CARICOM member states are characterized by relatively high wages. This reflects mainly the fact that most of the Caribbean countries are middle-income countries, their links with the United States labor market which for many workers is an outside option, as well as their low flexibility compared to other middle-income countries. Problems arise from two sources. First, high wages across skill levels and sectors appears to be rising faster than productivity and are reflected in high unemployment rates. Second, the sub-region suffers from skill mismatching and shortages.

---

5. Using HS 6-digit mirror data.

6. This refers to the top five exports, which account for the highest share of total exports at the SITC 4-digit level.

Table 3. The Similarity between Caribbean Exports and Partners' Exports

Export Similarity Index 2005

Country	ESISA	ESICA	ESIUSA	ESIChina	ESIEU	ESIJapan	ESI Caribbean
Antigua and Barbuda	6.42	88.03	6.31	5.12	6.35	5.39	7.98
Bahamas	6.75	38.95	7.48	2.94	10.90	8.13	18.44
Barbados	18.52	15.08	15.01	8.65	19.57	9.69	28.17
Belize	10.98	21.29	8.27	6.44	9.53	6.83	19.53
Dominica	9.62	28.43	12.51	7.98	13.00	8.85	12.18
Dominican Rep.	9.41	28.28	14.49	18.00	13.20	10.26	11.49
Grenada	4.53	12.72	8.43	4.19	8.72	7.37	7.88
Guyana	8.52	32.47	4.24	3.34	4.82	2.43	7.31
Haiti	4.22	7.04	4.27	5.64	3.94	2.54	7.98
Jamaica	7.77	79.11	7.11	4.78	7.60	5.36	14.74
Saint Kitts and Nevis	4.12	6.01	9.07	7.57	10.57	11.48	6.75
Saint Lucia	7.11	11.93	9.05	4.13	10.84	6.91	19.17
Saint Vincent and the Grenadines	4.67	43.19	3.84	3.41	4.46	4.47	10.34
Suriname	6.87	60.65	4.27	2.53	4.02	2.12	10.45
Trinidad and Tobago	20.74	39.46	6.95	4.14	9.09	4.27	10.13
Caribbean (aggregate)	22.42	48.01	15.58	13.89	18.14	10.91	1.00
Caribbean (average)	8.68	34.18	8.09	5.92	9.11	6.41	12.84

Export Similarity Index 1997

Country	ESISA	ESICA	ESIUSA	ESIChina	ESIEU	ESIJapan	ESI Car 97
Antigua and Barbuda	20.59	49.49	9.28	7.42	9.86	8.32	13.68
Bahamas	8.31	33.36	6.13	5.84	7.00	6.08	12.11
Barbados	8.18	20.62	12.95	9.26	13.83	10.63	12.76
Belize	9.97	27.58	4.90	4.41	4.91	2.90	7.04
Dominica	11.58	25.43	13.41	9.07	15.22	10.31	9.01
Dominican Rep.	10.01	24.87	9.24	17.55	10.77	5.94	4.88
Grenada	4.43	11.90	5.15	4.09	5.86	4.40	6.63
Guyana	6.18	32.55	4.15	4.02	4.12	1.57	6.97
Haiti	7.61	22.59	4.53	11.25	5.32	2.65	9.85
Jamaica	11.21	23.87	7.00	9.89	9.10	4.39	17.85
Saint Kitts and Nevis	3.61	6.67	7.53	4.57	7.31	7.56	3.82
Saint Lucia	17.36	31.67	6.40	8.51	7.46	4.33	12.22
Saint Vincent and the Grenadines	6.26	49.67	7.00	8.20	7.94	8.38	10.64
Suriname	14.44	19.76	4.40	4.59	4.19	2.24	15.07
Trinidad and Tobago	22.04	43.47	8.01	7.87	11.19	4.63	20.03
Caribbean (aggregate)	21.17	38.42	14.23	21.99	17.79	9.64	100.00
Caribbean (average)	10.79	28.23	7.34	7.77	8.27	5.62	10.84

Source: Comtrade HS 6-digit 1992 classification and authors' calculation.

While there has been significant tariff reduction and tariff alignment in the Caribbean, there is still important tariff dispersion. The Bahamas, Barbados and Dominica still have more than 50 tariff lines with tariffs over 50 percent. Most of the tariff peaks are on agricultural products. In addition, there are high tariffs on beverages, and on manufactured goods. Trade costs are relatively high in the Caribbean, potentially impeding trade. Overall average Caribbean freight and insurance costs to the United States are relatively high, at 9.4 percent of total product cost in 2005–06. It is estimated that on average a country that exports the same composition of goods as the Caribbean faces lower trade costs of nearly 3 percentage points (see Chapter 3).

The small size of the Caribbean economies also limits the region's competitiveness. Economies of scale are limited as production capacity of most of the countries is limited to small scale. As the result, unit costs are relatively higher than comparable developing countries.

National Trade Policies Remain Weak and Have Had Mixed Outcomes

There has been significant tariff reduction and tariff alignment in the Caribbean. Average applied MFN tariffs fell from over 20 percent in 1996 to just below 10 percent in 2005. Still, there is some tariff dispersion, with average tariffs on 10 percent of goods over 20 percent. While the progress to date is admirable, there is still room for further reduction of tariffs and more uniformity in some of the countries.

While many Caribbean countries (most notably Trinidad and Tobago, Dominica Republic, and Jamaica) have undertaken policy measures to improve their trade policy, important weaknesses remain in five major areas: (i) measures affecting imports; (ii) measures affecting exports; (iii) investment incentives; (iv) competition policy; and (v) trade policy formulation and implementation.

Customs procedures and administration are weak in most Caribbean countries. Customs valuation methods are not effective because of limited capacity at the customs departments in many Caribbean countries. With the exception of Trinidad and Tobago and Dominican Republic, export procedures and financing are not well developed in the Caribbean. Exporters have limited access to credits for exports and credit insurance. Export promotion activities (export facilitation, information, image-building, and participation in fairs) are barely developed.

The legal framework for businesses including taxation is weak in many Caribbean countries. Registration time of businesses is relatively long and registration fees are relatively high. Taxation systems need improvements. Many Caribbean countries apply a range of incentives to promote investment, including duty concessions, tax exemptions and holidays, loss write-offs, and training support. However, most of them have not developed a comprehensive investment strategy.

A comprehensive competition policy does not exist in most of the Caribbean countries. Trinidad and Tobago (the most advanced country of the region) does not have a comprehensive competition policy legislation, although efforts to enhance the regulatory framework and reinforce consumer protection have been developed in recent years. Because of the relatively small size of the domestic market of many Caribbean countries, the level of competition in many areas is low, and *de facto* monopolies are present, particularly in services.

National institutions in charge of trade policy formulation and implementation are weak. Ministry of commerce and industry and trade institutions lack staff and expertise in policy formulation. Linked to the limited expertise is the limited negotiation power. As a result trade agreements either bilateral or multilateral are negotiated and signed with little awareness of their implications. A point in case is the recently negotiated CARIFORUM-EC Economic Partnership Agreement (EPA). Many Caribbean countries felt unprepared as they were engaging in a reciprocal trade negotiation. The entity responsible for leading CARICOM external trade negotiations such as the EPA, the Caribbean Regional Negotiating Machinery (CNRM), does not oversee the implementation of these agreements. In this context, implementation of trade agreements has generally been slow.

Trade policies have thus had limited outcomes. Trade costs are relatively high in the Caribbean, potentially impeding trade. Using world cost insurance freight (cif) Free-on-board (fob) ratios for the same composition of exports, the freight rate is only 6.6 percent. This implies that an average country that exports the same composition of goods as the Caribbean faces lower trade costs of nearly 3 percentage points. Similarly, trade costs were 7.8 percent for Central America in the same products in 2005–06.[7] Only Grenada and St. Vincent and the Grenadines have transport costs below the world average for the products that they export. In 60 percent of the 785 HS 6-digit products that the Caribbean exported to the United States their average freight and insurance costs were higher than world costs.

A New Global and Regional Trade Environment is Emerging with Critical Challenges to the Caribbean Countries which Face Large Fiscal and External Imbalances, High Level of Unemployment, and Major Structural Constraints . . .

The Caribbean is in the process of redefining its relations with its main trading partners, including the European Union and the United States, through the recently signed EPA and exploring the possibility of moving from unilateral to reciprocal arrangements with the United States and Canada. At the same time, the region is also redesigning the process of regional trade integration with the ongoing implementation of the Caribbean Single Market Economy (CSME). It is worth noting that this report does not prejudge in either way what the implications of the EPA would be for the Caribbean countries.[8] The two parallel processes (global integration and regional integration), which complement each other, will shape the region's trade environment during the next few years. But global integration is being conducted in a context of macroeconomic and financial imbalances. The region experienced large current account and fiscal deficits, as well as high levels of indebtedness, which in the past, slowed trade reforms and, are currently a major concern in the evolving trade environment (see Chapter 1). The fragility of the current macroeconomic and fiscal stance of most Caribbean countries raises the issue of the capacity of the region to afford the current pace of trade liberalization. Potential revenue losses raise the issue of the *sequencing*

---

7. Central America includes Costa Rica, El Salvador, Guatemala, Honduras, and Nicaragua.

8. A partial equilibrium modeling of the impact of the EPA on Caribbean countries was carried by M. Gasiorek and J. Chwiejczak (2007). It concludes that welfare gains associated with the liberalizations are typically very small. Under perfect competition the net welfare gain, depending on the underlying elasticities used, ranges from between 0.07% to 0.99% of base total imports. Under imperfect competition the welfare gains range from 0.45% to 1.48% when the monopoly profits accrue to the EU suppliers, and from 1.95% to 3.16% when the monopoly profits accrues to domestic distributors. In contrast full MFN liberalization, under perfect competition leads to higher welfare gains, at 2.69% of base imports on average for all CARIFORUM countries, and 2.26% for the OECS economies.

of trade reforms and the need of compensatory measures. It also calls for a reflection on the role that *foreign aid* could play as a *compensatory scheme* (see Chapters 1 and 7).

Global trade liberalization is also being done in a context of high unemployment in the Caribbean region. In contrast to human development indicators, high growth rates have not translated into increased employment. Unemployment rates are high, amounting to 10 percent on average for the region as a whole over 2002–06. Most of the countries (Bahamas, Barbados, Belize, Jamaica, and Suriname) exhibit double digit or nearly double digit unemployment rates on average over the past five years. Trinidad and Tobago appears to be the only exception to this trend. The issue for the Caribbean is to create jobs so as to reduce high unemployment rates and poverty. However, the potential social costs (loss of jobs in the sectors benefiting from trade preferences) associated with trade liberalization in the context of EPAs renders this objective more challenging—at least in the short term. Given this potential effect of EPAs, the need for fiscal adjustment, which may involve some reductions in public employment, and the continued decline in agriculture (still accounting for a significant share of the labor force), one of the key challenges will be to raise the skill levels of the poor and the unemployed, as well as the population in general. But this will take time. There may thus be an urgent need for the Caribbean to improve social protection and safety net programs during the transition period. The EPAs could offer a framework where these programs and social packages could be negotiated and put in place.

The current evolving trade environment is also constrained by structural weaknesses, most notably the poor level and quality of infrastructure of the region. Despite recent improvement, the region's level and quality of infrastructure remain weak. This, in turn, constitutes an important obstacle to both intra-regional and external trade. While some Caribbean countries, particularly Jamaica, Antigua and Barbuda, Bahamas, Barbados, and Trinidad and Tobago have levels of access to basic infrastructure that is better than what is predicted by income levels others including Haiti, still struggle with a poor infrastructure base. Intra-regional and external trade is also hampered by the poor quality of roads. With the exception of Barbados, Jamaica, and St. Vincent and the Grenadines, most of the Caribbean countries have low levels of paved roads (see Chapter 1). Transportation of goods suffers from the deteriorated condition of existing roads, which often lack basic maintenance services. The Caribbean countries have adequate physical infrastructure capacity in ports and runways. However, airport and port charges remain a small fraction of the total cost of transporting people and goods to and from Caribbean countries. Transports costs are thus relatively high and limit the potential for expanding regional trade.

Because of infrastructure, institutional and political constraints, intra-regional integration has been slow. The implementation of the common external tariff (CET), the cornerstone of the Caribbean Single Market (CSM), originally scheduled for 1981 has been delayed. The CET contains a number of loopholes and some countries have yet to apply it fully. There is wide dispersion in the range of actual tariffs implemented by CARICOM members on imports from non-members. This reflects the large number of exemptions from CET that CARICOM members can use. Average tariffs range from 7.2 percent in Jamaica to 30.7 percent in the Bahamas. Maximum tariffs are even more dispersed, ranging from 40 percent to 400 percent. Significant non tariff barriers (NTBs) appear to exist on certain categories of imported products from outside CARICOM. The Bahamas, where tariffs are about double the average rate in the Caribbean, has not joined the CSME. CARICOM reported several instances of discriminatory environmental taxes in Antigua and Barbuda, Barbados, Grenada, Belize, Guyana, and Dominica. Intra-regional trade is very limited and skewed toward few countries and products. Trinidad and Tobago has long been the dominant intra-regional exporter, with 85 percent of total exports. Barbados is the second largest exporter with only 6 percent of total exports, followed by Guyana with 4 percent. The OECS countries as a group account for about 5 percent of the value of intra-regional exports.

In sum, trade liberalization in the Caribbean is being implemented in a fragile macroeconomic and structural environment. Trade liberalization (and more specifically the EPA process) should pay more attention to these constraints, which go beyond trade issues per se and cover a large range of issues, such as macroeconomic imbalances, small economic size, infrastructure deficiencies, and economic vulnerability of the Caribbean. Thus, for many countries of the region, reaping the benefits of greater openness will require that complementary reforms and policies be implemented prior to, and in conjunction with, trade reform. Seen in this context, supporting trade adjustment and integration in the Caribbean will also require a shift toward more efficient transfer/assistance mechanisms with support directed at priority areas defined in national development plans and strategies. Put differently, if only from the perspective of the impact of infrastructure on trade performance, there is a strong case for an "aid for trade" strategy, as discussed in Appendix B. Failure to provide assistance will hamper the ability of Caribbean countries to respond to the opportunities that trade liberalization and integration can bring. At the same time, it must be recognized that although regional and global trade integration are key determinants of long-run growth and poverty reduction for all countries in the region, there are important differences among them that need to be considered in designing an "aid for trade" program for each individual country.

. . . Yet the New Trade Environment Offers Opportunities to the Caribbean

The new trade environment offers opportunities to the Caribbean to reposition itself as a growing and competitive region. Trade liberalization under the EPA may have significant economic and social gains for the Caribbean region. Simulations of the impact of the EPA on the Caribbean region show that the full application of the market access elements of the agreement (excluding sugar) leads to an increase (though small) in welfare as represented by a rise in absorption of 0.04 percent (see Table 4 and for more detail Chapter 6). Similarly, there is a small rise in demand for exports (0.76 percent), in demand for imports (0.4 percent), and in unskilled labor demand (0.29 percent). All but four sectors experience an increase in output, and most notably "vegetables, fruit and nuts" which benefits from the removal of a 30 percent EU import tariff and sees output rise by 4.4 percent in response to a rise in EU export demand by 25 percent.[9]

When the simulations include the removal of EU sugar tariffs, a similar pattern emerges of aggregate changes, with a slightly higher increase in aggregate absorption which is now 0.18 percent. Moreover, under a full liberalization of EU sugar imports the Caribbean producers are no longer quantity constrained and can increase their exports to the EU substantially. The changes in output are again slightly different when the changes in the EU sugar tariff are introduced– and not surprisingly this is particularly so for sugar cane

---

9. These results are those of the CGE GLOBE Model. See Chapter 6 for further details. It is worth noting that these simulations remain a theoretical exercise. The results therefore should be taken with caution. Nonetheless, they provide a good indication of potential effects of the EPA in Caribbean countries using rigorous quantitative frameworks.

Table 4. Aggregate Results with Balanced Macro, Factor Tax Adjustment, Unemployed Unskilled Labor

Trade Policy Scenarios	CARIB 4	CARIB 5	CARIB 10	CARIB 11
% Change on Reference Equilibrium	Bilateral Tariff Reduction 2033	Bilateral Tariff Redux 2033 inc Sugar	Combined Service Liberalization	Goods and Services Liberalization
Absorption	0.04	0.18	4.98	5.02
Private Consumption	0.08	0.27	6.96	7.04
Import Demand	0.40	0.84	2.61	3.02
Export Supply	0.76	0.81	6.29	7.09
GDP	0.11	0.15	2.38	2.49
Unskilled Labor Employment	0.29	0.41	6.62	6.92

Source: World Bank staff and Institute of Development Studies (IDS).

and sugar beet which sees production expand by just over 20 percent, and sugar which sees production expand by over 40 percent.

The welfare gains associated with service trade liberalization are more substantial. In aggregate, the services liberalization alone leads to an absorption (welfare) gain of just under 5 percent, and this welfare gain is reflected in an increase in imports from both the United States and the EU15; as well as an increase in exports to both of these. This is then also reflected in an increase in output for all sectors, and an increase in employment of unskilled labor of just under 7 percent (see Table 4 and for more detail Chapter 6). Along the same lines, policy experiments using the Jamaican Model reveal that a productivity increase in the "commerce" sector, which includes tourism, results in welfare gain. Aggregate absorption increases by 2.1 percent and employment of unskilled labor increases by 4.0 percent. Aggregate exports and imports increase, mostly with the EU. When the simulations add the increase in sugar prices (JAM-6) and the assumption that the EPA is associated with increased investment in Jamaica (JAM-7), to the point where the profit rate stays at its initial value, the results are more beneficial. With the increase in sugar prices, absorption increases by 2.8 percent (see Table 5). Employment of unskilled labor goes up by 5.4 percent, with synergy between gains from increased export revenue and employment. Simulation JAM-7 adds an open capital market, with increased foreign investment that keeps the profit rate at its base level. The result is an increase in the capital stock of 9.6 percent and increased employment of unskilled labor of 11.3 percent. Aggregate absorption increases by 7.3 percent (see Table 5 and for more detail Chapter 6).

These results show the importance of trade liberalization under the EPA most notably the liberalization of services trade. They confirm that trade in services is a niche where the Caribbean comparative advantage could help the region position itself as a major player within this niche in the international market. As the CARIFORUM countries face declining preferences in their key markets for goods, many have been seeking to promote service industries for some time now. Although, market access commitments on services and investments are still to be negotiated under any future FTA with the United States or Canada, market access for their service firms in key overseas markets is one part of the strategy to promote growth and development of service industries.

Table 5. Aggregate Results for Jamaica CGE Model (Percent change from base value)

% Change from Base	Value Base 2008	JAM 1	JAM 2	JAM 3	JAM 4	JAM 5	JAM 6	JAM 7
Absorption	492.1	20.1	20.1	20.1	0.3	2.1	2.8	7.3
Consumption	295.9	20.1	20.2	20.2	0.5	2.1	2.7	7.6
Investment	130.4					3.2	3.9	9.0
Government	65.8					0.4	0.5	2.3
Exports	147.6	20.1	0.1	0.1	0.8	6.0	6.9	13.9
Imports	229.6	20.2	20.2	20.2	1.3	3.6	5.2	9.7
Price indices								
Exchange rate	100.0	0.6	0.7	0.7	20.5	0.2	20.9	20.5
Export Price Index	100.0	20.8	20.8	20.8	0.8	20.8	0.8	0.8
Import Price Index	100.0	20.3	20.3	20.3	0.2	20.3	0.2	0.2
Intl terms of Trade Index	100.0	20.5	20.5	20.5	0.4	20.5	0.4	0.4
Producer price index	100.0	0.0	0.0	0.0	0.4	20.1	0.2	0.1
Consumer price index	100.0							
Agricultural terms of Trade	100.0	20.5	20.5	20.5	0.6	20.5	0.6	0.6
Investment/GDP ratio	31.8	0.1	0.0	0.0	20.2	20.1	20.2	20.5
Trade deficit/GDP ratio	20.0	0.2	0.2	0.2	−0.2	−0.4	−0.9	−1.8

Source: Bank staff and IDS.

Services sector is dominated by tourism, which stands out as an area of opportunity. For the CARIFORUM as a whole, over the period 1997–2002 tourism comprised about 70 percent of total services exports on average. For instance, for the Dominican Republic tourism accounted for 91.4 percent of total services exports in 2006; and about half (46 percent) of Trinidad and Tobago's services exports. Travels accounted for nearly 70 percent of the service receipts of Bahamas, Jamaica, and Barbados. Yet though the tourism sector is well developed in several CARIFORUM economies, traditional tourism has failed to foster linkages with national economies, and few Caribbean-owned tourism businesses have flourished. The region's traditional tourism product, beach resorts, has matured and faces challenges from competitors in other regions such as Asia, and the rapidly changing nature of global tourism demand. The region also faces issues related to its strategy for managing and marketing the sector. However, several reports have identified higher-end tourism as a major area of emerging opportunities for the Caribbean (World Bank 2005a). Given the rapidly changing nature of global tourism demand, an area of new opportunities for CARIFORUM countries include adventure tourism, nature-based tourism, cultural, meetings and conferences, and community tourism. However, exploring other new areas of opportunity such as high value financial services, telecommunications, and maritime transport would be a critical step to expand the range of opportunities in services sector. The EPA provides a liberalization framework and advantages for the Caribbean in the service sector. The *asymmetric nature* of the liberalization process between CARIFORUM and the European Commission also gives the Caribbean countries leeway to prepare for the changing environment. It also gives them the opportunity to redeploy their service development strategy. But the region would still need to strengthen infrastructure (notably IT and communication) for exports, and address issues of incentives regime most notably for small firms to be able to export services abroad.

But a Trade Strategy for Growth and Enhanced Competitiveness is Currently Missing

Seizing the new trade opportunities would require designing a full-fledged trade and growth strategy. Unfortunately, there has not been a clearly designed competitiveness strategy, which would enable the region to reap the benefits of global trade integration. The CSME, which is the cornerstone of the regional integration agenda of CARICOM focuses mainly on four areas: (i) the free movement of goods; (ii) common external tariff and trade policy; (iii) sectoral development policies and (iv) macroeconomic policies.[10] While important progress has been made in freeing the movement of goods, the CSME agenda has shown few results in the areas of harmonization of trade policies, sectoral development policies, and macroeconomic convergence.

More importantly, a common trade policy in relation to non-CARICOM countries does not effectively exist. The CARICOM Treaty does not explicitly prohibit individual member states from negotiating bilateral trade agreements with third countries.[11] Specifically, Belize benefits from a special provision in the Treaty by which it retains the right to enter into bilateral agreements with neighboring countries in Central America. As a result, the principle of a customs union (and, by extension, a single market) is somewhat blurred. The challenge for the coming years is for CARICOM countries to design a common trade policy. Ultimately, the success of the CSME will depend largely on the effective implementation of a common trade policy.

This trade strategy should focus on three key elements: (i) addressing the issue of high trade costs which undermine the region's competitiveness; (ii) providing priority to the services sector which has proven to be a sector with important potential; and (iii) developing and strengthening the incentive regimes (tariff reforms and investment code) to attract private sector.

Thrust, Objectives, Scope, and Structure of the Report

The main objective of this report is to help policymakers in the Caribbean design an agenda of policy actions to accelerate trade integration and growth and reduce poverty. *This trade report is a joint response from the World Bank and the Organization of American States (OAS) to a demand statement formulated by the Caribbean Regional Negotiating Machinery and the CARICOM Secretariat* to strengthen the analytical underpinnings of the linkages between trade, economic growth, and poverty. It aims at centering the Caribbean's next round of trade reforms and its overall agenda around trade on these key thematic areas.

---

10. It is worth noting that there is not a unique way to divide the CSME implementation agenda. For instance, a recent needs assessment for CARICOM commissioned by the CARICOM Secretariat divides the CSME implementation agenda into four areas: (i) the institutional and legal framework; (ii) market access; (iii) sectoral development policies; and (iv) macroeconomic framework. See Brewster, 2003.

11. The CARICOM Treaty only requires that individual member states which have negotiated bilateral trade agreements with third countries seek approval of the relevant CARICOM Ministerial Council.

The strategic focus of the trade report is on the linkages between trade, growth and poverty. This focus is motivated by four main reasons. First, many reports have been prepared on regional integration issues in the Caribbean. The Economic Commission for Latin America and the Caribbean (ECLAC) has published a series of reports, covering a wide range of regional issues in the Caribbean, including: (i) trade and investment flows; (ii) fiscal trends and policy issues; (iii) issues of implementation of the CSME; (iv) special and differential treatment; (v) the impact of foreign direct investment; and (vi) issues, effects and implications of the Free Trade Area of the Americas (FTAA) agreement for CARICOM economies. More recently, the Bank has published three reports, which deal with the development challenges facing the Caribbean region: "A Time to Choose: Caribbean Development in the 21st Century" (2005); "Organisation of Eastern Caribbean States: Towards a New Agenda for Growth" (2005); and "Crime, Violence, and Development in the Caribbean" (2006). These reports provide a broad overview of regional integration issues and development challenges facing the Caribbean region. However, little attention has been paid to the interactions between trade, growth, and poverty in the Caribbean. Specifically, the channels through which trade reforms could lead to higher growth rates, and ultimately to lower poverty rates have not been sufficiently analyzed. Second, the current trade environment of the Caribbean countries is characterized by the erosion of trade preferences to allow for a flexible liberalization of trade in goods and services in the context of the renegotiations of the EPA with the European Union.[12] Analyzing the potential impact of this changing trade environment is critical as it could help the CARIFORUM design a strategy to compensate for the forgone public revenue and loss of growth, and to limit the poverty impact. Third, after years of mixed performance, regional integration in the Caribbean is at the crossroads. The CSME could bring a new impetus to regional integration in CARIFORUM and be the engine for a strategy for higher growth and poverty reduction. Fourth, the findings and policy recommendations of the report would help the policymakers of the region to determine the next generation of trade reforms in the CARIFORUM.

The report provides an overview of the economic and trade system context of the Caribbean, under which the new trade environment is operating. It then discusses the opportunities and challenges for the Caribbean associated with the new trade environment. It finally quantifies the gains from global trade integration using a dynamic macroeconomic analysis.

The report provides policy priorities to accelerating Caribbean integration into the world economy and to reap the benefits of global competition. Each part of the report

---

12. Under the Cotonou Agreement the EU and the ACP countries are committed to negotiating Economic Partnership Agreements (EPAs). The objective of these EPAs is to facilitate the integration of the ACP countries into the world economy. Specifically, it is intended that this will be achieved through: the EPAs fostering and supporting greater regional integration, allowing a flexible liberalization of trade in goods and services, building up institutional capacities and the establishment of simple and transparent rules for business, and via development assistance provisions. While Haiti requested more time to review the CARIFORUM-EC EPA before signing it, the agreement was signed on October 15, 2008 by most CARIFORUM states and on October 20, 2008 by Guyana. Provisional application of the EPA became effective on December 29, 2008.

Currently the Caribbean countries have access to the US market via the CBI, which was initially launched in 1983 through the Caribbean Basin Economic Recovery Act (CBERA), and substantially expanded in 2000 through the U.S.-Caribbean Basin Trade Partnership Act (CBTPA) Note that the CBTPA process is due to expire on September 30, 2010, or possibly sooner if in the interim there is an alternative free trade agreement between the USA and the Caribbean. As with the EPA's this would imply reciprocal market access.

focuses on a key question and *adds value* by providing an in-depth analysis of the issues raised and laying the foundations for policy recommendations described in the last chapter of the report:

- Part I (Overview of economic and trade system context): Is Caribbean's economic and trade system sound enough to sustain the new era of its global trade relations which is being shaped?
- Part II (New opportunities and challenges): What are the opportunities and challenges that the new trade environment offers to the Caribbean?
- Part III (Macroeconomic framework): What are the gains in terms of growth and poverty reduction of the recently negotiated EPA?

The structure of the report reflects this design. Part I presents the economic and trade context of the Caribbean. This part of the report adds value by analyzing how the Caribbean's economic and trade context has prevented the region from accelerating trade reforms and regional integration. It also raises and analyses an issue more often neglected in trade reports on the Caribbean: how the current macroeconomic imbalances and structural and political constraints may constitute a major obstacle to the region's ability to reap the benefits of the current international trade environment. This part of the report argues that trade liberalization (and more specifically the EPA process) should pay more attention to these constraints, which go beyond trade issues per se and cover a large range of issues, such as macroeconomic imbalances, small economic size, infrastructure deficiencies, and economic vulnerability of the Caribbean. The report adds value by analyzing the issue of appropriate sequencing of trade liberalization in a context marked by macroeconomic imbalances. Thus, for many countries of the region, this part of the report argues that reaping the benefits of greater openness will require that complementary reforms and policies be implemented prior to, and in conjunction with, trade reform. To this end, aid for trade would play a critical role.

Part II focuses on the analysis of the new opportunities and challenges of the new trade environment. Along the lines of the 2005 Bank report "A Time to Choose," this part of the report identifies services (mainly tourism) as a key sector of opportunity for the Caribbean. However, this report adds value by expanding the analysis to financial services viewed as a new area of opportunity. Moreover, this part of the report discusses the opportunities that the provisions of the EPA in the area of services could provide to the Caribbean. It adds value by providing the main features of a long term trade strategy for the Caribbean strategy to seize the opportunities of the global economy. It discusses the respective role that regional integration, national policies, and foreign aid could play in a long term trade strategy. Because of the short-term costs associated with trade liberalization, this part of the report also discusses the strategy to manage them. Finally, it lays out the ways to alleviate the structural constraints to trading to reinforce the long-term strategy's chances of success.

Part III presents an assessment of the impact of the EPA on growth and poverty using two types of macroeconomic models. This part of the report adds value by quantifying the impact of trade liberalization under the main provisions of the EPA on growth and poverty and other MDGs in the Caribbean region. The findings of this part of the report provide policymakers of the Caribbean with the first quantitative assessment of the potential implications of the EPA, which would help inform their policy decisions. Various policy simulations are conducted which provide policymakers of the Caribbean with a broad range of policy actions. Finally, this part of the report adds value by providing the first—to our best knowledge—thorough quantitative analysis of the potential implications of "aid for trade" for the Caribbean region.

Certain aspects of trade and competitiveness have been omitted or not sufficiently developed in the report due to the programmatic approach of this trade report. They will be addressed in future work. They include: (i) Trade logistics; (ii) Quality of trade; and (iii) Bilateral trade agreements.

Top Five Strategic Policy Priorities to Accelerating Trade Integration and Growth and Reducing Poverty in the Caribbean

Based on its key findings, the report recommends the following five policy priorities to accelerate trade integration and growth and reduce poverty in the Caribbean. These priorities will be discussed with the CARICOM Secretariat, the CRNM, the Governments of member states of CARIFORUM, and the donor community.

Reducing Macroeconomic and Fiscal Imbalances and Investing in Infrastructure to Enhance Integration in the Global Economy

Caribbean's economic context is marked by macroeconomic imbalances, which limit its potential to integrate into the global economy. Caribbean countries have been experiencing macroeconomic and fiscal imbalances, which affect their competitiveness and integration. The trend in the region is one of persistent double-digit merchandise and current account deficits. The merchandise deficit for the region as a whole consistently reached above 22 percent of GDP over the past decade 1997–2006, and the current account deficit stood at an average of 11.5 percent of GDP over the same period (see Chapter 1 Tables 1.3 and 1.4). The region has been experiencing persistent fiscal deficits. The region's overall fiscal balance deteriorated consistently between 1997 and 2002. Despite a slight improvement in 2005, the deficit stood on average at about 4 percent of GDP over 2001–06 (see Chapter 1 Table 1.5). Most Caribbean countries have exhibited a weak fiscal position over the past years, marked by large overall deficits. Moreover, a large burden of debt has been the dominant feature of the Caribbean region's macroeconomic stance over the past years. The average public sector external debt of the Caribbean region increased by 10 percentage points on average from an average of 42.1 percent of GDP during the period 1997–2000 to 52 percent of GDP over 2001–06.

The appropriate *sequencing* of trade liberalization in view of integrating the Caribbean into the world economy would first require reducing these macroeconomic imbalances. Appropriate policy responses will help reduce large fiscal and current account deficits and high indebtedness levels and debt overhang. In the *short term*, the authorities' ability to reduce spending is constrained by the current global economic downturn. Priority spending in social sectors (education and health) and basic infrastructure should be protected to minimize the social costs of the current economic crisis. However, expansionary fiscal policy is further constrained by limited fiscal space and borrowing headroom. The high debt and debt servicing burdens of many Caribbean countries could make them vulnerable to a tightening in global liquidity conditions. In the *medium term*, the objective should be the accumulation of primary surpluses, which together with foreign aid would finance future investment in infrastructure in the region. Correcting current macroeconomic imbalances in the region could be done at the national level through the improvement of domestic policies. However, the long practice of inappropriate macroeconomic policies could be difficult to reverse at the national level. A regional dimension of these policy responses could help the Caribbean countries. Implementing the macroeconomic convergence framework of CARICOM could help bring down the deficits and act as a *peer pressure mechanism.* As the *composition of expenditure reduction* matters, macroeconomic stability policy should be guided by the principle of *selectivity,* which involves protecting expenditure on infrastructure and social sectors.

Investing in infrastructure to alleviate the structural constraints to trading both between countries of the region and between the region and its international trading partners.   Many of the Caribbean countries (and notably the poorest in the region, such as Haiti and Guyana) remain ill-equipped to take full advantage of new trade opportunities because of significant supply-side constraints. Despite recent improvement, the region's level and quality of infrastructure remain weak. This in turn constitutes an important obstacle to both intra-regional and external trade. While some Caribbean countries, particularly Jamaica, Antigua and Barbuda, Bahamas, Barbados, and Trinidad and Tobago have levels of access to telecommunication services that is better than what is predicted by income levels, other countries still struggle with international rates that are well above cost; prohibitive rates constitute a tax on internationally conducted business. Intra-regional and external trade is also hampered by the poor quality of roads. To the exception of Barbados, Jamaica, and St. Vincent and the Grenadines, most of the Caribbean countries have low level of paved roads. Transportation of goods suffers from the deteriorated condition of existing roads, which more often lack the basic maintenance services. The Caribbean countries have adequate physical infrastructure capacity for ports and runways. However, airport and port charges remain a small fraction of the total cost of transporting people and goods to and from Caribbean countries. Transport costs are thus relatively high and limit the potential for expanding regional trade. Internet services are more costly than in countries with comparable income levels. For instance, the cost of 20-hour dial-up access in St. Lucia is US$22.22 compared to US$8.42 in Malaysia (ITU 2004). As a result of these high prices, internet density is particularly low in the Dominican Republic, Haiti, Suriname and St. Vincent and the Grenadines, at 3.64, 0.96, 4.16 and 5.98 users per 100 inhabitants, respectively. Other countries like Jamaica and St. Kitts and Nevis have relatively higher usage rates of more than 20 users per 100 inhabitants. Yet, those usage rates are all substantially lower than in countries like the United States, Singapore, and New Zealand. In terms of access to electricity, sustained policy efforts to expand access to electricity in the English-speaking Caribbean have achieved electrification rates above 80 percent in these countries. In contrast, the Dominican Republic and Haiti have only been able to achieve rates below 70 percent and 40 percent, respectively. Air transport is also underdeveloped. Goods carried through air transport are relatively small as evidenced by freight services. The Caribbean average of freight is far below that of East Asia and Pacific, Latin America and Caribbean (LAC) and even Sub-Saharan Africa (see Table 6).

Build and/or rehabilitate infrastructure, including roads, irrigation schemes, water and sanitation facilities, electricity distribution and ICT networks would help fill the Caribbean region's infrastructure gap and would facilitate increased economic activities and improved access by the population to social services. More importantly by reducing production costs, infrastructure building or enhancement would improve competitiveness and facilitate penetration into the global economy.

Table 6. Air Transport, Freight (million tons per km)

	1997	1998	1999	2000	2001	2002	2003	2004	2005	Ave. 1997–2000	Ave. 2001–05	Ave. 1997–2005
Antigua and Barbuda	0.2	0.2	0.2	0.2	0.2	0.2	0.2	0.2	0.2	0.2	0.2	0.2
Bahamas	0.5	1.1	1.5	1.6	1.8	1.6	1.6	0.6	0.6	1.2	1.2	1.2
Guyana	3.3	3.3	2.2	2.3	1.6	—	—	—	—	2.8	1.6	1.4
Jamaica	20.9	23.8	29.5	29.2	26.4	56.6	48.9	37.7	15.8	25.8	37.1	32.1
Suriname	29.5	26.9	31.8	30	27.6	24.3	24.3	28.2	27.1	29.5	26.3	27.7
Trinidad and Tobago	19.6	49	54.7	45.5	41.8	35.6	34.3	41.8	47.9	42.2	40.3	41.1
Caribbean Average	12.3	17.4	20	18.1	16.6	23.7	21.9	21.7	18.3	17	20.4	18.9
East Asia & Pacific	6,481	6,136	7,219	8,424	8,618	9,708	10,566	12,562	13,285	7,065	10,948	9,222
Latin America & Caribbean	4,591	4,689	4,188	4,623	4,183	3,930	4,035	4,648	4,518	4,522	4,263	4,278
Sub-Saharan Africa	1,374	1,444	1,687	1,736	1,699	1,500	1,643	1,822	1,903	1,560	1,713	1,645

Source: World Bank, World Development Indicators, 2007 and Bank staff's calculations.

Accelerating National Trade Policy Reforms and Improving Investment Incentives

Policy reforms should be accelerated in five major areas of weaknesses, including: (i) import policies; (ii) export policies; (iii) investment incentive policies; (iv) competition policy; and (v) trade policy formulation and implementation. Customs procedures and administration should be reinforced as well as the legal framework for businesses including taxation policy. The CARIFORUM countries would also need to create or strengthen incentives to promote investment. Trinidad and Tobago's incentive policy could serve as an example for the other CARIFORUM countries.

The success of trade reforms would require that the countries develop a comprehensive competition policy, which is currently missing in most of the CARIFORUM countries. However, trade policy would not produce expected outcomes unless national institutions in charge of formulating trade policies, negotiating and implementing trade agreements are reinforced. The first step and perhaps the most important element of success of a trade policy in the Caribbean is to reinforce the capacity of ministries of commerce and industry and trade related institutions to formulate trade policy, negotiate, and implement trade agreements. In this regard, donors should provide assistance in the context of the "Aid for trade" agenda. Technical assistance should be provided to help technical staff and policy-makers of the Caribbean better understand the implications of trade agreements, design implementation action plans, and follow-up mechanisms.

Assessing the outcomes of trade reforms would require that data are available. Unfortunately, in many Caribbean countries trade data (in particular services data) are more often scarce, outdated or missing. Strengthening the capacity of national statistics departments to regularly produce and publish trade data should be a priority of a trade policy in the Caribbean countries. Donors should provide assistance in that area. The EPA offers a good opportunity and framework to design a comprehensive technical assistance to the Caribbean countries in the area of trade data.

Adjusting to Preferences Erosion, Accelerating the Implementation of the CSME, and Using the EPA for Enhanced Competitiveness and Global Trade Integration

As the report indicates, the Caribbean region is facing three major trade developments which will shape the region's trade environment over the next decades. First, unilateral trade preferences are eroding as a result of other trade agreements (AGOA, CAFTA-DR, FTAs) that Caribbean's major trading partners (European Union and the United States) are concluding. Second, the region's competitors are increasing their global market share at the detriment of the Caribbean, reflecting the region's competitiveness problems (see above). Third, the region is also redesigning the process of regional trade integration with the ongoing implementation of the Caribbean Single Market Economy (CSME).

The region has little leverage on the erosion of preferences and fierce competition from other developing countries. The question is therefore: what can be done at the country and regional levels to cope with the "new" trade environment and enhance the region's competiveness? What can the EPA bring to the competitiveness agenda?

The report argues that policy actions should center around three elements: (i) adjusting to the erosion of trade preferences; (ii) accelerating the implementation of the CSME agenda; and (iii) seizing the opportunities of the EPA.

Adjusting to the erosion of trade preferences. For the past three decades, the Caribbean has pursued an external trade policy anchored on preferential access to the European and North American markets. However, the Caribbean is facing a situation where preferential access for traditional products is being eroded. Most notably, the reciprocity character of the EPA, which requires the Caribbean to reduce tariff and nontariff barriers on trade in goods, services, and the movement of capital with the EU, ends the preferences that the Caribbean countries had enjoyed over the past decades. However, the gradual approach of dismantlement of the preferences offers to the Caribbean the time to adjust to the new environment. In the *short term*, the Caribbean region would need to reinforce their competitiveness during the transition period. This requires the implementation of good macroeconomic policies, to firm up the basis of macroeconomic stability. Second, the region would need to address the short-term costs of the erosion of preferences in particular, the losses of Government's revenue following trade liberalization. Short-term compensatory measures should be explored to help losers (mainly exporters benefiting from preferences) to cope with revenue losses. The issue is the costs and the additional burden that these compensatory measures could imply for the Governments' revenues. Aid for trade could help alleviate the financial burden on the Governments' resources and thus encourage the liberalization reform process. In the *long term*, the focus should be on finding new niches of exports where the Caribbean countries have comparative advantages or segments of existing niches.

Unilateral liberalization could be an option for individual Caribbean countries to integrate the world economy. However, given the similarities of the Caribbean countries and the common development agenda of these countries, regional integration should be used as a tool to integrate the world economy. This, in turn, implies advancing the CARIFORUM's regional integration agenda.

Accelerating the implementation of the CSME to make it the cornerstone of trade integration and economic development of the Caribbean's region. The implementation of the CSME has been slow. While, the region has been successful at eliminating tariffs on goods originating in common market countries, CARICOM has still yet to be a single market economy. The CSME agenda has shown little results in the areas of harmonization of trade policies, sectoral development policies, and macroeconomic convergence (see Chapter 2). For the CSME to become the driver of integration and economic development of the region, CARICOM would need to accelerate the implementation of the main provisions of a single market economy. In the *short term (next two years)*, the focus should be on reducing tariff dispersion, advancing the free movement of labor, adopting a regional financial service and investment code, and establishing a regional stock exchange (Phase I of the CSME's implementation process). In the *medium term (next three to five years)*, the region would need to develop a common trade policy, which does not effectively exist and would be the backbone of a full and well-functioning single market. In the *long term*, the region should advance the harmonization of the regulatory regime and economic policies to complete the single economy and implement a CARICOM monetary union (Phase II of the CSME's implementation process).

Using the EPA framework to reinforce competitiveness. One of the main goals of the EPA is to promote competitiveness and development of Caribbean countries. Both the EU and the CARIFORUM countries acknowledge the importance of increasing the competitiveness of Caribbean economies, developing their capacity to access high quality markets. However, the EPA framework does not define a clear competitiveness strategy for the Caribbean. The challenge is for the Caribbean to use the relevant provisions of the EPA framework to reinforce competitiveness. The 25 years transitory period that the framework provides for full liberalization, gives time to the Caribbean to take policy actions to enhance competitiveness, including: regulatory and legal reforms to improve the "doing business" environment, controlling wages increases to match labor productivity, investing in infrastructure to reduce production costs. Some specific provisions of the EPA could be exploited to reinforce competitiveness and industrial development. The EPA framework excludes sensitive industrial sectors and contains an "infant industry clause" which allows CARIFORUM to reinstate tariffs in the future to protect growing industry and/or industries. There are also provisions on technical assistance towards developing the capacity to export successfully in EU markets. This was achieved with agreement on the Trade Partnership for Sustainable Development (Development Chapter) which includes support for infrastructure and the CARICOM Development vision. The Joint Declaration on Development Cooperation includes a commitment to channel EPA support through the CARICOM Development Fund.

The EPA also offers the opportunity for the Caribbean countries to improve the competitiveness of potentially *viable* production, including downstream processing, through innovation, training, promotion of linkages and other support *activities,* in agricultural and fisheries products, including both traditional and non traditional export sectors. Within the framework of European Community funding instruments, both Parties will decide on the programming of funds, in complementarity to the actions already funded, and with respect to the still available funds under the Special Framework of Assistance (SFA), to help the CARIFORUM banana industry to further adjust to the new challenges, including activities aimed at increasing the productivity and competitiveness in areas of viable production, the development of alternatives both within and outside the banana industry, addressing social impact arising from changes in the sector and for disaster mitigation.

Develop a Long-Term Trade Strategy with a Focus on Increased Competitiveness and New Areas of Opportunities

Seizing the new trade opportunities would require designing a full-fledged trade and competitiveness strategy. The strategy should focus on targeting sectors with high export and growth potential such as tourism, financial services, telecommunications, and maritime transportation. More broadly, the region's efforts should focus on the following strategic directions: (i) expansion of value-added activities with a broader participation of the private sector; (ii) modernization of trade transaction system and concerted export strategy; and (iii) facilitation of sectoral development and provision of favorable investment climate. Priority should be given to the following actions. First, the Caribbean governments will need to invest in the production and marketing infrastructures of the sectors and in the technical and operational capacities of the private sector operators. Specific actions include among others, targeting the infrastructure for facilitating exports of services. Second, the governments' interventions should facilitate access to finance by exporters and traders through proper institutional arrangements. Third, the governments should also promote the dissemination of knowledge and information on markets and market standards.

A regional trade and growth strategy should also focus primarily on removing the constraints to competitiveness. Addressing the specific issue of high production costs would require improving labor policies to enhance labor productivity and investing in infrastructure to reduce infrastructure bottlenecks to exports. Investing in *regional public goods* (transports, telecommunications, water and sanitation, and so forth) would reduce the costs of production of goods and services. It would also facilitate the mobility of goods and persons across countries of the region. Building and/or rehabilitating regional infrastructures would be needed to strengthen the region's competitiveness. Reinforcing human skills to favor labor productivity would help the region compete on the global economy.

Because of the large disparities between CARIFORUM countries, a regional trade and competitiveness strategy should enable least developed countries of the region to benefit from specific provisions so as to help them catch up. This is consistent with the current approach adopted by CARICOM member states. CARICOM countries have recognized that economic divergence among member states could be an impediment to advance regional integration. The CARICOM Treaty thus rightly attributes special treatment of less developed countries in terms of their obligations under the Treaty. The Treaty calls for the establishment of a Regional Development Fund that would help disadvantaged countries, regions and sectors cope with CSME-related adjustment.[13] A US$250 million fund was

---

13. See Article 158 of Chapter VII of the CARICOM Treaty.

launched in July 2008 with an initial $60 million towards its $250 million target.[14] While this initiative is laudable, past experiences within and outside the LAC region showed that development banks either national or regional have generally failed.

Reinforcing Cariforum Regional Institutions with a Focus on Implementation

Perhaps one of the most critical weaknesses identified within the Caribbean regional and international trade negotiations construct has been the endemic failure of the regions institutions both at the national and regional levels to take advantage of the market access opportunities presented through either one-way preferential arrangements or in more recent times, negotiated trade agreements with international partners. In an effort to overcome this problem and to effectively coordinate necessary activities that will emanate from the signing of the EPA, and indeed future agreements such as the CARICOM/Canada FTA, this report proposes the creation of a *Regional Implementation Mechanism* (RIM).

This structure can be placed within any of the existing regional governing institutions, or be created as a separate entity. The proposed body can coordinate the regional objectives and activities with national bodies; which can mirror the regional structure. The entity will be comprised of units charged with the following responsibilities.

- *Market Research Division.* This unit will undertake the analytical work required to identify niche markets (both existing and potential) in the EU for CARIFORUM exporters; the potential barriers to trade in each market area; identify the potential "winners" where market penetration will be most quickly gained; the costs associated and the necessary measures needed both nationally and regionally to engage these markets.
- *Legal Division.* This division will examine the legislative requirements to facilitate service providers and potential investors who may wish to transact business in the EU; conduct negotiations with regard to facilitating entry and also examine the areas for mutual recognition agreements, among other variables.
- *Private Sector Division.* This unit would seek to develop the necessary cooperative relationships between the Caribbean private sector firms. In addition this division would be the conduit through which private sector firms would be able to communicate their concerns and needs regarding barriers to the markets as well as potential investment opportunities available. These would then be translated into finite and concrete proposals to enhance the building of productive capacity in the country/region.
- *National Implementation Liaison Division.* This unit would coordinate the activities with the national implementation bodies in an effort to better facilitate use of funding, share knowledge, and allow the individual countries to raise their concerns and areas of interest.

---

14. The Fund, currently being held in an escrow account at the Caribbean Development Bank (CDB), will promote business development, among other areas. Member States would contribute $120 million of the Fund through a formula that would take into account size, per capita income and other minor indices. The remainder of the funds would come from contributions by development partners. Disadvantaged countries will be the main targets of the Fund and which could receive allocations from the Fund in the forms of loans, grants and interest subsidy grants.

■ *The Project Fund Development Unit.* This unit would be responsible for the development of "sellable" projects in line with the prescribed format required by the EU, vetting of and assisting in the preparation of national projects, and lobbying of the EU on issues pertinent to ensuring a more viable framework for the disbursement of funds.

Implications for the Aid for Trade Agenda

Findings and Policy Issues

Increasing the volume and predictability of foreign aid. The proposed policy agenda to accelerate trade integration and growth in the Caribbean region has important implications for the conduct of macroeconomic policy and the strategic focus of the development agenda in the Caribbean over the next decade. Macroeconomic management would be crucial to reduce the existing macroeconomic and fiscal imbalances if the Caribbean countries have to better integrate into the global economy. The trade and growth strategy would also require investment in trade infrastructure to enable the Caribbean countries to seize the opportunities of the global trade environment.

Given their limited resources, the Caribbean countries are unlikely to significantly increase their global trade penetration and thus achieve higher growth rates and reduce poverty without significant financing from donors. The growth experience over the past decades shows that even during period of good economic policies, global trade penetration was relatively low and economic growth rates were not sustained over a long term.

The trade and growth strategy proposed here requires significant support from the international community. Foreign aid could play a catalytic role as *compensation* for the revenue losses during the transition period of implementation of trade reforms. Simulations using the GLOBE Model show that a lump-sum government-to-government budget transfer between 0.08 percent and 0.31 percent of benchmark CARIFORUM GDP provided by the EU to compensate the CARIFORUM region (for tariff revenue shortfalls on EU imports after the implementation of the EPA tariff cuts) leads to welfare gains of a magnitude of between 0.13 percent and 5.43 percent. Aggregate real imports, real consumption and domestic absorption rise (see Table 7 and for more details Chapter 6). Foreign aid could also play a major role in financing the strategy. More and predictable aid flows would be required to finance much needed trade infrastructures and help the CARIFORUM member states finance the proposed trade and growth strategy. In this context, foreign aid could play a critical role as a *joint compensation-promotion scheme.* Simulations using the GLOBE Model show that a lump-sum government-to-government budget transfer between 0.08 percent and 0.31 percent of benchmark CARIFORUM GDP provided by the EU to compensate the CARIFORUM region for tariff revenue shortfalls on EU imports after the implementation of the EPA tariff cuts leads to welfare gains of a magnitude of between 0.13 percent and 5.43 percent. Real GDP per capita increases at a rate of 2.4 percent in 2009 and about 1 percent in the subsequent 3 years. The expansion in labor demand leads to a significant drop in unemployment as well after 2009. Poverty falls throughout the simulation period, by more than one percentage point between 2010 and 2013, and the composite human development indicator improves eventually by about 4 percentage points (see Table 8 below and for more details Chapter 6).

A legitimate question that could be asked is to what extent the Caribbean economies can absorb huge inflows of foreign aid as this concerns the potential destabilizing macroeconomic

Table 7. Macro Results for GLOBE Model Experiments (Closure: Balanced Macro Closure, EU Budget Transfer, Unemployed Unskilled Labor)

Trade Policy Scenarios	CARIB 2	CARIB 3	CARIB 4	CARIB 5	CARIB 11
% Change on Reference Equilibrium	Bilateral Tariff Reduction 2013	Bilateral Tariff Reduction 2023	Bilateral Tariff Reduction 2033	Bilateral Tariff Redux Services 2033 inc Sugar	Goods and Services Liberalization
Absorption	0.13	0.31	0.32	0.44	5.43
Private Consumption	0.18	0.44	0.46	0.63	7.60
Import Demand	0.30	0.80	0.83	1.26	3.63
Export Supply	0.01	0.10	0.11	0.14	6.20
GDP	0.04	0.09	0.10	0.13	2.50
Unskilled Labor Employment	0.12	0.27	0.29	0.37	6.96

Source: Bank staff and IDS.

effects associated with large inflows of foreign aid: real exchange rate appreciation (Dutch Disease) and disincentive effect on tax collection (moral hazard). The Dominican Republic SPAHD Model shows that an increase in foreign aid to not only compensate for tariff loss from trade liberalization under the EPA but also to finance public investment, leads to a real exchange appreciation. This translates into a fall in the share of exports into GDP as well as a large increase in the share of total imports to GDP. As a result, the trade balance deteriorates quite significantly during the first few years of the adjustment process (see Chapter 6).

Should the region achieve its goal of attracting large amounts of foreign aid, improving macroeconomic management would be critical to prevent the potential destabilizing macroeconomic effects of huge flows of foreign aid. Good macroeconomic policies will be crucial for reducing the potential short-term Dutch Disease effects of increased foreign aid. This means that the Caribbean countries will have to continue implementing macro-stabilization programs to ensure that inflation, fiscal and current account deficits are under control. Moreover, effective management of aid flows is critical to ensure that their potential trade and growth-enhancing, and poverty-reducing effects materialize. Improving *accountability, transparency,* and *efficiency* in the use of public resources is crucial to ensure that public investment translates into accumulation of capital and growth. Increasing efficiency of public investment in Caribbean countries is directly related to the ability of the government of Caribbean countries to improve governance. The implementation of the governance reforms (e.g. in Haiti), together with procurement and public enterprise reforms, will help advance public finance reforms, and thereby improve economic governance. Decisive complementary actions to fight corruption, improve the rule of law, and advance judiciary reforms is also needed to decisively improve governance in the Caribbean region.

Implementation Roadmap

The success of an aid for trade agenda in the context of the EPA in the Caribbean would require that the region design an operational implementation roadmap. This implementation roadmap or plan of action could be designed over the next two to three years as follows.

Table 8. Dominican Republic: Human Development Indicators—Deviations from Baseline, 2008–2020

	2008	2009	2010	2011	2012	2013	2014	2015	2016	2017	2018	2019	2020
Poverty rate (2003 = 63) *(% of population living under the poverty line)*													
IMMPA Method	−0.09	−0.84	−1.31	−1.39	−1.64	−1.04	−0.89	−0.64	−0.47	−0.56	−0.48	−0.33	−0.18
Literacy rate *(% of educated labor in total population)*	0.00	0.00	0.00	0.02	0.04	0.08	0.13	0.19	0.24	0.29	0.34	0.38	0.42
Infant mortality (2004 = 27.4) *(Infant mortality rate per 1000 live births)*	−0.04	−0.42	−0.92	−1.28	−1.62	−1.62	−1.49	−1.35	−1.22	−1.10	−0.99	−0.89	−0.81
Malnutrition (2002 = 5.3) *(Malnutrition prevalence, weight for age)*	−0.02	−0.01	−0.09	−0.15	−0.20	−0.26	−0.23	−0.21	−0.19	−0.18	−0.17	−0.16	−0.15
Life expectancy (2004 = 67.8) *(Life expectancy at birth, years)*	0.01	0.12	0.25	0.34	0.43	0.42	0.39	0.35	0.32	0.28	0.26	0.23	0.21
Access to safe water (2002 = 93) *(Percentage of population with access to safe water)*	0.01	0.19	0.25	0.28	0.33	0.20	0.20	0.18	0.15	0.13	0.11	0.09	0.07
COMPOSITE MDG INDICATOR (2006 = 100) *(A rise denotes an improvement)*	0.15	0.99	2.25	3.19	4.35	4.49	4.39	4.16	4.02	4.23	4.23	4.08	3.90

Source: UNDP Human Development Report.

Note: Malnutrition prevalence is in % of children under 5.

Preparation of Comprehensive Needs Assessment.   This needs assessment would be prepared country by country, building on what already exists and incorporating the specific issues identified by the EPA Agreement, the OECD questionnaire, and the national export strategies. The UNDP's Need Assessment Guide on Aid for Trade and the Bank's Diagnostic Trade Iintegration Study (DTIS) methodology could provide a good framework to help the Caribbean countries complete such an exercise.

National Validation of the Needs Assessment.   The needs assessments should be validated in national workshops consisting of all stakeholders involved in aid for trade (that is, government, private sector, multilateral agencies, regional institutions, and so forth).

Preparation of an EPA Implementation Program.   Once the needs assessments are completed, an EPA implementation program of action would be developed and costed with clear priorities. Twenty-two specific areas have been identified as priority areas for immediate work under the Regional Preparation Task Force (RPTF) work program for the EPAs. It is important that the focus be on these areas so that terms of references are prepared and implementation actions are taken. This implementation program should have clear timelines with expected results and performance indicators. The implementation program will identify institutions responsible for implementing actions.

Preparation of "bankable" project documents.   This should enable the effective implementation of the EPAs and all Caribbean trade agreements.

Policy Matrix for Enhanced Competitiveness and Trade Integration

Policy Theme	Priority Recommended Policy Actions (Over Next 2 Years)	Medium and Long-Term Recommended Ppolicy Actions (Next 3–5 Years)
1. Strengthening macroeconomic framework	▓ Reduce Government expenditure by tightening fiscal policy while protecting expenditure for infrastructure and social services. ▓ Reduce Government's recourse to external debt by limiting borrowing at non concessional terms, and seeking grant financing, in particular for poorest countries of the region. ▓ Increase the scope of domestic revenue by introducing new revenue measures (e.g. VAT). ▓ Control price increase by an appropriate macropolicy mix.	▓ Improve the efficiency of Government's spending by improving the allocation of resources across sectors. ▓ Improve the collection of Government's revenues by improving tax administration. ▓ Reduce fiscal vulnerability by reducing dependence on trade taxes. ▓ Enhance coordination of macroeconomic policies by harmonizing monetary and fiscal policies. ▓ Reinforce macroeconomic convergence by (i) implementing economic convergence criteria; and (ii) increasing the influence of the Caribbean Centre for Money and Finance (CCMF) on macroeconomic policies (i.e. implementing CCMF's policy recommendations).
2. Accelerating national trade policy reforms and improving investment incentives	▓ Prepare comprehensive national and regional competition policies. ▓ Prepare comprehensive national and regional investment strategies, with particular attention to regional public goods. ▓ Prepare comprehensive national and regional trade policy.	▓ Improve customs procedures and administration by enhancing customs valuation methods and reinforcing the capacity at the customs departments. ▓ Increase exporters' financing capacity by increasing their access to credits for exports and credit insurance. ▓ Develop export promotion activities by developing export facilitation, information, image-building, and participation in fairs. ▓ Enhance the legal framework for business including taxation by reducing the registration time and fees. ▓ Improve tax systems by revisiting the incentive measures, including duty concessions, tax exemptions and holidays, loss write-offs, and training support. ▓ Strengthen national trade institutions by reinforcing their technical capacity to formulate, negotiate, and implement trade policies.

(Continued)

Policy Matrix for Enhanced Competitiveness and Trade Integration (*Continued*)

Policy Theme	Priority Recommended Policy Actions (Over Next 2 Years)	Medium and Long-Term Recommended Ppolicy Actions (Next 3–5 Years)
3. Accelerating the implementation of the CSME	▨ Accelerate full implementation of the CET by reducing the wide dispersion in the range of actual tariffs implemented by CARICOM members on imports from non-members (i.e. reduce the large number of exemptions from CET that CARICOM members can use). ▨ Reduce non-tariff barriers (NTBs) on certain categories of imported products from outside CARICOM. ▨ Accelerate the implementation of stage 1 of the CARICOM Single Economy, scheduled to take place between 2008 and 2009 by: (i) implementing the schedule for the removal of unauthorized import duties and discriminatory taxes; (ii) speeding up the removal of barriers to the right of establishment and provision of services; and (iii) issuing CARICOM passports in countries, which have not yet done so.	▨ Implement stage 2 of the CSME scheduled to take place between 2010 and 2015 by: (i) putting in place a common regime for electronic commerce; (ii) developing regional rules for Government procurement; (iii) establishing an effective regional system of company registration to facilitate harmonization and oversight; (iv) reducing restrictions on access to property; (v) agreeing on a schedule for removal of restrictions on air and maritime transports, and financial services; (vi) establishing a common services regime; (vii) accelerating the liberalization of capital flows by abolishing exchange controls in countries which have maintained them, and developing a regional stock exchange; and (viii) fully implementing the free movement of skills by developing and implementing a regional policy on harmonization and transferability of social security benefits, eliminating the need for passports for travel within the region, and developing common entry/departure forms. ▨ Promote common sectoral policies and programs in main development sectors, including industry, agriculture, transport, and human development by: (i) increasing technical, human, and financial resources to implement common sectoral policies; and (ii) addressing infrastructure weaknesses to set up a common regional development policy.

4. Implementing the EPA and Reinforcing integration with the United States	▪ Establish national commissions for implementation of the EPA in each CARIFORUM countries. ▪ Set up a Regional Implementation Mechanism of the EPA. ▪ Develop national implementation strategies of the EPA. ▪ Establish national commissions for implementation of the Caribbean Basin Trade Partnership Act (CBTPA). ▪ Develop national implementation strategies of the CBTPA.	▪ Prepare a regional implementation strategy of the Free Trade Area Agreement with the United States.
5. Developing a long-term trade strategy with a focus on increased competitiveness	▪ Design a full-fledged trade and competitiveness strategy with focus on targeting sectors with high export and growth potential, such as tourism, financial services, telecommunications, and maritime transports. ▪ Improving labor policies. ▪ Maintain and invest in infrastructure. ▪ Provide more resources to the Caribbean Export Development Agency (CEDA).	▪ Expand value-added activities with a broader participation of the private sector. ▪ Modernize trade transaction system and concerted export strategy. ▪ Facilitate sectoral development and promote a favorable investment climate. ▪ Invest in the production and marketing infrastructures of the sectors and in the technical and operational capacities of the private sector operators. ▪ Facilitate access to finance by exporters and traders by improving institutional arrangements. ▪ Promote the dissemination of knowledge and information on markets and market standards. ▪ Invest in regional public goods (transports, telecommunications, water and sanitation, etc.).

(Continued)

Policy Matrix for Enhanced Competitiveness and Trade Integration (*Continued*)

Policy Theme	Priority Recommended Policy Actions (Over Next 2 Years)	Medium and Long-Term Recommended Ppolicy Actions (Next 3–5 Years)
6. Reinforcing regional institutions with a focus implementation	▨ Strengthen CARICOM Secretariat's capacity to formulate, supervise the implementation of trade reforms and drive the integration through: (i) technical training in the macroeconomic dimension and implications of trade policy, as well as macroeconomic simulation models for the analysis and quantitative evaluation of the growth and poverty effects of trade reform; (ii) hiring new staff; and (iii) upgrading working material of staff of the Secretariat ▨ Reinforce Caribbean Regional Negotiating Machinery (CRNM)'s capacity to negotiate trade agreements by: (i) providing training to staff of the (CRNM) in the areas of trade and macroeconomic issues; (ii) increasing the numbers of technical staff of the CRNM; (iii) upgrading working material of staff of the Secretariat ▨ Request technical assistance of donors to support CARICOM Secretariat and CNRM during trade negotiations. ▨ Prepare a framework which clarifies the respective mission, duties, and accountability of the CARICOM Secretariat and the Caribbean Regional Negotiating Machinery (CNRM).	▨ Strengthen the capacity of the CARICOM Secretariat to help CARIFORUM countries implement the newly negotiated EPA and other trade agreements. ▨ Implement the principle adopted of automatic financing of the regional institutions. ▨ Prioritize the activities of the regional institutions (CARICOM Secretariat, CRNM, etc.), improve communication, and avoid duplication of activities.

| 7. Mobilizing "aid for trade" | ▓ Prepare comprehensive needs assessment by country, which quantifies envelop of foreign aid needed to implement the EPA and advance regional integration.

▓ Validate the needs assessment at country and regional levels.

▓ Present the needs assessment and financial requirements to the donor community during an aid for trade workshop.

▓ Prepare "bankable" projects.

▓ Validate the projects at national and regional levels.

▓ Present the projects at various forums to attract private sector financing. | ▓ Develop a Caribbean framework for securing aid for trade commitments by donors.

▓ Set up a mechanism for assessing impact of aid for trade on Caribbean's competitiveness. |

PART I

Overview of Economic and Trade System Context

CHAPTER 1

Macroeconomic and Structural Constraints on Trade Reform in the Caribbean

Caribbean countries are entering a new type of relationship with their main trade and development partners through the recently negotiated Economic Partnership Agreements (EPA) with the European Union and the prospects of negotiating free trade agreements with Canada and the United States. These new trade relationships will fundamentally modify the trade environment of these countries, and are likely to have a significant and sustained economic and social impact. The EPA provides a framework for the support by the EU to the Caribbean countries, mainly in the broad context of aid for trade programs. This chapter analyses the constraints associated with the macroeconomic and structural context under which this new trade architecture is being forged.

Understanding this context is of critical importance for three reasons. First, macroeconomic imbalances and structural impediments are major constraints on trade reform and integration in the Caribbean. Second, the effectiveness of new trading relations with its main partners will depend on the region's ability to successfully manage the potential transitional economic costs involved in a shift toward a new trading regime. Third, the new trade environment offers the opportunity to the Caribbean to adjust its macroeconomic challenges and address its structural weaknesses to reap the full benefits of trade integration—while at the same time enhancing its longer-run growth prospects.

This chapter provides an analysis of the macroeconomic and structural constraints on trade reforms in the Caribbean. It aims at describing the macroeconomic and structural environment in which the current trade negotiations and the new dynamics of regional integration within the Caribbean are taking place.

The key findings of this chapter are summarized as follows. First, Caribbean countries have been experiencing macroeconomic and fiscal imbalances, which affect their competitiveness and integration. Second, the growth performance observed in the region in the past two decades has led to improvement in social indicators. However, high growth rates have not translated into employment. Unemployment rates are high, amounting to 10 percent on average for the region as a whole over 2002–06. Moreover, one of the largest countries of the region, Haiti is the poorest country in Latin American and Caribbean and among the poorest in the world. Third, macroeconomic challenges are compounded by structural and physical constraints, which are either physical/geographical (small economic size and location), infrastructure-related, or climatic (exposure to climatic hazards such as hurricanes) and play a critical role in the region's capacity to trade. Fourth, for many countries of the region, reaping the benefits of greater openness will require that complementary reforms and policies be implemented prior to, and in conjunction with, trade reform. Seen in this context, supporting trade adjustment and integration in the Caribbean will also require a shift toward more efficient transfer/assistance mechanisms with support directed at priority areas defined in national development plans and strategies. Put differently, if only from the perspective of the impact of infrastructure on trade performance, there is a strong case for an "aid for trade" strategy.

Caribbean Economy and Macroeconomic Constraints

Over the past decade, the Caribbean as a whole experienced relatively robust growth. Real GDP grew by 3.6 percent over the 1997–2006 period, driven mainly by the strong performance of Trinidad and Tobago (8.6 percent), Belize (6.2 percent), and the Dominican Republic (6.0 percent). Growth in OECS countries was relatively strong as well, averaging 3.5 percent over 1997–2006. This outcome reflects mainly the good performance of Antigua and Barbados (4.8 percent) and Grenada (4.3 percent). At the same time, inflation rates have fallen in most of the Caribbean countries, particularly in those with fixed exchange rate regimes (11 out of 15 countries).[15] Average inflation fell below 7 percent over the period 1997–2006. Many countries recorded a significant drop in their inflation rates down to single digit levels in 2005–06, compared to double digits levels in the late 1990s and early 2000s. OECS countries stand out as the best performers, with inflation rates hovering in the 1 to 4 percent range on average during 1997–2006.[16]

Against this background, the long-term sustainability of growth has been hampered by significant macroeconomic imbalances, including large current account and fiscal deficits, as well as high levels of indebtedness. Moreover, Caribbean countries have been affected by the recent rise in food and energy prices.[17] Box 1 provides an assessment of the

---

15. Countries with fixed exchange rate regime include Antigua and Barbuda, The Bahamas, Barbados, Belize, Dominica, Grenada, St. Kitts and Nevis, St. Lucia, St. Vincent and the Grenadines, and Suriname. Countries with flexible exchange rate regime include the Dominican Republic, Guyana, Haiti, Jamaica, and Trinidad and Tobago.

16. However, high food and fuel prices have manifested themselves in sharply rising inflation in many Caribbean countries. For instance, in Haiti, inflation rose to 15.6 percent in May 2008, up from 7.9 percent in September 2007, reflecting higher prices for food, fuel, and public transportation, which together account for two-thirds of Haiti's CPI.

17. In Haiti, the prices of rice, corn, beans, cooking oil and other foodstuffs have increased significantly since late 2007. Food inflation increased from 6.4 percent in July 2007 to 20.8 percent in April 2008, while overall inflation rose to 16.5 percent in April 2008. This jump was explained by higher prices for food, fuel, and public transportation.

Table 1.1. Caribbean Economies: Real GDP Growth, 1997–2006 (annual percent)

	1997	1998	1999	2000	2001	2002	2003	2004	2005	2006*	Average 1997–2000	Average 2001–06	Average 1997–2006
Average (All 15 countries)	4.1	4.3	3.6	3.4	0.5	2.2	3.8	3.7	4.6	5.9	3.9	3.5	3.6
Average OECS	3.7	4.7	3.7	2.5	−1.4	1.3	3.8	4.3	5.9	6.3	3.7	3.4	3.5
Average Non-OECS	4.3	3.9	3.6	4.0	1.8	2.8	3.9	3.3	3.8	5.7	4.0	3.6	3.7
Standard Deviation (All 15 countries)	2.5	3.2	3.0	3.8	3.6	2.7	4.1	4.5	3.7	3.1	3.1	3.6	3.4

Source: ECLAC database and Bank staff's calculations.
Note: *Preliminary figures.

effects of the current financial crisis on trade and economic growth in the Caribbean. The main transmission channels of the crisis to Caribbean economies are analyzed. These include: (i) lower tourism activities; (ii) lower remittances; (iii) reduced exports; (iv) reduced foreign direct investment flows; (v) reduced ability of highly-indebted countries to access financial market to fulfill their borrowing needs; and (vi) heightened cost of financing for the corporate sector. The macroeconomic imbalances, combined with high

Table 1.2. Caribbean Economies: Inflation Rates, 1997–2006 (Variation in consumer prices, December-December)

	1997	1998	1999	2000	2001	2002	2003	2004	2005	2006*	Average 1997–2006	Average 2001–06	Average 1997–2006
Average (All 15 countries)	5.4	4.9	10.6	9.1	2.7	5.6	8.6	8.8	7.0	4.8	7.5	6.3	6.8
Average OECS	2.9	2.3	1.6	1.5	0.9	1.2	2.0	2.6	4.9	3.0	2.1	2.4	2.3
Average Non-OECS	7.1	6.6	16.6	14.1	3.8	8.6	13.0	12.9	8.5	6.0	11.1	8.8	9.7
Standard Deviation (All 15 countries)	6.1	5.7	28.5	19.2	2.8	7.5	12.6	13.1	4.3	2.7	14.9	7.2	10.3

Source: ECLAC database and Bank staff's calculations.
Note: *Preliminary figures.

Box 1: Effects of the Financial Crisis on Trade and Economic Growth in the Caribbean

Economic growth in the Caribbean countries is expected to slow down relative to 2007 as these economies have been hit hard by recent shocks including a recession in the U.S. economy, the global financial crisis, and a period of high food and fuel prices—although prices are currently declining. As for most Caribbean countries, the economy and financial system are very dependent of the U.S. economy and financial markets conditions. Estimates of GDP growth in Jamaica have been revised down to between 0 and 1 percent for 2008, 2 to 3 percent for 2007, in Haiti down to around 2 percent for 2008 from 3.7 percent in 2007; in Dominican Republic to 5–6 percent in 2008 compared to 7–8 percent in 2007; and in the OECS 4.6 percent for 2007 compared to 7.2 percent in 2006.

The main channels of transmission of the financial crisis to the economy are through (i) Tourism, (ii) remittances, (iii) exports, (iv) reduced ability of highly indebted government to access financial market to fulfill their borrowing needs, (v) heightened cost of financing for the corporate sector, (vi) reduced FDI flows and capital flows affecting investment and most likely growth, and (vii) margin calls from foreign banks' parent company further drying up domestic liquidity.

In the Caribbean, the tourist season is already receiving lower than expected advanced bookings. Economic slowdown in North America and Europe would affect the tourism demand in the short term reducing travel revenues which would have a negative impact on the current account. In the current environment, growth in visitor arrivals is likely to be stymied, based on reduced airlift from the United States in the latter part of 2008 as well as in a decrease in disposable income of potential tourists from North America and Europe.

Remittances have dropped mainly due to the effect of the housing conditions in the United States and failed investment in pyramid schemes that have affected many remittance senders in the United States. Second order effects of the decline in remittances might slightly depress consumption of households' recipient of those funds. In Jamaica, where remittances represent approximately 16 percent of GDP, the official forecast for FY2008/09 has been revised down to 6–7 percent from 10–11 percent.

The global economic slowdown and in particular lower demand from North America and Europe are likely to affect export revenues for many Caribbean countries. Lower economic growth and consumption in North America and Europe could affect their import demand for main OECS's agricultural main products like bananas, cocoa and nutmeg. In the Dominican Republic, there is already some evidence that textile exports to the United States are shrinking. Similarly, lower economic growth could affect U.S. import demand for Haiti's assembly industry. In Jamaica, exports revenues mainly in Bauxite levies have dropped in the past year, affecting the government revenues.

Lower growth and consumption in North America and Europe could slow tourism demand and FDI in the Caribbean. The acute tightening of global liquidity conditions could have a negative impact on FDI flows thus slowing down tourism related projects. In many Caribbean countries, FDI is a significant component of the capital account, covering large portions of the current account deficit.

The authorities' ability to respond to these events is restricted as fiscal policy is constrained by limited fiscal space and borrowing headroom. The high debt and debt servicing burdens of many Caribbean countries could make them vulnerable to a tightening in global liquidity conditions. The level, structure, and composition of debt imply substantial rollover risks for the Caribbean countries—in view of the on-going global financial crisis. While debt to GDP ratios in the Caribbean countries have been going down, they remain at extremely high levels—126 percent for Jamaica, 101 percent average for the OECS and about 50 percent for Dominican Republic.

Corporate spreads have also shot up leading to substantially higher costs of financing for the private sector. Credit growth to the private sector has been slower in the past three months for all countries. It is expected that decreased availability of funding and higher financing costs will particularly affect the tourism sector.

The recent financial market turmoil is likely to have a negative impact directly on the banking sector by weakening bank portfolios as corporations and households ride the downturn with increasingly limited and more expensive funding. Central banks may find themselves in a position in which they will need to provide liquidity to domestic banks to, for example, meet margin calls on their trading portfolios. Another source of risk for the banking system in the sub-region is the presence of large foreign banks whose parent companies may need to call liquidity back from operations in the Caribbean.

Source: Based on "Caribbean Macro Monitoring Notes, 2008–09" (World Bank).

Table 1.3. Caribbean Economies: Merchandise Trade Balance, 1997–2006 (Percent of GDP)

	1997	1998	1999	2000	2001	2002	2003	2004	2005	2006	Average 1997–2000	Average 2001–06	Average 1997–2006
Average (All 15 countries)	−22.6	−22.7	−21.6	−22.4	−22.0	−22.2	−23.8	−23.0	−25.3	−24.1	**−22.3**	**−23.4**	**−22.9**
Average OECS	−35.2	−34.5	−34.5	−34.5	−32.6	−31.3	−35.4	−36.3	−37.9	−38.2	**−34.7**	**−35.3**	**−35.0**
Average Non−OECS	−14.2	−14.8	−13.1	−14.4	−14.9	−16.2	−16.0	−14.2	−16.8	−14.7	**−14.1**	**−15.5**	**−14.9**
Standard Deviation (All 15 countries)	14.6	13.3	14.8	15.4	12.8	11.2	15.0	17.3	17.9	19.6	**14.5**	**15.6**	**15.2**

Source: LDB and IMF Article IV Consultations, and Bank staff's calculations.

levels of unemployment and widespread poverty, have slowed trade reform and are a major concern in the current evolving trade environment.

Large Merchandise and Current Account Deficits

The trend in the region is one of persistent double-digit merchandise and current account deficits. The merchandise deficit for the region as a whole reached consistently above 22 percent of GDP over the past decade 1997–2006, and the current account deficit stood at an average of 11.5 percent of GDP over the same period (see Table 1.3 and 1.4). Comparative figures for the OECS are usually much worse than averages for the region.

Table 1.4. Caribbean Economies: Current Account Balance, 1997–2006 (Percent of GDP)

	1997	1998	1999	2000	2001	2002	2003	2004	2005	2006*	Average 1997–2000	Average 2001–06	Average 1997–2006
Average (All 15 countries)	−11.0	−11.9	−9.5	−10.4	−13.3	−13.3	−8.6	−9.8	−13.7	−13.1	**−10.7**	**−12.0**	**−11.5**
Average OECS	−18.7	−15.8	−16.6	−15.7	−18.9	−21.1	−22.5	−17.6	−23.7	−25.0	**−16.7**	**−21.5**	**−19.6**
Average Non-OECS	−5.8	−9.2	−4.7	−6.8	−9.6	−8.1	0.6	−4.6	−7.1	−5.1	**−6.6**	**−5.7**	**−6.0**
Standard Deviation (All 15 countries)	8.4	8.5	7.9	8.4	9.7	10.0	15.1	10.1	12.5	14.6	**8.3**	**12.0**	**10.5**

Source: ECLAC database, IMF Article IV Consultations, and Bank staff's calculations.
Note: *Preliminary figures.

For this group of countries, the merchandise deficit has been above 30 percent of GDP throughout the period while the current account deficit stood above 20 percent of GDP in most years (see Tables 1.3 and 1.4). Trinidad and Tobago is the only country in the region that has achieved surpluses on both its merchandise and current accounts for the past five years (2002–06). More recently, this country has enjoyed large current account surpluses, averaging 18 percent of GDP during the years 2005–06 (See Appendix Table A4). With petroleum accounting for more than 40 percent of its GDP and fuels representing more than 70 percent of its exports, Trinidad and Tobago's current account surpluses are largely associated with a sharp improvement in its terms of trade. Higher energy prices (namely oil and gas) and chemical prices (namely ammonia, methanol, and urea), combined with stronger production volumes, led to a surge in the merchandise surplus, despite an increase in capital goods imports associated with infrastructure investments on the island. However, most Caribbean countries have recorded double digit current account deficits. Eight out of 15 countries (including Antigua and Barbuda, Bahamas, Dominica, Grenada, Guyana, St. Kitts and Nevis, St. Lucia, and St. Vincent and the Grenadines) exhibit deficits that range between 12–30 percent of GDP on average over 2001–06.[18] In addition, three countries (Barbados, Belize, and Jamaica) recorded nearly double digit current account deficits (see Appendix Table A4).

Large current account deficits may not be an issue if they are a temporary phenomenon, reflecting for instance temporary terms of trade shocks or growth spurs. They may also not be a major concern if they mirror the import of capital goods in the context of a fast growing economy, because over time growth will translate into an increased capacity to service the external debt brought about by these deficits. Moreover, current accounts may be sustainable if they are financed through foreign direct investment. Unfortunately, these three situations do not apply to the Caribbean region. Current account deficits are an issue in the specific context of the Caribbean economies for three reasons.

First, they are a persistent phenomenon, which is a reflection of the trade structure of Caribbean countries. Most Caribbean countries present a narrow export base (generally dominated by exports of services) and are highly dependent on oil imports. In this context, rising oil prices experienced over the past years have resulted in trade deficits in the Bahamas, Barbados, Belize, Jamaica, Guyana[19], and the OECS countries, as growth in merchandise exports (when and where it occurred) was not enough to offset growth in merchandise imports, which was driven by higher fuel prices. The deterioration of the services balance due to a weakening of the tourism sector, and deficit on the income account coupled with trade deficits resulted generally in current account deficits in most Caribbean countries. Large net transfers (remittances and foreign aid) recorded in most Caribbean countries did not fully compensate for the structural deficits in the trade and services balances. In addition, when countries recorded a current account surplus, it tended to be short-lived. A case in point is the Dominican Republic. After running a surplus for two

---

18. It worth mentioning that the six OECS countries belong to the group of Caribbean countries, with double digit current account deficits.

19. In the case of Guyana, the import bill increased by over 21 percent in 2006, reflecting higher oil prices, flood rehabilitation and the higher demand generated by an expanded infrastructure program, partly linked to the Cricket World Cup.

years (2003–2004)[20], the BOP current account reverted to a negative balance in 2005, moving from a surplus of 6.1 percent of GDP to a deficit of 0.5 percent.[21]

Second, large and long lasting trade and current account deficits signal the lack of appropriate policy response on account of policymakers in the region. In fact, there is little evidence that policies have been designed to tackle this issue. When policy actions were taken, they were more short-term reactions to a crisis than deep-seated responses to address the underlying structural causes of current account deficits. This was the cases of Belize and Barbados in 2006. These two countries recorded an improvement in their merchandise and current account balances that contributed to a small overall balance of payment surplus. The factors underlying this performance were short term in nature. Faced with an imminent crisis related to external debt service, Belize responded with a sharp contraction in capital expenditures. This together with the start-up of oil exports, along with higher export earnings from sugar and other agricultural products, strong tourism performance and inward remittances, helped to reduce the current account deficit. Barbados used instead a counter-cyclical monetary policy that started in 2005 to reduce external imbalances.

Third, in the wake of trade negotiations and a changing trade environment, current account deficits in the Caribbean countries are a critical issue as trade liberalization could further widen the deficits, at least temporarily. This potential risk raises the issue of the *sequencing* of trade reforms in the context of the current EPA process, and what can be done to finance a temporary degradation of the trade balance.

Large Fiscal Deficits

The region has been experiencing persistent fiscal deficits. The region's overall fiscal balance deteriorated consistently between 1997 and 2002. Despite a slight improvement in 2005, the deficit stood on average at about 4 percent of GDP over 2001–06 (see Table 1.5). Most Caribbean countries have exhibited a weak fiscal position over the past years, marked by large overall deficits. A first group comprises seven out of fifteen countries, which have an overall deficit ranging between 4–8 percent of GDP on average over 1997–2006. These include four OECS countries (Antigua and Barbuda, Dominica, Grenada, and St. Kitts and Nevis) and three non-OECS countries (Belize, Guyana, and Suriname). A second group, which includes Bahamas, Barbados, Dominican Republic, Haiti, St. Lucia, and St. Vincent and the Grenadines, consists of countries with relatively moderate fiscal deficits: 1–3 percent of GDP on average over the period 1997–2006. Trinidad and Tobago stands out as the only country that has maintained a surplus, mainly due to its good performance during 2003–06. This is mainly the reflection of oil price increases, which have led to growth in Government's revenue.

Persistent growth in expenditure has generally outstripped growth in revenue in the first and second groups of countries. In Guyana, expenditure rose by about 10 percentage points of GDP on average between 1997–2006, while in Grenada and St. Kitts and Nevis, it increased by about 7 percentage points over the same period. At the same time, revenue

---

20. BOP current account surpluses in 2003 and 2004 reflect the combination of the collapse in domestic demand which led to a fall in imports and thus an improvement in the trade balance, growing influx of tourists, which yielded a large surplus in the services balance, and growing family remittances.

21. This reflects an increase of US$ 1.529 billion on the trade deficit, equivalent to a variation of 78 percent.

Table 1.5. Caribbean Economies: Overall Fiscal Balance, 1997–2006 (Percent of GDP)

	1997	1998	1999	2000	2001	2002	2003	2004	2005	2006	Average 1997–2000	Average 2001–06	Average 1997–2006
Average (All 15 countries)	−3.2	−3.8	−3.6	−3.9	−5.4	−6.2	−4.5	−3.3	−1.1	−2.2	**−3.6**	**−3.8**	**−3.7**
Average OECS	−3.8	−3.7	−4.2	−4.8	−7.0	−9.5	−5.5	−3.9	1.5	−2.6	**−4.1**	**−4.5**	**−4.3**
Average Non-OECS	−2.8	−3.9	−3.2	−3.3	−4.3	−4.1	−3.9	−3.0	−2.8	−1.6	**−3.3**	**−3.3**	**−3.3**
Standard Deviation (All 15 countries)	2.7	3.7	2.9	4.3	4.2	5.5	3.2	2.4	7.1	5.4	**3.4**	**4.6**	**4.1**

Source: ECLAC database and Bank staff's calculations.

increased twice less than expenditure, by some 5 percentage points in Guyana, and less in Grenada and St. Kitts. The same story applies to Barbados, Dominican Republic, Jamaica, and Haiti, though to a lesser extent. This reflects the fact that some of the more fiscally stressed economies of the region did not make sufficient effort at fiscal consolidation over the period under review. More broadly, while revenue increased slightly or remained flat in most of the Caribbean countries, expenditure grew faster. Only few countries (most notably Trinidad and Tobago) achieved a sustained improvement in their fiscal stance. Trinidad and Tobago recorded an overall fiscal surplus of more than 2 percent on average over 2001–06. This reflects the fact that the country benefited from strong oil prices and higher returns from natural gas due to a large expansion in exports. This facilitated an increase in revenue that reached more than 27 percent of GDP on average over 2001–06, which largely outpaced an increase in expenditure of about 25 percent of GDP (see Appendix Table A6).

A few other countries, including Suriname, Guyana, and Belize also experienced recently an improvement in their fiscal position. In the case of Suriname, the fiscal surplus recorded in 2006 reflects higher revenue associated with high international prices of oil, gas, and minerals while in Guyana, the decline in the fiscal deficit is the result of improved revenue administration, especially the Integrated Financial Management and Accounting System (IFMAS) and debt forgiveness under the Multilateral Debt Relief Initiative (MDRI). In Belize, tax receipt improved thanks to higher proceeds from the general sales tax (GST) and taxes on income and profits. Meanwhile, growth in spending was held in check due to the containment of public sector wages and reduced debt servicing, following debt restructuring.

Fiscal deficits reflect the structure of public finances of most Caribbean countries, dominated by relatively high levels of expenditure. In fact, the region's revenue performance is quite remarkable. Income-to-GDP stands at levels between 25–30 percent on average over 2001–06 in five countries, including Antigua and Barbados, Belize, St. Lucia, Suriname, and Trinidad and Tobago, while it stands between 30–35 percent in four countries, including Barbados, Grenada, Jamaica, and St. Vincent and Grenadines. Three countries, including Dominica, Guyana, and St. Kitts recorded income-to-GDP higher than 35 percent (see Table 1.5).[22] These performances mirror important revenue efforts recently made by most of the Caribbean countries, including improving revenue collection, increasing tax rates, and introducing new revenue measures (VAT). The issue of fiscal deficits is thus not a reflection of a fundamental lack of revenue. Instead, it reflects high levels of expenditure associated with payments of wages and salaries and allocations of expenditures to goods and services. On average, the region total expenditure reached 32 percent of GDP over 2001–06 while income-to-GDP stood at 28 percent of GDP.

As the scope for increasing revenue may be limited, the issue is thus to what extent the region is able to mobilize additional resources, if only temporarily, in replacement of potential revenue foregone following a trade liberalization policy in the context of the EPA with the EU. Caribbean policymakers face two alternative policy choices: First, the choice of a fiscal adjustment in the form of a drastic cut in expenditure to maintain current fiscal deficits under control. The difficulty of reducing wages and salaries implies that the eventual cut of expenditure is more likely to fall on expenditure on goods and services, at the expense of the quality of services delivery, or on capital expenditure, at the expense of future growth.[23] Second, the Government could recourse to a widening of fiscal deficits by maintaining expenditure at unchanged levels. It does not seem that any of these policy choices could bring gain for the Caribbean. Foreign aid could thus play a key role in support of trade reforms. The role of foreign aid is further discussed in the report.

The underlying issue raised here is the issue of the *sequencing* of trade reforms. Can trade liberalization produce economic and social gains in a context of high fiscal deficits? Can the region afford the current pace of trade liberalization under its fiscal burden? What role can foreign aid play to *compensate* revenue losses and to *promote* trade in the region? These issues are further discussed in this report.

High Levels of Indebtedness and Debt Overhang Issues

A large burden of debt has been the dominant feature of the Caribbean region's macroeconomic stance over the past years. The average public sector external debt of the Caribbean region increased by 10 percentage points on average from an average of 42.1 percent of GDP during the period 1997–2000 to 52 percent of GDP over 2001–06. The dramatic worsening of the debt situation reflects a shift in the policy of financing growth in the region, most notably for OECS countries. In the 1980s, growth was supported by large public investments, primarily financed by aid flows. During the late 1990s and early 2000s, most Caribbean countries (in particular the OECS governments) made efforts through increased public investment to offset exogenous shocks and the contraction in private investment. In the face of sharply reduced aid flows, the increase in public investment in the late 1990s and early 2000s were not financed by raising revenues, but through expensive commercial borrowing (both domestic and external) and growing fiscal deficits.[24] As a result, this policy led to significant build-up of debt in the Caribbean countries to levels that test the limits

---

22. Only Haiti recorded a low revenue performance: about 9 percent of GDP on average over 2000–05.

23. It is worth noting that the fiscal adjustment could also involve reducing the waste of resources through a more efficient use of public resources.

24. IMF (2005) notes that interest payments increased for more indebted OECS countries during 1998–2003, even when global interest rates were declining.

Table 1.6. Caribbean Economies: Public Sector External Debt, 1997–2006 (Percent of GDP)

	1997	1998	1999	2000	2001	2002	2003	2004	2005	2006*	Average 1997–2000	Average 2001–06	Average 1997–2006
Average (All 15 countries)	41.2	41.6	42.1	43.5	47.6	54.6	56.6	55.9	51.5	46.0	**42.1**	**52.0**	**48.1**
Average OECS	33.8	37.5	44.9	46.7	52.2	67.2	71.5	72.1	62.7	56.3	**40.7**	**63.7**	**54.5**
Average Non-OECS	47.5	44.7	40.3	41.3	44.6	46.1	46.6	45.2	44.0	39.2	**43.5**	**44.3**	**44.0**
Standard Deviation (All 15 countries)	44.9	44.5	37.1	32.7	32.4	36.4	33.6	34.0	36.1	29.8	**39.8**	**33.7**	**36.2**

Source: ECLAC database and Bank staff's calculations.

of sustainability. In 2005, the six OECS countries were ranked among the top 16 most indebted economies in the world.

Nevertheless, disparities in debt burdens appear between Caribbean countries. Some countries, including Antigua and Barbuda, Bahamas, Belize, Guyana, and Trinidad and Tobago, were able to bring down their debt levels either by fiscal consolidation, or debt restructuring and debt write-offs. In Bahamas, debt fell slightly from 7.6 percent of GDP on average over 1997–2000 to 6.1 percent of GDP in 2001–05 while Guyana's debt-to-GDP ratio dropped from an average of 170.6 percent of GDP to 139.1 over the same period. Trinidad and Tobago experienced the most dramatic decline in debt: the average debt-to-GDP ratio fell by half from 24 percent over 1997–2000 to 12.8 percent over 2001–05. This improvement of the debt situation in Trinidad and Tobago was mainly due to new receipts of oil revenue and efforts at fiscal consolidation. Meanwhile, Guyana benefited from debt relief of US$ 254 million under the MDRI which helped to bring down the external debt ratio from 143.1 percent of GDP in 2005 to 107.8 percent of GDP in 2006 (see Appendix Table A5).

Notwithstanding recent improvements in the debt situation in a few countries, the picture is still dominated by high levels of indebtedness in the Caribbean region. Debt levels expanded in Barbados, Belize, Dominican Republic, Haiti, Jamaica, Grenada, and St. Vincent on account of factors varying from borrowing on commercial terms, public sector wage settlements and accelerated public capital spending associated with the upgrading of public infrastructure (see Appendix Table A5). External debt takes away a large part of Governments' resources. Debt servicing continued to pose a serious challenge to growth and productive capacity in the region, as these costs diverted scarce resources that could have been devoted to the promotion of growth and social spending. Potential revenue losses associated with trade liberalization may result in the short term in higher debt ratios and exacerbate debt management problems in the Caribbean.[25] This raises the issue of short term corrective or compensation measures.

---

25. This debt prospect may not necessary applies to Haiti and Guyana, which are HIPC countries and should benefit over the next years from grant financing. Their debt profile and ability to borrow are being put under scrutiny in the context of HIPC and MDRI debt relief.

Table 1.7. Unemployment Rates in Selected Caribbean Countries, 2002–06 (Percent)

	2002	2003	2004	2005	2006*	Average 2002–06
Bahamas	9.1	10.8	10.2	10.2	7.6	9.6
Barbados	10.3	11.0	9.8	9.1	8.7	9.8
Belize	10.0	12.9	11.6	11.0	9.4	11.0
Jamaica	14.2	11.4	11.7	11.3	10.3	11.8
Suriname	10.0	7.0	8.4	11.2	12.1	9.7
Trinidad and Tobago	10.4	10.5	8.4	8.0	6.2	8.7
Average	10.7	10.6	10.0	10.1	9.0	

Source: ECLAC Data and Bank staff's calculations.
Note: *Preliminary.

Social Development, High Unemployment and Poverty

High growth rates experienced in the Caribbean over the past decades have resulted in significant human development improvement in all countries except Haiti.[26] Life expectancy has improved significantly. The Human Development Index (HDI) has improved steadily since 1980 for countries for which information is available. At present, with the exception of Haiti, all countries rank among the medium and high HDI categories. Progress towards meeting the Millennium Development Goals (MDGs) has been quite good. Most countries except Haiti are likely to achieve universal primary enrollment. Similarly, the region scores very high in terms of eliminating gender disparity in primary and secondary schools.[27] The goal of reducing child mortality rates by two-thirds by 2015 is on track for all countries, with seven having already achieved the goal. In other categories, the region seems less poised to meet its MDG goals. For example, maternal mortality rates, which must be reduced by three-quarters by 2015, have not improved since 1990.

In contrast to human development indicators, high growth rates have not translated into employment. Unemployment rates are high, amounting to 10 percent on average for the region as a whole over 2002–06. Most of the countries (Bahamas, Barbados, Belize, Jamaica, and Suriname) exhibit double digit or nearly double digit unemployment rate on average over the past five years. Trinidad and Tobago stands as the only exception to this trend. The unemployment rate stood at less than 9 percent on average over that period.

High unemployment mirrors the *mismatch* between the shift in the production structure away from agriculture to industry and services, and the capacity of these two sectors to create jobs in the region. Although the contribution of agriculture to Caribbean economies has been declining for the past two decades, it remains an important source of employment, in particular in most of the OECS countries. Agriculture still accounts for a

---

26. For more detail see World Bank. A Time to Choose. Op. Cit.

27. It is worth mentioning that the indicators used to measure this goal are believed not to capture persistent gender inequality (UNDP 2003).

significant 16 percent of employment in the sub-region—over a quarter of the labor force in Dominica, and one fifth in St. Lucia. The concentration of the workforce in this rapidly declining sector has resulted in rising unemployment rates. However, recent developments are encouraging. Some Caribbean countries managed to reduce their unemployment rates during the past two years. For example, in Bahamas, unemployment fell sharply from a stable figure of 10 percent to 7.6 percent in 2006, mostly owing to hotel project construction. In Barbados, unemployment in 2006 was at its lowest in 16 years at 8.7 percent. Reports indicate that job creation occurred in tourism, construction and utilities sectors while losses were recorded in manufacturing, government services and the finance, insurance, and business services sectors. In Belize, unemployment dropped from 11 percent in 2005 to 9.4 percent in 2006. Most of the new jobs were created in tourism-related services. Trinidad and Tobago is the best performer, with an unemployment rate on a continuously declining trend since 2002. Unemployment decreased considerably in 2006 (to 6.2 percent) following the creation of 12,000 new jobs throughout the year. This reduction has occurred in a context of rising domestic demand, resulting from an increase in banking credit and fiscal expenditure. The challenge now is for these countries to maintain a sustained declining trend in unemployment.

More generally, the issue for the Caribbean is to create jobs so as to reduce high unemployment rates and poverty. However, the potential social costs (loss of jobs in the sectors benefiting from trade preferences) associated with trade liberalization in the context of EPAs renders this objective more challenging—at least in the short term. Given this potential effect of EPAs, the need for fiscal adjustment, which may involve some reductions in public employment, and the continued decline in agriculture (still accounting for a significant share of the labor force), one of the key challenge will be to raise the skill levels of the poor and the unemployed, as well as the population in general. But this will take time. There is an urgent need for the Caribbean to improve social protection and safety net programs during the transition period. The EPAs could offer a framework where these programs and social packages could be negotiated and put in place.

Despite higher growth rates in some countries, progress toward reducing poverty has been relatively slow and remains uneven in the region. In the larger Caribbean countries, an estimated one quarter to one third of the population is living below the poverty line. The three most populous countries of the region (excluding Cuba) have poverty rates—based on the US$1/day poverty line—of 16.4 percent (Dominican Republic), 44.1 percent (Jamaica), and 54 percent (Haiti). Jamaica experienced a decline in poverty of 15 percentage points between the early 1990s and the early 2000s, while in the Dominican Republic poverty increased significantly, especially after the financial crisis of 2002–03 (World Bank 2006a, 2006c). In Belize, Dominica, Grenada, Guyana, St. Kitts and Nevis, and St. Vincent and the Grenadines, poverty rates remain in the 30–40 percent range. The deterioration of poverty indicators in some countries has been largely the consequence of severe external economic shocks (such as the removal of European preferences for ACP banana exports, in the case of St. Lucia and Dominica) and natural hazard occurrences (such as Hurricane Ivan, in the case of Grenada in 2004). In some cases (such as in the Dominican Republic, following the 2002–03 financial crisis), increases in poverty and unemployment have been positively correlated.

In sum, the *scope* (goods and services), the *sequencing* (appropriate timing) and *strategy* (type of approach) of liberalization stand out as issues that have not been given enough attention. High external indebtedness, fiscal imbalances, and large current account deficits remained three of the most important challenges confronting most Caribbean economies. This puts squarely on the front burner the need for fiscal consolidation and the achievement of sustainable levels of debt consistent with economic adjustment, restructuring and transformation necessary for catalyzing growth and development in the region. In addition, poverty and unemployment are also important considerations in many Caribbean countries that further constrain the capacity of the region to move forward trade reforms.

Structural and Physical Constraints

Macroeconomic constraints facing the Caribbean region can be alleviated with the implementation of appropriate policies and reforms aimed at achieving macroeconomic stability. Current account deficits may be brought under control by implementing appropriate monetary, fiscal and exchange rate policies, which strengthen the region's competitiveness. Fiscal deficits can be avoided by improving the composition of, and transparency and efficiency in the allocation of, government expenditure, and reinforcing revenue-enhancing measures so as to expand *fiscal space*. Implementing prudent borrowing policies will help reduce the high levels of indebtedness in the region. Overall, appropriate macroeconomic policies and reforms could alleviate the burden of macroeconomic constraints on Caribbean countries as evidenced by recent economic and financial development (2005–06) in the region.

However, the issue is that the macroeconomic constraints are compounded by structural and physical constraints, the solution to which goes beyond the quality and degree of appropriateness of macroeconomic policies. These constraints, which are either physical/geographical (small economic size and location), infrastructure-related, or climatic (exposure to climatic hazards such as hurricanes) play a critical role in the region's capacity to trade. The current trade negotiations seem not to have appropriately weighted the degree to which these factors operate as binding constraints, which may limit the outcomes of trade liberalization.

Small Economic Size

With an aggregate GDP of about US$70 billion in 2005[28] and a population of about 25 million people in 2006, the 15 Caribbean countries present a relatively small economic size, three times lower than the size of Ireland's economy. The region exhibits important similarities and differences. Most of the countries are typically small in terms of GDP and population. GDP ranges from US$283.6 million in Dominica to US$31.6 billion in the Dominican Republic. GDP for the Dominican Republic, the largest of the CARIFORUM countries, and for Trinidad and Tobago (US$16.2 billion), the largest of the CARICOM islands, thus is more than 100 times and more than 50 times higher than that of Dominica, the smallest

---

28. This data does not include Bahamas, whose data are lacking.

economy of the CARIFORUM countries. Population ranges from 48,393 in St. Kitts and Nevis to more than eight and nine million inhabitants in Haiti and the Dominican Republic, respectively. The ratio of per capita income of the richest CARICOM state (The Bahamas) and the poorest (Haiti) is about 37:1. Growth has averaged more than 3 percent per annum in the OECS countries over the past decade, about 7 percent in Trinidad and Tobago, but only about 1 percent in Haiti.

The small economic size of the Caribbean countries results in relatively high production costs, which coupled with undiversified production sectors limit the region's ability to compete on international markets. Caribbean countries are not big enough to afford large national industries. Small market size tends to raise costs because of the preference of monopolies and, hence, lack of domestic competition. Small Caribbean firms cannot realize economies of scale, nor can they spend significant funds on marketing, research and development. Their capacity to adjust to changes in the global market place is often limited.[29] Economic openness renders small CARICOM economies vulnerable to external shocks such as fluctuations in international commodity prices or policy changes abroad. Vulnerability is compounded by the fact that most CARICOM countries depend for their export earnings on a very limited number of products—another common characteristic of small developing economies. This argument is further discussed below.

Because of size constraint, trade liberalization in the context of an EPA may not produce its expected results as the small Caribbean countries may not reap the full benefits of the proposed liberalization process. In fact because of the small size of Caribbean economies, the potential economic and social costs of the *phasing-out* of preferences may be high as the *space of burden sharing* is relatively limited. *Fiscal space* is limited. Finding appropriate compensating measures may not be an easy task in the short term, and may take time. Moreover, the small Caribbean economies would find it hard in the short term, to adjust their infant industries, the viability of which has been highly dependent on trade preferences. Foreign aid could play a catalytic role as a *compensatory scheme* during the transition period to help these countries cope with the transitional costs of trade liberalization (see Chapter 2).

Infrastructural Weaknesses and Trade in the Caribbean Region

Linkages over the long term between infrastructure capital and economic growth are well documented (OECD 2003; World Bank 1994; Aghion and Schankerman 1999).

---

29. See for example, Bernal (2003). There is a lot of debate among economists on whether or not small size acts as an obstacle to development. One of the most comprehensive studies on this subject is a report issued by the World Bank/Commonwealth Secretariat Joint Task Force on Small States (2000), entitled Small States: Meeting the Challenges in the Global Economy. This report is available at: http://www.worldbank.org. The report argues that small states face a number of specific challenges that combine to make them particularly vulnerable. High income volatility and difficult access to capital are highlighted as common features of many small island states; the lack of domestic competition is noted as a key feature of the small economies. Alan Winters (2000) points out the strong potential economic disadvantage of small size. See A. Winter, Beautiful but Costly: Business Costs in Small Economies. For more research on small states, see the World Bank Small States website (http://www.worldbank.org); Small Island Developing States Network (http://www.sidnet.org), and the Commonwealth website on Small States (http://www.commonwealthsmallstates.org).

Infrastructure, particularly when it is publicly provided, is usually viewed as promoting growth through two main channels: (i) increase in marginal productivity of private inputs[30]; and (ii) impact on private capital formation.[31] In addition to these conventional effects, core public infrastructure may spur growth through a variety of other channels. As discussed by Agénor and Moreno-Dodson (2007), these channels include: (i) reduction in the magnitude of adjustment costs associated with increases in private capital formation, following shocks to relative prices[32]; (ii) improvement in the durability of private capital[33]; and (iii) significant impact on health and education outcomes.[34] Technical Appendix A provides a detailed review of the externalities associated with (public) infrastructure. This section summarizes the status of infrastructure in the Caribbean region and its implications for trade and growth performance of the region.

Despite recent improvement, the region's level and quality of infrastructure remain weak. This in turn constitutes an important obstacle to both intra-regional and external trade. In most of the infrastructure indicators, Caribbean region fares less than comparable developing countries, including Mauritius, Korea, Singapore, and Taiwan (see Table 1.8). However, some Caribbean countries, particularly Jamaica, Antigua and Barbuda, the Bahamas, Barbados, and Trinidad and Tobago have levels of access to telecom services that is in better than comparable developing countries. In Jamaica, the earliest and most successful country to embrace a competitive telecommunications sector, mobile phone use has increased tenfold since the liberalization in 2000. As a result, fixed line and mobile phone subscribers per 100 people reached more than 117 on average over the period 2004–06, a rate higher than that of Mauritius, Malaysia, and Thailand (see Table 1.8). Caribbean countries that invited competition in international calling and mobile telephony now have tariffs that compare favorably with competitive, developed countries.[35] Other countries, including Haiti, still struggle with international rates that are well above cost; prohibitive rates constitute a tax on internationally conducted business.

Intra-regional and external trade is also hampered by the poor logistics and high transport costs. To the exception of Barbados, Jamaica, and St. Vincent and the Grenadines, most of the Caribbean countries have low level of paved roads far below the levels of Mauritius,

---

30. If production inputs are gross complements (as is normally the case), infrastructure tends to increase the marginal productivity of private inputs, thereby lowering production costs.

31. Infrastructure increases the marginal productivity of production inputs; in so doing, it raises the perceived rate of return on, and may increase the demand for, physical capital by the private sector.

32. By facilitating the reallocation of capital across sectors following from shocks to relative prices (e.g., an increase in the relative price of tradables, which would draw resources away from the nontradables sector), public infrastructure may reduce the magnitude of adjustment costs associated with increases in private capital formation.

33. The durability of private capital may be significantly enhanced by improving the availability, and quality, of core public infrastructure.

34. Studies have also found that access to clean water and sanitation has a significant effect on the incidence of malaria, and more generally on child mortality. In the cross-section regressions for developing countries reported by McGuire (2006) for instance, average years of female schooling have a statistically significant impact on under-five mortality rates. In addition, studies have shown that the quality of education tends to improve with better transportation networks in rural areas, whereas attendance rates for girls tend to increase with access to sanitation in schools.

35. Since the introduction of competition in the mobile phone market, costs both in terms of acquisition and usage have fallen, resulting in increased subscription. For example, as of 2006 in Trinidad and Tobago there were 1.7 million mobile subscribers in a country with a population of 1.3 million.

Table 1.8. Selected Infrastructure Indicators of Caribbean Countries and Comparable Developing Countries, 2004–06

	Fixed Line and Mobile Phone Subscribers (Per 100 People)	Improved Sanitation Facilities (% of Population with Access)	Improved Water Source (% of Population with Access)	Internet Users (Per 100 People)	Price Basket for Internet (US$ Per Month)	Roads, Paved (% of Total Roads)
Antigua and Barbuda	168.9	95.0	91.0	38.1	22.0	33.0
Bahamas, The	111.6	100.0	97.0	31.9	25.0	57.4
Barbados	116.8	100.0	100.0	54.8	25.6	100.0
Belize	51.1	47.0	91.0	11.4	12.7	17.0
Dominica	87.9	84.0	97.0	36.1	16.5	50.4
Dominican Republic	57.2	78.0	95.0	20.8	12.3	49.4
Grenada	68.3	96.0	95.0	18.2	22.0	61.0
Guyana	52.9	70.0	83.0	21.6	12.5	7.4
Haiti	6.9	30.0	54.0	6.9	12.0	24.3
Jamaica	117.7	80.0	93.0	46.4	26.5	73.9
St. Kitts and Nevis	74.5	95.0	100.0	21.4	22.0	—
St. Lucia	—	89.0	98.0	33.9	22.0	—
St. Vincent and the Grenadines	92.1	—	—	8.4	22.0	70.0
Suriname	88.2	94.0	92.0	7.1	16.2	26.3
Trinidad and Tobago	149.1	100.0	91.0	12.3	12.6	—
Caribbean	**88.8**	**82.7**	**91.2**	**24.6**	**18.8**	**47.5**
East Asia & Pacific	57.8	50.6	78.5	11.1	5.8	11.4
Latin America & Caribbean	72.8	77.0	90.9	18.4	12.2	24.3
Comparators						
Benin	209.0	13.0	33.0	67.0	8.0	11.0
Korea, Rep.	138.5	—	92.0	70.5	34.6	76.8
Malaysia	91.2	94.0	99.0	43.2	2.7	81.3
Mauritius	90.1	94.0	100.0	14.5	16.2	100.0
Singapore	148.1	100.0	100.0	38.3	13.2	100.0
Taiwan, China	165.4	—	—	63.6	1.5	95.5
Thailand	75.5	99.0	99.0	13.3	5.8	98.5

Sources: World Bank, World Development Indicators, 2008 and Bank staff's calculations.

Table 1.9. Logistic Performance Index Caribbean Countries and Comparable Developing Countries

Country	LPI	Customs	Infrastructure	International Shipments	Logistics Competence	Tracking & Tracing	Domestic Logistics Costs	Timeliness
Caribbean								
Dominican Republic	2.38	2.33	2.18	2.34	2.25	2.28	3.05	2.89
Jamaica	2.25	2.35	2.03	2.13	2.07	2.24	3.5	2.65
Haiti	2.21	2.08	2.14	2.2	2.11	2.16	2.78	2.6
Guyana	2.05	1.95	1.78	1.8	1.95	2.35	3.5	2.5
Caribbean Average	**2.22**	**2.18**	**2.03**	**2.12**	**2.10**	**2.26**	**3.21**	**2.66**
Comparators								
LAC	2.57	2.38	2.38	2.55	2.52	2.58	2.97	3.02
East Asia	2.62	2.47	2.41	2.66	2.58	2.58	3.06	3.07
Benin	2.45	1.80	1.89	2.78	2.56	2.89	3.22	2.78
Hong Kong, China	4	3.84	4.06	3.78	3.99	4.06	2.66	4.33
Malaysia	3.48	3.36	3.33	3.36	3.4	3.51	3.13	3.95
Mauritius	2.13	2	2.29	2.2	1.75	2.25	2.67	2.33
Singapore	4.19	3.9	4.27	4.04	4.21	4.25	2.7	4.53
Taiwan, China	3.64	3.25	3.62	3.65	3.58	3.6	3.1	4.18
Thailand	3.31	3.03	3.16	3.24	3.31	3.25	3.21	3.91
Uganda	2.49	2.21	2.17	2.42	2.55	2.33	3.63	3.29

Source: World Bank Trade Logistics and Facilitation, Logistics Performance Index.

Korea, Singapore, and Taiwan (see Table 1.8). Transportation of goods suffers from the deteriorated condition of existing roads, which more often lack the basic maintenance services. The Caribbean countries have adequate physical infrastructure capacity for ports and runways. However, inefficiencies (including port charges) are sometimes an impediment to trade for importers and exporters. According to the 2008 Doing Business survey, import and export costs are particularly high in Belize, Haiti and Jamaica. Furthermore, the Logistics Performance Indicator, which measures key dimension of logistics for developing and industrialized countries, indicates that Dominican Republic, Haiti, Jamaica and Guyana are performing below the LAC regional average as well as Hong Kong, Singapore, Taiwan, and Thailand in term of infrastructure, customs, and timeliness. Transports costs are relatively high and limit the potential for expanding regional trade. Internet services are much costlier in Caribbean than in countries with comparable income levels. For instance, the cost of 20-hour dial-up access in St. Lucia is US$22.22 compared to US$8.42 in Malaysia (ITU 2004). As a result of these high prices, internet density is particularly low in Trinidad and Tobago, St. Vincent and the Grenadines, Haiti, Suriname, at 12.8; 8.4; 7.1; and 6.9 users per 100 inhabitants, respectively. Other countries like Barbados, Antigua and Barbuda, and the Dominica have relatively higher usage rates of more than 30 users per 100 inhabitants. But these rates are all substantially lower than in countries like Korea and Taiwan (see Table 1.8).

In terms of access to electricity, sustained policy efforts to expand access to electricity in the English-speaking Caribbean have achieved electrification rates above 80 percent in these countries. In contrast, the Dominican Republic and Haiti have only been able to achieve rates below 70 percent and 40 percent, respectively. Per capita consumption of electric power is relatively high in Barbados, Jamaica, Suriname, and Trinidad and Tobago compared to the remaining CARICOM countries (see Table 1.10). Air transport is also underdeveloped. Goods carried through air transport are relatively small as evidenced by freight services. The Caribbean average of freight is far below that of East Asia and Pacific, Latin America and Caribbean (LAC) and even Sub-Saharan Africa (see Table 1.11).

Table 1.10. Per Capita Consumption of Electric Power (Per capita Kilowatt/hour)

	1995	2000	2002	2003	2004	2005	Average 1995–2005
Barbados	2186.8	2636.9	2890.9	2916.6	2998.3	3115.2	2790.8
Grenada	764.6	1111.3	1266.9	1340.3	1301.3	1355.6	1190
Guyana	589.9	942.8	943.9	858.3	875.8	901.7	852.1
Haiti	29.8	34.8	29.6	32.1	36.2	36.2	33.1
Jamaica	1967.9	2334.6	2410.5	2479.8	2450.6	2431.8	2345.9
Dominican Republic	479.4	707.1	1308.6	1648.6	1357.5	1291.5	1132.1
Suriname	3016.8	3006.9	2999.1	3016.3	3022.1	3149.1	3035.1
Trinidad and Tobago	2877	3738.2	3832.1	4523.5	4569.4	4750.4	4048.4
Average	1489	1814.1	1960.2	2101.9	2067.4	2128.9	1926.9

Source: World Bank, World Development Indicators, 2007, and Bank staff's calculations.

Table 1.11. Air Transport, Freight (million tons per km)

	1997	1998	1999	2000	2001	2002	2003	2004	2005	Aver. 1997– 2000	Aver. 2001– 2005	Aver. 1997– 2005
Antigua and Barbuda	0.2	0.2	0.2	0.2	0.2	0.2	0.2	0.2	0.2	0.2	0.2	0.2
Bahamas	0.5	1.1	1.5	1.6	1.8	1.6	1.6	0.6	0.6	1.2	1.2	1.2
Guyana	3.3	3.3	2.2	2.3	1.6	—	—	—	—	2.8	1.6	1.4
Jamaica	20.9	23.8	29.5	29.2	26.4	56.6	48.9	37.7	15.8	25.8	37.1	32.1
Suriname	29.5	26.9	31.8	30	27.6	24.3	24.3	28.2	27.1	29.5	26.3	27.7
Trinidad and Tobago	19.6	49	54.7	45.5	41.8	35.6	34.3	41.8	47.9	42.2	40.3	41.1
Caribbean Average	12.3	17.4	20	18.1	16.6	23.7	21.9	21.7	18.3	17	20.4	18.9
East Asia & Pacific	6,481	6,136	7,219	8,424	8,618	9,708	10,566	12,562	13,285	7,065	10,948	9,222
Latin America & Caribbean	4,591	4,689	4,188	4,623	4,183	3,930	4,035	4,648	4,518	4,522	4,263	4,278
Sub-Saharan Africa	1,374	1,444	1,687	1,736	1,699	1,500	1,643	1,822	1,903	1,560	1,713	1,645

Source: World Bank, World Development Indicators, 2007 and Bank staff's calculations.

With regard to access to water and sanitation, access to improved water source is generally reported to be on average higher than that of East Asia and Pacific and LAC (see Table 1.8). The English-speaking countries as well as Dominican Republic and Suriname have levels in excess of 90 percent, close to those observed in Korea, Mauritius, Malaysia, Singapore, and Thailand. By contrast, in Haiti, less than 60 percent of the population has access to improved water sources. In most countries, the combination of high losses as a result of leakage, theft and under-billing (in excess of 50 percent) and inadequate investment in production and treatment infrastructure have resulted in water rationing, at least at certain times of the year and certain districts. Sewage networks are much less extensive than water supply networks, and waste water is often inadequately treated prior to discharge, which can cause health problems as well as environmental damage (for example, degradation of coral reefs).

The Caribbean countries have adequate physical infrastructure capacity for ports and runways. However, airport and port charges remain a small fraction of the total cost of transporting people and goods to and from Caribbean countries.

Infrastructure weaknesses can impinge on trade performance through transportation costs, the quality of the labor force, and adjustment costs to tariff cuts. Box 1 below summarizes the gains for external trade performance resulting from improved access to infrastructure, and draws the main policy lessons for the Caribbean region. It calls for the Caribbean to invest in core infrastructure (most importantly, electricity, roads, and sanitation). The cost of not investing in infrastructure can be high, given its impact on growth as well as poverty (World Bank 2005a). A few examples in different sectors illustrate this point. In Jamaica, for instance, a 1999 study found that investments valued at US$500 million—mostly for tourism and housing projects—were being held up by lack of water; yet the capital cost of providing the water would have been only around US$30 million. In Guyana and elsewhere, the failure to invest in expanding mobile telecommunications means that these countries are missing out on the productivity gains experienced by Jamaica and other countries that liberalized telecommunications and attracted additional investment. In Haiti, the lack of power, water, and other infrastructure makes it difficult for businesses to succeed and grow.

Box 2: Infrastructure, Trade and Growth: Linkages and Implications for the Trade Agenda of Caribbean Countries

---

Arguments

There are three specific channels through which infrastructure can impinge on trade performance: through transportation costs, the quality of the labor force, and adjustment costs to tariff cuts.

- *Infrastructure constraints, production costs, and exports.* From the perspective of international trade, the reduction in production costs that improved infrastructure may lead to is the most direct effect. Eliminating infrastructure constraints, such as water shortages, electricity outages and difficult road access, can facilitate the process of shifting private resources to more productive sectors, for instance from nontradables to tradables, or from agriculture to services and manufacturing. In addition, by facilitating the movement of people and goods, improved infrastructure can lead in the medium term to higher investments in the rural sector and greater agricultural diversification, by raising expected rates of return.

- *Infrastructure, labor force quality, and trade opportunities.* To the extent that, as discussed in the Appendix, core infrastructure exerts positive effects on health and education outcomes, improved access to infrastructure services can generate significant benefits for export activities in terms of a more productive/higher quality labor force. Moreover, if infrastructure capital enhances the degree of complementarity between skilled labor and physical capital, it will also increase private incentives to invest in the accumulation of knowledge. This may in turn create new opportunities for trade (by opening up new areas of specialization) and economic growth.

- *Trade liberalization and infrastructure.* Following a cut in tariffs, improved access to infrastructure may reduce adjustment costs by facilitating the reallocation of capital from the nontradable to the tradable sector. Moreover, by lowering not only production costs (at a given level of the stock of capital) but also adjustment costs related to investment, improved provision of infrastructure services will tend to raise expected rates of return and therefore stimulate private capital formation.[36] At the same time, by enhancing the ability of the private sector to respond to price signals, lower adjustment costs may be accompanied by efficiency gains, which may translate into permanent growth effects.

Implications for Trade Reform in the Caribbean

The positive externalities associated with improved access to core infrastructure may be substantial in Caribbean countries and must be accounted for in the design of trade reforms aimed at fostering

---

36. In that sense, there is again a complementarity effect between public infrastructure and private investment, but this time it operates through overall adjustment costs, rather than solely through the direct rate of return on private capital.

growth and reducing poverty. Many of these countries (and notably the poorest in the region, such as Haiti and Guyana) remain ill equipped to take full advantage of new trade opportunities because of significant supply-side constraints. For instance, among the constraints that agriculture suffers from in Caribbean countries (in addition to limited and fragmented fertile land and relatively high labor costs) is an inadequate and costly transport infrastructure, which translates into high international transport costs for both inputs and outputs. Moreover, some specific considerations are worth mentioning. First, because of large disparities across the Caribbean countries, without improved access to infrastructure, the poorest countries of the region will not only be unable to compete effectively on international markets, they will also find it difficult to reap the benefits from intra-regional integration. Second, to help to overcome the disadvantages faced by most Caribbean islands due to their small economic size and foster integration through increased intra-regional trade, there is a need for governments to foster the development of regional public goods in infrastructure, mainly regional transport links. Third, because the Caribbean region is highly susceptible to natural disasters such as hurricanes, landslides, and earthquakes, Caribbean countries must improve their ability to cope with infrastructure vulnerability. With growing risks of more violent weather in the next 10 to 50 years due to climate change, the scope for large losses in physical assets may increase dramatically—with consequent pressure on public finances. This, in turn, may increase macroeconomic instability and real exchange rate volatility, thereby distorting critical signals in relative prices for producers. Not only must the region take appropriate measures to improve warning systems and prevention, but the contingent liabilities associated with these losses must be accounted for in designing fiscal policy.

Source: Bank staff.

Investing in infrastructure is thus critical to accelerate trade and growth in the Caribbean region. However, despite the infrastructure weaknesses and the importance of infrastructure for trade and growth (see Box 1), Caribbean government often cannot afford to borrow for infrastructure investment. As seen earlier (Section 1.1 C), many Caribbean countries have debts that are at or approaching unsustainable levels. High debt levels mean that traditional Government borrowing to finance infrastructure is no longer sustainable for highly indebted countries like Antigua and Barbuda, Dominica, Grenada, Haiti, Jamaica, and St. Kitts and Nevis. Because of the limited scope of private sector, most infrastructures will need to be self-financed through public spending. However, limited Government resources, the inability of many Caribbean countries to significantly increase Government revenues in the short term, as well as the limited scope of private sector, make difficult the strategy of self-financing of infrastructure investments. This issue is more complicated because of the high exposure of the Caribbean region to natural disasters and the associated *contingent liabilities* that may occur: each time a natural disaster occurs; scarce resources must be redirected to rebuilding damaged infrastructure assets, investing in new ones to help the development of the region's economic base. In this context, foreign aid could thus play a catalytic role in support of Governments' own efforts to finance infrastructure. The *aid for trade* framework contained in the recently negotiated EPA between the Caribbean countries and the EU offers an opportunity for the Caribbean to benefit for financial assistance to support the investment required to address infrastructure bottlenecks, which affect trade performance of the region. This issue is further discussed in the report. Appendix B provides a detailed analysis of the issues associated with aid for trade in the specific case of Caribbean countries.

Economic Vulnerability

The literature on economic vulnerability of small states is controversial. On the one hand, several recent studies (Easterly and Kraay 2000; Favaro 2004; World Bank 2003) conclude that there is no evidence that small states are more vulnerable than others and suffer growth disadvantages because of their small sizes. Along the same lines, the recent World Bank Report "A Time to Choose. Caribbean Development in the 21st Century" (2005) draws a weaker relationship between the small size of the Caribbean countries and their economic vulnerability. Using an empirical analysis of the relationship between state size (in terms of population) and volatility (defined by the standard deviation of GDP growth) based on world-wide sample over the period 1981–2000, the report concludes that volatility in the Caribbean has been broadly comparable to other regions, rather than exceptional.[37] On the other hand, a study by Briguglio et al (2004) shows that small island developing states (to which most Caribbean countries belong to) tend, when compared with other countries, to be more vulnerable as they tend to be more exposed to international trade, have higher export concentration, be more dependent on strategic imports, and have relatively higher transport costs.

Leaving aside the debate and arguments regarding the relationship between small size and economic vulnerability of the Caribbean countries, it is true that the region, particularly the OECS countries, stand out as among the *most hazard prone* in the world, with a very high frequency of violent windstorms. The Caribbean region is highly susceptible to natural disasters such as hurricanes, landslides, and earthquakes. The OECS countries rank among the top 10 countries by number of disasters per land area and per population.

These factors and the structure of their economies make small Caribbean countries economically vulnerable. First, the greater trade openness, due to small size of domestic markets and the need to achieve economies of scale makes them vulnerable to fluctuations on the international markets. Second, their greater exposure to terms of trade risks, due to their dependence on fewer export commodities, increases their economic vulnerability. Third, their large government sector, due to the large fixed cost in providing public goods and services, takes up a significant part of public resources. Moreover, physical factors also contribute to economic vulnerability of the Caribbean. The degradation of the environment in the Caribbean countries increases the likely impact of natural disasters. Excessive deforestation makes the countries more susceptible to floods, landslides and soil erosion.

The economic vulnerability of Caribbean countries translates into significant economic losses. A recent paper by Rasmussen (2004) shows that incidents—that affect at least 2 percent of a country's population or inflict damage of at least 2 percent of GDP—seem to occur in the region once every 2.5 years. In a study of the impact of damage and losses in six Caribbean countries (Bahamas, Cayman Islands, Dominican Republic, Grenada,

---

37. The state size is defined in terms of population and volatility is defined by the standard deviation of GDP growth. The report indicates that to the extent that specific factors such as natural disasters cause them to be more volatile, their effects are mitigated by the relative advantages in other areas (factors strengthening resilience. It also concludes that the inter-relationship between government size and volatility needs to be looked at carefully—since government size is highly endogenous to many of the determinants of volatility, an empirical framework that assumes exogenous government size is subject to potential endogeneity bias.

Haiti, and Jamaica) associated with hurricanes during 2004, ECLAC estimated that 76 percent of the total impact was constituted by actual physical damage to assets, both private (houses and businesses) and public (roads and bridges, utilities, schools, hospitals and clinics). By themselves, damage and losses to infrastructure and utilities (such as electricity, water and sanitation, and transport) represented 15.6 percent. For Grenada alone, the total loss represented 19.6 percent to core infrastructure assets, education and health systems. This loss of assets translated into a sizable loss in terms of annual flows as well, due to disruptions in activity. In terms of GDP, it is estimated that total damage and losses (inflicted mostly by Hurricane Ivan) amounted to more than twice the size of Grenada's GDP in the previous year.[38]

In sum, trade liberalization in the Caribbean is being implemented in a fragile macroeconomic and structural environment. Trade liberalization (and more specifically the EPA process) should pay more attention to these constraints, which go beyond trade issues per se and cover a large range of issues, such as macroeconomic imbalances, small economic size, infrastructure deficiencies, and economic vulnerability of the Caribbean. Thus, for many countries of the region, reaping the benefits of greater openness will require that complementary reforms and policies be implemented prior to, and in conjunction with, trade reform. Seen in this context, supporting trade adjustment and integration in the Caribbean will also require a shift toward more efficient transfer/assistance mechanisms with support directed at priority areas defined in national development plans and strategies. Put differently, if only from the perspective of the impact of infrastructure on trade performance, there is a strong case for an "aid for trade" strategy, as discussed in Appendix B. Failure to provide assistance will hamper the ability of Caribbean countries to respond to the opportunities that trade liberalization and integration can bring. At the same time, it must be recognized that although regional and global trade integration are key determinants of long-run growth and poverty reduction for all countries in the region, there are important differences among them that need to be considered in designing an "aid for trade" program for each individual country.

---

38. In the Cayman Islands, damage and losses exceeded by more than one third the country's estimated GDP of the previous year.

CHAPTER 2

Caribbean Regional and Global Trading Relations

The Caribbean is in the process of redefining its relations with its main trading partners, including the European Union and the United States, through the recently signed EPA and the upcoming discussions on the future of the CBI. At the same time, the region is also redesigning the process of regional trade integration as it strives to implement the Caribbean Single Market Economy (CSME).[39] The underlying motivation for this is the belief that enhanced regional integration will enable the Caribbean countries to become more efficient and competitive, and thus ultimately to be able to integrate more successfully into the world economy. Hence regional integration is seen as a key step towards dealing in the first instance with any EPA-induced liberalization, and in the second instance with the challenges posed by increased globalization.

The two parallel processes (regional integration and global integration), which complement each other, will shape the region's trade environment during the next few years. It is worth noting that this report does not prejudge in either way what the implications of the EPA would be for the Caribbean countries. It is thus important to understand the underpinnings of these new trade developments to better assess the benefits and costs that they may bring about for the Caribbean region. The impact of the EPA will not only depend on the extent and nature of integration among the Caribbean economies themselves, but also on the formal nature of their trading relations with other countries, notably the EU, the United States, and Canada. In addition, the structural and institutional constraints to trading, together with the macroeconomic and financial imbalances (analyzed in Chapter 1),

---

39. There is also a strong emphasis in the EPA on the need to foster, encourage, and strengthen the process of regional integration.

may hamper the capacity of Caribbean countries to reap the full benefits of the recently signed EPA, as well as slow the regional integration process.

This chapter describes the main features of the new trade architecture, highlights the issues associated with new trade developments, and analyzes the constraints to trading and integration in the Caribbean region. Where relevant, the specificities of the OECS countries are highlighted.

The key findings of this chapter are as follows. First, the process of economic integration has been slow and intra-regional trade is skewed towards few countries (Trinidad and Tobago, Jamaica, Barbados, and Guyana) and products (natural gas and petroleum, chemicals, motor vehicles, telecommunications equipment, and construction equipment). Second, the implementation program of the CET has resulted in a significant reduction in the region's import tariffs. However, some critical issues remain unsolved, including the introduction of revenue-compensation measures, large scope of tariff suspension and reductions, and national derogations from the common tariff. In addition, tariff dispersion in the CET remains high, resulting in additional efficiency costs and further complicating the group's market access negotiations with other countries and regions. This complicates the region's joint negotiating efforts with third countries, creates additional transaction costs and reduces transparency of market access for exporters targeting the CARICOM market. Third, a common trade policy in relation to non-CARICOM countries does not effectively exist. Moreover, the CARICOM Treaty does not explicitly prohibit individual member states from negotiating bilateral trade agreements with third countries. Specifically, Belize benefits from a special provision in the Treaty by which it retains the right to enter into bilateral agreements with neighbouring countries in Central America. As a result, the principle of a customs union (and, by extension, a single market) is somewhat blurred. Fourth, the move toward greater hemispheric integration has deepened the Caribbean countries' resolve to accelerate their own regional integration process. But it is also true that the liberalization of CARICOM's import market for both goods and services will have important consequences for import-competing industries and fiscal revenues. The hemispheric integration process also risks diluting the CARICOM program because it has promoted bilateral actions by some member countries. Fifth, Caribbean's integration into the global economy has mainly been driven by trade preferences granted to the region by its main partners, resulting in highly open economies. However, penetration into the world economy has been slow and declining. Sixth, the Caribbean is facing a key challenge as preferential access for traditional products is being eroded. Foreign aid could play a catalytic role to compensate for revenue losses and support trade reforms. Seventh, the current trade environment offers the region a unique opportunity to strategically reposition itself to be a dynamic exporter of services to key markets.

Intra-Caribbean and Regional Integration Issues

The rationale for intra-Caribbean integration has mainly been driven by the countries' awareness of the constraints that their small economic size poses to the development of their economies. From the early days of their independence, the Caribbean countries sought to overcome the constraints of small economic size through regional economic integration. The economic arguments in favor of intra-Caribbean integration point out the potential costs of the small size of the Caribbean economies, as discussed in Chapter 1.

These include the costs of the presence of monopolies, the lack of domestic competition, and the lack of economies of scale, as well as the limited capacity to adjust to changes in the global marketplace.

Moreover, the constraint of small size calls for the need for *foreign policy coordination*, which aims at increasing the *negotiation power* of the small Caribbean economies vis-à-vis their main trading partners: The USA, the EU, and Canada. It also calls for the need for *functional cooperation* to ensure cost savings and quality enhancements in the common provision of economic goods and social services to the region. Intra-Caribbean integration has also been influenced by the common history and culture of the member countries of CARICOM, and the key role that external powers have played to influence the regional integration process in the region.

This section provides a review of the main developments and features of the regional integration process. It focuses on the issues and achievements to date.

Process of Regional Integration and Key Issues

Slow Integration Process.   The process of regional integration among the Caribbean countries has been gradual and has followed different steps, which began with the creation in 1973 of CARICOM, culminating in the establishment of the CARICOM Single Market in 2006. Box 2 summarizes the history to date of intra-Caribbean integration. It reveals that the process has been relatively slow. It took nearly a decade to transform the Caribbean Free Trade Association (CARIFTA) into CARICOM in 1973, and from that date, more than three decades to create the CARICOM Single Market in 2006. This reflects less the absence of willingness of the Head of Governments of Caribbean countries than the wide disparities between the member states. Faced with diverse economic and social situations, regional integration has not been perceived as a development priority for all Caribbean countries; and neither was its potential for spurring growth through increased regional trade. This can be seen at the very beginning of the integration process. When CARIFTA was created in 1968, only four countries (Antigua, Barbados, Trinidad and Tobago, and Guyana) participated in its formation at the outset. The other countries joined the regional grouping later in the process. This also applies to the transformation of CARIFTA to CARICOM. While Barbados, Guyana, Jamaica, and Trinidad and Tobago signed the Treaty of Chaguaramas in 1973, the other former CARIFTA members show little enthusiasm in the first place to accede to the treaty.[40]

The specific case of the small and least developed Caribbean countries has also added to the complexity and the delay in advancing intra-Caribbean integration. In 1968, seven of smaller and less developed members of CARIFTA formed the Eastern Caribbean Common Market (ECCM) as a precondition for entry into CARIFTA. In 1981, the Organisation of Eastern Caribbean States (OECS) came into being when seven Eastern Caribbean countries signed the Treaty of Basseterre agreeing to cooperate with each other and promote unity and solidarity among the Members. One of the objectives of the alliance is to promote economic cooperation and regional integration. The OECS countries are currently in the process of establishing an economic union which would allow for the free circulation of goods, services, labor, capital and the establishment of a common external tariff.

---

40. They joined the treaty one year latter in 1974.

Box 3: History of Regional Integration in the Caribbean: Key Dates and Developments

---

- 1958 marks the first attempt to regional integration in the Caribbean. On that year, the Federation of the West Indies whose members included all the Commonwealth territories except the Bahamas, Belize and Guyana, was created, to a large extent under the impetus of the United Kingdom.

- In 1962, the Federation of the West Indies was demised, mainly as the result of the internal conflicts within the Caribbean islands and the perception that the Federation was externally imposed. Upon gaining independence in 1962, both Trinidad and Tobago and Jamaica withdrew and the Federation collapsed. A few regional organizations continued to exist after the dissolution of the Federation, including the University of West Indies (created in 1948), the Regional Shipping Services (set up in 1962), and the Caribbean Meteorological Service (established in 1963).

- In 1965, following a series of Heads of Government Conferences, the Heads of Government of Antigua, Barbados and British Guyana signed an Agreement to set up the Caribbean Free Trade Association (CARIFTA). In 1967, at the Fourth Heads of Government Conference, it was agreed to establish CARIFTA formally and to include as many Commonwealth countries as possible. The Free Trade Association was to be the beginning of what would become the Caribbean Common Market (CCM), which would be established for the achievement of a viable Economic Community of Caribbean Territories (ECCT). Subsequently, CARIFTA was formed on May 1st 1968 with the participation of Antigua, Barbados, Trinidad and Tobago and Guyana. Latter in 1968, Dominica, Grenada, St. Kitts/Nevis/Anguilla, Saint Lucia and St. Vincent, Jamaica and Montserrat joined. Belize, which was called British Honduras at that time, joined in May 1971.

- In 1972, at the Seventh Heads of Government Conference, the Caribbean Leaders decided to transform CARIFTA into a Common Market and establish the Caribbean Community of which the Common Market would be an integral part.

- In 1973, CARIFTA became CARICOM when Barbados, Guyana, Jamaica and Trinidad and Tobago signed the Treaty of Chaguaramas. The other former CARIFTA members acceded to the Treaty in 1974. Seven of the smaller and less developed members of CARIFTA formed the Eastern Caribbean Common Market (ECCM) in 1968 as a precondition for entry in to CARIFTA. The 1973 Treaty of Chaguaramas established two organizations, the Caribbean Community and the Caribbean Common Market.

- In 1989, the West Indian Commission was created with the objective to recommend a way forward to move regional integration in the Caribbean.

- In 1992, at a special meeting of the Conference of Heads of Government, based on the recommendations by the West Indian Commission, it was decided to establish the CARICOM Single Market Economy (CSME), and to set up an intergovernmental task force to supervise the revision of the Treaty of Chaguaramas to allow for the establishment of the CSME.

- As of the latest update on the implementation of the CSME, only 12 members of CARICOM have signed and ratified the revised treaty In July 2005, The Bahamas announced that it would not become a member of the CSME. In July 2006, after 28 months of suspension, Haiti joined the ranks of CARICOM. Haiti's parliament ratified the Revised Treaty of Chaguaramas clearing the way for the country's full participation in the CSME although it has been given considerable flexibility with implementing the Treaty given its economic circumstances. Montserrat (a British Territory), is awaiting entrustment from the United Kingdom.

Source: Bank staff based on Kenneth Hall (2001), *The Caribbean Community-Beyond Survival.*

The majority of the OECS members-states are already participants of the Eastern Caribbean Central Bank (ECCB) monetary authority under which they share a common currency.

The recognition of the differences in levels of economic development between the Caribbean countries is well reflected in the treaty that established CARICOM and subsequently the CSME. The treaty distinguishes between the more developed countries (MDCs) and the less developed countries (LDCs).[41] This translates effectively into the recognition of special and differential treatment of the LDCs. It is true that the provision of special and differential treatment of the LDCs is in line with the spirit of regional integration and the objective of achieving a more balanced development in the region. The argument here is one that has been commonly made in many regional trading arrangements, where it is felt that certain countries are more likely to gain from the integration process, while others are more likely to lose. Along these lines, within the Caribbean the argument is thus sometimes made that the prerequisites for integration are more likely to be present in the "more developed" countries, such as Barbados, Jamaica, and Trinidad and Tobago, in particular. But there is one caveat to this argument that often emerges in discussion of the Caribbean regional integration process, which has also led some to question how effectively integrated the region really is. Indeed, it is also true that the special and differential treatment in particular with regard to tariff and non-tariff barriers, which serve to introduce intra-regional trade barriers, limits the extent of integration in the region.

Limited Trade and Economic Integration.   Economic integration has stalled in the region. The 1973 Treaty of Chaguaramas called for the establishment of a common market. More than 30 years later, that goal is still rather far from being met. Target dates have often been postponed, while the objectives themselves have expanded. Implementation of the common external tariff (CET), originally scheduled for 1981, was delayed by more than a decade, and most countries missed the 1998 deadline for full implementation. Even today, the CET contains a number of loopholes and some countries have yet to apply it fully. There is wide dispersion in the range of actual tariffs implemented by CARICOM members on imports from non-members. This reflects the large number of exemptions from the CET that CARICOM members can use. Average tariffs range from 7.2 percent in Jamaica to 30.7 percent in the Bahamas. Maximum tariffs are even more dispersed, ranging from 40 percent to 400 percent. Significant NTBs appear to exist on certain categories of imported products from outside CARICOM. The Bahamas, where tariffs are about double the average rate in the Caribbean, has not joined the CSME. In October 2004, CARICOM reported several instances of discriminatory environmental taxes in Antigua and Barbuda, Barbados, Grenada, Belize, Guyana, and Dominica.

Intra-regional trade is very limited and skewed toward few countries and products. In 2006, CARICOM intra-regional exports reached their highest level, climbing to US$2.5 billion from US$2.3 billion in 2005. Trinidad and Tobago has long been the dominant intra-regional exporter, with 85 percent of total exports. Barbados was the second largest exporter with only 6 percent of total exports, followed by Guyana with 4 percent. The OECS countries as a group account for about 5 percent of the value of intra-regional exports.

---

41. It is important to note that the classification between MDCs and LDCs does not depend on conventional criteria such as per capita income levels or social development indicators. It is related to economic size. The MDCs are: Barbados, Guyana, Jamaica, Suriname, and Trinidad and Tobago. The remaining countries are considered LDCs. The LDCs are those countries which are seen as being particularly vulnerable either due to their size, or due to their levels of economic development. Hence, for example, Antigua and Barbuda has one of the highest GDP per capita level in the region but is still considered an LDC. All of the OECS countries are considered as LDCs.

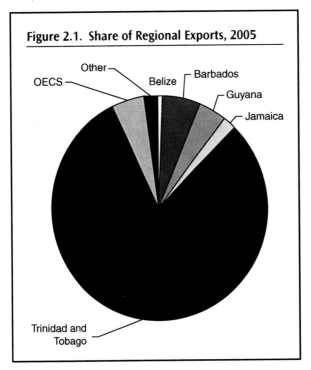

Figure 2.1. Share of Regional Exports, 2005

Source: Authors based on COMTRADE database, 2006.

Jamaica is the largest market for the region's imports, with a share of 39 percent followed by Barbados and Guyana. Intra-regional trade in goods is dominated by natural gas and petroleum, chemicals, motor vehicles, telecommunications equipment, and construction equipment. If it wasn't for Trinidad and Tobago, regional trade between CARICOM countries would be very limited.

In the 1989 Grand Anse Declaration, Caribbean Heads of Government committed themselves to establishing a single market and economy "in the shortest possible time" and agreed on a number of actions to be completed by 1993. However, that deadline was never met. In 1998, Heads of Government agreed again to work toward completing the implementation of the major elements of the CSME, this time by 1999. That deadline also was not met. December 2005 was set as the deadline for implementing the most important single market provisions, but once again this deadline was not met. The year 2008 has been set for implementing the single economy.

The Caribbean Single Market Economy (CSME) is today the cornerstone of economic integration, and aims at creating a single economic space to support competitive production

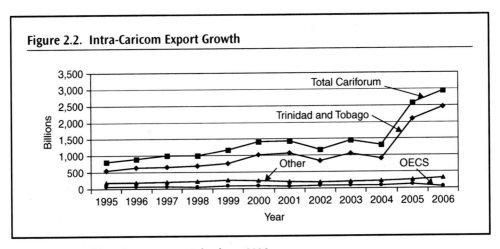

Figure 2.2. Intra-Caricom Export Growth

Source: Bank staff based on COMTRADE database, 2006.

within CARICOM, for both regional and extra-regional markets.[42] The CSME is to be implemented in two phases. Phase I took effect on January 1, 2006 and was formalized at the launch of the Caribbean Single Market (CSM) on January 30, 2006 in Kingston, Jamaica. The CSM removes barriers to trade in goods, services, and several labor categories. The second phase of the process is the implementation of the CARICOM Single Economy by the end of 2015. Stage 1 is to take place between 2008 and 2009 with the consolidation of the Single Market and the initiation of the Single Economy. Stage 2 is to take place between 2010 and 2015 and consists of the consolidation and completion of the Single Economy and policies to implement a CARICOM monetary union.

What progress has been made? Thirteen member states of CARICOM have signed and ratified the Revised Treaty of Chaguaramas, which entered into force in January 2006. The Bahamas and Montserrat are not members of the CSME. All thirteen members, except Haiti, have enacted the treaty into domestic law. Overall, Barbados, Jamaica and Trinidad and Tobago are the most advanced in implementation. The region has been most successful at eliminating tariffs on goods originating in common market countries such that most products have been circulating duty free since the 1990s. Many non-tariff barriers have also been removed and there is a schedule in place that calls for the removal of unauthorized import duties and discriminatory taxes. However, the removal of barriers to the right of establishment and provision of services has progressed slowly. Member states have taken stock of their respective barriers to services trade and have established a program for the removal of restrictions.

All members have enacted legislation to permit free movement of university graduates, media workers, sports persons, artists and musicians, and certain categories of high level staff circulating to provide a service or establish a business. Members are discussing whether to expand these categories to include workers in the hospitality area, artisans, domestics, nurses and teachers who are non-graduates. The CARICOM passport has been introduced by ten states[43] to facilitate both intra regional and international travel. The expectation is that all the member states will have introduced the CARICOM passport by 2008. A number of regional bodies have been established to facilitate aspects of regional integration, including the Caribbean Court of Justice and the CARICOM Regional Organization for Standards and Quality (CROSQ).

Yet, CARICOM has still yet to be a single market economy. The main provisions of a single market economy have yet to be implemented. A final decision on governance and institutional reform is still pending. In July 2002, government leaders agreed to inaugurate the Caribbean Court of Justice "by the second half of 2003". The inauguration took place in April 2005, with some controversy continuing to surround the Court's appellate jurisdiction. It is not clear how the process will be moved forward.

CARICOM countries have recognized that economic divergence among member states could be an impediment to advance regional integration. The CARICOM Treaty thus rightly attributes special treatment of less developed countries in terms of their obligations

---

42. The rationale for the CSME is that the free movement of goods, services, capital and skilled people across the region will facilitate a more efficient allocation of resources, easier access to capital, skills and other inputs from across the region and, thus, more competitive production of goods and services.

43. These states are Antigua and Barbuda, Barbados, Dominica, Grenada, Guyana, St. Kitts and Nevis, St. Lucia, St. Vincent and the Grenadines, Suriname and Trinidad and Tobago.

under the Treaty. The Treaty calls for the establishment of a Regional Development Fund that would help disadvantaged countries, regions and sectors cope with CSME-related adjustment.[44] The US$250M fund was launched in July 2008 with an initial $60M towards its $250M target. The Fund, currently being held in an escrow account at the Caribbean Development Bank (CDB), will promote business development, among other areas. Member States would contribute $120M of the Fund through a formula that would take into account size, per capita income and other minor indices. The remainder of the funds would come from contributions by development partners. Disadvantaged countries will be the main targets of the Fund and which could receive allocations from the Fund in the forms of loans, grants and interest subsidy grants.

The slow pace and limited economic integration may stem partly from the fact that the Caribbean governments may have underestimated the scope and complexity of legal, institutional and administrative work that has to be done to make the CSME operational in all member states. But other factors, including structural, institutional and political factors have also influenced the integration process. Section 2.3 of this chapter reviews the role that these factors have played in the Caribbean economic integration process.

Implementation of the CSME: Issues and Challenges

The single market covers the free movement of goods, services, capital and skilled workers across the region, the right of establishment, and the implementation of a common external tariff and trade policy. The CSME implementation agenda covers four main areas: (i) the free movement of goods; (ii) common external tariff and trade policy; (iii) sectoral development policies and (iv) macroeconomic policies.[45] While important progress has been made in freeing the movement of goods, the CSME agenda has shown little results in the areas of harmonization of trade policies, sectoral development policies, and macroeconomic convergence.[46]

The Free Movement of Goods is Advanced. CARICOM has made good progress to free the movement of goods. Over the past decades, intra-regional trade has been free of tariff restrictions, and since the early 1990s, many tariff barriers have also been removed. CARICOM has also put in place a schedule for removing the remaining restrictions, including among others, unauthorized import duties, export duties, discriminatory internal taxes and other fiscal charges, and unauthorized import licenses and quantitative restrictions on goods of Community origin.[47] Moreover, efforts are being made to harmonize across the region the application of authorized non-tariff trade regulations.

---

44. See Article 158 of Chapter VII of the CARICOM Treaty.

45. It is worth noting that there is not a unique way to divide the CSME implementation agenda. For instance, a recent needs assessment for CARICOM commissioned by the CARICOM Secretariat divides the CSME implementation agenda into four areas: the institutional and legal framework; market access; sectoral development policies; and macroeconomic framework. See Brewster, 2003.

46. Some of the background materials of this section are drawn from the report: CARICOM Report No. 2. Inter-American Development Bank. August 2005.

47. Fiscal charges such as environmental levies, taxes and surcharges, bottle deposit levies, inspection fees, consent fees, consumption taxes, and special produce import taxes are scheduled to be removed.

However, the free movement of goods is still hampered by a number of issues that CARICOM needs to address, for the CSME to be an effective instrument of trade integration within the region. First, the treaty still lacks an agreement on how to treat goods produced in, and shipped from, free zones. Second, CARICOM does not have yet a regime for free circulation of goods. Third, there is no common regime for electronic commerce, which is emerging as an important sector of economic activity, both in intra-regional and international business transactions. Fourth, the integration process has not yet covered government procurement. As a result, the regional market remains segmented in favor of nationals, and cannot therefore impact fully on the regional economy.

Common External Tariff and Trade Policy.   In 1992, CARICOM governments established a four-phase implementation program for the CET. Unfortunately, the speed of implementation has varied substantially among member states: only two countries met the established deadline of June 1998. As of today, eleven member states have fully implemented the program, while two others (Antigua and Barbuda, St. Kitts and Nevis) have reached phase three. Member states are now in the process of implementing the revised structure of the CET based on the 2002 Harmonized System (HS). Barbados, Guyana, Jamaica, Montserrat and Trinidad and Tobago have already completed that process. Haiti and the Bahamas retain their own import tariff regimes, the former because it has not yet adopted the CET, the latter because it does not intend to do so.

The implementation program of the CET has resulted in a significant reduction in the region's import tariffs, from an unweighted average of 20 percent in the early 1990s to 10 percent today. However, some critical issues remain unsolved. First, many countries (mainly the OECS), which rely heavily on trade taxes as a source of government revenue, have introduced revenue-compensation measures to mitigate the revenue losses stemming from the introduction of the CET. These include, among others: import-related levies such as stamp duties, import surcharges, and discriminatory rates of the consumption tax.[48] Second, the CET offers broad scope for tariff suspensions and reductions, as well as for national derogations from the common tariff. This complicates the region's joint negotiating efforts with third countries, creates additional transaction costs and reduces transparency of market access for exporters targeting the CARICOM market. Third, the level of tariff dispersion in the CET remains high, resulting in additional efficiency costs and further complicating the group's market access negotiations with other countries and regions. Fourth, although CARICOM's tariffs are lower than a decade ago, they are still relatively high, particularly in the food and manufacturing sectors, where products remain highly protected from external competition (see Table 2.1).

This raises concerns about *trade diversion* and calls on the member states to reform the CET to eliminate exceptions and derogations, reduce tariff dispersion, and pursue further tariff reduction where possible. However, the scope for tariff reduction is linked to the capacity of CARICOM member states to design and implement fiscal reforms that will reduce dependence on trade taxes over the long term, and on the availability of additional financial support from the international community in the short and medium term.

---

48. In some countries, these charges have spurred anti-trade bias, and have therefore been declared illegal by the WTO.

Table 2.1. CARICOM: CET and National Applied Tariffs in Selected Countries, 2003

HS Sec	Simple Average (%) Description	CET	Barbados	Guyana	Jamaica	St. Kitts & Nevis	Trinidad & Tobago
01	Live animals/products	24.9	53.3	27.1	25.3	11.5	24.3
02	Vegetable products	18.2	28.0	18.4	16.4	13.2	16.2
03	Animal vegetable fats	26.7	32.1	25.8	23.9	21.9	24.0
04	Processed foods/tobacco	19.7	34.2	25.0	15.5	16.1	16.2
05	Mineral products	4.8	6.9	6.2	2.6	2.4	3.0
06	Chemical/industrial products	5.4	6.6	6.1	2.0	5.6	2.3
07	Plastic/rubber	7.4	9.1	8.7	5.6	6.7	6.3
08	Animal hides/skin	8.2	9.6	9.2	5.6	7.6	5.8
09	Wood/wood articles	9.6	10.6	9.5	6.8	9.7	6.9
10	Paper/cellulose material	7.3	8.9	8.0	4.8	8.1	5.2
11	Textiles	10.4	10.8	10.8	7.6	11.1	7.9
12	Footwear/misc. articles	16.6	16.2	16.0	15.4	18.5	15.2
13	Stone/glassware	8.8	9.6	8.8	6.2	9.8	8.4
14	Precious/semi-precious metals	20.1	29.7	28.6	16.8	14.4	14.7
15	Base metals	5.6	6.8	6.7	2.7	6.2	4.6
16	Machinery/electrical equipment	6.5	7.8	7.5	3.5	7.7	4.9
17	Motor vehicles/vessels	9.6	10.0	9.4	6.4	9.7	7.2
18	Precision instruments	11.5	14.4	14.2	8.9	10.8	9.9
19	Arms/munitions	38.1	47.7	44.7	22.7	46.8	22.9
20	Misc. manufactured articles	16.2	16.2	15.8	15.2	19.3	15.7
21	Art/antiques	20.5	20.0	20.0	20.0	25.0	20.0
	Average tariff (%)	10.1	13.1	11.0	7.2	9.4	7.9
	Standard deviation	14.7	26.4	12.9	12.4	12.1	12.3

Sources: Inter-American Development Bank, CARICOM Report No. 2, August 2005.

The urgency of fiscal reforms in the region, where most of the countries experienced large fiscal deficits over the past decade (see Chapter 1), is more pronounced in the context of eroding trade preferences and following the recent signing of EPA. While it is true that Caribbean countries should make every effort to expand their domestic revenue base, it is also true that foreign aid could play a catalytic role as a compensation scheme for revenue forgone from trade liberalization in the short to medium term. Aid for trade could also be used as a promotion scheme in the long term (see Box 3).

A common trade policy in relation to non-CARICOM countries does not effectively exist. The CARICOM Treaty does not explicitly prohibit individual member states from negotiating bilateral trade agreements with third countries.[49] Specifically, Belize benefits from a special provision in the Treaty by which it retains the right to enter into bilateral agreements with neighbouring countries in Central America. As a result, the principle of a customs union (and, by extension, a single market) is somewhat blurred. The challenge for the coming years is for CARICOM countries to design a common trade policy, which is the backbone of a full and well-functioning single market. Ultimately, the success of the CSME will depend largely on the effective implementation of a common trade policy.

Right of Establishment and the Free Movement of Services, Capital, and Labor.   One of the most fundamental aspects of the single market is the right of establishment, which allows Community nationals to establish a business presence anywhere in the CSME. However, two main obstacles limit the provision of the right of establishment. First, there is no regional system of company registration to facilitate harmonization of regulation and oversight. Several countries have extra requirements for non-nationals in the process of registration, which are discriminatory and often slow the registration process. Second, there are restrictions on access to property which seriously affect the right of establishment. While CARICOM has just started to address the issue of the regional system of company registration, the limitations to landholding remain challenging. An effective CSME would need implementation of clear provisions regarding access to property.

Free Movement of Services.   The integration approach adopted in this area has consisted in the adoption by CARICOM member states of a negative list, whereby all sectors and measures are to be liberalized unless otherwise specified.[50] The CARICOM Treaty gives nationals of member states the right to provide services by any of the four modes of supply recognized in Article 36 of the Treaty.[51]

Services are a critical area for Caribbean trade integration because this is an area where CARICOM countries have the greatest opportunities to expand trade and foster economic growth. However, key issues would need to be addressed for trade in services to become a cornerstone of intra-regional trade integration. First, air and maritime transports and

---

49. The CARICOM Treaty only requires that individual member states who have negotiated bilateral trade agreements with third countries seek approval of the relevant CARICOM Ministerial Council.

50. A positive list approach, which is usually less "liberalizing", would mean that countries limit their liberalization commitment to specific sectors or measures.

51. These four modes are identical to the modes under Article 1(2) of the WTO General Agreements on Trade and Services (GATS).

financial services are facing critical constraints. Existing restrictions are not well identified; and agreement on a schedule for their removal is not done. Second, CARICOM lacks a common services regime and this limits its capacity to negotiate and implement services agreements with external trade partners.

Liberalization of Capital Flows.   Progress in this area has been mixed. Few countries (Guyana, Jamaica, and Trinidad and Tobago) have abolished exchange controls; the other members have maintained them. National stock exchanges have been established in few countries, including the Bahamas, Barbados, Guyana, Jamaica, Trinidad and Tobago, and the OECS. However, cross listing and trading take place only among three of them. CARICOM is in a process of developing a regional stock exchange. But, discussions are still ongoing on the structure that would guarantee the most effective integration of the regional capital market.[52] CARICOM has also established a Caribbean Credit Rating Agency (CCRA) in Trinidad and Tobago, with a view to accelerate integration of the regional securities industry. In addition, member states agreed to develop a CARICOM Financial Services Agreement, which would help streamline the cross-border operations of financial institutions and reduce barriers to cross-border financial flows. But the effectiveness of that agreement has been delayed.

CARICOM's efforts to advance financial integration broaden and deepen the scope of potential integration within the region; and this is a good approach. Yet, infrastructure weaknesses limit the potential of financial integration within the region. Financial transactions cannot be well processed and expanded unless there is a sound and high quality telecommunications and transports services. Unfortunately, as documented in Chapter 1, this is an area where the Caribbean region has performed poorly. Financial integration and infrastructure building are thus ultimately related. This, in turn, calls for a more comprehensive approach to regional integration, which should put infrastructure development as an important step in the sequencing of policy actions—both at the national and regional levels.

Free Movement of Skills.   CARICOM has rightly given priority to the free movement of skilled workers as a central element of the CSME. However, overall progress in this area has been slow. Concrete policy actions have been scarce or have remained at the level of the implementation of specific legislations only. For instance, eleven countries have implemented legislation and the regulatory and administrative arrangements needed to foster the free movement of university graduates. Ten countries have done the same with respect to the movement of artists, media workers, musicians and sport persons. Antigua and Barbuda, Montserrat, and St. Kitts and Nevis, still need to fulfil their obligations.

The free movement of skills is limited by key factors, including among others, the lack of a regional policy on harmonization and transferability of social security benefits, the elimination of the need for passports for travel within the region, common entry/departure

---

52. A Regional Capital Markets Committee is working closely with CARICOM's Ministerial Council for Finance and Planning (COFAP) and has put forward four proposals: (i) cross listing and cross trading; (ii) the OECS model; (iii) the creation of a new entity; and (iv) a scheme modeled on the European EURONEXT. It seems that there is a preference to go with the EURONEXT model. However, there has not been a final decision yet.

forms, and a CARICOM passport. Moreover, administrative processes remain cumbersome and additional restrictions still exist. These, together with poor infrastructure, limit the incentive of workers to move within the region.

Lack of Macroeconomic Coordination and Convergence.   Cognizant that an effective CSME requires the coordination of macroeconomic policies, the CARICOM Revised Treaty calls on member states to harmonize their monetary and fiscal policies.[53] Unfortunately, achievement to date in this area has not gone beyond meetings of CARICOM finance ministers (COFAP) and central bank governors. Binding rules and procedures for policy coordination and implementation are not yet in place. Institutional arrangements still lack implementation and enforcement mechanisms. CARICOM member states do not appear to have integrated the convergence criteria into their budgetary and policy formulation process.[54] As a result, convergence criteria are not met and substantial dispersion exists among CARICOM countries.[55]

The lack of macroeconomic convergence also mirrors the lack of influence of the Caribbean Centre for Money and Finance (CCMF) on macroeconomic policies implemented by CARICOM countries. CCMF's policy recommendations are not followed by concrete policy actions to reinforce regional coordination and macroeconomic convergence between Caribbean countries.

Fiscal policy harmonization is still at an infancy stage while investment policy harmonization has yet to materialize. There is important work to be done in the areas of harmonization and rationalization of tax systems, harmonization of systems of investment incentives, as well as financial policy.

Overall, the success of macroeconomic convergence within the region will depend on the capacity of CARICOM to set up binding rules and procedures for policy coordination and ensure that enforcing mechanisms exist and function effectively.

Lack of Progress on Sectoral Policies.   CARICOM Revised Treaty gives an important emphasis on policies for sectoral development.[56] The Treaty covers the main development sectors, including industry, agriculture, transport, and human development. The objective is to create a common development policy, which could help the region grow faster, reduce poverty, and achieve long-term and sustainable development.

However, little has been achieved. In fact, sectoral policies have not moved beyond the good intentions of CARICOM member states to promote common policies. Three reasons

---

53. See Articles 44 and 70 of the Revised Treaty.

54. The Caribbean Centre for Money and Finance (CCMF) is in charge of measuring economic convergence among member states' economies. In this regard, it uses a set of eligibility criteria for entry into a monetary union: (i) reserve cover, set at three months import cover for the past 12 months; (ii) exchange rate stability, with fluctuations in the exchange rate remaining within a 1.5 percentage point band for countries with floating exchange rate regimes, and zero fluctuations for those with fixed exchange rate regimes, over a period of 36 months; (iii) debt service ratio below 15 percent; (iv) average fiscal deficits of no more than 3 percent of GDP; and (v) an inflation convergence standard, defined as the median inflation rate for the three countries with the lowest, but positive, inflation rate, plus or minus 1.5 percent.

55. According to the CCMF, only one convergence criteria—the import cover standard—has been consistently met by member countries.

56. See Chapter IV and VI of the Revised Treaty.

could be put forward to explain the meager outcomes so far. First, limited technical, human, and financial resources have impeded the implementation of common sectoral policies. Second, infrastructure weaknesses limit the ability of CARICOM member states to set up a common regional development policy. Third, weak political will at the national level and limited cooperation among member states result in countries putting little emphasis on regional development policies and more on national strategies and policy measures.

Sectoral development policies and programs are critical for the success of the single market. One cannot expect the removal of restrictions to trade and the creation of new governing structures to enforce rules and monitor regional activities to bring benefits unless the economic sectors that are to drive the integration process are strong. This *sequencing of integration* is well understood by CARICOM member states. The challenge for CARICOM is to reconcile the need for a regional development strategy and the pressing national needs of many countries of the group to allocate their scarce resources to national priorities. This in turn is related to the issue of multiple dimensions of the obstacles to regional integration, which cover the physical, resource and human constraints as well as the political economy of regionalization (see below).

Hemispheric Integration

Launched in the late 1990s, but put on hold since early-2004, the hemisphere-wide FTAA aimed at creating a balanced, WTO-consistent agreement covering trade in agriculture and industrial goods, services, investment, government procurement, dispute settlement, intellectual property, competition policy, and subsidies, antidumping and countervailing duties. The FTAA played a key role in convincing the CARICOM countries to deepen their own regional integration and to look at opportunities for integration with the wider hemisphere.

The general acceleration of trade liberalization in the Western Hemisphere also provided a fresh incentive for Caribbean integration. Indeed, much of the perceived urgency in implementing the CSME today results from the belief that, in economic terms, the Community must prepare itself for greater competition in Western Hemispheric markets, through deeper integration among its members. In political terms, it must preserve a Caribbean identity and economic space that, unless grounded in deeper integration, could risk being weakened or made somewhat redundant by the general liberalization trend in the hemisphere.

In general, the move toward greater hemispheric integration has deepened the Caribbean countries' resolve to accelerate their own regional integration process. As the first truly comprehensive external trade negotiation experience for the Caribbean countries, the FTAA contributed toward greater coordination of foreign trade positions and negotiations resources, as evidenced by the creation in 1997 of the Caribbean Regional Negotiating Machinery (CRNM). But it is also true that the liberalization of CARICOM's import market for both goods and services will have important consequences for import-competing industries and fiscal revenues. The hemispheric integration process also risks diluting the CARICOM program because it has promoted bilateral actions by some member countries that do not seem to have occurred in relation to Europe. One example is the free trade area that Trinidad and Tobago negotiated with Costa Rica (it was later expanded to CARICOM as a whole). Another example is the growing cooperation among South American Countries; in which Guyana and Suriname are increasingly involved (both countries are members of the Initiative for the Integration of Regional Infrastructure in South America (IIRSA)).[57] While such actions clearly have their own merit, they also have the potential to weaken the Caribbean integration process, particularly if full CSME implementation is delayed.

The Caribbean and the Global Trading Environment

For the past three decades the Caribbean has pursued an external trade policy anchored on preferential access to the European and North American markets. Under the Lomé and Cotonou agreements, Caribbean countries received preferential access to the EU for traditional agricultural exports. Similarly, the region has enjoyed 30 years of preferential access to the United States for certain products under the Caribbean Basin Initiative (CBI). Although these preferential trading arrangements were established as a development tool to stimulate and diversify Caribbean exports, the prevailing consensus is that much more needs to be done to promote export diversification and growth.

The Caribbean is facing a situation where preferential access for traditional products is being eroded. This situation is exacerbated by the region's comparatively high production costs (particularly labor and transport) and small size which make it difficult to achieve economies of scale to competitively export certain products. In the new era of globalization and integration, preferential arrangements that were the cornerstone of Caribbean trade policy can no longer represent key elements of a viable trade and growth strategy. Rather, the region must take steps to strategically reposition itself to take advantage of new market opportunities, particularly in services, where it has consistently demonstrated comparative advantage.

The region has a unique opportunity to strategically reposition itself to be a dynamic exporter of services to key markets. CARICOM countries recently concluded comprehensive EPA negotiations with the EU and are expected to begin negotiating a free trade agreement with Canada. Moreover, CARICOM and the United States have discussed the possibility of establishing a free trade agreement, which would further strengthen economic ties and possibly open up new areas for exports of services. The region's challenge will be to leverage this new architecture of trade agreements to bring about sustained growth.

External Trade Structure

Caribbean countries are generally very open economies. Trade as a percentage of GDP averaged 111 percent for the region over the period. Haiti being the country where trade represents the lowest percentage of GDP, while Guyana is the most dependent on trade. On average, the OECS countries are only marginally more open than the rest of the region. With respect to trade performance, Caribbean countries'share of world trade has been

---

57. For more information on IIRSA, see its official website at http://www.iirsa.org.

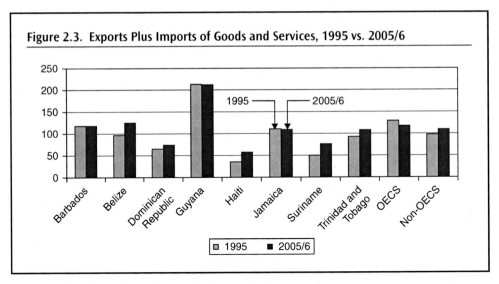

Figure 2.3. Exports Plus Imports of Goods and Services, 1995 vs. 2005/6

Source: Bank staff. World Development Indicators Database.

declining over the past decade (see Chapter 3). While merchandise exports increased in Trinidad and Tobago driven in large part by the surge in oil and natural gas exports, in contrast, over the past 10 years, merchandise exports in Dominica, St. Lucia, and St. Vincent declined by up to 40 percent due to preference erosion.

The importance of the services sector cannot be overstated for many Caribbean economies. On average, the region derives 45 percent of its GDP from trade in services. This figure is much higher for services-based economies of the OECS, where trade in services (particularly tourism and financial services) accounts for almost 60 percent of GDP. The role of services is less prominent in countries such as the Dominican Republic and Haiti.

The United States have historically been the region's largest trading partner, accounting for two-thirds of exports and 40 percent of imports. The Caribbean is a significant

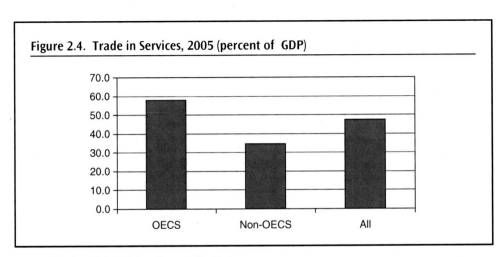

Figure 2.4. Trade in Services, 2005 (percent of GDP)

Source: Bank staff. World Development Indicators.

Table 2.2. Share of Mercahndise Exports by Country, 2006 (percent)

CARIFORUM Countries	US	EU	CARICOM	Canada	Others
Antigua and Barbuda	8%	23%	23%	0.3%	46%
Belize	54%	27%	11%	0.1%	8%
Barbados	18%	17%	54%	2.4%	8%
Dominica	4%	28%	60%	0.2%	8%
Dominican Republic	80%	10%	1%	1.7%	7%
Grenada	21%	24%	47%	2.5%	5%
Guyana	18%	44%	24%	1.2%	12%
Jamaica	26%	24%	3%	19.4%	28%
St. Kitts and Nevis	92%	3%	4%	0.0%	1%
St. Lucia	14%	28%	54%	0.3%	4%
Trinidad and Tobago	59%	7%	22%	1.1%	12%
St. Vincent and the Grenadines	9%	27%	62%	0.3%	1%
All countries	51%	11%	21%	3.3%	14%

Source: Bank staff. World Development Indicators Database.

source of natural gas, petroleum products and aluminum to the United States. Other important tradable goods include clothing and medical instruments from the Dominican Republic, and bauxite from Jamaica. The European Union is the region's second most important trade partner, averaging 11.7 percent of exports and 13 percent of imports, although its shares have been on a slight downward trend over the years. Sugar and bananas remain important exports to the EU for Dominica, Guyana, and Belize where in 2007 these goods accounted

Figure 2.5. CARIFORUM Main Export Partners, 2001–06

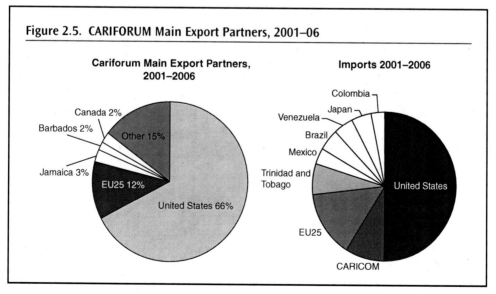

Source: Author's based on COMTRADE 2008.

for 44 percent, 51 percent, and 75 percent of their EU trade respectively. However, for the region as a whole, bananas and sugar account for only 11 percent of exports to the EU.

Intra-regional trade in goods accounts for a substantial share of CARICOM trade. The share of intra-regional exports is double the share of exports to the EU. Intra-regional exports are dominated by Trinidad and Tobago, which has become the region's main supplier of natural gas, petroleum, and light manufacturing and food products. Jamaica and Barbados are the main consumer markets for Caribbean export products (after the United States and the EU). In 2006, Jamaica accounted for 31 percent of regional imports, followed by Barbados (18 percent), Guyana (12 percent), and Suriname (11 percent). Regional trade is less important for the Bahamas, Belize, Haiti, and the OECS countries.

In recent years, the Caribbean has been expanding its exports to new markets such as China, Mexico, and Colombia. The region has increased its exports of metals and ores, petroleum products, and iron and steel. On the import side, Brazil, Venezuela, China and Colombia are becoming more important suppliers of goods to the Caribbean, such as construction and mining machinery, iron ore, refined petroleum products and clothing.

Caribbean and European Union Economic Partnership Agreement: From Preference Dependence to Reciprocity

Negotiations on an Economic Partnership Agreement between the European Union and CARICOM and the Dominican Republic (negotiating as CARIFORUM) began in September 2003 and were concluded in December 2007, The CARIFORUM-EC EPA marks the first reciprocal trade agreement between the two parties. It is a WTO-compatible trade agreement, built on the principles of trade and development afforded under the Cotonou Agreement. It is expected to further strengthen EU-CARIFORUM ties, as the EU is the region's second most important trade partner. For Dominica, Barbados, St. Lucia, and St. Vincent and the Grenadines, the EU is still the dominant export market for agricultural exports.

For 25 years, the Lomé agreement and its subsequent revisions were the main trade accord through which ACP countries received unilateral preferential access to the EU market, particularly for exports of sugar and bananas. In 1999, the EU's preferential regime for ACP states was challenged under the WTO and subsequently declared illegal under international trade law. As per the "Enabling Clause", WTO rules permit unilateral preferential treatment for only two groups of countries: LDCs or all developing countries. Since the Cotonou agreement, which followed the Lomé agreement in 2002, did not apply to all developing countries, nor were all ACP countries LDCs, the regime could not qualify for an exemption under WTO rules. As a result, the EU and ACP countries agreed to negotiate comprehensive economic partnership agreement by January 1, 2008, to bring their trade regime in line with WTO rules.

Objectives of the EPAs. The Caribbean region is the first regional ACP regional group to conclude EPA negotiations with the EU. The agreement was negotiated between CARICOM and the Dominican Republic (participating as CARIFORUM), and the 27 member states of the European Union. The CARIFORUM EPA is a comprehensive agreement covering trade in goods, services as well as areas related to government procurement, investment, trade facilitation, competition policy, and intellectual property rights. The objective of the EPA is to contribute to poverty reduction by establishing a trade partnership that is consistent with sustainable development and the development principles of the Cotonou Agreement. Promoting regional integration, economic cooperation and good governance, and the gradual integration of CARIFORUM states in the world economy, are some of its core principles. The EPA is seen as a vehicle for improving trade capacity and supporting the conditions for competitiveness and economic growth in the Caribbean. Within this context, the EPA aims to establish a transparent and predictable framework for trade and investment between the EU and CARIFORUM states. Although the EPA is a reciprocal agreement, both parties recognize that the difference in levels of development calls for *progressive* and *asymmetric* liberalization, of trade in a way that is supportive of development.

What is in the Agreement? Although the EPA was negotiated to reinforce and build on the principles of the Cotonou Agreement, it represents a deeper and broader framework for trade than its precursor. First, and perhaps most importantly, the agreement is reciprocal, which requires the Caribbean to reduce tariff and nontariff barriers on trade in goods, services, and the movement of capital with the EU. Second, the EPA is a free trade agreement that will offer both sides the predictability and transparency of legally binding market access commitments. By virtue of its status as a free trade agreement (as opposed to a unilateral preferential arrangement), both parties are able to lock in market access and guard against further challenges under the WTO. Third, the EPA expands coverage by bringing new trade-related areas under discipline. The agreement includes the Singapore issues—customs and trade facilitation, and transparency in government procurement, investment, and competition policy. It also includes a chapter on intellectual property rights and their enforcement.

Under the EPA, the EU has committed itself to immediate duty free and quota free access for 98.5 percent of goods trade. In services, the EU will liberalize 94 percent of services sectors, including business services, financial services and tourism and recreation services which are potential export areas for Caribbean providers. This includes removing investment barriers (mode 3), such as limitations on foreign shareholdings, and any measures which require joint ventures. Similarly, in cross-border supply of services (modes 1 and 2), the EU has removed limitations on the number of service suppliers, volume of transactions, and economic needs tests. In the case of temporary movement of service providers (mode 4), the EU has granted market access temporary entry for contractual Caribbean professionals, provided they have secured a contract, in 29 sectors and entry for independent/self employed Caribbean service providers has been liberalized in 11 sectors. There are no quotas on the number of service suppliers than can enter the EU market.

The Caribbean, on the other hand, will liberalize 87 percent of its trade relations with the EU according to a phased approach. CARIFORUM will liberalize 61 percent of trade in the first 10 years, 83 percent within 15 years, and the remainder within 25 years. Within the first ten years of implementation, this represents only an additional 10 percent of trade since 51 percent of EU imports to the Caribbean were already liberalized. For the first three years, the agreement includes a moratorium on all tariffs. High revenue imports such as motor vehicles, parts, and gasoline will benefit from a 10-year grace period. In addition, there are exclusions and long phase in periods for import competing goods such as fish, meat, fruits, vegetables, beverages, ethanol, rum, spices, and vegetable oils. In services, liberalization commitments by the Caribbean region cover 75 percent of sectors for non-LDCs and 65 percent for LDCs. These are sectors such as tourism, environmental services, business services, and maritime services where liberalization has the greatest prospect for increasing investment and economic growth. Public services sectors are excluded from the agreement.

There is therefore effectively an exclusion list for 13.1 percent of EU imports into CARIFORUM, where by and large the CARIFORUM opted not to liberalize most agricultural products and other important locally produced products. In principle also the exclusion list is meant to be common across countries. Indeed CARICOM itself constitutes a Customs Union and hence the external tariffs of each of the CARICOM countries should be the same; while the external tariff of the Dominican Republic can differ. In practice the exclusions, defined at the 8-digit HS level are numerous and it is very difficult to ascertain the extent to which they are common across countries. This is an issue which would require more detailed research. The official position of the negotiating parties is that at the end of the liberalization period (i.e. after 25 years), there is very little difference in the exclusions across the countries.

There is also, a "regional preference clause" in the agreement which is presumably designed to facilitate the process of intra-regional CARIFORUM de facto and de jure integration. The regional preference clause essentially states that any concession with regard to both goods and services, which is offered to the EU, must also be offered to all the other CARIFORUM countries.

Sensitive industrial sectors have also been excluded and an "infant industry clause" has been agreed where CARIFORUM will be allowed to reinstate tariffs in the future to protect growing industry and/or industries. Some simplification of Rules of Origin has been made, notably with regard to textiles and fishing and also allow for wider cumulation of inputs.

The agreement also has safeguard clauses, which can be seen as being somewhat soft in terms of the conditions in which it can be invoked. Either party is allowed to apply duties where there is "serious injury" or "disturbances in a sector." The latter in particular is somewhat lax and open to wide interpretation. It is quite likely that the clause was inserted at the request of the CARIFORUM grouping precisely in order to provide protection for domestic industries in the face of a rise in EU imports. There is a danger that the clause may be invoked too easily by both parties to the agreement.

The treatment of sugar and bananas in the EPA is of critical importance for Caribbean producers. In 2007 EU sugar imports from CARICOM totaled €$238 million. As per the new agreement, sugar will enter the EU duty free and quota free from end September 2009 after the EU completes internal reform to sugar under its Common Agricultural Policy (CAP). In the interim, an additional transitional quota of 60,000 tons will be made available to Caribbean sugar exporters.[58] This commitment could yield substantial benefits to sugar producers in Guyana, Belize and Barbados, who will no longer be bound by quantitative restrictions. Sugar remains an economically important crop in these countries and accounts for 35 percent or more of their trade with the EU.

Caribbean banana exporters will have immediate duty-free and quota-free access to the EU. In effect, the EPA is expected to neutralize the WTO dispute settlement panel ruling

---

58. CARIFORUM gained an additional 60,000 tones in additional sugar quotas which will be spilt equally between the Dominican Republic and CARICOM.

against the banana protocol. Current banana exports to the EU totaled US$57 million or 4 percent of the value of total CARICOM exports to the EU. In 2007, EU imports of bananas from the CARIFORUM countries totaled €$219 million or 5.5 percent of total EU imports from CARIFORUM. The EPA contains a comprehensive Joint Declaration on Bananas, which acknowledges the importance of the industry to several CARIFORUM countries. In the Declaration, the EU commits itself to providing funding to assist the industry in adjusting to the new trading environment. However, any long-term plan for the banana industry in OECS countries is unlikely to be sustainable unless producers receive significant assistance and gain a strong foothold in niche markets, such as organic or fair trade bananas. Trade in bananas still accounts for a large proportion of trade with Europe for Belize, Dominica, and St. Lucia.

There is potentially great value if the EU delivers increased aid for trade to help with implementation and adjustment issues. The arguments underlying a call for "Aid for trade" in the context of the EU-Caribbean EPA are discussed in the Technical Appendix B of the report. Box 3 below summarizes the main points. The agreement was widely expected to have a significant development dimension. The EPA's joint declaration on development cooperation includes a commitment to channel EPA support through a Caribbean Regional Development Fund. The fund would provide resources to support EPA implementation programs as well as support adjustment measures and economic reforms. The EU has also committed to more than doubling aid to the region, from €57 millions (2002–07) to €165 millions (2008–13) under the 10th EDF (European Development Fund). This goes in the direction of *aid for trade as a promotion scheme*, not only as *aid for trade as a compensatory scheme*. Indeed, a call for an *aid for trade as a compensatory/promotion scheme* centered around five arguments: (i) assistance to offset adjustment costs, such as fiscal support to help countries make the transition from tariffs to other sources of revenue; (ii) technical assistance; (iii) capacity building, including support for trade facilitation;

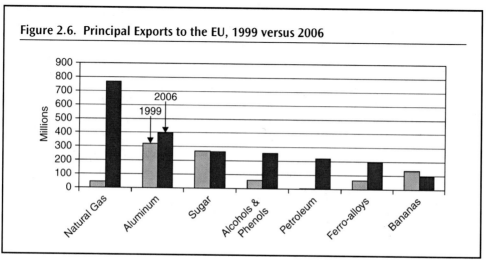

Figure 2.6. Principal Exports to the EU, 1999 versus 2006

Source: Bank staff. World Development Indicators Database.

(iv) institutional reform; and (v) investments in trade-related infrastructure.[59] At the same time, *aid for trade could play a catalytic role as a promotion scheme* and be designed to help Caribbean countries realize the full benefits of new market opportunities (see Box 3). In that perspective, the first argument is that aid may help countries invest in infrastructure (both at the national and regional level) so as to alleviate supply-side constraints. The second is that it may help to support capacity building and strengthen the institutional environment. The third is that it may help to support structural reforms that are complementary to trade reforms, such as labor market reforms, which may condition the impact of trade reform on unemployment and poverty.

However, disbursement of aid flows and linkages between aid and trade as described in the CARIFORUM-EC EPA agreement needs further clarification. The evidence so far related to the DOHA Round suggests that these linkages have proven difficult to establish, partly because of the lack of coordination among donors and inadequate integration of trade issues in development programs (see Technical Appendix B). Indeed, a review of existing PRSPs for the region shows that trade issues are largely neglected. For instance, Guyana's PRSP barely mentions trade as a critical area for the country's development strategy while Haiti's PRSP completely ignores trade issues.

What New Opportunities in Services Does the EPA Create?   With respect to services, the EPA covers many of those sectors where Caribbean firms can sharpen their competitive advantage, particularly in business, communications, construction, financial, transport and tourism services. The agreement provides for all modes of supply: cross-border supply, consumption abroad, commercial presence, and movement of people. Public services and utilities are not open to foreign participation and CARIFORUM has special carve outs in place to reserve market share for small and medium enterprises in certain sectors. With respect to mode 4, the Caribbean negotiated market access for employees of Caribbean firms and independent professionals (including entertainment professionals) to have temporary entry to supply services in the EU for a period of up to 90 days in a year. This commitment goes beyond what the EU has liberalized under the WTO, and although it is small, it indicates that there is potential for small countries to gain market access for temporary movement in these specialized areas. Over the next five years, both parties have agreed to work together to further improve access to services and investment commitments, through further negotiations.

Simulations using the GLOBE Model show that the welfare gains associated with service trade liberalization are substantial (see Chapter 6). In aggregate, the services liberalization alone leads to an absorption (welfare) gain of just under 5 percent, and this welfare gain is reflected in an increase in imports from both the United States and the EU15; as well as an increase in exports to both of these. Along the same lines, policy experiments using the Jamaican Model reveal that a productivity increase in the "commerce" sector, which includes tourism, results in welfare gain (see Chapter 6).

---

59. As noted by Stiglitz and Charlton (2006, p. 8), until recently the existing aid for trade approach was to provide modest amount of aid on an *ad hoc* basis—primarily to cope with specific bottlenecks, or to support participation in WTO negotiations.

Box 4: Aid for Trade: Rationale and Implications for Trade Reform in the Caribbean

Arguments

Arguments in favor of an "aid for trade" agenda center around five dimensions: (i) assistance to offset adjustment costs, such as fiscal support to help countries make the transition from tariffs to other sources of revenue; (ii) technical assistance; (iii) capacity building, including support for trade facilitation; (iv) institutional reform; and (v) investments in trade-related infrastructure. These arguments could be summarized in two key roles of aid for trade: (i) "*aid for trade as a compensatory scheme*"; and (ii) "*aid for trade as a promotion scheme*" (for further details, see Technical Appendix B).

Aid for Trade as a Compensatory Scheme

- *Mitigating Revenue-induced Cuts in Productive Expenditure.* Caribbean countries rely on tariffs as a source of revenue far more than do developed countries largely because tariffs are an administratively efficient way of raising revenues. To the extent that trade liberalization may reduce tariff revenue, that replacing lost tariff revenue with other sources may take time and may have high associated costs, and that revenue losses may have an adverse effect on productive public expenditure, tariff reforms may need to be accompanied by a temporary increase in aid. This will provide "breathing space" for governments to implement measures aimed at strengthening the domestic tax system (by reducing tax collection costs, fighting tax evasion, etc.) and other reforms on the expenditure side (such as improving the efficiency of public spending).

- *Mitigating Adjustment Costs and Implementation Costs.* Although implementation costs are hard to quantify, there is a risk that changes in the regulatory environment that are mandated by trade agreements draw money away from development budgets (and possibly from more productive uses), as pointed out by Stiglitz and Charlton (2006) in a broader context. The role of aid in this context is not only to facilitate job creation in areas most adversely affected by trade liberalization, or to help those who have lost their jobs obtain alternative employment (as is commonly argued), but also to mitigate the risk that the implementation of the regulatory agreements that are required as part of trade arrangements may lead to "resource diversion."

Aid for Trade as a Promotion Scheme

- *Facilitating Domestic Investment in Infrastructure and the Provision of Regional Public Goods.* Some countries need to invest in the necessary exporting infrastructure (e.g. efficient ports, adequate roads, reliable electricity and communications) to stimulate private investment in productive capacity. Thus, by supporting domestic infrastructure investment, aid for trade programs may foster the ability of the private sector to take advantage of changes in competitiveness and more general enhance its role in promoting development. In addition, as also noted in Technical Appendix A, aid for trade is particularly important for regional public goods in infrastructure. Coordination failures often create a gap in the optimal provision of these goods. In addition, for regions where countries are relatively small (as is the case in the Caribbean), size is an important incentive for governments to pool resources for the provision of efficient, cost-effective common services. Regional investments supported by foreign grants may generate therefore potentially large returns.

- *Supporting Capacity Building and Institutional Reform.* When implementing trade reforms, capacity building and institutional reforms are essential in a range of areas, including: (i) strengthening tax administration and enforcement capability; (ii) acquiring knowledge to meet product standards prevailing in high value markets; (iii) building supply capacity to fostering the development of a favorable business climate to help private sector enterprises capitalize on new trade opportunities and identifying infrastructure bottlenecks. To benefit fully from trade liberalization, developing countries may also need to strengthen regional institutions. A well-designed aid for trade program, which avoids the "diversion risk" alluded to above, may promote all these objectives.

- *Financing Complementary Structural Reforms.* The need for complementary reforms may involve not only the labor market but also the financial sector. In countries with underdeveloped

(Continued)

Box 4: Aid for Trade: Rationale and Implications for Trade Reform in the Caribbean (*Continued*)

---

financial sectors, inadequate access to finance—whether to finance short-term capital needs or physical investment—is a major factor inhibiting exports. Difficulties in assessing the creditworthiness of (and the value of collateral pledged by) small exporting firms, in particular, may constrain access to formal sector loans, with an adverse effect on employment and poverty. To foster the expansion of exports, therefore, credit bureaus. Again, a well-designed aid for trade program may help to alleviate these constraints.

Implications for Trade Reform in the Caribbean

- *Tariff Reforms May Lead to Fiscal Revenue Losses.* Thus, to avoid possible adverse effects of revenue losses on productive government spending (as noted earlier), temporary financing in the form of increased aid may be necessary to increase incentives to implement (and sustain) trade reform.

- The Economic Partnership Agreement (EPA) recently completed between the European Union and the CARIFORUM Group EPA contains explicit provisions related to compliance with, and adoption of, international technical, health, and quality standards pertaining to food production and marketing (agricultural goods, fish and fish products, etc.). Compliance with these (at times very demanding) standards will impose a significant burden on governments in the region; to avoid the "diversion risk" alluded to earlier, a "trade for aid" program is likely to be essential. This need is well recognized in the EPA.

- There are significant supply-side and institutional constraints that prevent a number of Caribbean countries from taking full advantage of new trade opportunities. Thus, there is a strong case for increased assistance to Caribbean countries, in the form of grants or loans (with disbursements perhaps over a 4–5 year horizon), to cover a wide range of needs—from investments in infrastructure (at both the domestic and regional levels), to capacity building and institutional reform, and support for complementary reforms—to alleviate key obstacles to trade expansion.

Some Specific Issues for Caribbean Countries

- *Additionality Issue.* The issue is that there is a risk that aid allocated to promote trade may substitute for other allocations of aid, some with potentially higher return in terms of growth and welfare—such as education and health.

- *Delivery and Monitoring Issue.* The experience with "aid for trade" programs under the DOHA round suggests that there is a need to improve coherence and coordination of action among donors to improve the delivery of aid. In addition, ensuring that trade is adequately integrated into broader development and poverty reduction strategies remain actually a challenge in the Caribbean region.

- *Dutch Disease Issue.* If aid is at least partially spent on nontraded goods, it may put upward pressure on domestic prices and lead to a real exchange rate appreciation. In turn, a real appreciation may induce a reallocation of labor toward the nontraded goods sector, thereby raising real wages in terms of the price of tradables. The resulting deterioration in competitiveness may lead to a decline in export performance, unsustainable current account deficits, and an adverse effect on growth. However, if aid raises public investment in infrastructure, then the longer-run effect on the real exchange rate may turn out to be positive (that is, a real depreciation).

- *Aid Volatility.* It is important to ensure any aid-for-trade initiative that involves a sizable increase in spending on trade-related infrastructure makes aid flows predictable over the medium term, to secure sustained commitment in the region.

What are the Risks Associated with the EPA? Although the completion of an EPA is a milestone in the region's efforts to strategically reposition itself in the global economy, there are some significant risks associated with EPA implementation that must be addressed. The simulations of the Jamaican Model show that an EPA or some kind of FTA or preferential trading agreement with a single partner (EU or USA) may benefit Jamaica,

Table 2.3. Comparing the Frameworks: The EPA versus the Lomé/Cotonou Agreement

EU-CARIFORUM EPA	Lomé/Cotonou Regime
Comprehensive reciprocal free trade agreement between 16 Caribbean countries and the EU	International agreement offering non reciprocal, unilateral trade preferences to 79 ACP members.
Binds current levels of EU preferences and liberalization commitments	Non binding preferential provisions
Comprehensive technical disciplines covering: ▇ Goods ▇ Services ▇ Intellectual property ▇ Investment ▇ Procurement ▇ Competition Policy ▇ Trade Facilitation ▇ Standards and Certification ▇ Technical Barriers to Trade.	Minimal provisions (but no liberalization commitments) to strengthen and cooperate on regulatory frameworks in areas such as: services intellectual property, standards and phytosanitary standards, trade and environment, labor standards, consumer policy
Immediate duty and free quota free access for 98.5% of exports including bananas. Sugar and rice subject to transitional quotas with full duty and quota free access by 2010.	Duty free access for 98% of exports meeting rules of origin requirements. Duty free quotas for sugar, and preferential access for beef, rice other agricultural products
Increased development assistance commitments to be channeled through EDF and new Caribbean regional development fund.	Development assistance delivered under EDF

Source: Bank staff.

but it does lead to trade diversion and less benefit than could be achieved by lower MFN tariffs (see Chapter 6).

Because many Caribbean countries depend on customs duties as a significant source of government revenue, implementation of the EPA could create fiscal and macroeconomic risks for countries as they lower tariffs and taxes on trade with the EU. For example, in Antigua and Barbuda, St. Vincent, St. Lucia, and St. Kitts, the share of tariffs in government revenue is greater than 40 percent. To safeguard against any immediate negative impacts, there is a 3 year moratorium on tariff reduction and many tariff sensitive goods have long phase-out periods. As EPA implementation progresses, reducing the reliance on trade taxes is nevertheless an urgent priority. The EU has pledged assistance under the EDF to support this process, but very likely additional financing (at highly concessional terms) will be needed in the transition to a new tax regime, to prevent further pressures on fiscal balances. Nonetheless, the excessive dependence on customs duties indicates clearly that many countries in the Caribbean need substantive tax reforms. Some of these reforms have already been carried out in Barbados and Trinidad and Tobago where a well functioning value-added tax regime was implemented.

Caribbean and the WTO and DOHA Round

All sovereign members of CARICOM are members of the WTO, with the exception of the Bahamas, which currently has observer status. CARICOM countries believe that full participation in the multilateral trading system is an essential element for achieving their development goals. With respect to the key negotiating areas, the Caribbean has been most active in services and agriculture and fisheries. As noted earlier, the Caribbean has a keen interest in greater services liberalization, particularly in mode 4.

The Caribbean has been a vocal advocate in the WTO DOHA Round for special and differential treatment, and recognition of the challenges facing small vulnerable economies in the multilateral trading system. Many Caribbean countries had become particularly jaded by the WTO after the devastating rulings against the EU-ACP protocols on bananas and sugar. This was compounded by the dispute settlement case brought against Antigua and Barbuda by the United States on internet gambling services. The Caribbean felt as though both its traditional livelihood (agriculture) and its future source of economic growth (services) were under attack in the global trading system.

In their statements at the Fifth WTO Ministerial Meeting in Hong Kong, Caribbean countries underscored their expectation for flexibility and policy space in any agreement that is the result of the DOHA Round. Caribbean countries advocated longer time periods and greater flexibility and policy space in implementing commitments. They continued to lobby for market access for products and services of particular export interest to developing economies, and increased technical and financial resources (aid for trade) to help them (as well as other developing countries) implement trade rules, manage trade disputes, and capitalize on the opportunities presented by the world trading system. Some preference-affected countries, such as Guyana, have said that WTO members should endeavor to put in place measures to mitigate the impact of reform on low income non-LDC preference receiving countries.

Caribbean Trade Relations with the USA

The United States is the largest trading partner for CARICOM as a region. It is also a very important source of foreign direct investment in the tourism sector and other services industries. Trade and economic cooperation between the United States and CARICOM goes back to 1983 with the establishment of the Caribbean Basin Initiative (CBI) under the Caribbean Basin Economic Recovery Act (CBERA) which intended to facilitate the economic development and export diversification of the Caribbean Basin economies. The CBI was substantially expanded in 2000 through the enactment of another piece of legislation, the Caribbean Basin Trade Partnership Act (CBTPA), which offers duty- and quota-free entry for apparel assembled in CBI countries from fabrics and yarns of U.S. origin. This decision was aimed at encouraging additional U.S. exports of fabric and U.S. investment in the region, thereby improving competitiveness of the U.S. textile industry. Currently, the CBI provides 19 countries with duty-free access to the U.S. market for a wide range of goods. In contrast to CBERA, which is permanent, the CBTPA benefits by statute expire on September 30, 2010. The U.S. Administration intends to conduct an extensive review of all 19 CBI beneficiary countries to determine the extent to which the program is being utilized effectively.

Table 2.4. Caribbean Bilateral and Regional Trade Architecture

Entry into Force	Name of Agreement
1975	Lomé I
1979	Lomé II
1984	Lomé III
1984	United States Caribbean Basin Economic Recovery Act (CBERA)
1986	CARICOM-Canada Trade and Economic Co-operation Agreement (CARIBCAN)
1989	Lomé IV
1995	Lomé IV (revision)
1993	CARICOM–Venezuela (non reciprocal)
1995	CARICOM–Colombia Agreement on Trade, Economic and Technical Cooperation
2000	CARICOM–Cuba Trade and Economic Cooperation Agreement
2001	CARICOM–Dominican Republic
2002	Cotonou
2005	CARICOM–Costa Rica[60]
2008	CARIFORUM–EC EPA
Ongoing	WTO DOHA Round
Ongoing	CARICOM–Canada Free Trade Agreement
On hiatus	Free Trade Area of the Americas (FTAA)
Ongoing	CARICOM-Central America[61]

Source: Bank staff.

U.S. exports to the CBI beneficiary countries more than doubled between 1988 and 2006, reaching $25.8 billion in 2006 (2007 Report to Congress). Trinidad and Tobago became the leading source of U.S. imports entered under CBI preferences in 2006, displacing the Dominican Republic, the long-time leader. The United States imported US$3.1 billion under CBI preferences from Trinidad and Tobago in 2006, an increase of 32.8 percent from 2005. Jamaica's exports to the United States under CBI preferences grew significantly by 61.5 percent in 2006 to US$246 million. The United States continues to have a small value of bilateral trade with many of the Caribbean economies. While the overall value is small, CBI-preference imports account for relatively significant proportions of total U.S. imports from these countries. Apparel products, electrical switches, and cane sugar were some of the leading categories of CBI preference imports from the smaller Caribbean economies.

---

60. The agreement came into effect between Costa Rica and Trinidad and Tobago on November 15, 2005, with Guyana on April 30, 2006 and with Barbados on August 1, 2006. In the other CARICOM countries the internal process of approval of the agreement has still to be concluded.

61. In a communiqué dated August 8, 2007, CARICOM reported the launch of FTA negotiations with the Central American countries, including Panama. A Ministerial meeting was held at Port-of-Spain, Trinidad and Tobago, to formally launch negotiations to be carried out on the basis of an existing free trade agreement between the Caribbean Community and Costa Rica.

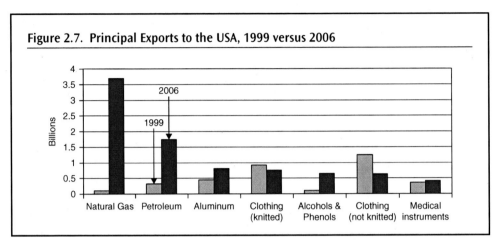

Figure 2.7. Principal Exports to the USA, 1999 versus 2006

Source: Bank staff. World Development Indicators.

Another component of the CBI is the Haitian Hemispheric Opportunity through Partnership Encouragement (HOPE) Act, which provides special access for Haiti. In December 2006, the U.S. Congress enacted the Haitian Hemispheric Opportunity through Partnership Encouragement Act of 2006 (HOPE Act) giving preferential access benefits to Haitian apparels under the Caribbean Basin Economic Recovery Act (CBERA) of 1983. Haiti has experienced rapid increases in exports to the United States under CBI preferences, with increases of 39.0 percent in 2005, and 25.1 percent in 2006 to $379 million. This growth has resulted mainly from CBPTA apparel provisions. In May 2008, the U.S. Congress passed amended legislation (referred to as HOPE II Act) to grant new and special rules of origin for selected apparel and textile imports from Haiti into the United States for a total of ten years. The HOPE II Act grants duty-free treatment for select Haitian apparel imports that are wholly assembled or knit-to shape from less expensive third-party countries yarns and fabrics. The competitive advantage to Haitian apparel firms is the ability to use the less expensive inputs and still receive duty-free treatment for the extended time period. The preferential treatment is conditioned on eligibility criteria related to labor, human rights and anti-terrorism policies. HOPE II Act took effect in October 2008 and it provides: (a) All of the benefits of HOPE Act (2006); (b) Extended duty-free treatment for ten years; (c) Duty-free treatment for apparel imports in limited quantities (tariff preference levels-TPLs); and (d) Co-production with the Dominican Republic.

Looking into the future, Caribbean countries have expressed interest in negotiating a free trade agreement with the United States. Depending on the liberalization commitments and provision, an FTA with the United States could increase trade and investment flows, making the Caribbean an attractive region for U.S. business. Some of the key interests of Caribbean countries would be market access for services and service providers, as well as permanent market access for the region's key exports such as energy products, apparel, and iron ores.

Relations with Other Countries in the Americas

Negotiations on a new trading arrangement between CARICOM and Canada are expected to begin in 2009. Formal economic relations between CARICOM and Canada began as far back as 1986, with the signature of an economic and trade development assistance program: the Commonwealth Caribbean Country Tariff (CARIBCAN).[62] The current framework for trade between the two parties (CARIBCAN) is a non-reciprocal preferential agreement granted by Canada for goods. Items exempted under the arrangement include some textiles, clothing and footwear, as well as certain agricultural products including products subject to tariff rate quotas. The current waiver granted by the WTO General Council for the implementation of CARIBCAN expires at the end of 2011. CARICOM's objectives in redefining its trade relationship with Canada include broadening the country coverage to include Haiti and Suriname, the expansion of Canadian investment flows into the region, and the creation of a comprehensive framework for development cooperation.

The Caribbean also continues to pursue a strategy of developing trade links with its Central and South American neighbors. The region has signed bilateral agreements with Cuba, Costa Rica, Venezuela, Colombia and the Dominican Republic. The CARICOM Member States have also held preparatory meetings with MERCOSUR and the Central American countries in anticipation of advancing bilateral trading arrangements.

Structural, Institutional, and Political Constraints to Trade Integration

Structural Constraints

Structural disparities are often cited as an important impediment to deeper integration among Caribbean countries. Caribbean countries differ widely in terms of their level of economic development, macroeconomic conditions and performance, as well as the importance of the regional market. Altogether these disparities have constrained trade and economic integration among them.

Differences in Levels of Economic Development.   A key feature of CARICOM grouping is the large differences in economic size of its member states (see Chapter 1). CARICOM members also display highly dissimilar levels of economic development and income differences have widened over time, leading to greater economic divergence. This reflects the fact that trends in growth performance have differed considerably from one member state to the other (see Chapter 1). Differences in levels of development mirror differences in production and export structures. In Trinidad and Tobago, economic activity is heavily concentrated on the oil and natural gas sector. Jamaica and Suriname have large mineral sectors, while agriculture plays a dominant role in the Guyana and Belize. The OECS countries, the Bahamas, and Barbados, are mainly service-based economies. Divergent production structures make it difficult for governments to agree on a common development strategy for the region, which, in turn, is necessary to guide the definition of regional policies related to specific economic sectors such as agriculture, mining, and tourism.[63]

Varying production structures result in varying export structures and make it difficult for the Caribbean governments to agree on a common strategy for external trade.

---

62. Beneficiaries are Anguilla, Antigua and Barbuda, the Bahamas, Barbados, Belize, Bermuda, Cayman Islands, Dominica, Grenada, Guyana, Jamaica, Montserrat, St. Kitts and Nevis, St. Lucia, St. Vincent and the Grenadines, Trinidad and Tobago, Turks and Caicos Islands, and the British Virgin Islands.

63. It is also worth noting that at the same time, there are regional public goods that require common policies—in infrastructure development, most notably.

Moreover, CARICOM countries differ substantially in terms of direction of their exports. Many of the smaller OECS countries depend disproportionately on the European market as a supplier of tourists and a consumer of their agricultural commodities. For these countries, maintaining their trade preferences is a significant objective in their external trade negotiations. Other countries, such as Trinidad and Tobago, are much more focused on North America and have a strong interest in expanding their access to that and other Western Hemisphere markets through greater trade liberalization. In terms of foreign policy coordination, OECS countries have sometimes argued that their positions are not sufficiently reflected in the region's trade negotiations with third countries, and that agencies such as the RNM, which coordinates the group's external trade talks, are dominated by the agendas of the larger CARICOM countries. This perception has at times weakened their commitment to regional efforts at foreign policy coordination on trade and other matters.

Varying Macroeconomic Conditions and Performance.   Over the past decade, macroeconomic conditions and performance have varied largely from one CARICOM country to another (see Chapter 1). This has made it difficult for CARICOM countries to achieve progress in the areas of macroeconomic policy coordination, macroeconomic convergence, and ultimately the formation of a monetary union.

Economic disparity and divergence among Caribbean countries have also led to differences in the perceived benefits of integration. On the one hand, small countries have generally felt that intra-regional market liberalization could harm their country's domestic industries. In addition, fiscal concerns and the perception of inequitable distribution of the cost and benefits of integration may have limited incentives for small Caribbean countries to pursue aggressively a strategy to foster closer regional trade links. On the other hand, more advanced countries have also sometimes questioned the usefulness of regional integration as it could bring additional constraints (need of transfers of resources to less advanced countries, financial contributions to regional bodies, and so forth). Neither group of countries may therefore have sufficiently invested in advancing trade integration within the region. At the same time, it is notable that smaller Caribbean countries (namely, OECS countries) have favored regional integration on a smaller scale.

Difference in Degree of Importance of the Regional Market.   The integration process is also affected by variations among member countries in the importance of the regional market for their economies. For Barbados and Trinidad and Tobago, CARICOM is a significant market, which absorbed about 45 percent and 22 percent, respectively, of their total merchandise exports in the past five years. Several OECS countries are also heavily dependent on the CARICOM market: over a third of their exports are intra-regional, although most of these are intra-OECS or destined for Barbados. On the contrary, for Belize, Jamaica, and Suriname, CARICOM market plays only a marginal role. In these countries, the share of intra-regional exports in total exports ranges from 5 to 7 percent.[64] The Bahamas has virtually no trade with any other CARICOM member, which partly explains its reluctance to join the single market.[65]

---

64. In the period 2000–02, Belize exported only 40 products to CARICOM (equal to 6 percent of its total merchandise exports); Barbados exported almost 585 products (46 percent of its total good exports).
65. Other factors for consideration include concerns over the free movement of labor in the CSME.

Box 5: Principal Organs and Bodies of CARICOM

The *Conference of Heads of Government* is the supreme organ of the Community and as such provides overall policy direction for the Community. It consists of Heads of Government of all member states.

The *Bureau of the Conference* composed of the current, immediately outgoing and immediately incoming Chairman of the Conference and the Secretariat General of CARICOM, initiates proposals for development and approval by the ministerial councils, informs the Conference of upcoming issues, supports implementation of Community decisions and provides policy guidance to the Secretariat.

The distribution of responsibilities for portfolios is as follows:

Antigua and Barbuda: Services	Jamaica: External Trade negotiations
The Bahamas: Tourism	St. Lucia: Sustainable Development
Barbados: CSME	St. Kitts and Nevis: Health, HIV/AIDS and HR development
Belize: Justice and Governance	St. Vincent and the Grenadines: Transport
Dominica: Labor	Suriname: Community development and cultural cooperation
Grenada: Science and Technology	Trinidad and Tobago: Security and Energy
Guyana: Agriculture	

The *Community Council of Ministers,* composed of Ministers responsible for Community Affairs in each member state, has primary responsibility for the development of Community strategic planning and coordination in the areas of economic integration, external relations and functional cooperation.

The *Conference* and the *Community Council* are assisted by four ministerial councils:

- Council for Finance and Planning (COFAP), responsible for economic policy coordination and financial and monetary integration;
- Council for Trade and Economic Development (COTED), responsible for the promotion of trade and economic development in the Community;
- Council for Foreign and Community Relations (COFCOR), responsible for relations between the Community and international organizations and Third States; and
- Council for Human and Social Development (COHSOD), responsible for the promotion of human and social development in the Community.

The *Community comprises three bodies:* (i) the *Legal Affairs Committee,* comprising ministers responsible for legal affairs or attorney generals of the member states, provides Community organs with legal advice; (ii) the *Budget Committee,* which consists of senior member state officials and oversees the Community budget and work program; and (iii) the *Committee of Central Bank Governors,* composed of Heads of Central Banks of all member states and charged with providing recommendations to COFAP on monetary cooperation, integration of capital markets and other financial matters.

The CARICOM Secretariat is the Community principal administrative organ. It services the meetings of Community organs, follows up on agreements emerging from such meetings, conducts technical work and assists member states with implementation of Community decisions, among other things.

Source: Adapted from IADB, CARICOM Report No. 2, August 2005.

Institutional and Governance Weaknesses

In preparation of the CSME, CARICOM member states made important efforts toward institution building to reinforce chances of successful implementation. Actions were taken to improve the decision-making process, most notably by shifting the unanimity requirement for Ministerial Councils' decisions to a qualified majority, and by making all its decisions binding. Additional bodies have been created to facilitate enforcement of the Community's decisions. Box 3 below summarizes the key organs and bodies of the Community. Yet, institutional inefficiencies continue to delay the integration process. However, while CARICOM governments established a Prime-Ministerial Expert Group on Governance in early 2003, concrete actions are lacking in this area.

Although some flexibility has been introduced since the Revised Treaty entered into force in 1997, decisions are still taken by consensus and through inter-governmental cooperation. With the exception of the Caribbean Court of Justice, none of the agencies or bodies created to support the regional integration process has been given any form of supra-national decision-making power. Contrary to the European Union, where common legislative instruments such as EU regulations and directives drive implementation, CARICOM has not yet developed an appropriate range of instruments that would enable Community decisions to become law. Currently, most of the actions needed to implement the CSME require a separate legislative or administrative decision by every member state. This, in turn, opens the way for significant delays in implementation—unless efficient enforcement mechanisms are in place. Enforcement, however, has been a long neglected part of the regional integration process. It was only a few years ago that member states began to make concerted efforts at introducing stronger enforcement mechanisms into the process.

The persistent weakness of regional institutions is also a key feature of the inter-governmental decision-making structure. Most of the CARICOM's regional institutions lack sufficient funding to execute their mandates efficiently. The CARICOM Secretariat, the administrative organ of the Community, and other important agencies such as the RNM, rely on financial contributions from member states.[66] Yet, payments are sometimes late or fail to materialize. Many regional institutions continue to rely heavily on donor support, the availability of which may have generated "moral hazard" and further compromised the willingness of governments to contribute to funds. This, in turn, has led donors to question the sustainability of the institutions and, in some cases, to interrupt funding. An illustrative example of this is the recent difficulties of the Caribbean Export Development Agency (CEDA).

Member states adopted the principle of automatic financing of the regional institutions as a mean to help them fulfill their mandates and make them more efficient. However, a number of issues have remained unresolved, including: (i) the level of financing required; (ii) the sources of funding, including a resource base and a revenue stream; and (iii) the mechanism for the automatic transfer of resources.

An environment prone to crime and violence may also have compounded institutional inefficiencies in CARICOM. It is reported that the location of the CARICOM's Secretariat in Guyana has made it difficult for the Secretariat to attract and retain talented staff, particularly in periods of political conflict and elevated crime in Guyana. Many staff positions in the Secretariat are currently vacant, and have been for some time. In addition, organizational and administrative inefficiencies, including inadequate prioritization of activities, internal communication problems and duplication of activities have also hampered the

---

66. The size of the contributions is determined by a CARICOM formula.

Secretariat's work as well as that of
other regional agencies, contributing
to delays in implementation of Community decisions.[67]

In sum, the proliferation of
institutions has not significantly
improved the capacity of CARICOM
to deliver tangible regional outcomes.
Part of the problem is that the creation of new institutions without the
ability to enforce the decisions taken
by member states does not translate
into concrete actions. The issue is less
the creation of institutions than the
empowerment of these institutions
with required authority to move forward the regional integration process.
This is related to the political economy of regional integration.

Political Economy of Regional Integration

Regional integration between countries with large disparities in economic structure inevitably produces
losers and winners, at least in the
short and medium term. Trade reforms

Table 2.5. Financing of CARICOM Secretariat: Member State Contributions (Share of total member state contributions, 2002)

All Member States	Share (in %)
Trinidad and Tobago	25.0
Jamaica	22.8
Barbados	10.7
The Bahamas	9.8
Guyana	7.0
Suriname	7.0
Haiti	3.0
Belize	2.9
OECS (combined)	**10.9**
o.w. Antigua and Barbuda	1.8
Dominica	1.8
Grenada	1.8
St. Kitts and Nevis	1.8
St. Lucia	1.8
St. Vincent and Grenadines	1.8
Montserrat	0.4
Associate Members	0.8
Total	**100.0**

Source: Adapted from IADB, CARICOM Report No. 2, August 2005.

may benefit advanced countries of the
regional group while they may add to the fiscal burden of less advanced countries in the
short term. For this reason, poor countries of CARICOM often resist to commit to regional
reforms that could advance the regional process more quickly. Exceptions to the implementation of regional provisions are numerous within the CARICOM; and the OECS
countries are granted specific clauses in order to protect them against some of the adverse
effects of regional integration.

The willingness of CARICOM member countries to transfer some national decision-
making power to a supra-national level and to give regional institutions the clout they need
to develop, implement and enforce the Community's decisions also comes into question.
Many countries in the region have not clearly showed their willingness to abandon their
national sovereignty in favor of regional bodies. The fear of loss of national sovereignty has
been one of the most important constraints to regional integration in the Caribbean region.

---

67. Until recently, the Secretariat was housed in several different building and communication was
suboptimal. It worth noting that some of these problems will likely be solved once the Secretariat's new
headquarters building in Georgetown is fully operational.

That feeling is exacerbated by the fact that economic divergence between CARICOM countries means that the Community's decisions diverge from specific national interests. Countries weigh the perceived costs of loss of sovereignty against the benefits of belonging to the regional group. For a country such as Trinidad and Tobago, the benefits of regional integration have been clear as the country has taken the advantage of CARICOM's free trade area to boost its manufactured exports to the region. But for other countries, in particular the OECS countries, the benefits of regional integration have been less tangible and may only materialize in the longer term. Meanwhile, the economic costs and the costs in terms of loss of sovereignty are more often immediate and difficult to overcome in the short term.

Sovereignty and national interest issues raise the question of how far regional integration can go in the Caribbean region. It seems that the vision of leaders of the region and thus the future of the regional grouping do not go beyond the implementation of the CSME. Yet, the implementation of the CSME has stalled and could continue to be a protracted process at the expense of regional integration. In fact, deepening regional integration in the Caribbean requires addressing the daunting challenges posed by the reluctance of most countries in the group to lose their prerogatives in critical areas of their sovereignty. Part of this problem is related to the fact that CARICOM countries have not undertaken a full "cost-benefit" analysis of their integration arrangement to assess its net benefits to their economies and the region as a whole, with proper account of the distribution of benefits and costs over time.[68] In addition, the complexity of the regional process, the scarcity of resources to support it, and the perceived inequitable distribution of the costs and benefits of economic integration do not give countries adequate incentives to fully abandon their control in critical areas of national economic management in favor of regional bodies.

---

68. From the regional perspective, a number of organisations have undertaken empirical analysis of the regional integration process and proffered support for the process (for example, ECLAC, European Union).

CHAPTER 3

Trade Patterns and Flows, and Competitiveness Issues

Trade plays a critical role in the economies across the Caribbean region. As small island states the Caribbean countries rely on export income to create jobs, buy imports, and maintain an overall healthy balance in external accounts. The countries are relatively open and have made significant progress in opening to trade, but tariffs remain high in some economies and some sectors.

The production and trade structures of the Caribbean countries show that they are predominantly services economies. Services related sectors contribute over 50 percent in the CARICOM countries and in some cases such as that of Antigua and Barbuda over 90 percent of GDP, while industry (including manufacturing) accounts for roughly 2–17 percent of output. Caribbean countries mostly export services and import goods. Services exports account for almost 53 percent of the region's total exports (excluding Trinidad and Tobago), from a 51 percent share in the 1995. For the past decade, goods have accounted for 79 percent of total imports into the Caribbean region.

The importance of trade in Caribbean countries is also evident in their dependence on international trade taxes as a source of fiscal revenues. Revenue from international trade transactions accounts for 50 percent of total revenue in Antigua and Barbuda, Grenada and St. Lucia, 45 percent in Dominica, and 47 percent in the Bahamas.

This chapter analyses trade patterns of Caribbean countries and recent trade flows in the region, and discusses the region's competitiveness issues. The chapter also highlights the binding constraints to trading in the region, with a particular focus on costs of inputs and infrastructure costs.

The key findings of the chapter are the following. First, after a period of stagnation (1995–99) and slight decline (2000–02), CARICOM merchandise exports and imports have been rising since 2002. However, the region's export performance has been relatively weak compared with other developing countries, including countries in South America and East Asia. In addition, OECS's overall merchandise export performance has been relatively weak. Second, the analysis of the composition of trade by sectors shows a changing trend in the export structure of CARICOM member states over the past half decade, marked by declining manufactured and food exports, while exports of fuels grew. Third, a breakdown of the composition of exports by destination shows that the CARICOM exports mostly manufactured goods to the United States and mostly food products to the European Union. Between 2001 and 2006, 44 percent of exports to the EU were food products while 42 percent were manufactures. Conversely, 15 percent of exports to the United States were food products while 52 percent were manufactures. The composition of CARICOM imports by sector shows that most goods coming into the region are manufactured products. Between 2001–06, approximately 60 percent of total imports were manufactures, while another 17 percent share were food and raw agricultural products. The remaining imports were fuels (22 percent) and ores and metals (1 percent). The analysis of the composition of imports by destination also yields similar results. CARICOM imports from the United States and the EU are predominantly manufactured products (74 and 78 percent respectively). The remaining goods from the EU are mostly food products. From the United States, they include food, raw agricultural and fuel products. Fourth, the analysis of the region's export structure shows increased concentration of products. In 1997, the top 20 products accounted for 51 percent of total exports; and this share increased to 70 percent in 2006. The increase in concentration appears to be related to a decreasing dependence on bananas but increased dependence on fuels and metals as a source of foreign exchange, particularly in Trinidad and Tobago. Export structures are most concentrated in The Bahamas (90 percent), St. Kitts and Nevis (85 percent), Suriname (94 percent), and Trinidad and Tobago (87 percent). Fifth, Caribbean access to the global economy has been low and declining. Penetration into the world economy declined from 0.5 percent in 1980 to less than 0.2 percent in 2006, while Asia region has been increasing its share of the world trade (more than 12 percent in 2006). Sixth, the analysis of similarity of export structure of the capacity of Caribbean countries to compete with their main trade partners shows that the Caribbean's export structure is very similar to Central America's, especially for Antigua and Barbuda, Jamaica, and Suriname. However, for the other trade partners competition is relatively weak. Seventh, binding constraints to CARIFORUM's competitiveness include high cost of inputs and factors of production, as well as high costs of trade, including transport and insurance costs.

Trade Performance, Trade Flows, and Patterns

Growth and Patterns in the Direction of Trade

CARIFORUM merchandise trade has been characterized by rising exports and imports. After a period of stagnation (1995–99) and slight decline (2000–02), merchandise exports have been rising since 2002 to reach more than US$23 billion in 2006 (see Figure 3.1). This trend reflects mainly the performance of non-OECS countries, which have experienced relatively strong export value growth of more than 12 percent over the period 2003–06.

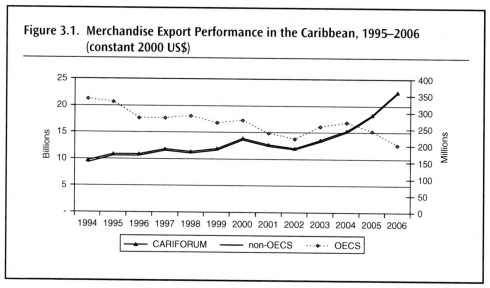

Figure 3.1. Merchandise Export Performance in the Caribbean, 1995–2006 (constant 2000 US$)

Source: COMTRADE Database and Authors' calculations.

Exports to the USA/Canada and EU have been rising since 2002 increasing in real terms by 34 percent on average over 2003–06. Imports of goods have also been growing reaching a value of nearly US$35 billion in 2006, mainly driven by non-OECS CARIFORUM countries (see Figure 3.1).

OECS merchandise trade has followed a different trend. The sub-region's overall merchandise export performance was relatively weak. Merchandise exports stagnated while imports rose over the period. Goods destined to non-OECS CARICOM partners grew the fastest (9.8 percent a year). Exports to the EU displayed the worst performance, declining by an annual average of 11 percent since 1995. Exports to the USA and Canada have been volatile over the past decade but grew on average 7 percent each year.

While the Caribbean countries export performance has been strong compared with the world, it has been relatively weak compared with other developing countries (Figure 3.2). With respect to the rest of Latin America, the Caribbean has performed better than Central America in recent years, but not as well as South America (See Figure 3.3).

This general trend hides differences between countries' performance. Some member states performed better than others. Trinidad and Tobago, Suriname, and Haiti enjoyed relatively high export growth over the past 5 years. Among the OECS, Antigua and St. Lucia displayed relatively robust growth of 10.8 percent and 10.4 percent a year, respectively while other OECS member states such as Dominica, Grenada, and St. Vincent saw their total good exports decline during this period.

The CARICOM countries rely on markets that grant them preferential access to their major export destination. The EU, the United States, and Canada account for a 68 percent share of CARICOM good exports. United States and Canada are the most important destination accounting for over one-half of exports. The EU accounts for 15 percent. However, this mark has declined by 17 percentage points in the mid-1990s. The figures are more striking for the OECS region. For this group of countries, CARICOM (including the OECS

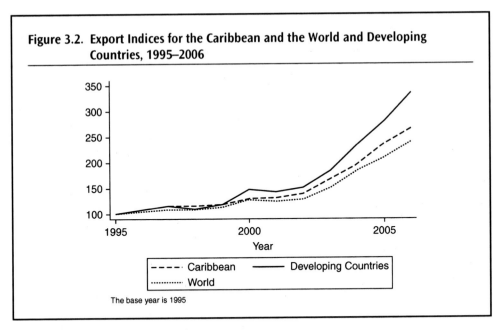

Figure 3.2. **Export Indices for the Caribbean and the World and Developing Countries, 1995–2006**

Source: IMF Direction of Trade Statistics.

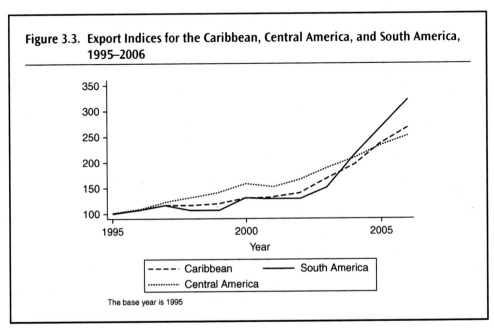

Figure 3.3. **Export Indices for the Caribbean, Central America, and South America, 1995–2006**

Source: IMF Direction of Trade Statistics.

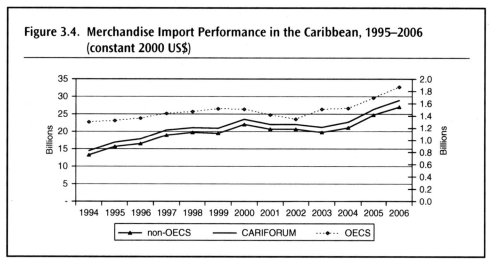

Figure 3.4. Merchandise Import Performance in the Caribbean, 1995–2006 (constant 2000 US$)

Source: COMTRADE Database and Bank staff's calculations.

sub-region) is the most important destination of exports and accounts for 41 percent of the region's exports. The EU accounts for another third while USA and Canada hold a 25 percent share of OECS good exports, up from 20 percent a decade earlier. The remaining goods are destined to Latin America and other surrounding European territories in the Caribbean.

CARICOM has increased the share of intra-merchandise exports relative to extra-regional partners. Intra-regional exports increased to 11 percent in the period 2005–06 compared to 8 percent in 1995–96. A closer look at intra-regional trade flows shows that CARICOM relies mainly on Trinidad and Tobago, Barbados and Jamaica as destinations for the region's exports. There is evidence of growing trade links between the OECS and Belize and Suriname. OECS's exports to these two partners have displayed the fastest growth. OECS'S sub-regional partners account for about 40 percent of OECS's intra-regional exports, with Antigua and Barbuda and St. Lucia each accounting for a 10 percent share of sales.

During the period 1995–2006, CARICOM good imports grew at an annual average of 7 percent to reach US$ 29 billion. The region's total imports displayed stronger growth in the first half of the decade (over 9 percent a year) than in the second half (4 percent a year). Imports from Latin America (mostly Brazil, Venezuela and Colombia) and China region displayed the fastest growth of 20 and 24 percent a year, respectively.

The most important source of goods for the CARICOM countries is the United States and Canada—sourcing 41 percent of imports, although this share has declined in recent years. Another 13 percent of imports arrive from the European Union. This general trend also applies to OECS countries, for which United States and Canada account for about 40 percent of imports while the EU make up about 30 percent of imports on average. Non-OECS CARICOM members account for another 15 percent, while OECS sub-region holds a 3 percent share. Latin America and other countries source 4 percent and 10 percent of OECS goods imports, respectively.

Intra-CARICOM's share of imports is small and increasing—currently 14 percent, up from 11 percent a decade earlier in 1995. The goods sourced from the CARICOM region come predominantly from Trinidad and Tobago. Roughly 80 percent of intra-CARICOM's imports come from Trinidad and Tobago, up from 61 percent share in 1995. Trinidad and Tobago accounts for at least a 60 percent share of intra-regional imports of Grenada, St. Kitts and Nevis, St. Lucia and St. Vincent and the Grenadines, and roughly 80 percent of regional imports for Jamaica, Barbados, and Suriname.

Composition of Trade by Sectors and Destination of Exports

The analysis of the composition of trade by sectors shows a changing trend in the export structure of CARIFORUM member states over the past decade. In 1995 on average 20 percent of CARICOM exports were food products, and more than 60 percent were manufactures. Over the last decade, manufactured and food exports declined, while exports of fuels grew. As a result, in 2006 manufactured and food products account for less than 30 percent and 10 percent of total exports respectively, while fuels exports make up nearly two-thirds of total exports (see Figure 3.5 below). The share of exports of fuels rose as a result of rising kerosene exports by St. Lucia and Trinidad and Tobago. Exports of ores, metals, and raw agricultural materials (category "other" in Figure 3.5) are negligible and have remained stable at about 2 percent of total exports in 2006.

The analysis of exports by destination shows no changing pattern in the destination of CARIFORUM exports over the past decade. The United States and Canada remain the main markets of CARIFORUM exports. Together they account for more than half of CARIFORUM exports while the EU absorbs only about 15 percent of the region's exports in 2006 (see Figure 3.6). Exports to USA/Canada and Europe are currently dominated by natural gas, petroleum and aluminum products (see Figures 3.7 and 3.8). In addition, agriculture products (sugar and alcohol) are also exported to the EU. Intra-CARICOM exports increased over the past decade from about 12 percent of total exports in 1995 to 18 percent

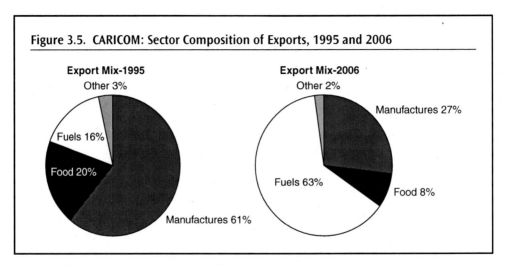

Figure 3.5. CARICOM: Sector Composition of Exports, 1995 and 2006

Export Mix-1995
Other 3%
Fuels 16%
Food 20%
Manufactures 61%

Export Mix-2006
Other 2%
Manufactures 27%
Fuels 63%
Food 8%

Source: COMTRADE Database and Bank staff's calculations.

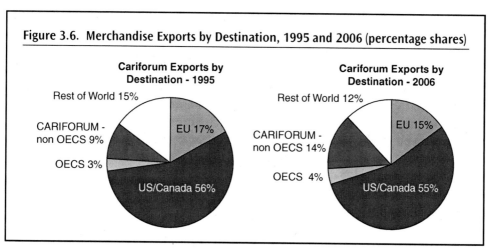

Figure 3.6. Merchandise Exports by Destination, 1995 and 2006 (percentage shares)

Source: COMTRADE Database and Bank staff's calculations.

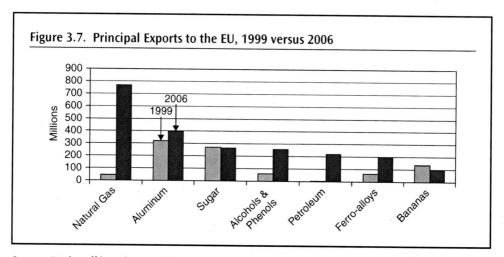

Figure 3.7. Principal Exports to the EU, 1999 versus 2006

Source: Bank staff based on World Development Indicators Database.

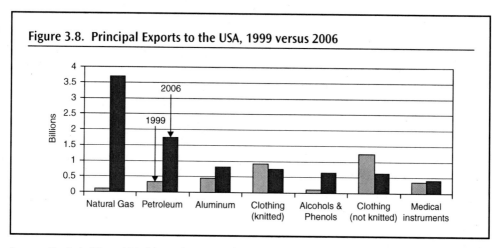

Figure 3.8. Principal Exports to the USA, 1999 versus 2006

Source: Bank staff based World Development Indicators.

in 2006. Intra-regional exports are relatively diversified, roughly 27 percent of exports are manufactures and another 22 percent are food products. Exports of fuels, ores and metals and raw agricultural products account for the other half of exports, led in large part by Trinidad and Tobago's oil exports and St. Lucia's kerosene exports (or re-exports).

During the period 2001–06 Barbados, Dominica, St. Lucia and Grenada demonstrated a relatively balanced export structure by sector, with food and manufactured products each accounting for an equal proportion of merchandise exports. Manufactured exports by these three countries have, similarly to the overall CARICOM trend, increased their importance at the expense of food products. Antigua and Barbuda, Suriname, Jamaica, and St. Kitts and Nevis, display a highly manufactures-intensive export structure. On the other hand, Guyana, Belize, and St. Vincent and the Grenadines are highly food-intensive exporters.

The composition of CARICOM's imports by sector shows that most goods coming into the region are manufactured products. Between 2001–06, approximately 60 percent of total imports were manufactures, while another 17 percent share were food and raw agricultural products. The remaining imports were fuels (22 percent) and ores and metals (1 percent). Fuels increased their share over the past decade while manufactured imports declined. Food and raw agricultural products—also declined slightly in importance at the expense of fuels. This could be the result of price effects (higher international fuel prices), rather than real changes in the quantity traded.

The analysis of the composition of imports by destination also yields similar results. CARICOM's imports from the United States and the EU are predominantly manufactured products (74 and 78 percent respectively). The remaining goods from the EU are mostly food products. From the United States, they include food, raw agricultural and fuel products. Between 2001 and 2006, 39 percent of OECS imports; from CARICOM Partners were manufactures; 25 percent were food products; and another 34 percent were fuels. It is important to note that CARICOM imports more than 20 percent of its fuels needs from Trinidad and Tobago while also importing significant amounts from Venezuela and the United States.

Export Concentration and Principal Products

The analysis of the region's export structure shows increased concentration of products. In 1997, the top 20 products account for 51 percent of total exports; and this share increased to 70 percent in 2006.[69] The increase in concentration appears to be related to a decreasing dependence on bananas but increased dependence on fuels and metals as a source of foreign exchange, particularly in Trinidad and Tobago. A breakdown of the top 20 exports to the world during 2001–06 shows that four are agricultural and food products, six are minerals and ores, four are manufactures and six are a fuel-related product.

The export concentration of individual CARICOM member states varies significantly. Export structures are most concentrated (that is, the top five [SITC 4-digit] exports account for the highest share of total exports) in The Bahamas (90 percent), St. Kitts and Nevis (85 percent), Suriname (94 percent), and Trinidad and Tobago (87 percent). The calculations of the HHI for CARICOM member states yield similar results, namely that Suriname,

---

69. Using HS 6-digit mirror data.

Grenada, St. Kitts and Nevis, have the most concentrated structures while Barbados, Guyana and the Dominican Republic are some of the least concentrated.[70] Product diversification can also be measured using a proxy—the total number of product lines exported in a given time period. Most countries managed to increase the number of product lines exported. Grenada diversifies its exports moving from exporting 121 different products in 1995 period to 182 products a decade later. Trinidad increased its exports of product lines from 385 to 481. Dominica's performance was more modest, exporting 262 products at the beginning of the decade, with a small increase to 274 products in 2006.

While some new products were discovered, growing exports of existing goods still accounted for by far the largest share of trade growth. Even at a finer level of disaggregation, the six-digit HS level, new goods were on average responsible for just 10 percent of export growth over the period and only 7 percent of manufacturing export growth. The countries with the highest export growth, Antigua and Barbuda, Bahamas, Haiti and Trinidad and Tobago, all experienced export growth largely through increased exports of existing goods.

The CARICOM intra-regional export structure is less concentrated than the world, and the concentration is generally improving. The top 10 products account for 29 percent of intra-regional merchandise exports, down from a 47 percent share during the period 1995–2000. Countries such as Trinidad and Tobago and Barbados have a relatively diversified regional export basket in which the top 10 exports account for only 16 percent and 60 percent of the total. However, in the OECS countries the situation is reversed, as a few products dominate intra-regional export structures. In Dominica, the top five exports to CARICOM are chemical products such as soap and disinfectants. Together, these five products represent almost 75 percent of Dominica's intra-regional exports. Grenada's intra-regional exports are dominated by one product (flour of wheat), while in St. Kitts and Nevis this is the case with lemonade, flavored waters and margarine. In both countries, these products make up more than two-thirds of intra-regional exports, while in St. Vincent and the Grenadines this share is held by five food products exported to the world and the region.

Caribbean exports show relatively little change in technology content, especially compared with other regions. Table 3.1 shows an index of the average real wage of exports for the Caribbean and other regions and countries in 1990–94 and 2000–04.[71] In 2000–04, Caribbean's exports have an average real wage associated with them of $6,574. That implies that their exports, on average, are representative of exporters with a per capita income of $6,574. The average per capita income in the Caribbean, weighted by total exports, is over

70. Other well known export concentration ratios include: the Hirschman index, the Olive index, the entropy index, the Herfindahl index. For more details, See Attaran and Zwick (1987); ECA (2006).

71. For each product, the average wage associated with it is the sum of all exporters GDPPC at PPP weighted by the revealed comparative advantage of the exporters. For example, if apparel weighs heavily in the export basket of low income countries it will have a low index. The index is defined in detail in Hausman, Hwang, Rodrik (2005). Once an industry average wage is known, the average real wage associated with a country or region's export basket is calculated as the weighted average of the indexes in the industries in which it exports. For example, a country with many low wage industries that weigh heavily in its export basket will have a low wage index. The average wage associated with exports is calculated by country or region, using average bilateral 4-digit SITC trade and average GDPPC at PPP data from 2000–2004 and 1990–1994.

Table 3.1. Index of Average Wage of Exports

	1990–1994	2000–2004	Percent Change
Caribbean	6,661	6,574	−1.31
LAC	8,143	9,128	12.10
South America	7,312	7,764	6.18
Central America	6,169	7,302	18.37
Mexico	10,451	11,389	8.98
China	8,308	9,963	19.92
World	10,679	11,108	4.02

Source: Freund and Ozden 2008.

$7100, indicating that their exports are somewhat below their income level. LAC exports have an average real wage associated with them of $9,128. The average per capita income in LAC, weighted by total exports, is $8,311, indicating that their exports are somewhat above their income level.[72] Hausman, Hwang, Rodrik (2005) argue that the fact that China's export wage index is so far above their per capita income may be responsible for China's strong growth. The intuition is that China is getting into sophisticated products, which have high productivity growth. The Caribbean's export basket does not offer a positive indicator.

How has the average wage associated with exports changed over time? Of interest, the average wage of exports declined in the Caribbean by about one percent. This suggests that the Caribbean may be moving down the value ladder. In contrast, the average wage in LAC is $8,143 in 1990–94—about 12 percent lower—indicating that LAC has moved toward relatively high-wage products in the last 10 years. Using world export shares, the average world wage also increased from $10,679 to $11,108, only a 4 percent rise. In part this is because of the large increase in exports by poor countries that compete primarily in low wage products.

Competitiveness, Specialization, and Complementarity

Market Access and Penetration

Caribbean's access to the global economy has been low and declining (see Figures 3.9 and 3.10). Penetration into the world economy declined from 0.5 percent in 1980 to less than 0.2 percent in 2006, while Asia region has been increasing its share of the world trade (more than 12 percent in 2006).

The CARICOM's preferential access in major export markets has had mixed impact on the region's competitive position relative to its competitors. The region receives preferential

---

72. Using the same data, this is calculated as the sum over the LAC countries in the sample of (share of LAC total exports)*(GDPPC at PPP).

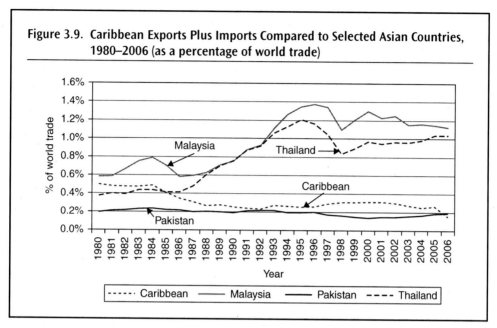

Figure 3.9. Caribbean Exports Plus Imports Compared to Selected Asian Countries, 1980–2006 (as a percentage of world trade)

Source: Bank staff based on World Development Indicators.

treatment in all its major export markets through the Cotonou Agreement (EU), the Caribbean Basin Initiative and Caribbean Basin Trade Partnership Act (U.S.), the CARIBCAN (Canada), and the Generalized System of Preferences (both in the EU and U.S.). Over the last decade, the CARICOM countries have lost relative competitiveness, either through the

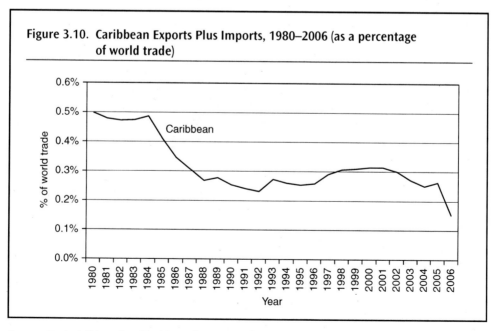

Figure 3.10. Caribbean Exports Plus Imports, 1980–2006 (as a percentage of world trade)

Source: Bank staff based on World Development Indicators.

erosion of preferences or through the expansion of preferential treatment to competitors, in its major export markets.

The CARICOM's market penetration in the European Union has improved marginally over the last decade to reach 0.11 percent of total EU imports. Of the 443 different product lines exported to the EU between 1995–2006, 259 of them have gained market share. Those products that gained the most market share included rice, spices, vegetable and natural gas. However, some of the products have lost significant market penetration including sugar, bananas, bauxite and alcohols and phenols. For OECS countries, bananas and sugar have lost significant market penetration: bananas (1.2 to 0.2 percent share) and sugar (0.5 to 0.2 percent share). However, some OECS's exports have gained market penetration. Ships and floating structures have increased their share by 2 percentage points to 2.5 percent, spices have increased their share by almost 1 percentage point, while feedstuffs have increased by 0.1 percentage points.

Penetration into the U.S. market has also improved, as the CARICOM share in total U.S. imports has risen from 0.35 percent to 0.58 percent since 1995 year, boosted by energy exports and minerals. Of the 351 products exported to the United States, 205 lost market share. The products that gained the most market share were resource based, including metals, ores, chemicals and natural gas. Among the biggest "losers" in market penetration were bauxite, clothing, and citrus fruits. This trend also applies to the OECS. The OECS lost market share in 7 of the top ten export products to the United States, including zinc, fresh tomatoes, and electrical circuits. It is interesting to note that the top three products exported to the United States in 1993–96—dresses, jerseys and pullovers, and brassieres – all lost significant market shares to reach almost zero in 2006. This could be the result of preference erosion in apparel production vis-à-vis Mexico and other Central American competitors.

International Competitiveness of Exports and Specialization of Exports

The CARICOM's export performance and international competitiveness can also be evaluated using the export specialization index (ESI).[73] The CARICOM region appears to be specialized in 90 out of a total of 526 products exported to the world between 1995 and 2006. Of these 90 products, 16 of them either increased or maintained their ESI from earlier in the decade (1995): their breakdown is relatively diversified between food and agricultural products (6 of them), fuels materials (3), and industrial goods and manufactures (7).

The CARICOM was specialized in 48 out of 347 products exported to the EU in 1995, only two of these having increased their ESI from up until 2006 period (essential oils and

---

73. The export specialization index measures a country's (or region's) international specialization in specific products by dividing that product's share in a country's (or region's) total exports, by its share in world imports. It is assumed that if a specific product's share in CARICOM's exports is greater than the product's share in world imports, that is, and ESI greater than one, then the region is specialized in production and appears to be an efficient producer of that product. Trends in ESI over time and across different markets can help identify increasing (or decreasing) specialization, comparative advantages and sectors where promotional resources can be targeted.

alcoholic beverages). For OECS region, two products, sugar and bananas, either maintained or decreased their specialization, a sign of preference erosion and weakening competitiveness over the last decade. In the U.S. market, the CARICOM appears specialized in 72 out of the 320 products exported to that destination from 1995, with the majority of these (mostly manufactures) have experienced a decrease in their ESI by 2006. Thirteen products have increased their specialization—three of them are food and agricultural products, four are crude materials, and six are manufactures.

For OECS region, Vignoles (2005) ranks exports into four categories based on supply-side performance (measured through their growth in world market share) and demand-side trends (measured through growth in global imports). The four categories include: "champions"; "achievers in adversity"; "underachievers" and "declining sectors."[74] The study shows that 79 product groups accounting for 36 percent of total exports are classified as "champions." In the top 20 exports, there are eight "champions": three of these products are food and agricultural products, while the other five are manufactures. Fourteen products groups representing 4 percent of total exports are "achievers in adversity." One product (flour wheat) dominates this category. Eighty-nine products accounting for 53 percent of total exports are "underachievers." One export sector (fruit and nuts) accounts for half of all underachievers (in value terms) and has lost an average 12 percent per year in world market share. Fifteen products representing 6 percent of total OECS exports are "declining sectors." Two of these products are sugar and rice.

The study also identifies for the individual OECS member states the sectors that could benefit from additional national resources: the "champions." For instance, in Dominica, two "champions" displaying significant increases in world market shares are perfumery and cosmetics, and non-alcoholic beverages. In Grenada, spices (namely nutmeg), as well as equipment for distributing electricity, and paper and paperboard are stand out as "champions." St. Kitts and Nevis had seven "champions," with electrical switches and electrical machinery representing the majority of this category. For St. Lucia, alcoholic beverages, kerosene, and telecommunications equipment experienced strong growth in world market shares.

Trade Complementarity, Similarity, and Intensity

Analyzing trade complementarity is important to get a measure of how a country's (or region's) export supply fits into the import demand of its trading partners. In addition, examining how similar export patterns are shows how much competition there is between regions or countries.

Table 3.2 shows the complementarity between CARICOM exports and its major trade partners using HS 6-digit data for 1997 and 2005. This is usually measured by an export-import

---

74. "Champions" refers to export sectors that increase their world market shares and face growing global demand. "Achievers in adversity" represents sectors that increase their world market shares while global demand falls. "Underachievers" refers to sectors facing growing demand but with supply-side constraints leading to declines in market share; and "declining sectors" represent those export sectors facing constraints in both supply and demand, with falling market shares and decreasing growth in global imports.

Table 3.2. The Similarity between Caribbean Export and Partners' Imports

Country	ESISA	ESICA	ESIUSA	ESIChina	ESIEU	ESIJapan
Export-Import Similarity 2005						
Antigua and Barbuda	6.56	7.24	6.69	3.46	7.94	5.76
Bahamas	5.62	19.69	9.26	4.40	10.40	7.00
Barbados	20.65	28.49	21.94	11.77	21.69	16.76
Belize	8.84	14.80	10.44	5.96	11.01	9.98
Dominica	10.39	20.84	12.04	7.12	11.42	11.17
Dominican Rep.	9.54	17.28	16.44	9.61	16.90	14.05
Grenada	5.44	6.41	7.72	4.24	8.56	5.76
Guyana	3.31	8.65	4.04	4.02	5.58	5.95
Haiti	3.62	4.94	5.98	2.58	6.25	5.66
Jamaica	4.76	6.37	8.07	3.66	8.24	6.96
Saint Kitts and Nevis	6.16	4.96	8.49	8.00	9.55	7.46
Saint Lucia	6.78	16.32	10.46	4.86	10.00	7.28
Saint Vincent and the Grenadines	4.10	26.43	3.24	3.35	4.25	3.03
Suriname	4.02	3.89	4.38	3.84	5.05	4.93
Trinidad and Tobago	15.00	23.01	20.56	11.83	20.32	22.87
Caribbean (aggregate)	19.75	30.59	25.54	15.23	26.27	26.10
Caribbean (average)	7.65	13.95	9.98	5.91	10.48	8.98
Export-Import Similarity 1997						
Antigua and Barbuda	10.72	27.74	14.10	10.00	13.16	17.97
Bahamas	6.54	19.07	8.03	5.38	7.95	7.53
Barbados	10.66	13.50	12.37	8.12	14.12	9.31
Belize	4.28	6.12	4.64	4.72	5.57	6.98
Dominica	11.24	12.50	13.98	8.44	15.06	10.87
Dominican Rep.	6.29	12.90	14.50	5.34	12.63	11.76
Grenada	4.68	5.09	5.34	2.99	5.90	4.54
Guyana	3.37	23.00	4.20	3.20	4.85	6.39
Haiti	3.26	6.29	8.82	3.51	6.70	7.63
Jamaica	5.52	14.25	10.12	4.66	10.32	9.42
Saint Kitts and Nevis	5.29	3.59	7.07	6.30	7.03	5.96
Saint Lucia	8.02	9.78	13.95	8.62	11.11	16.71
Saint Vincent and the Grenadines	7.58	11.72	8.36	4.63	7.93	6.47
Suriname	6.73	7.06	10.49	7.87	8.54	12.76
Trinidad and Tobago	13.52	27.25	15.11	12.66	14.20	19.35
Caribbean (aggregate)	16.12	26.10	23.05	14.41	22.72	21.44
Caribbean (average)	7.18	13.32	10.07	6.43	9.67	10.24

Source: Comtrade HS 6-digit 1992 classification and Bank staff's calculation.

similarity index.[75] It shows that overall the region has a relatively high degree of complementarity with Central America, the EU, the United States, and Japan. However, this result is largely coming from Barbados and Trinidad and Tobago. The table also shows that complementarity has remained roughly unchanged since 1997.

Table 3.3 shows the similarity of export structure between the Caribbean countries and their main trade partners.[76] It provides an indication of how much countries are likely to compete with one another. It shows that the Caribbean's export structure is very similar to Central America's, especially for Antigua and Barbuda, Jamaica, and Suriname. However, for the other trade partners competition is relatively weak. In the last column, the similarity with the rest of the Caribbean (i.e. the Caribbean total excluding the countries own exports) is shown for each exporter. Even among Caribbean countries, there is little similarity in export structure. Since 1997, export similarity has remained roughly constant, with two important exceptions. The Caribbean region countries look more different from China, i.e. are competing less with China now than in 1997, and have become more similar to Central America.

A way to gauge the importance of complementarity versus similarity in trade is to examine whether the Caribbean's export structure is closer to the export or import structure of its trade partner. In 2005, for Central America and South America, Caribbean exports are more similar to their exports than to their imports, suggesting competition. However, Caribbean exports are more similar to the imports of the United States, the EU, Japan, and China, suggesting a relatively high level of complementarity.

Binding Constraints to Competitiveness

Costs of Inputs and Factors of Production

Labor Market Rigidities and High Labor Cost.   Labor markets in CARICOM member states are characterized by relatively high wages and low flexibility compared to other middle-income countries. Problems arise from two sources. First, high wages across skill levels and sectors appears to be rising faster than productivity and are reflected in high unemployment rates. Second, the sub-region suffers from skill mismatching and shortages.

The misalignment between wages and productivity can be attributed to four main factors. First, CARICOM countries are characterized by strong unions. It is estimated that unionization rates range from 12 to 47 percent of the labor force in St. Vincent and the Grenadines, and Grenada, respectively. The labor unions have a large influence on wage

---

75. An export-import similarity index is an index between 0 and 100, such that 100 reflect that the Caribbean's export shares across industries are identical to the import shares in the other country or region. Zero reflects no complementarity: the importer only imports products that the exporter does not export. The Finger and Kreinin similarity indices, which describe how similar two economies is defined by the formula $ESI = \{\Sigma \underset{i}{Minimum}[S_{iA}, S_{iB}]\}100$, where S_{ij} is the *share* of product i in j's exports to the world. If the product-share distribution of A's and B's exports are identical ($S_{iA} = S_{iB}$ for each i), the index will take on a value of 100. If A's and B's export patterns are different the index will be zero. Similarly, the index can be calculated using the import shares from one country and the export shares of another to determine complementarity of two trade partners.

76. Again, an index of 100 reflects identical structures and an index of 0 reflects very different structures.

Table 3.3. The Similarity between Caribbean Exports and Partners' Exports

Country	ESISA	ESICA	ESIUSA	ESIChina	ESIEU	ESIJapan	ESI Caribbean
Export Similarity Index 2005							
Antigua and Barbuda	6.42	88.03	6.31	5.12	6.35	5.39	7.98
Bahamas	6.75	38.95	7.48	2.94	10.90	8.13	18.44
Barbados	18.52	15.08	15.01	8.65	19.57	9.69	28.17
Belize	10.98	21.29	8.27	6.44	9.53	6.83	19.53
Dominica	9.62	28.43	12.51	7.98	13.00	8.85	12.18
Dominican Rep.	9.41	28.28	14.49	18.00	13.20	10.26	11.49
Grenada	4.53	12.72	8.43	4.19	8.72	7.37	7.88
Guyana	8.52	32.47	4.24	3.34	4.82	2.43	7.31
Haiti	4.22	7.04	4.27	5.64	3.94	2.54	7.98
Jamaica	7.77	79.11	7.11	4.78	7.60	5.36	14.74
Saint Kitts and Nevis	4.12	6.01	9.07	7.57	10.57	11.48	6.75
Saint Lucia	7.11	11.93	9.05	4.13	10.84	6.91	19.17
Saint Vincent and	4.67	43.19	3.84	3.41	4.46	4.47	10.34
Suriname the Grenadines	6.87	60.65	4.27	2.53	4.02	2.12	10.45
Trinidad and Tobago	20.74	39.46	6.95	4.14	9.09	4.27	10.13
Caribbean (aggregate)	22.42	48.01	15.58	13.89	18.14	10.91	1.00
Caribbean (average)	8.68	34.18	8.09	5.92	9.11	6.41	12.84
Export Similarity Index 1997							
Antigua and Barbuda	20.59	49.49	9.28	7.42	9.86	8.32	13.68
Bahamas	8.31	33.36	6.13	5.84	7.00	6.08	12.11
Barbados	8.18	20.62	12.95	9.26	13.83	10.63	12.76
Belize	9.97	27.58	4.90	4.41	4.91	2.90	7.04
Dominica	11.58	25.43	13.41	9.07	15.22	10.31	9.01
Dominican Rep.	10.01	24.87	9.24	17.55	10.77	5.94	4.88
Grenada	4.43	11.90	5.15	4.09	5.86	4.40	6.63
Guyana	6.18	32.55	4.15	4.02	4.12	1.57	6.97
Haiti	7.61	22.59	4.53	11.25	5.32	2.65	9.85
Jamaica	11.21	23.87	7.00	9.89	9.10	4.39	17.85
Saint Kitts and Nevis	3.61	6.67	7.53	4.57	7.31	7.56	3.82
Saint Lucia	17.36	31.67	6.40	8.51	7.46	4.33	12.22
Saint Vincent and the Grenadines	6.26	49.67	7.00	8.20	7.94	8.38	10.64
Suriname	14.44	19.76	4.40	4.59	4.19	2.24	15.07
Trinidad and Tobago	22.04	43.47	8.01	7.87	11.19	4.63	20.03
Caribbean (aggregate)	21.17	38.42	14.23	21.99	17.79	9.64	100.00
Caribbean (average)	10.79	28.23	7.34	7.77	8.27	5.62	10.84

Source: Comtrade HS 6-digit 1992 classification and Bank staff's calculation.

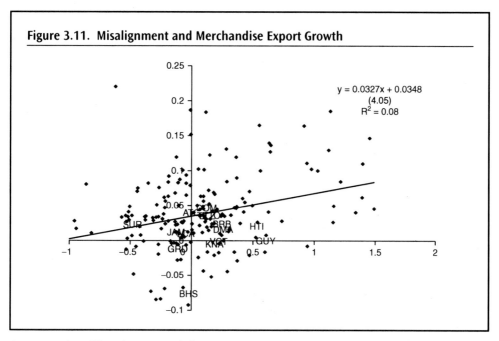

Figure 3.11. Misalignment and Merchandise Export Growth

$$y = 0.0327x + 0.0348$$
$$(4.05)$$
$$R^2 = 0.08$$

Source: Bank staff based on IMF statistics.

determination through their political and bargaining power during collective negotiations. Second, CARICOM countries have large public sectors that impact wage setting across the economy. The public sector employs more than 20 percent of the labor force. As a result, increases in government wages for specific labor groups also push up wages for private sector firms seeking similar services. Third, rigid labor regulations such as minimum wage laws make it difficult to hire and fire workers. This affects the ability of firms to adjust their labor allocation to changes in productivity. Finally, remittances also impact the functioning of labor market by raising reservation wages (the specific rate an individual requires to work in given market) since their income is supplemented by external sources.

The Exchange Rate. Figure 3.9 shows a scatter plot of the countries' average real exchange rate misalignment and real total merchandise export growth from 2000–2004 and Figure 3.10 shows the relationship between misalignment and manufacturing export growth.[77] The fitted line shows that a ten percent increase in undervaluation increases average annual export growth by about 0.3 percentage points and average annual manufacturing export growth by 0.7 percentage points. Most of the countries in the Caribbean have not experienced extensive overvaluation in this period. There is some indication that undervaluation has aided the manufacturing exports of Haiti and Guyana.

---

77. This part uses data from the Penn World Tables, which is only available through 2004. The horizontal axis represents the percent of undervaluation of the currency. For example, 0.2 indicates the currency is 20 percent undervalued. It shows that export growth is limited by an overvalued exchange rate. Misalignment is measured adjusting for the Balasa-Samuelson effect. The real exchange rate at PPP is regressed on real per-capita GDP, and the extent of misalignment is measured as the difference between the log of the real exchange rate at PPP and the log of the fitted value from the regression (as in Rodrik 2007).

Table 3.4. Average Tariffs in the Caribbean

Country	1996	1997	1999	2000	2001	2002	2003	2004	2005
Antigua and Barbuda	21.58		19.11	10.76	9.63	9.64	9.63		9.69
Bahamas, The			31.15			30.64			
Barbados	21.61		19.19	19.18	13.06	13.05	13.05		
Belize	22.21		19.71		10.53	10.53	10.53		
Dominica	21.05		18.49	17.16	9.90	9.89	9.89		
Dominican Republic		14.77		18.05	8.48	8.55	8.55	8.49	
Grenada	21.33		18.91		18.90	10.45	10.45		10.22
Guyana	23.03		20.75	20.73	11.02	11.02	11.02		
Jamaica	21.19		18.76	7.20	7.22	7.22	7.22		
St. Kitts and Nevis	21.22		18.69	9.36	9.28	9.35	9.35		9.15
St. Lucia	21.12		18.67	18.67	8.91	8.91	9.34		
St. Vincent and Grenadines	20.74		17.67	18.96					
Suriname	21.17								
Trinidad en Tobago	9.71					6.33			
Average	20.50		20.10	15.56	10.69	11.30	9.90		9.69

Source: WITS. Note: Many country-years are not available, country-years with fewer than observations are also dropped (9 cases).

Trade Policy.   Table 3.4 shows average tariffs in the Caribbean from 1996 to the present, for years for which data are available. There has been significant tariff reduction and tariff alignment in the Caribbean. Average applied MFN tariffs fell from over 20 percent in 1996 to just below 10 percent in 2005. Still, there is some tariff dispersion, with average tariffs on 10 percent of goods over 20 percent. Tariffs (bound at 58 on average) are binding less than one percent of the time, where binding is defined as a tariff overhang of less than 3 percent (Bound rate—MFN rate < 3). The Bahamas, Barbados and Dominica still have more than 50 tariff lines with tariffs over 50 percent. Most of the tariff peaks are on agricultural products, such as fruits, vegetables, tobacco, meat (especially poultry), and fish. In addition, there are high tariffs on beverages, including: juices, beer, and liquor, as well as on crude oil and revolvers and pistols. On manufactured goods, there are high tariffs on some auto parts, motorcycles, jewelry and few other products. While the progress to date is admirable, there is still room for further reduction of tariffs and more uniformity in some of the countries.

While many Caribbean countries (most notably Trinidad and Tobago, Dominican Republic, and Jamaica) have undertaken policy measures to improve their trade policy, important weaknesses remain in five major areas: (i) measures affecting imports; (ii) measures affecting exports; (iii) investment incentives; (iv) competition policy; and (v) trade policy formulation and implementation.

Customs procedures and administration are weak in most Caribbean countries. Customs valuation methods are not effective because of limited capacity at the customs departments in many Caribbean countries. To the exception of Trinidad and Tobago and Dominica

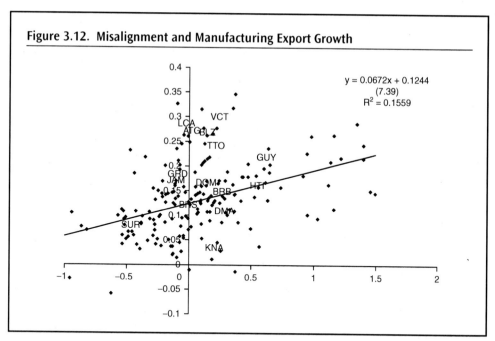

Figure 3.12. Misalignment and Manufacturing Export Growth

$$y = 0.0672x + 0.1244$$
$$(7.39)$$
$$R^2 = 0.1559$$

Source: Bank staff based on IMF statistics.

Republic, export procedures and financing are not well developed. Exporters have limited access to credits for exports and credit insurance. Export promotion activities (export facilitation, information, image-building, and participation in fairs) are barely developed.

The legal framework for businesses including taxation is weak in many Caribbean countries. Registration time of businesses is relatively long and registration fees are relatively high. Taxation systems need improvements.

Many Caribbean countries apply a range of incentives to promote investment, including duty concessions, tax exemptions and holidays, loss write-offs, and training support. However, most of them have not developed a comprehensive investment strategy.

A comprehensive competition policy does not exist in most of the Caribbean countries. Trinidad and Tobago (the most advanced country of the region) does not have a comprehensive competition policy legislation, although efforts to enhance the regulatory framework and reinforce consumer protection have been displayed in recent years. Because of the relatively small size of the domestic market of many Caribbean countries, the level of competition in many areas is low, and de facto monopolies are present, particularly in services.

National institutions in charge of trade policy formulation and implementation are weak. Ministry of commerce and industry and trade institutions lack staff and expertise in policy formulation. Linked to limited expertise is the limited negotiation power. As the result trade agreements either bilateral or multilateral are negotiated and signed with little awareness of their implications. A point in case is the recently negotiated EPA. Many Caribbean countries were unprepared to this new framework. Negotiations were conducted by the CRNM which itself lacks the necessary expertise. In this context, implementation of trade agreements has generally been slow.

Trade Costs.   Trade costs are relatively high in the Caribbean, potentially impeding trade. Trade costs are estimated using CIF-FOB ratios for each HS 6-digit product that a country exports to the United States.[78] The CIF-FOB ratio represents the ratio of costs including freight and insurance relative to costs of the customs value of the product. A CIF/FOB ratio of 1.1 indicates that freight and insurance charges are 10 percent.

Overall average Caribbean freight and insurance costs to the United States are relatively high, at 9.4 percent in 2005–06. Using world CIF-FOB ratios for the same composition of exports, the freight rate is only 6.6 percent. This implies that an average country that exports the same composition of goods as the Caribbean faces lower trade costs of nearly 3 percentage points. Similarly, trade costs were 7.8 percent for Central America in the same products in 2005–06.[79] Only Grenada and St. Vincent and the Grenadines have transport costs below the world average for the products that they export. In 60 percent of the 785 HS 6-digit products that the Caribbean exported to the United States their average freight and insurance costs were higher than world costs. Given the proximity of the Caribbean countries to the United States this raises some questions about the shipping and insurance costs these countries are facing.

Transport costs for imports to the Caribbean tend to be high relative to other countries in the region. A study by Hoffman (2001) estimates that 1997 costs of insurance and maritime freight in the Caribbean were 11.2 percent of import value as compared with 9.3 percent for Central America and 5.2 percent for the world. One issue with these estimates though is that they do not take into account the composition of trade, differences could stem from higher cost products. Port handling costs tend to be much higher in the Caribbean than in other countries in Latin America, ranging from US $200–400 in 1997 as compared with about US$150 in Argentina (ECLAC 1997). Some of the problems include scale, low productivity of labor, little competition among shipping companies, poor technology, security costs and excessive waiting periods. For example in the Dominican Republic, the median customs clearance time is 7 days (Micco and Perez 2002). Djankov, Freund, and Pham (2008) calculate that on average each day of waiting is equivalent to a reduction in trade of about one percent. While countries may be less concerned about trade facilitation for imports, which tends to be significantly worse than for exports, this has important implications for firms wanting to use imported inputs.

---

78. The U.S. is the only country with data on trade costs, and is the major trading partner of the Caribbean.
79. Central America includes: Costa Rica, El Salvador, Guatemala, Honduras, and Nicaragua.

PART II

Challenges and New Opportunities

CHAPTER 4

New Areas of Opportunities and Challenges

A s CARIFORUM countries face declining preferences in their key markets for goods, many have been seeking to promote service industries for some time now. Trade in services stands out as an area of opportunity for the Caribbean countries. Moreover, an important part of the recently negotiated EPA includes rules and market access commitments on services. Both CARIFORUM and the European Union engaged in significant GATS-plus liberalization of services in the EPA. The simulations using the GLOBE Model show that the welfare gains associated with service trade liberalization in the context of the EPA would be substantial. In aggregate, the services liberalization alone leads to an absorption (welfare) gain of just under 5 percent, and this welfare gain is reflected in an increase in imports from both the United States and the EU15; as well as an increase in exports to both of these (see Chapter 6).

By and large, tourism accounts for the vast majority of services exports from the Caribbean. Other areas of opportunity include off-shore banking, financial services, and telecommunications. However, apart from the tourism industry, little attention has been paid to these areas of opportunities in the services sector. Also, the tourism sector and the emerging areas of opportunity face key challenges, which limit their potential to translate into high and sustained growth and poverty-reducing sectors.

This chapter reviews the services sector, analyzes its strengths and the challenges it faces. The key findings of the chapter are as follows. First, services are by far the most important component of economic activity in most economies in the Caribbean. The smaller the economy, the more important is the contribution of services to exports. Services account on average for 60 percent of GDP for OECS countries, while they make up 45 percent GDP for CARICOM as a whole. The service sector is dominated by tourism, which is as a major generator of foreign exchange of many Caribbean countries. Second, although the tourism sector is well developed in several CARIFORUM economies, traditionally tourism has failed to sustain high growth rates, and few Caribbean-owned tourism businesses have flourished. Higher-end tourism stands out as a major area of emerging opportunities for the Caribbean. Unfortunately, the Caribbean seems not to have a clear long-term strategy to move to new types of tourism services and diversify the tourism sector. Third, the financial sector is rapidly growing and its deepening has generally followed a trend common in many emerging economies. The financial services industry in the Caribbean is divided between the offshore and onshore sectors. In most instances, the greatest international linkages are in the offshore sector while the onshore banking and insurance industry is usually limited to satisfying domestic demand. Financial liberalization has strengthened the importance of financial services in Caribbean countries: an example of success is Trinidad and Tobago. In that country, financial services now account for 11.5 percent of the domestic economy and the government is seeking to expand the sector in an attempt to diversify from the dependence on the energy sector (which account for 45 percent of GDP). Trinidad and Tobago has become a leading financial services center in the CARICOM region. Fourth, the asymmetric liberalization of services recently concluded under the EPA is an opportunity for Caribbean countries to boost their export sector so as to sustain higher growth rates for poverty reduction. But the issue is that Caribbean services sector faces significant constraints to its development. Infrastructure for export services is not developed. Firms involved in services export are small and generally face daunting challenges to export abroad. Incentives regime are limited. Fifth, reaping the full benefits of service liberalization would require a comprehensive strategy. However, the Caribbean countries do not have a full-fledged and well articulated strategy to promote trade in services. The development of such a strategy becomes a policy priority if the region is to make trade in services a niche for higher trade performance.

Trade in Services

Overview and Importance of Services Sector

Data on services are scarce and more often not updated. Nonetheless, available data suggests that services are by far the most important component of economic activity in most economies in the Caribbean.[80] The smaller the economy, the more important is the contribution of services to exports. Services account on average for 60 percent of GDP for OECS countries, while they make up 45 percent GDP for CARICOM as a whole. On average, they account for more than 75 percent of total exports of OECS countries, but about 55 percent of CARIFORUM exports.

These general trends hide differences between countries of the region. While services account for more than three-fourths of total exports in Antigua and Barbuda, Barbados, St. Lucia, St. Vincent, they make up only about 16 percent and less than 10 percent of those of Suriname, and Trinidad and Tobago, respectively (see Table 4.1).

---

80. The situation is different in the strong manufacturing economy of Trinidad and Tobago which has significant natural resources, and in the Dominican Republic due to the export processing zones. In the case of Guyana and Suriname the service sector is under-developed and this is reflected both in terms of its lower contribution to GDP and particularly to exports.

Table 4.1. Trade in Services Contribution to GDP and Exports in CARIFORUM

	Trade in Services as % of GDP 2005	Share of Total Exports (%) 2006	
		Goods	Services
Antigua and Barbuda	89.0	13.4	86.6
Bahamas, The	57.2	22.1	77.9
Barbados	70.2	20.6	79.4
Belize	40.5	54.6	45.4
Dominica	45.1	33.4	66.6
Grenada	41.2	22.0	78.0
Guyana	43.9	80.1	19.9
Haiti	13.7	70.8	29.2
Jamaica	41.7	44.6	55.4
St. Kitts and Nevis	55.9	29.7	70.3
St. Lucia	65.9	16.8	83.2
St. Vincent and the Grenadines	63.1	21.5	78.5
Suriname	31.3	83.4	16.6
Trinidad and Tobago	9.5	91.5	8.5
Dominican Republic	18.2	60.4	39.6
CARICOM (Average)	47.7	43.2	56.8
OECS (Average)	60.0	22.8	77.2
CARIFORUM (CARICOM + DR)	45.8	44.3	55.7

Source: ECLAC, IMF, ECCB.

Services sector is dominated by tourism, which is as a major generator of foreign exchange in many Caribbean countries. However, other areas of opportunities are emerging. Construction, commerce, and communications have grown particularly fast and contributed to the rapid growth that some Caribbean countries have enjoyed. For instance, since the mid-1990s, growth rates in the Dominican Republic have been particularly high in communication and tourism-related services, such as transport and the hotel and restaurant industry. However, inefficiencies and lack of competition persist in certain services activities. There are still chronic problems in these areas of opportunities in most of the Caribbean countries, which are an impediment for the rest of the economy. First, the cost of capital for domestic investment is relatively high although the Dominican economy has survived the financial crisis in the banking system. Second, infrastructure weaknesses constrain the development of these sectors. Third, there has not been a full-fledged strategy to develop and diversify services away from the tourism sector.

Contribution of Tourism to Caribbean Economies

Services sector is dominated by tourism and trade related services. Many Caribbean countries have developed large tourism industries owing to their year-round warm climates,

Table 4.2. Tourism Contribution to CARICOM Countries

Country	Estimate of the Percentage Generated by the Travel and Tourism Industry (Both Directly and Indirectly) in 2007	Tourism Services Exports as a Percentage of GDP in 2005	Tourism Exports Annual Average Growth Rate (Percent) 2000–05
Antigua and Barbuda	75.8	38.5	2.9
Bahamas	53.6	34.6	3.6
Barbados	43.4	29.0	4.4
Belize	26.0	18.4	13.0
Dominica	25.0	23.1	2.9
Grenada	35.2	14.0	−5.0
Guyana	9.5	4.3	−14.1
Haiti	7.5	2.0	−9.1
Jamaica	31.1	16.4	3.0
St. Kitts and Nevis	33.4	25.2	13.5
St. Lucia	46.0	40.5	4.9
St. Vincent and Grenadines	32.3	24.4	5.0
Trinidad and Tobago	17.2	3.0	16.3

Source: World Trade and Tourism Council. "Caribbean Travel and Tourism Navigating the Path Ahead", 2007. IMF, Balance of Payment Statistics Database, February 2008 Edition and IMF, World Economic Outlook Database, October 2007.

beaches, and natural beauty, as well as their proximity to the United States, the world's second largest importer of tourism services (supplier of tourists). In countries with highly developed tourism industries, tourism services exports often account for a large percentage of GDP. Table 4.2 shows the contribution of tourism and travel-related services to GDP in selected CARICOM countries, for which data were available. In 2007, travel and tourism industries as a share of total GDP ranged from a low of 8 percent for Haiti to more than 75 percent in Antigua and Barbados. In general, the largest components of exported tourism services are meals and lodging expenditures. Some Caribbean countries also are developing several important niche areas of tourism. For instance, St. Vincent and the Grenadines has developed smaller, but highly lucrative, luxury and yacht-based tourism.

Tourism exports are also an important contributor to GDP for most of the Caribbean countries. In 2005, tourism exports as a share of GDP ranged from a low of 2 percent for Haiti to more than 40 percent in St. Lucia. In aggregate, tourism services exports accounted for more than 22 percent of total GDP in CARICOM countries (excluding Trinidad and Tobago, the largest regional economy). From 2000 through 2005, average annual growth of tourism services exports in about one-half of the CARICOM countries was between 3 to 6 percent (see Table 4.2). These rates are below the 7 percent average annual growth in global tourism services exports over the same period. In contrast to the overall trend, three countries (Belize, St. Kitts and Nevis, and Trinidad and Tobago) experienced rapid growth in tourism services exports while another three (Grenada, Guyana, and Haiti) experienced little or negative growth. In two of the three countries that experienced rapid growth (Belize and Trinidad and Tobago), tourism services exports have not traditionally accounted for more than 15 percent of GDP. This figure contrasts with the majority of CARICOM countries where tourism is the largest industry. Moreover, in Trinidad and Tobago, the growth in tourism services exports was primarily in business travel, rather than leisure travel, which is the traditional tourism base in these countries. Grenada saw below average growth in tourism exports following natural disasters, while two countries, Haiti and Guyana, experienced civil disorder that discouraged tourist visits.

Aside from the direct contribution of tourism services exports to GDP, the tourism services industry also has significant spillover effects in many CARICOM countries. Spillover effects accrue to the transportation industry, especially airlines and port services, as well as to local producers of intermediate inputs consumed by both the accommodations and transportation industries. WTTC (2004) reported that additional spillovers include government spending on tourism infrastructure, such as spending on national parks, immigrations and customs bureaus, or construction of airports; consumption of accommodations and transportation services by nationals; and, in certain limited circumstances, some spending on intra-regional tourism by residents of Caribbean countries. According to WTTC (2007), the direct and indirect effects of the global travel and tourism industry account for slightly more than 10 percent of global GDP.

Although the tourism sector is well developed in several CARIFORUM economies, traditional tourism has failed to sustain high growth rates, and few Caribbean-owned tourism businesses have flourished. The region's traditional tourism product, beach resorts, has matured and faces challenges from competitors in other regions such as Asia, and the rapidly changing nature of global tourism demand. The region also faces issues related to its strategy for managing and marketing the sector.

However, several reports have identified higher-end tourism as a major area of emerging opportunities for the Caribbean. For the tourism sector to drive sustained growth and become an engine of economic development, the challenges for the Caribbean countries is to develop new types of products, including adventure tourism, nature-based tourism, cultural, meetings and conferences, and community tourism. Unfortunately, there does not seem to have a clear long-term strategy to move to new types of tourism services and diversify the tourism sector.

More generally, services have traditionally enjoyed little importance and still appear to have very low priority in terms of external trade policy and incentives for industrial development in CARIFORUM. This may be partly due to the fact that the national governments themselves do not pay sufficient attention to service sector development. Foreign investment in other service sectors that have potential for exports has not grown significantly in the last decade.[81] Most domestic service firms are small and lack the capital base to develop into exporters. Also, Caribbean governments have apparently not focused on promoting the services sector through their industrial and trade policies. CARIFORUM economies need to diversify their services export portfolio. There may be a clear case for reorientation of the focus of industrial and trade policy on the services sector in this region.

---

81. The liberalization of some telecommunications services since 2000 in several CARICOM states has resulted in considerable foreign investment in the infrastructure for mobile or cellular telephone services.

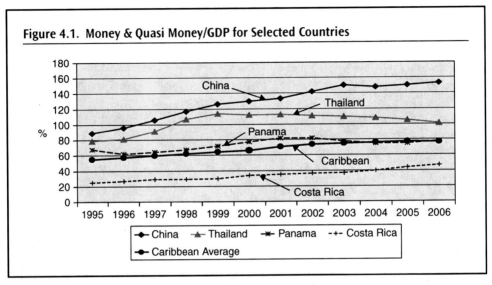

Figure 4.1. Money & Quasi Money/GDP for Selected Countries

Source: Bank staff based on World Bank World Development Indicators.

This requires significant investment in new service sectors and a concerted effort to move from relying on natural comparative advantage (in tourism) to enhancing the competitive advantage of the region.

Financial Services

Overview of Financial Services in the Caribbean

There is no clear indication of the size or composition of the financial services sector in CARIFORUM countries but available data reveals that it is rapidly growing. The region's financial deepening has generally followed a trend common in many emerging economies (see Figures 4.1 and 4.2).

The financial services industry in the Caribbean is divided between the offshore and onshore sectors. In most instances, the greatest international linkages are in the offshore sector while the onshore banking and insurance industry is usually limited to satisfying domestic demand.[82] In recent years several countries have been aiming to develop regional centers for financial services. These include the Dominican Republic, Trinidad and Tobago, and Jamaica. The current internationally recognized centers for offshore banking and finance in the region include: the Bahamas, Barbados, Bermuda, Cayman Islands, Curacao, and the Dominican Republic. However, there is also some offshore financial services activity in Anguilla, Antigua and Barbuda, Belize, British Virgin Islands, Dominica,

---

82. Offshore banking is an activity in which entities in a certain country provide deposit taking, lending, and other banking services to non-residents. Offshore financial centers are characterized by an absence of corporate and personal income taxes, minimal controls on exchanges between nonresidents, and proximity to a major market such as the United States.

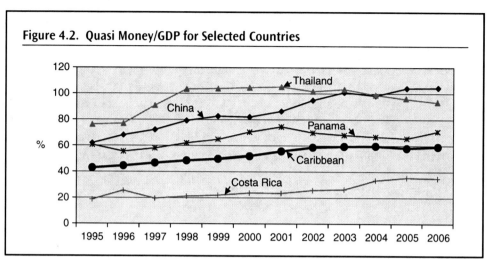

Figure 4.2. Quasi Money/GDP for Selected Countries

Source: Bank staff based on World Bank World Development Indicators.

Grenada, St. Lucia, St. Kitts and Nevis, St. Vincent and the Grenadines, and the Turks and Caicos.

The importance of this business sector to many Caribbean economies is reflected by net foreign assets relative to GDP. Net foreign assets are particularly dominant in The Bahamas, St. Kitts and Nevis, and Antigua and Barbuda, respectively accounting for 1,352 percent, 69 percent, and 65 percent relative to these countries' GDP in 2005. By comparison, for the United States, the ratio of net foreign assets to GDP was 10 percent in that same year. Canadian banks, which have always had a major presence in the Caribbean, have recently increased their holdings in the Caribbean region. Most notably, they have increased their presence with the purchase of the Royal Bank for Trinidad and Tobago (RBTT) by Royal Bank of Canada in March 2008, and the acquisition of some of the assets of Banco de Ahorro y Credito Altas Cumbres in the Dominican Republic in February 2008 by Scotiabank through the purchase of a Chilean bank based in Guatemala.[83]

While some countries have relatively limited foreign participation in the banking and financial services sector (Trinidad and Tobago, Suriname, Belize, and Guyana), the situation is completely different in others such as the OECS where foreign banks always operated in competition with local banks. It is slowly becoming more open in the wider Caribbean. Since 2002, many Caribbean countries have been reforming and liberalizing their financial services. For instance, the Dominican Republic passed a monetary and financial law that provides for national treatment of investors in most of the sector. The law also established a regulatory regime for monetary and financial institutions and allows for foreign investment in financial intermediary activities in the Dominican economy. Liberalization of the financial sector also takes place in the context of the WTO. Many Caribbean countries have also ratified the Fifth Protocol to the GATS on financial services and have committed to allow foreign banks to establish branches or local companies to supply deposit-taking, lending, and credit card services.

---

83. Reuters, February 4, 2008. *Trinidad Express*, March, 2008.

Financial liberalization has strengthened the importance of financial services in Caribbean countries. An example of success is Trinidad and Tobago. In that country, financial services now account for 11.5 percent of the domestic economy and the government is seeking to expand the sector in an attempt to diversify from the dependence on the energy sector (which account for 45 percent of GDP). Trinidad and Tobago has become a leading financial services center in the CARICOM region. It has succeeded in expanding its leadership in the banking sector within the region, with RBTT representing that success (see Box 5 on the next page). The Government of Trinidad and Tobago has set the goal of transforming itself into a Pan-Caribbean financial hub by 2020. To that end, the country is pursuing reforms that would further strengthen oversight of financial markets, promote greater competition within the industry, and devote resources to the improvement of technological infrastructure and workforce skills.

Status of Financial Liberalization in the CARICOM

Caribbean countries have also made efforts to use regional integration as a vehicle to develop financial services. In 2001, member governments agreed to create a single market for services and capital and allow free movement of people under the CARICOM Single Market and Economy (CSME) process. The liberalization of trade in services among CARICOM is codified in Chapter III of the Revised Treaty of Chaguaramas. In February 2002, the proposal for the removal of restrictions to trade in services and the movement of capital was finally elaborated and presented to the Heads of Government. It identified the sectors in which restrictions exist and when they would be removed.[84] According to the proposal, trade in services through the four modes of supply were supposed to be totally liberalized by the end of 2005. However, the legal and administrative tasks involved in this process, and the political determination needed to carry it forward, proved to be major obstacles; the deadline was not met. Yet, all CARICOM states except Haiti indicated that by July 2007 the majority of barriers would have been removed.[85]

However, by March 2008 it appeared that some restrictions had not yet been removed. With respect to liberalization relating to free movement of goods, services, capital and establishment, the 19th inter-sessional Heads of Government meeting of CARICOM called on the member states which continue to maintain restrictions inconsistent with the Program for Removal of Restrictions, to eliminate them by the appropriate measures including the bringing into force of relevant laws. Antigua and Barbuda have yet to implement the Statutory Instrument of the Caribbean Community Skilled Nationals Act and the Movement of Factors Act. Although St. Vincent and the Grenadines passed the Caribbean Community Skilled Nationals Act and the Movement of Factors Act, this law is still to be proclaimed. In Suriname, the law establishing the Accreditation body had been passed in

---

84. About 340 restrictions affecting trade in services, the movement of persons and capital in CARICOM had to be removed.

85. Incidentally, while Haiti had been granted special dispensation to implement the obligations under the Revised Treaty at a later date than the other Members, in January 2008, the Haitian authorities indicated that they are now in a position to start implementing the Common External Tariff (CET). It will be quite some time before Haiti is in a position to implement the single market regime for services and allow for the free movement of capital.

Box 6: Financial Services in Trinidad and Tobago: Leveraging the Regional Market to Succeed

The Royal Bank of Trinidad and Tobago (RBTT) is one of the leading banks in the Trinidad and Tobago, registering US$7.6 million in assets in 2007. It is among the largest financial services firms in the Caribbean region with more than 100 branches and offices in 12 countries throughout the region*. The company provides a comprehensive range of commercial and retail financial services through its multiple subsidiaries, which include a merchant bank and a trust company. RBTT was established in Trinidad and Tobago in 1902 to provide financing for thriving trade between Canada and the West Indies, though it eventually expanded to provide increasingly sophisticated banking services locally. Formerly majority-owned by Trinidad and Tobago nationals, RBTT was purchased in 2007 by the Royal Bank of Canada for $2.2 billion, reflecting the firm's strategic importance in the region.

RBTT owes much of its domestic and regional success to strong economic growth that oil- and natural gas-rich Trinidad and Tobago has experienced since the 1970s. Increased profitability and domestic liquidity heightened demand for financial services and provided the country's banks with sufficient capital to expand their operations. In the 1990s, financial sector liberalization, telecommunications improvements, and an increasing focus on globalization spurred a consolidation trend within Trinidad and Tobago's banking sector. As the domestic market became saturated, the larger firms, including RBTT, sought market growth in neighboring countries. RBTT subsequently engaged in a series of mergers and acquisitions that significantly enlarged its regional footprint. RBTT has benefited from a general lack of interest in the Caribbean market by many of the multinational banks that have traditionally focused on larger, more profitable markets. However, interest in the region is slowly rising as these firms increasingly seek new opportunities for growth, and this has been evidenced by the Royal Bank of Canada's recent acquisition of RBTT.

The Government of Trinidad and Tobago has established the goal of transforming itself into a Pan-Caribbean financial hub by 2020. To that end, the country is pursuing reforms that would further strengthen oversight of financial markets, promote greater competition within the industry, and devote resources to the improvement of technological infrastructure and workforce skills. If those policies are successful, it is likely that RBTT will continue to expand its reach throughout the region.

Source: Central Bank of Trinidad and Tobago, 2006 Annual Economic Survey: Review of the National Economy; EUI, Country Profile: Trinidad and Tobago, 2007 and United States International Trade Commission: "Caribbean Region: Review of Economic Growth and Development, Investigation No. 332-496, USITC Publication 4000, May 2008.

*In addition to its presence in Trinidad and Tobago, RBTT has operations in Antigua, Aruba, Barbados, Curacao, Grenada, Jamaica, the Netherlands Antilles, St. Kitts and Nevis, St. Lucia, St. Vincent and the Grenadines, and Suriname. The Bank also has representative office in Costa Rica.

Parliament; but its implementation has yet to start. Barbados and Belize have to remove exchange controls that restrict the free movement of capital.

The implementation of various aspects of the single market for services is slow. By January 2008, eleven member states had notified the CARICOM Secretariat of the Competent Authority for registration of service suppliers. However, it was not clear if the administrative and procedural arrangements were in effect in Member States to actually allow free movement of service suppliers. Anecdotal evidence or complaints from service suppliers in some countries seemed to indicate that while the legislative changes for establishing the single market for services had been made, the administrative and regulatory changes were far from complete. There are as yet no formal details on the status of actual implementation of the regime for allowing the temporary entry of services suppliers or contact information for the national Competent Authorities for registration of services suppliers. This means that in different countries service suppliers may not yet be able to take advantage of their rights under the Treaty although the regime has been approved for over a year now and the Single Market entered into its third year of operation on January 1, 2008.

To date, there has been no formal information from CARICOM member states on the implementation of Regime for CARICOM National Exercising the Right of Establishment, including contact information of the Competent Authorities in each jurisdiction. The COTED and COHSOD therefore requested in January 2008 that countries indicate whether the entry procedures for Right of Establishment have been implemented and provide details on the relevant authority. They also urged Member States, as applicable, to fully implement the approved regime for Right of Establishment as soon as possible.

With regard to free movement of skilled community nationals, anecdotal reports seem to indicate that university graduates are able to move but there is some level of differentiation across the region in terms of the procedures that they must follow (the level of automaticity of acceptance of CARICOM Skills Certificates, and so forth). As a result, in July 2007, the Twenty-Eighth Meeting of CARICOM Heads of Government urged all Member States to implement with immediate effect, the decision that CARICOM nationals entering with a Certificate issued by another Member State should be allowed to work immediately, pending the verification of their qualifications by the receiving Member State. However, mutual recognition of professional qualifications is still not in place across CARICOM. Free movement of artists and cultural workers has yet to happen.

Another issue associated with the provision of services in the CSME is related to domestic regulations. Under the CSME framework, all participating CARICOM member states are obligated to liberalize their professional services market. However, a regulatory framework has yet to be put in place and implemented sectors which are not yet regulated. There is also a need to modernize and harmonize the regulations for sectors which are already regulated.

Services in the Cariforum-EC Economic Partnership Agreement

The recently concluded EPA between CARIFORUM and the European Union has resulted in significant GATS-plus market opening at the bilateral level and specific rules on services trade between the two regions. The EPA contains a comprehensive *Title II on Investment, Trade in Services and E-commerce*. It includes the Bahamas and Haiti in the Agreement but they must submit their commitments on investment and services within six months of the signature of the EPA.

In the case of services, there are specific rules in the EPA in the following areas: courier, telecommunications, financial services, maritime transport, and tourism. In the case of tourism, large firms will be prevented from behaving in an anti-competitive manner in order to safeguard the interests of the mainly small firms in the Caribbean. There are also provisions for cooperation and mutual recognition of qualifications as well as technical assistance for building the capacity of service suppliers in CARIFORUM states. Over time these will address a range of needs in the Caribbean such as developing regulatory regimes, building the capacity of regional services firms, market intelligence, interaction with EU firms, among other activities.

There is asymmetry in the level of liberalization between CARIFORUM and the European Commission. While the EC opened more than 90 percent of service sectors, in the case of CARIFORUM, the sectoral coverage is much less at about 65 percent for the LDCs and about 75 percent by the MDCs using a generous methodology in CARIFORUM's favor. The main sectors that most CARIFORUM states have liberalized to some extent in the EPA are: accounting, auditing and bookkeeping services; architecture; engineering; computer and related services; research and development; management consulting; services incidental to manufacturing; related scientific and technical consultant services; telecommunications; convention services; courier services; environmental services; hospital services; tourism and travel-related services; entertainment services; maritime transport.

In terms of market access, perhaps the most significant gains for CARIFORUM are in temporary movement of natural persons (Mode 4). The EC has granted market access for Caribbean professionals in twenty nine sectors for employees of Caribbean firms (Contractual Service Suppliers–CSS) to be able to enter the EU to supply services once they have a valid contract. These are subject to conditions stipulated in the Services chapter of the EPA but the stays are for up to six months in a calendar year. As well, the EU has liberalized eleven sectors for temporary entry by Independent Professionals (IPs) or self employed persons. The EPA also provides for negotiations on mutual recognition of qualifications between European and Caribbean professionals within three years of the EPA entering into force.

The liberalization of services is an opportunity for the Caribbean countries to boost their export sector so as to sustain higher growth rates for poverty reduction. The issue is that Caribbean services sector faces significant constraints to its development. Infrastructure for export services is not developed. Firms involved in services export are small and generally face daunting challenges to export abroad. Incentives regime are limited. In the case of tourism, it appears that most countries except Suriname have subsidies in the form of tax incentives for new investments. Duty is waived on inputs for businesses in free zones.[86] However, incentives are quite limited in other service sectors.

Jamaica has the most comprehensive incentive program for service industries which covers the following sectors: tourism, maritime transport, banking, other financial services, software/information technology, recreation, culture and sports, and audiovisual services. The Jamaican government has stimulated some significant investment and job creation in the ICT sector by a range of incentives as well as negotiating special rates for telecommunications services supplied to ICT firms in the Montego Bay area of Jamaica.[87] The incentives in CARICOM states which are considered services subsidies are mainly tax incentives and duty free inputs/free zones. No CARIFORUM government gives direct grants to firms. The challenge is thus for these countries to respond to the growing demand and opportunities in the EC market that the EPA agreement will offer.

---

86. Tourism incentives are the most common across WTO Members as well.

87. JAMPRO reported in 2003 that the ICT industry has some 96 companies and affiliates which are operating as: software distributors and dealers; system consultants, technical support and software developers; Internet service providers/Web content; computer training companies; export service providers of data entry, telemarketing, CAD/CAM and customer software. Of these companies, 44 percent are export-oriented service providers originating mainly from North America.

Reaping the full benefits of service liberalization would require a comprehensive strategy. However, the Caribbean countries do not have a full-fledged and well articulated strategy to promote trade in services. The development of such a strategy becomes a policy priority if the region is to make trade in services a niche for higher trade performance. But because of the complexity of the issues associated with trade in services, most notably the provisions of trade liberalization under the EPA, the design of an effective trade strategy in services would require external assistance. Moreover, the recurrent problem is how to attract investment (whether domestic or foreign) in the service sectors. Given the Caribbean's limited resources for investment and the very slow pace of the CARICOM Single Market, which was supposed to stimulate greater intra-CARICOM investment, it appears that not much will change in terms of investment in new service sectors unless foreign aid is sought to support the required investment. In addition, foreign aid could be used to provide technical assistance to the Caribbean countries to implement the provision of trade in services embedded in the EPA agreement.

CHAPTER 5

Capitalizing on a Changing International Environment

A s indicated in the previous chapters, the current changing environment offers opportunities to the Caribbean countries. Capitalizing on this changing environment
would require designing a long-term trade strategy, aimed at positioning the
Caribbean countries in the world economy. This strategy should rely on the three dimensions of development strategy in countries with close regional links and highly integrated
into the international market: (i) national dimension; (ii) regional dimension; and
(iii) international dimension. The quality of national policies and the depth of domestic reforms
are crucial to the success of a trade strategy, which will position the Caribbean region in the
global market (*national dimension*). Regional coordination, harmonization of national policies, and development of regional public goods will play a critical role in ensuring that the
regional building blocks of the trade strategy facilitate its success (*regional dimension*). The
nature of Caribbean economies, which depend highly on international trade calls for a trade
strategy, which lays out an agenda of multi-lateral liberalization and external competitiveness in the current context of worldwide trade liberalization (*international dimension*).

Trade reforms tend to produce transitional costs. The current trade environment
dominated by the erosion of preferences and the liberalization of trade regimes in the
Caribbean could imply short term transitional costs: revenue losses and adjustment and
implementation costs (see Box 3 and Technical Appendix B). How successful the
Caribbean countries will cope with these short term constraints will determine the success
of a long term trade strategy.

Given the resource implications of a long-term strategy and the actions to cope with
short-term costs, seeking foreign aid will be important for Caribbean countries. However,
structural and institutional weaknesses can constrain the success of such a strategy.
Addressing these constraints will be important for its success.

This chapter provides the main features of a long term trade strategy for the Caribbean strategy to seize the opportunities of the global economy. It discusses the respective role that regional integration, national policies, and foreign aid could play in a long term trade strategy. Because of the short-term costs associated with trade liberalization, the chapter discusses the strategy to manage them. Finally, it lays out the ways to alleviate the structural constraints to trading to reinforce the long-term strategy's chances of success.

The main findings of the chapter can be summarized as follows. First, a long-term strategy consists of positioning the Caribbean region to compete in the global economy and reap the full benefits of world trade integration. But the long-term strategy faces daunting challenges related to the size of Caribbean countries, the cost of doing business in the region, and the erosion of preferences. Second, the region could use its external trade relationships as an impetus to implement internal reforms to promote trade, economic growth, and poverty reduction. The implementation of these trade agreements can help the region attract foreign direct investment by strengthening its competitiveness. However, this requires that the region design and implement an investment strategy, which addresses the weaknesses and constraints to investment in the region. Third, regional integration will play a critical role in the long-term trade strategy in the Caribbean. It can help the Caribbean countries, and most notably the OECS countries enhance efficiency and improve their international competitiveness. As such, accelerating the implementation of the CSME is crucial to reinforce external competitiveness. Fourth, increasing the region's competitiveness will also depend on the capacity of CARIFORUM countries to build, and enhance the provision of, regional public goods. Building infrastructure to last would be critical for regional trade as it would facilitate the mobility of goods, labor, and capital across the region. Fifth, positioning the Caribbean region in the global economy and strengthening Caribbean countries' external competitiveness would require substantial external support. Foreign assistance would help the countries implement appropriate competitiveness policies, make the necessary investments, and strengthen the institutions to support trade. Aid for trade is particularly important for regional public goods in infrastructure. Coordination failures often create a gap in the optimal provision of these goods. Sixth, managing transitional costs associated with trade liberalization would require both strengthening national policies and mobilizing foreign aid to facilitate the implementation of in-depth trade reforms as well as the design of a long term trade strategy. Seventh, because of structural and institutional weaknesses of Caribbean countries, when implementing trade reforms, capacity building and institutional reforms are essential in a range of areas. Strengthening tax administration and enforcement capability is essential for Caribbean countries in the medium term to mitigate the impact of tariff reductions on revenues.

Longer-term Trade Strategy and Challenges

Long-Term Vision and Challenges

A long-term strategy consists of positioning the Caribbean region to compete in the global economy and reap the full benefits of world trade integration. However, the long-term strategy faces daunting challenges related to the size of Caribbean countries, the cost of doing business in the region, and the erosion of preferences. The small size of markets and firms operating in the region makes competing with foreign firms difficult. It also limits the potential of economies of scale thereby reducing the ability of the firms of the region to compete with larger and more efficient foreign enterprises.[88] Caribbean countries have undiversified economies and are largely dependent on few export products for foreign exchange. The presence of monopolies and the lack of domestic competition, especially in trade-related services translate into additional costs for firms and make them vulnerable to compete on the global economy.

The Caribbean's business environment remains relatively weak. Most of the Caribbean countries' overall performance of doing business ranks below that of comparable developing countries, including Mauritius, Hong Kong, Malaysia, and Singapore (see Table 5.1). Time for and cost to export of most Caribbean countries, are relatively higher than those of comparable countries. For instance the cost to export of Trinidad and Tobago (best performer of the region) is higher to that of Vietnam (the second worst performer of the selected comparable sample of countries). The same observation applies to time for and costs to import.

The high cost of doing business in the Caribbean countries puts enterprises of the region at a comparative disadvantage relative to main competitors. Firms operating in the region face high cost structures as a result of relatively high wages and limited flexibility in labor markets, high cost and poor access to capital, and high at-the-border costs for many imports used in production. At the same time, poor reliability and high cost of infrastructure across the region create an additional burden to firms to compete in domestic and foreign markets. High cost structures affect both merchandise and services firms. In goods sectors, the high cost of capital makes it difficult for firms to develop new niche products, identify buyers and market their goods effectively. High infrastructure cost also impact the provision of services. For example, the tourism industry faces relatively high electricity and transport costs, making it difficult to compete with other low-cost competitors offering a similar tourism product. As a result, competitors have been gaining visitor arrival market shares. Over the last decade, the Hispanic Caribbean destinations have gone from holding 28 percent to 37 percent of total Caribbean stopover arrivals, and from 8 percent to 17 percent of cruise passenger arrivals. Reducing the high cost of doing business in most of the Caribbean countries would impact all sectors of the economy and improve the capacity of both goods and services firms to compete.

The erosion of preferences for agricultural products entering the EU markets is an important challenge for the Caribbean. Two agricultural products facing increasing erosion of preferences in the EU market are sugar and bananas. St. Kitts and Nevis's economy is one the most dependent on sugar as a source of foreign exchange since raw sugar exports account for 13 percent of total exports. The erosion of preferences and the uncompetitive nature of the island's sugar production prompted officials to shut down the state-owned sugar industry in July 2005. It is estimated that the government of St. Kitts incurred annual

---

88. For example, Caribbean banana producers are characterized as small (less than 1 hectare); often family-owned ventures operating on mountainous terrains that lack mechanized technology. On the other hand, Latin American and African producers are large, highly mechanized plantations between 50 and 5,000 hectares. It is worth noting that three multinational firms (Chiquita, Dole and Del Monte) control a majority of Latin America and African banana producers. See NERA/OPM (2004).

Table 5.1. Doing Business: Selected Indicators Caribbean and Comparable Developing Countries

Country	Overall Doing Business Rank 2008	Overall Trading Across Borders Rank 2008	Time for Export (Days)		Cost to Export (US$ per Container)		Time for Import (Days)		Cost to Import (US$ per Container)	
			2007	2008	2007	2008	2007	2008	2007	2008
Caribbean										
Antigua and Barbuda	41	55	13	19	1,057	1,107	15	19	1,467	1,174
Belize	59	116	23	23	1,800	1,800	26	26	2,130	2,130
Dominica	77	80	11	16	1,478	1,197	17	18	1,512	1,107
Dominican Republic	99	35	17	12	770	815	17	13	990	1,015
Grenada	70	52	19	19	820	820	23	23	1,178	1,178
Guyana	104	101	30	30	850	850	35	35	856	856
Haiti	148	153	52	52	1,650	1,650	53	53	1,860	1,860
Jamaica	63	92	21	21	1,750	1,750	22	22	1,350	1,350
St. Kitts and Nevis	64	22	15	15	750	750	17	17	756	756
St. Lucia	34	88	18	18	1,375	1,375	21	21	1,420	1,420
St. Vincent and the Grenadines	54	75	15	15	1,770	1,770	16	16	1,769	1,769
Trinidad and Tobago	67	49	14	14	693	693	26	26	1,100	1,100
Comparators										
LAC Average	—	—	23	22	1080	1107	28	26	1,236	1,228
East Asia Average	—	—	26	24	778	775	28	25	945	917
Hong Kong, China	4	3	6	6	525	525	5	5	525	525
Malaysia	24	21	18	18	432	432	14	14	385	385
Mauritius	27	17	16	17	683	728	16	16	683	673
Singapore	1	1	5	5	416	416	3	3	367	367
Thailand	15	50	24	17	848	615	22	14	1,042	786
Vietnam	91	63	24	24	669	669	23	23	881	881

Sources: Bank staff based on various Doing Business reports.

losses of 3 percent of GDP to sustain sugar industry operations. Bananas account for a large share of merchandise exports in three Caribbean countries: Dominica (20 percent of exports), St. Lucia (31 percent), and St. Vincent and the Grenadines (32 percent). The effects of preference erosion have already been felt across the sub-region as banana exports for these three countries, together, have fallen 75 percent since the early 1990s, when the EU began removing protectionist measures for banana imports.

The erosion of preferential access to major export markets poses a significant problem for the Caribbean countries. Yet, it also creates an important opportunity to negotiate for adjustment and restructuring assistance for uncompetitive sectors. The region could explore moves to higher value-added agricultural products using branding as a way to develop competitive advantages.

Small size, geography and erosion of preferences are critical challenges for the region. Yet, the region has an opportunity to diversify its export base, a prerequisite for an improvement of its trade performance. A strategy for improved competitiveness should focus on the areas where the Caribbean countries have demonstrated comparative advantages and new avenue of potential exports, most notably services. Caribbean countries have established competitive advantages in export products such as electrical equipment, beverages, seafood and spices, using strategies of speed to market, branding and niche marketing. In agriculture, there is a need for the region to move to niches and higher value-added areas. These include, among others, organic production, oils and snacks for bananas; rum, ethanol and feedstuffs for sugar.

A long-term trade strategy should also focus on the development and diversification of the services sector to boost export sales for the Caribbean. Tourism is a sector which presents many opportunities for Caribbean region. However, the sector has been loosing market share in total tourism and cruise passenger arrivals to the Caribbean at the expense of more competitive Hispanic Caribbean destinations. A long-term strategy should focus on policy measures aimed at improving the price competitiveness of the Caribbean countries, most notably OECS countries, and addressing supply-side constraints such as airlift capacity. Other areas of explorations include health and education-related services, transportations and business services (such as high-end call centers and software development) that may be competitive and merit promotional efforts.

A long-term strategy to improve competitiveness of the Caribbean region will also require that the region move from a purely commodity-based economy to a more competitive knowledge-based economy. This in turn requires that the countries innovate and develop entrepreneurship. The Caribbean governments should facilitate the creation of an innovation-friendly environment by focusing on increasing educational attainment, improving the business climate and technology infrastructure. But the inability of the region to keep its more educated workers is a major constraint that the region should address. Available data suggest that on the whole, the total number of migrants from the Caribbean countries also increased by 51 percent from 1.9 million to 2.9 million during the same period, with the biggest percentage increase observed for Dominican Republic (94 percent) followed by Haiti (87 percent). The brain drain is becoming a serious issue for the Caribbean countries with potential adverse effects on the economic growth and development of the region. On average, about 13 percent of migrants from the Caribbean countries have a college degree with the highest portion observed for St. Kitts-Nevis (21 percent) followed by Antigua-Barbuda (18 percent). This is relatively high compared to Mexico or Central America; while in comparison migrants from Andean and South America are found to be more educated.

The Multilateral Agenda and the Pro-Competitiveness Policy

The Caribbean region is involved in a number of external multilateral trade agreements, including WTO DOHA Round, CARIFORUM-EU Economic Partnership Agreement, and other negotiations with countries in the Western Hemisphere (see Chapter 2). While the implementation of these external trade agreements is challenging for the Caribbean countries, they also offer an opportunity to the region to improve its competitiveness and broaden its market access for goods and services.

The region could use these trade agreements to implement internal reforms to promote trade, economic growth, and poverty reduction. First, high tariffs and dispersion undermine the region's competitiveness and facilitate trade diversion. The effective implementation of these trade agreements can be used to decisively lower tariff barriers in the region and facilitate the convergence process towards a common external tariff. Second, poor customs and port operation in the region has resulted in high trade costs. Policy measures aimed at improving customs and port operations and infrastructure can lower trade costs, and improve the region's external competitiveness. Third, multilateral liberalization may result in revenue losses as most of the Caribbean countries depend on international trade taxes as a source of fiscal revenue (see Chapter 2). However, it also provides the impetus to these countries to introduce more efficient tax regimes and harmonize with regional partners.

The implementation of these trade agreements can help the region attract foreign direct investment by strengthening its competitiveness. However, this requires that the region design and implement an investment strategy, which addresses the weaknesses and constraints to investment in the region. To this end, CARICOM Secretariat's investment policy under preparation rightly aims at attracting extra-regional FDI especially in the economic drivers by leveraging the synergies of the Single Market and Economy.[89] The centerpiece of this policy is the creation of the region as a single investment jurisdiction. The framework for this will be established by CARICOM Investment Code (CIC). The CIC will harmonize national incentives to investment in the industrial, agricultural and services sectors, with priority given to sustainable export industrial and services activities. New investments will be facilitated by the removal of bureaucratic impediments. The CIC will enable CARICOM to be marketed as a single investment jurisdiction to global firms, focused on attracting FDI to the priority activities that are the subject of common sectoral policies, while allowing for national targeting of FDI by individual member states and sub-regions.

The Role of Regional Integration

Regional integration will play a critical role in the long-term trade strategy in the Caribbean. It can help the Caribbean countries, and most notably the OECS countries

---

89. Sectors considered as economic drivers are: (i) agriculture; (ii) energy; (iii) tourism; and (iv) new export services. See CARICOM Secretariat. Towards the Single Economy. September 2006.

enhance efficiency and improve their international competitiveness. As such, accelerating the implementation of the CSME is crucial to reinforce external competitiveness. External trade policies such as the CET are in place, yet suffer from a number of tariff suspensions and national derogations (see Chapter 2). The right of establishment and the free movement of services, capital and labor are also important elements of the region's external competitiveness. In the context of the implementation of the CSME, member states have agreed to curtail introduction of new restrictions in these areas and have committed to a schedule for their removal. Yet, much remains to be done and the challenge is for CARICOM member countries to fully implement the provisions agreed upon to move forward the CSME.

As small economies which lack resources, Caribbean countries also face costs disadvantages. Deepening regional integration could help the member states of CARIFORUM overcome these disadvantages. It can provide reliable access to less costly inputs and other factors of production and trade (labor, capital, utilities and transport), and improve the capacity of Caribbean firms to compete with foreign competitors.

Increasing the region's competitiveness will also depend on the capacity of CARIFORUM countries to build, and enhance the provision of, regional public goods. Building infrastructure to last would be critical for regional trade as it would facilitate the mobility of goods, labor, and capital across the region. Investing in infrastructure (transports, energy, telecommunications, and so forth) would also reduce the cost of trading with external partners, thereby improving the region's competitiveness. For instance energy utility rates in CARICOM are among the highest in the world. Weaknesses of infrastructure have limited the region's capacity to penetrate the global economy (see Chapters 1 and 3). A shift to *trade quality* away from *trade quantity* would require investment in infrastructure. Specifically, investment in energy together with a regional energy policy will be a tool to optimize the use of energy resources and reduce the relative cost of energy to regional producers. A few regional initiatives are ongoing, including the creation of a Task Force on Regional Energy Policy; the Trinidad and Tobago Regional Energy Plan; the Caribbean Renewable Energy Development Programme (CREP) Project Pipeline and National Energy Policy Framework; GeoCaribe and PetroCaribe. The challenge is now to translate these initiatives into concrete action plans to design a comprehensive regional energy policy.

Investing in infrastructure requires that Caribbean governments increase domestic revenues and allocate more resources to finance infrastructure projects. However, most Caribbean countries have relatively limited fiscal space and revenue losses stemming from the erosion of preferences and trade liberalization have further shrunk their resource base. Thus, even with an improved revenue performance, it is unlikely that Caribbean governments will be able to finance the needed investments solely on their own resources. Foreign aid would be needed to complement domestic resources in support of investment in infrastructure.

The Role of Foreign Aid as a Promotion Scheme

Positioning the Caribbean region in the global economy and strengthening Caribbean countries' external competitiveness would require substantial external support. Foreign assistance would help the countries implement appropriate competitiveness policies, make the necessary investments, and strengthen the institutions to support trade.

Aid may be designed to help Caribbean countries realize the full benefits of new market opportunities. First, aid may help Caribbean countries invest in infrastructure (both at the national and regional level) so as to alleviate supply-side constraints. Second, aid may help to support capacity building and strengthen the institutional environment. Third, aid may help to support structural reforms that are complementary to trade reforms, such as labor market reforms.

As emphasized elsewhere in this Report, market access on its own is not sufficient to bring the benefits of trade to the Caribbean; many Caribbean countries are unable to take advantage of new trading opportunities because their supply capacity and competitiveness are limited. Caribbean countries need to invest in the necessary exporting infrastructure (e.g. efficient ports, adequate roads, reliable electricity and communications) to stimulate private investment in productive capacity. Thus, by supporting domestic infrastructure investment, aid for trade programs may foster the ability of the private sector to take advantage of changes in competitiveness and more general enhance its role in promoting development.

Aid for trade is particularly important for regional public goods in infrastructure (for example, regional transport and telecommunications networks, and energy systems). Coordination failures often create a gap in the optimal provision of these goods. In addition, for regions where countries are relatively small (as is the case in the Caribbean), the size is an important incentive for governments to pool resources for the provision of efficient, cost-effective common services (CARICOM 2007). Regional investments by Caribbean countries supported by foreign grants may generate therefore potentially large returns.

When implementing trade reforms in the Caribbean, capacity building and institutional reforms are essential in a range of areas. As noted earlier, strengthening tax administration and enforcement capability in Caribbean countries is essential in the medium term to mitigate the impact of tariff reductions on revenues. In addition, Caribbean countries often lack the necessary technology and knowledge to meet product standards prevailing in high value markets (sanitary measures, technical barriers, certification, etc.). Assistance to build supply capacity may involve fostering the development of a favorable business climate to help private sector enterprises capitalize on new trade opportunities and identify infrastructure bottlenecks. In turn, this may entail removing the obstacles that ineffective institutions place on the ability of firms with high export potential to grow by developing for instance more effective customs authorities, more accountable policing, and more efficient port authorities.[90] To benefit fully from trade liberalization, developing countries may also need to strengthen regional institutions. A well-designed aid for trade program, which avoids the "diversion risk" alluded to above, may promote all these objectives.

To achieve their full impact, trade reforms in the Caribbean will need to be accompanied by complementary structural reforms. It is well recognized, for instance, that the Caribbean countries need to invest in educational programs that enhance competitiveness and support diversification, by allowing workers (particularly those who lose their jobs in import-competing industries) to "retool" and adjust their skills to those required in the expanding sectors. More generally, there is good evidence suggesting that trade liberalization has stronger effects when labor markets are more flexible.

---

90. Institutional capacity can affect trade costs if customs procedures, inspections, and certifying bodies are run inefficiently.

The need for complementary reforms may involve not only the labor market but also the financial sector. With underdeveloped financial sectors, inadequate access to finance whether to finance short-term capital needs or physical investment is a major factor inhibiting Caribbean countries' exports. Difficulties in assessing the creditworthiness of (and the value of collateral pledged by) small exporting firms, in particular, constrain access to formal sector loans, with an adverse effect on employment and poverty. Again, a well-designed aid for trade program may help to alleviate these constraints.

Managing Transitional Costs

Nature of Transitional Costs

As discussed in Chapter 1, since 2000 many countries in the Caribbean have been grappling with difficult fiscal and public debt situations.[91] At the same time, some of these countries rely quite heavily on trade taxes as a source of current revenue. Given the current revenue structure of Caribbean countries, they are likely to experience short-run revenue shortfall as a consequence of trade liberalization. In an analysis of the fiscal effects of tariff reduction for the Caribbean Community, Peters (2005) concluded that the shortfall could be as much as a 45 per cent decline in customs duties.

A reduction in tariffs, unaccompanied by compensatory fiscal measures may lead to reduced government revenue in the short run. A fall in revenues associated with a reduction in tariffs may force Caribbean governments to implement concomitant cuts in expenditure in the short term. If these cuts take the form of reductions in social expenditure, they will have a direct effect on poverty, thereby mitigating the welfare gains from trade—at least in the short term. There is some empirical evidence suggesting that this has indeed been the case in other countries at the same level of development of Caribbean countries (see Winters, McCulloch, and McKay (2004)).

There is a risk that the loss of revenue results in cuts in public investment, in particular in infrastructure. Indeed, evidence suggests that the loss of revenue in other developing countries has led not only to cuts in current spending but at times to significant cuts in public investment, most notably in infrastructure (see Atolia (2007)). Given the importance of the externalities associated with public infrastructure (as discussed in Technical Appendix A), a sustained loss in tariff revenue may have an adverse effect on growth, which may offset the benefits of greater openness. Moreover, the positive effect of public capital on the marginal productivity of private inputs may hold not only for infrastructure but also for other components of public capital—such as in education and health, which may both affect the productivity of labor. Thus, cuts in productive expenditure in general may be particularly damaging to growth.[92]

---

91. In Antigua and Barbuda for instance, public debt in 2003 accounted for 142 percent of GDP; in the same year, this ratio reached 171 percent in St Kitts and Nevis, and 150 percent in Jamaica (with an interest bill of about 16 percent of GDP).

92. Other components of public spending, related for instance to the enforcement of property rights and maintenance of public order, could also increase productivity and exert a positive effect on private investment and growth, despite the fact that they may not be considered as being directly "productive."

The Role of Foreign Aid as a Compensatory Scheme

Caribbean countries rely on tariffs as a source of revenue far more than developed countries, largely because tariffs are an administratively efficient way of raising revenues. To the extent that trade liberalization may reduce tariff revenue, and given that replacing lost tariff revenue with other sources may take time and may have high associated costs, and that revenue losses may have an adverse effect on productive public expenditure, tariff reforms in the Caribbean may need to be accompanied by a temporary increase in aid. This will provide "breathing space" for governments to implement measures aimed at strengthening the domestic tax system (by reducing tax collection costs, fighting tax evasion, and so forth) and other reforms on the expenditure side (such as improving the efficiency of public spending).

Trade liberalization often entails large intersectoral movements in resources; Caribbean firms may incur sizable adjustment costs as a result of these movements. While it may take some time for the gains from trade to materialize (as they often depend on reform in other areas, as discussed elsewhere in this Report), adjustment costs tend to be "paid" upfront. For some countries, these adjustment costs (which include not only higher rates of unemployment in import-competing sectors but also pressures on the balance of payments and fiscal accounts) may be particularly significant. Even by spreading adjustment costs over a relatively long implementation period (say, 10 to 15 years); some countries may have limited capacity to bear them.[93]

There are also costs associated with the implementation of the regulatory reforms that are part of trade agreements.[94] While tariff reductions are relatively easy to implement, regulatory changes (customs reform, intellectual property rights, and sanitary and phytosanitary measures) may impose a burden that may be very large (at least in the short term) compared to the benefits that countries may receive from new market access opportunities. For instance, these regulatory changes may require higher expenditure on system design and drafting of legislation, capital expenditure on buildings and equipment, personnel training, as well as improvements in administration and enforcement capability. For some of the poorest Caribbean countries, the extent of reform of administrative systems that is required to meet agreed standards may be overwhelming.

Thus, although implementation costs are hard to quantify, there is a risk that changes in the regulatory environment that are mandated by trade agreements draw money away from development budgets (and possibly from more productive uses), as pointed out by Stiglitz and Charlton (2006) in a broader context. The role of aid in this context is not only to facilitate job creation in areas most adversely affected by trade liberalization, or to help those who have lost their jobs obtain alternative employment (as is commonly argued), but also to mitigate the risk that the implementation of the regulatory agreements that are required as part of trade arrangements may lead to "resource diversion."

---

93. Labor mobility costs can slow adjustment to trade liberalization significantly; see Artuc, Chaudhuri, and McLaren (2008) for some illustrative simulation results.

94. A case in point is the EPA recently signed between Caribbean countries and the European Union, as discussed later.

The second argument often used to justify "aid for trade" as a Compensatory Scheme applies with equal force to the current context of Caribbean countries. The Economic Partnership Agreement (EPA) recently completed between the European Union and the CARIFORUM Group EPA contains explicit provisions related to compliance with, and adoption of, international technical, health, and quality standards pertaining to food production and marketing (agricultural goods, fish and fish products, etc.).[95] Compliance with these (at times very demanding) standards will impose a significant burden on governments in the region; to avoid the "diversion risk" alluded to earlier, an "aid for trade" program is likely to be essential. This need is well recognized in the EPA.[96]

Another argument in favor of "aid for trade" as a Compensatory Scheme is related to the need to minimize supply-side and institutional constraints to trading in the Caribbean region. As noted elsewhere in this Report, as well as in Technical Appendix A, significant supply-side and institutional constraints prevent a number of Caribbean countries from taking full advantage of new trade opportunities. The ability of many Caribbean countries to compete in world markets is undermined by the absence or inadequacy of infrastructure services (such as roads and ports), a weak institutional environment (including modern and efficient customs), or simply knowledge about export market opportunities and how to access them. Furthermore, although trade reforms may be necessary to stimulate increases in productivity and output, reaping the full benefits of these reforms may require complementary reforms. This is one of the main messages, for instance, of a recent review of CARICOM's performance by the Inter-American Development Bank (2005). Thus, there is a strong case for increased assistance to Caribbean countries, in the form of grants or loans (with disbursements perhaps over a four- to five-year horizon), to cover a wide range of needs—from investments in infrastructure (at both the domestic and regional levels), to capacity building and institutional reform, and support for complementary reforms—to alleviate key obstacles to trade expansion.

The EPA recently concluded with the European Union recognizes these needs. In Part I, Article 8 states that development co-operation shall be primarily focused on the following areas: (i) The provision of technical assistance to build human, legal and institutional capacity in the CARIFORUM States so as to facilitate their ability to comply with the commitments set out in the Agreement; (ii) The provision of assistance for capacity and institution building for fiscal reform in order to strengthen tax administration and improve the collection of tax revenues with a view to shifting dependence from tariffs to other forms of indirect taxation;[97] (iii) The provision of support measures aimed at promoting private sector and enterprise development, in particular small economic operators, and enhancing the international competitiveness of CARIFORUM firms and diversification of the CARIFORUM economies; (iv) Diversification of CARIFORUM exports of goods and

---

95. The EPA, negotiated in individual regional groupings, replaces the Cotonou Agreement signed between the EU and ACP countries from January 1, 2008. The agreement also indicates that the EU will assist CARIFORUM States in establishing harmonized intra-regional sanitary and phytosanitary (SPS) standards.

96. The EPA also includes provisions to provide technical assistance for tax reforms aimed at reducing CARIFORUM States' reliance on trade taxes.

97. In Part II, the Agreement also recognizes that there may be a need for flexibility, regarding the phased elimination of customs duties; depending on progress toward necessary fiscal reforms.

services through new investment and the development of new sectors; and (v) Support for the development of infrastructure in CARIFORUM States necessary for the conduct of trade.

The Role of National Public Policies

"Aid for trade" could play a catalytic role in helping Caribbean countries cope with the short term costs of trade reforms (aid for trade as a compensatory scheme) and facilitating the implementation of in-depth trade reforms as well as the design of a long term trade strategy (aid for trade as a promotion scheme). Yet, it is also true that the national policies will play a critical role for successful trade reforms in the Caribbean region.

In order to mitigate the potential substantial effect of trade liberalization, there is a need to strengthen efforts at fiscal reform, paying particular attention to lowering tax exemptions, enhancing indirect tax systems (by implementing a broad based tax such as the VAT), improving tax collection and administration (with regard in particular to the personal income tax), and more generally modifying the tax structure to reduce dependence on trade taxes for fiscal receipts and create fiscal space for a reduction in tariffs.

However, developing non trade-based, fiscal revenue structures which are broad based and capable of generating revenues on a sustainable basis is likely to take significant time. Thus, to avoid possible adverse effects of revenue losses on productive government spending (as noted earlier), temporary financing in the form of increased aid may be necessary to increase incentives to implement (and sustain) trade reform. But increased foreign aid is also conditional to the implementation of good domestic policies including: policies to reinforce macroeconomic stabilization, and structural reforms in a broad based manner.

National policies should also play a critical role in mitigating the potential adverse effects of increased foreign aid, most notably Dutch disease effects. Assuming that there is no *additionality* problem, and that aid for trade translates into a sizable increase in aid flows, an important question that Caribbean countries may need to consider is whether an increase in these flows may have unintended negative consequences for trade—through a Dutch disease effect. The argument, essentially, is that if aid is at least partially spent on nontraded goods, it may put upward pressure on domestic prices and lead to a real exchange rate appreciation. In turn, a real appreciation may induce a reallocation of labor toward the nontraded goods sector, thereby raising real wages in terms of the price of tradables. The resulting deterioration in competitiveness may lead to a decline in export performance, unsustainable current account deficits, and an adverse effect on growth.

The international evidence does suggest that aid may lead to real exchange rate appreciation, and thereby reduce international competitiveness, in the short run. However, the capacity of Caribbean countries to manage foreign resources, and make them productive will determine the contribution of foreign aid to Caribbean countries' trade performance and ultimately the performance of their economies.[98] If aid raises public investment in infrastructure, then the longer-run effect on the real exchange rate may turn out to be favorable (that is, a real depreciation).[99] The reason, of course, is the supply-side effects

---

98. Limited capacity refers here to limited administrative, technical, human, and institutional capacity to manage effectively huge flows of foreign aid.

99. See Agénor and Yilmaz (2008) for a more detailed discussion.

that are associated with an increase in core infrastructure services (see Technical Appendix A). Put differently, once dynamic considerations are taken into account, the Dutch "disease" does not have to be a terminal illness; longer-run, supply-side effects may eventually outweigh short-term, adverse demand-side effects on the real exchange rate. It is therefore important for Caribbean countries to ensure that aid is properly allocated to investment. Ensuring that adequate attention is paid to other, nonprice aspects of competitiveness (such as product standards) is also important.

Finally, a possible concern for trade reform in Caribbean countries relates to aid volatility. This is a general issue associated with aid, as documented in a number of recent studies.[100] Of course, by their very nature, some types of aid (such as emergency aid or, to a lower extent, program aid) should indeed exhibit a high degree of volatility. By contrast, project aid should be relatively stable, given that it is designed to promote (directly or indirectly) investment in physical and human capital. Volatility in that category of aid could make it difficult for recipient governments to formulate medium-term investment programs to spur growth. In the specific context of Caribbean countries (especially among the poorest ones), it is therefore important to ensure any aid-for-trade initiative that involves a sizable increase in spending on trade-related infrastructure makes aid flows predictable over the medium term, to secure sustained commitment in the region.

Alleviating Structural and Institutional Constraints on "Old" and "New" Opportunities

As indicated in the report, the new trade environment offers new opportunities for the Caribbean, most notably in the area of trade in services. They can expand their trade basis and benefit from larger international markets. However, Caribbean countries often lack the necessary technology and knowledge to meet product standards prevailing in high value markets (sanitary measures, technical barriers, certification). Caribbean private sector enterprises may thus not be able to seize new market opportunities. Assistance to build supply capacity may involve fostering the development of a favorable business climate to help private sector enterprises capitalize on new trade opportunities and identifying infrastructure bottlenecks. In turn, this may entail removing the obstacles that ineffective institutions place on the ability of firms with high export potential to grow by developing for instance more effective customs authorities, more accountable policing, and more efficient port authorities.[101]

Because of structural and institutional weaknesses of Caribbean countries, when implementing trade reforms, capacity building and institutional reforms are essential in a range of areas. As noted earlier, strengthening tax administration and enforcement

---

100. Studies by Bulir and Hamann (2006) and Hudson and Mosley (2006) have found that the volatility of aid is much larger than the volatility of domestic tax revenues, with coefficients of variation in the range of 40–60 percent of mean aid flows. Both studies also found that aid volatility has actually increased since the late 1990s, as does Kharas (2007) for a large group of aid recipients. See Agénor and Aizenman (2007) for a more detailed discussion.

101. Institutional capacity can affect trade costs if customs procedures, inspections, and certifying bodies are run inefficiently.

capability is essential for Caribbean countries in the medium term to mitigate the impact of tariff reductions on revenues.

To benefit fully from new trade opportunities, Caribbean countries may also need to strengthen regional institutions, a point emphasized in chapter 2 of the report. First, regional institutions can help identify new trade opportunities for Caribbean private enterprises, by implementing an aggressive information policy and identifying the international market requirements. Second, regional institutions could help build the regional public goods, in particular much needed public infrastructure for trade. By doing so, they would reduce the cost of doing business and reinforce the region's competitiveness. Fourth, regional institutions could also help member countries implement harmonized and coordinated macroeconomic policies (macro-convergence policies) to strengthen macro-stabilization and competitiveness of the region. Finally, regional institutions could negotiate trade agreements in favor of Caribbean countries, and ultimately help member countries implement the agreements. But this requires that these institutions are provided clear mandate to negotiate and enough resources to oversee the implementation of the trade agreement. Given the limited domestic resources, financing Caribbean regional institutions is an issue as discussed in Chapter 2 of the report. Foreign aid should thus be sought.

PART III

Quantifying the Impact of Trade Reform on Growth, Job Creation, and Poverty

Quantifying the Gains from Global Trade Integration—A Dynamic Macroeconomic Analysis

T his chapter presents a quantification exercise of the impact of trade liberalization between the CARIFORUM countries and the EU, focusing on the potential effect of an EPA on CARIFORUM economies.

The assessment of an EPA between countries involves simulations of the impact of that process of trade liberalization in goods and services and any productivity or other changes that may arise from the agreement. The simulations can then be used to examine the changes in patterns of production within the economy and between regions, on the incomes received by factors of production, or on the welfare of different households in the economy. It is worth noting that these simulations remain a theoretical exercise. The results should therefore be taken with caution. Nonetheless, they provide a good indication of the potential effects of the EPA in Caribbean countries using rigorous quantitative frameworks. We have used three complementary models which are briefly outlined below and then more detail is provided in the Technical Appendixes D, E, and F.

The first model is a multi-country CGE model called GLOBE.[102] This model is based on the GTAP6 dataset for 2001 which has 57 sectors, five factors of production, one household and 87 regions or countries. The model aggregates the data to focus on issues in CARIFORUM region. This version of GLOBE has 19 sectors, 4 factors of production, 10 regions, and one household per region. This multi-country model supports analysis of inter-country linkages both between the proposed EPA partners and with other trading partners, and can be used for analysis of different liberalization scenarios: bilateral, regional, or global.

---

102. For a description of the GLOBE model and its roots, see McDonald, Robinson and Thierfelder (2005). For a recent application of the GLOBE model to the impact of rapid growth in China and India on other developing countries, see McDonald, Robinson and Thierfelder (2008).

The second model is a single country CGE model of Jamaica. This is based on a Social Accounting Matrix (SAM) for Jamaica for the year 2000. The Jamaica SAM was slightly modified for this study and has 23 sectors, four factors, one household, and imports/exports have three regions of origin/destination.

The third is a dynamic model applied to the Dominican Republic. It is used to discuss the transitional dynamics (in terms of growth, employment, and poverty) associated with the implementation of the EPA, and the role of public capital, and the externalities associated with some of its components (particularly infrastructure capital) to understand the importance of an "aid for trade" program for this country.[103]

The main findings of the chapter summarize as follows. First, the GLOBE model shows that the full application of the market access elements of the EPA (excluding sugar) in simulation CARIB4 leads to a very small increase in welfare as represented in a rise in absorption of 0.04 percent. When the simulations include the removal of EU sugar tariffs, a similar pattern of aggregate changes emerges, with a slightly higher increase in aggregate absorption which is now 0.18 percent.

Second, the liberalization of investment and service trade would result in significant welfare gains. The simulations show that the services liberalization alone leads to an absorption (welfare) gain of just under 5 percent, and this welfare gain is reflected in an increase in imports from both the United States and the EU15; as well as an increase in exports to both of these.

Third, aid for trade provided by the EU to CARIFORUM countries could help compensate for revenue shortfalls following the liberalization process under the EPA. In the "aid for trade concessions" simulations, the lump-sum transfer from the EU to CARIFORUM governments is just sufficient to offset tariff revenue losses while keeping real government expenditure and its composition unchanged.

Fourth, the analysis of further trade liberalization options for CARIFORUM reveals that the CARIFORUM region would be substantially better off under a trade liberalization agreement with the USA than under the EPA. The joint implementation of a trade agreement with the United States and the EPA might not be super-additive.

Fifth, policy experiments using the Jamaican model show that the welfare gains of trade liberalization under the EPA would come from services trade liberalization. Assuming a productivity increase in the "commerce" sector, which includes tourism, of 10 percent plus a fixed real wage of low skilled workers, welfare gains would increase by 2.1 percent and employment of unskilled labor increases by 4.0 percent. Aggregate exports and imports increase, mostly with the EU. Adding the increase in sugar prices, the assumption that the EPA is associated with increased investment in Jamaica, as well as an open capital market, with increased foreign investment that keeps the profit rate at its base level result in increase in aggregate absorption (welfare gain) by 7.3 percent. The results of the simulations on choice of major trading partner and on a MFN unilateral tariff cut show that, in the context of the small country assumption of no changes in world prices, the MFN tariff cut dominates in welfare terms any of the FTA arrangements considered. An EPA or some kind of FTA or

103. The analysis in this section was conducted in close collaboration with staff from the Ministry of the Economy, Planning, and Development in the Dominican Republic, to whom the Team expresses its sincere gratitude.

preferential trading agreement with a single partner (EU or USA) may benefit Jamaica, but it does lead to trade diversion and less benefit than could be achieved by lower MFN tariffs.

Sixth, in Dominican Republic, a fall in tariff revenues entirely offset by an immediate increase in indirect taxes would have negligible effect on growth and unemployment, and a moderate but persistent deterioration of the composite HD index. Yet, if the fall in tariff revenues is initially offset by an increase in aid, with domestic taxation implemented subsequently, poverty actually falls slightly during the first three years, but subsequently increases, because the increase in the indirect tax rate lowers real private consumption and reduces purchasing power. When aid is assumed to not only compensate for the tariff loss during 2008–10, but also to increase for four years, starting in 2009, by 2 percentage points of GDP, to finance public investment, growth increases significantly, poverty falls throughout the simulation period (by more than one percentage point between 2010 and 2013), and the composite HD indicator improves eventually by about 4 percentage points. When the increase in aid is assumed to be allocated totally to an increase in public investment in infrastructure, the implications for growth and trade flows are similar to those presented in the previous scenarios, but improvements in poverty and other HD indicators are less significant—the reason of course being that less spending on education and health implies less tangible results in terms of literacy, malnutrition, and infant mortality.

Seventh, it is important to stress that the experiments reported above are illustrative in nature. Nevertheless, they provide a good sense of the potential benefits of an "aid for trade" program associated with a trade agreement—even for a middle-income country. Indeed, even as a compensation scheme, a temporary increase in aid can be helpful, to the extent that it mitigates the direct effect of changes in taxation on the cost of living and poverty. From both a welfare and political economy perspectives, this may be an important consideration to ensure the sustainability of trade reforms. Moreover, if external support can also be provided to finance increases in public investment aimed at alleviating supply bottlenecks, domestic producers may be better able to capitalize on new trade opportunities.

Assessing the Gains from Trade: A Dynamic Multi-Country Analysis

The key characteristics of the first two CGE models (GLOBE and Jamaican models) are summarized in Technical Appendix D. To understand the scenario reported below, we need to highlight the macro closure rule of the models and the factor market-clearing assumptions.

Key Characteristics of the CGE Models

Macro Closure.   All economy wide models must incorporate the standard three macro balances: current account balance, savings-investment balance, and the government deficit/surplus. How equilibrium is achieved across these macro balances depends on the choice of macro "closure" of the model. The scenarios reported in this exercise assume a "neutral" or "balanced" set of macro closure rules. Changes in aggregate absorption are assumed to be shared equally (to maintain the shares evident in the base data) among private consumption, government, and investment demands. The underlying assumption is that there is some mix of macro policies that ensures an equal sharing of the benefits of any increase in absorption or the burden of any decrease among the major macro "actors" (households, government, and investment). To satisfy the savings-investment balance, the household savings rate adjusts to match required changes in investment. Government savings are held constant; factor income tax rates except taxes on unskilled labor income, or alternatively sales taxes, adjust to ensure that government revenue equals government spending plus government savings.

Current account balances are assumed to be fixed for each region (and must sum to zero for the world). Regional real exchange rates adjust to achieve equilibrium, as discussed earlier. The underlying assumption is that any changes in aggregate trade balances are determined by macroeconomic forces working mostly in asset markets, which are not included in the model, and these balances are treated as exogenous. This assumption ensures that there are no changes in future "claims" on exports across the regions in the model; that is, net asset positions are fixed. This macro closure ensures the model is focused on the effects of changes in relative prices on the structure of production, employment, and trade. Fuller analysis of the impact of trade liberalization on, for example, asset markets and macro flows is better studied using macro-econometric models which incorporate asset markets rather than using a CGE model which focuses on changes in equilibrium relative prices in factor and product markets. The strength of the multi-country CGE model is that it elegantly incorporates the features of neoclassical general equilibrium and real international trade models in an empirical framework, but it also abstracts from macro impacts working through the operation of asset markets.

Factor Market Clearing. The implications of two alternative factor market clearing conditions can be investigated. In the first, one can assume that there is full employment and full factor mobility in all factor markets. This specification can be viewed as an archetypal free market model; but the presumption of full employment in all economies is questionable. In common with many other models of developing countries, we assume that there are excess supplies of unskilled labor in the CARIFORUM region; the real wage is held constant and the supply of unskilled labor adjusts following a policy shock.

Regions, Sectors, Factors, and Households in the GLOBE Model. For its base data the GLOBE model uses a global SAM derived from the GTAP 2001 dataset which contains 87 countries or regions, 57 sectors, five factors of production and one household. Each country or region is linked by bilateral trade flows. Regions and sectors can be aggregated in GLOBE as desired. For the CARIFORUM EPA analysis there are 10 regions and 19 sectors, and a dummy regions GLOBE that is the global supplier of trade and transport services for international trade. Details of the aggregation are shown in Table 6.1.

Describing the Simulations Used in the GLOBE Regional CGE Model

Table 6.2 describes the policy experiments run with the GLOBE model of the CARIFORUM EPA.

The first five experiments focus exclusively on the goods market access components of the EU-CARIFORUM EPA. The first four of these (CARIB1-4) relate to the elimination of CARIFORUM and EU duties on traded goods from 2008 to 2033 with the exception of changes to the sugar regime. For these four experiments, the tariff equivalent for sugar is held at the 2008 levels. Only in experiment CARIB5 is the sugar tariff equivalent set to 0.

Table 6.1. Sectors, Factors and Regions in the GLOBE Model

	Sectors	Regions
Vegetables fruit nuts	Transport equipment and machinery	United States of America
Sugar cane and sugar beet	Electronic equipment	Other NAFTA
Other agriculture	Utilities and construction	South America
Forestry and fishing	Transport and communication	Central America
Minerals	Financial and business services	CARIFORUM
Beverages and tobacco	Recreation and other services	EU_15
Sugar	Public services	EU_10
Other food products	**Factors**	Other Europe and Transition
Textiles apparel leather	Land and Natural Resources	Asia
Petroleum coal products	Unskilled labor	ROW
Chemicals rubber plastic	Skilled Labor	
Metals	Capital	

Source: Bank staff and IDS.

Note: Model dataset, based on GTAP v.6.

Table 6.2. Experiments Description in the GLOBE Model, CARIFORUM

Trade Policy Scenarios	CARIB 1	CARIB 2	CARIB 3	CARIB 4	CARIB 5	CARIB 6	CARIB 7	CARIB 8	CARIB 9	CARIB 10	CARIB 11
Elimination of remaining EU duties on CARIFORUM imports	Yes										
Bilateral tariff cuts (according to the schedule for a given year)		2013	2023	2033	2033		2033				2033
Bilateral tariff cuts including sugar					Yes						
Productivity increase in CARIFORUM Non-Public Services (Transport and communication, Financial and Business Services, Recreation)						Yes	Yes			Yes	Yes
Reduction of CARIFORUM NTBs on Service Imports from EU								Yes		Yes	Yes
Reduction of EU NTBs on Service Imports from CARIFORUM									Yes	Yes	Yes

Source: Bank staff and IDS.

Note: all scenarios reported in this table have Balanced Macro Closure, unemployed unskilled labor and fiscal closure by either factor-tax adjustment or by sales-tax adjustment. The choice of fiscal closure is indicated in the presentation of results.

Thus, the experiments capture the tariff cut effects of the CARIFORUM EPA in two parts, all effects excluding sugar, and then all effects including sugar.

In addition to the goods trade liberalization scenarios CARIB1-5, the Appendix reports the results of further experiments for comparison with scenario CARIB4, namely (R3) a hypothetical CARIFORUM-U.S. partnership agreement *instead of the EPA* with the same final tariff rates on CARIFORUM-U.S. trade as in the EPA, (R4) a CARIFORUM-U.S. agreement as in R3 *in addition to the EPA tariff cuts* (as in CARIB4), (R5) the extension of the EPA import tariff cuts by CARIFORUM to all regions, and (R6) the complete elimination of all CARIFORUM tariffs on EU imports.

In the remaining experiments CARIB6-CARIB11 we also introduce the investment and services elements of the EPA. We do so in two ways. First, we allow for exogenously imposed productivity increases in the non-public CARIFORUM services sectors (on the order of 10 percent with sensitivity analyses around this figure reported in the Appendix) to capture the likely expected impact on economic efficiency in the region arising from the liberalization of investment and trade in services. Secondly, we allow for a reduction in tariff-equivalents in services. Here it should be noted that the underlying data on tariff equivalents in services is extremely poor. Indeed there are no underlying tariff equivalents in the GTAP dataset. We have therefore selected best "guesstimates" of tariff equivalents based on the study by Dee (2005). In these experiments the tariff equivalent for sugar is set back to the 2008 tariff equivalents so that the impact of the scenarios that affect only the service sectors can be seen as additional effects on top of the tariff changes excluding sugar.

For the remainder of this section, we report only the results for CARIB4 (full implementation of goods market access under the EPA without sugar); CARIB5 (full implementation of goods market access under the EPA with the changes in the sugar regime); CARIB10 (services trade and investment liberalization by both the EU and CARIFORUM); CARIB11 (full market access, services trade and investment liberalization without any changes in the sugar regime = CARIB4 + CARIB10). The full set of results provides a further decomposition of the various policy shocks and is available in Appendix tables A15-A30. The rates of the CARIFORUM duties on EU imports and EU duties on imports from CARIFORUM are shown for each of the experiments in Tables 6.3 and 6.4.[104]

In all simulations reported in this section, factor income tax rates except tax rates on unskilled labor adjust proportionally to balance government budgets. Appendix tables A23 to A30 reports the corresponding results under the alternative assumption of an endogenous sales tax adjustment. Furthermore, Tables A31 to A38 show results for the tariff cut scenarios CARIB2-5 and CARIB11 under the alternative assumption that the EU compensates the CARIFORUM region for tariff revenue shortfalls on EU imports after the implementation of the EPA tariff concessions in the form of a lump-sum government-to-government budget transfer.

---

104. For the CARIFORUM countries we obtained the tariffs for each country and each year at the HS 6-digit level from the annexes to the CARIFORUM-EC EPA. We then calculated weighted tariff averages for each of the CARIFORUM countries included in our model, at the appropriate level of aggregation for each of the simulated years. It is important to note that we have not therefore included the impact of any exceptions to the agreement which exist at the 8-digit level. While these exceptions are likely to be important for individual sectors and countries, with the level of aggregation we are working at in this report the results are highly unlikely to be significantly affected.

Table 6.3. Summary of Experiments: CARIFORUM Duties on EU Imports

GLOBE Commodities	Base	CARIB4	CARIB5	CARIB10	CARIB11
Vegetables fruit nuts	23.15	15.21	15.21	23.15	15.21
Sugar cane and sugar beet	14.53	0.00	0.00	14.53	0.00
Other agriculture	9.77	1.76	1.76	9.77	1.76
Forestry and fishing	14.46	4.26	4.26	14.46	4.26
Minerals	4.88	0.00	0.00	4.88	0.00
Beverages and tobacco	14.58	14.53	14.53	14.58	14.53
Sugar	20.60	20.60	20.60	20.60	20.60
Other food products	17.32	14.59	14.59	17.32	14.59
Textiles apparel leather	9.77	4.49	4.49	9.77	4.49
Petroleum coal products	26.42	0.00	0.00	26.42	0.00
Chemicals rubber plastic	10.66	1.99	1.99	10.66	1.99
Metals	9.96	0.53	0.53	9.96	0.53
Transport equipment and machinery	7.13	0.63	0.63	7.13	0.63
Electronic Equipment	8.16	0.00	0.00	8.16	0.00
Utilities and construction	3.00	0.00	0.00	3.00	0.00
Transport and communication	10.00	10.00	10.00	0.00	0.00
Financial and business services	5.00	5.00	5.00	0.00	0.00
Recreation and other services	5.00	5.00	5.00	0.00	0.00
Public services	0.00	0.00	0.00	0.00	0.00
Services productivity increases %					
Transport and communication (2)	0.00	0.00	0.00	10.00	10.00
Financial and business services (2)	0.00	0.00	0.00	10.00	10.00
Recreation and other services (2)	0.00	0.00	0.00	10.00	10.00

Source: Bank staff and IDS.

The cuts in the tariffs shown in experiments CARIB1-CARIB4 correspond to the tariff cuts in the agreement aggregated to the GLOBE model sectors and across time and CARIFORUM members for the years 2008 (base) 2013, 2023 and 2033. Experiment CARIBB5 shows the full effects of the EPA tariff changes combined. In experiments CARIBB6-CARIB10, the base tariffs and tariff equivalents are restored so that the analysis of the service sectors can be conducted with the EPA tariff effects isolated.

The Results of the GLOBE Regional CGE Model

The Main Scenarios.   Table 6.5 summarizes the main simulated impacts of the EPA on real macroeconomic aggregates for the CARIFORUM region. Not surprisingly, the corresponding macro effects on the EU or third regions are barely noticeable and are not tabulated here. The results in Table 6.5 are highly indicative. The full application of the market access elements of the agreement (excluding sugar) in simulation CARIB4 leads to a very small

Table 6.4. Schematic Summary of Experiments: EU Duties on CARIFORUM Imports

GLOBE Commodities	Base	CARIB 4	CARIB 5	CARIB 10	CARIB 11
Vegetables fruit nuts	30.47	0.00	0.00	30.47	0.00
Sugar cane and sugar beet	17.03	0.00	0.00	17.03	0.00
Other agriculture	0.00	0.00	0.00	0.00	0.00
Forestry and fishing	0.00	0.00	0.00	0.00	0.00
Minerals	0.00	0.00	0.00	0.00	0.00
Beverages and tobacco	0.00	0.00	0.00	0.00	0.00
Sugar (1)	114.54	114.54	0.00	114.54	114.54
Other food products	6.32	0.00	0.00	6.32	0.00
Textiles apparel leather	0.00	0.00	0.00	0.00	0.00
Petroleum coal products	0.00	0.00	0.00	0.00	0.00
Chemicals rubber plastic	0.00	0.00	0.00	0.00	0.00
Metals	0.00	0.00	0.00	0.00	0.00
Transport equipment and machinery	0.00	0.00	0.00	0.00	0.00
Electronic Equipment	0.00	0.00	0.00	0.00	0.00
Utilities and construction	0.00	0.00	0.00	0.00	0.00
Transport and communication	0.00	0.00	0.00	0.00	0.00
Financial and business services	5.00	5.00	5.00	0.00	0.00
Recreation and other services	10.00	10.00	10.00	0.00	0.00
Public services	0.00	0.00	0.00	0.00	0.00

Source: Bank staff and IDS.

Notes: 1. The 2001 EU tariff on sugar imports is a tariff equivalent estimated of the sugar tariff quota using the methodology in CEPII (2005). The sugar tariff equivalent for CARIFORUM imports into the EU for 2008 is reduced by 30 percent to reflect the ongoing CAP reforms between 2001 and 2008. 2. The productivity increase from additional investment used in the experiments is for illustrative purposes only.

Table 6.5. Aggregate Results with Balanced Macro, Factor Tax Adjustment, Unemployed Unskilled Labor

Trade Policy Scenarios	CARIB 4	CARIB 5	CARIB 10	CARIB 11
% Change on Reference Equilibrium	Bilateral Tariff Reduction 2033	Bilateral Tariff Redux 2033 incl. Sugar	Combined Service Liberalization	Goods and Services Liberalization
Absorption	0.04	0.18	4.98	5.02
Private Consumption	0.08	0.27	6.96	7.04
Import Demand	0.40	0.84	2.61	3.02
Export Supply	0.76	0.81	6.29	7.09
GDP	0.11	0.15	2.38	2.49
Unskilled Labor Employment	0.29	0.41	6.62	6.92

Source: Bank staff and IDS.

increase in welfare as represented in a rise in absorption of 0.04 percent. Similarly we see a small rise in demand for exports (0.76 percent), in demand for imports (0.4 percent), and in unskilled labor demand (0.29 percent). This result arises from considerable trade diversion, a switch in imports from competitive sources such as the United States to the EU15, as can be seen from Tables 6.6 and 6.7 below. These tables show that every sector sees a reduction in imports from the United States, and an increase in imports from the EU for most sectors.

Table 6.8 gives the changes in output by sector resulting from the simulations. All but four sectors experience an increase in output in the CARIB4 experiment, and most notably "vegetables, fruit and nuts" which benefits from the removal of a 30 percent EU import tariff and sees output rise by 4.4 percent in response to a rise in EU export demand by 25 percent.

Table 6.6. CARIFORUM Imports from the United States for GLOBE Model Experiments (Closure: Balanced Macro Closure, Factor Tax Adjustment, Unemployed Unskilled Labor)

Trade Policy Scenarios	CARIB 4	CARIB 5	CARIB 10	CARIB 11
% Change on Reference Equilibrium	Bilateral Tariff Reduction 2033	Bilateral Tariff Redux 2033 incl. Sugar	Combined Service Liberalization	Goods and Services Liberalization
Vegetables fruit nuts	−0.46	0.20	2.92	2.44
Sugar cane and sugar beet	0.07	13.80	3.39	3.46
Other agriculture	−0.08	1.86	4.13	4.05
Forestry and fishing	−0.36	0.36	3.21	2.84
Minerals	−0.21	1.40	5.50	5.29
Beverages and tobacco	−0.18	0.12	2.74	2.56
Sugar	−0.30	−7.13	3.59	3.28
Other food products	−0.53	0.07	2.43	1.88
Textiles apparel leather	−0.74	−0.19	2.89	2.13
Petroleum coal products	−0.54	−0.01	3.73	3.17
Chemicals rubber plastic	−1.86	−1.34	2.31	0.41
Metals	−2.16	−1.95	1.50	−0.69
Transport equipment and machinery	−2.41	−2.07	1.70	−0.75
Electronic equipment	−1.57	−1.23	1.86	0.26
Utilities and construction	−0.92	−0.50	0.30	−0.63
Transport and communication	−0.22	0.15	0.06	−0.17
Financial and business services	−0.16	0.19	−0.14	−0.30
Recreation and other services	−0.24	0.14	0.87	0.62
Public services	−0.28	0.10	2.24	1.95

Source: Bank staff and IDS.

Table 6.7. CARIFORUM Imports from the EU15 for GLOBE Model Experiments (Closure: Balanced Macro closure, Factor Tax Adjustment, Unemployed Unskilled Labor)

Trade Policy Scenarios	CARIB 4	CARIB 5	CARIB 10	CARIB 11
% Change on Reference Equilibrium	Bilateral Tariff Reduction 2033	Bilateral Tariff Redux 2033 incl. Sugar	Combined Service Liberalization	Goods and Services Liberalization
Vegetables fruit nuts	6.43	7.18	2.94	9.55
Sugar cane and sugar beet	20.16	34.44	3.76	24.67
Other agriculture	11.89	14.28	4.29	16.68
Forestry and fishing	8.92	9.79	3.48	12.71
Minerals	16.59	18.57	5.43	22.93
Beverages and tobacco	−0.16	0.29	2.72	2.55
Sugar	−0.32	−5.82	3.53	3.20
Other food products	2.83	3.68	2.55	5.45
Textiles apparel leather	8.60	9.29	2.93	11.78
Petroleum coal products	28.39	29.11	3.78	33.23
Chemicals rubber plastic	12.35	13.03	2.31	14.94
Metals	15.42	15.77	1.49	17.14
Transport equipment and machinery	9.84	10.33	1.72	11.73
Electronic equipment	17.18	17.72	1.88	19.38
Utilities and construction	2.39	2.85	0.29	2.68
Transport and communication	−0.24	0.17	10.58	10.31
Financial and business services	−0.18	0.21	4.85	4.65
Recreation and other services	−0.26	0.15	5.89	5.62
Public services	−0.30	0.10	2.24	1.94

Source: Bank staff and IDS.

Where we include the removal of EU sugar tariffs (CARIB5),[105] we see a similar pattern of aggregate changes, with a slightly higher increase in aggregate absorption which is now 0.18 percent. Once again this very low positive welfare impact appears to be driven by considerable trade diversion, but now the sectoral mix of that trade diversion is somewhat

---

105. Note that in this long-run scenario the EU is assumed to eliminate its sugar tariff on imports from all regions to take simultaneous account of preference erosion due to potential future EPAs with other sugar-producing regions, the impending liberalization of EU sugar imports from LDCs under the Everything But Arms initiative, and a potential Doha Round outcome. The CARIB5 scenario does not intend to capture the short-run effects arising from the expiry of the EU Sugar Protocol right after the start of the EPA, which would take place in any case and is not a genuine part of the agreement. Correspondingly, the reported changes in CARIFORUM sugar exports must be interpreted as changes relative to a base without Sugar Protocol preferences.

Table 6.8. Gross Output by Sector CARIFORUM for GLOBE Model Experiments (Closure: Balanced Macro Closure, Factor Tax Adjustment, Unemployed Unskilled Labor)

Trade Policy Scenarios	CARIB 4	CARIB 5	CARIB 10	CARIB 11
% Change on Reference Equilibrium	Bilateral Tariff Reduction 2033	Bilateral Tariff Redux 2033 incl. Sugar	Combined Service Liberalization	Goods and Services Liberalization
Vegetables fruit nuts	4.36	4.06	1.98	6.24
Sugar cane and sugar beet	0.16	21.90	4.02	4.17
Other agriculture	0.04	1.32	3.90	3.93
Forestry and fishing	−0.07	0.01	2.99	2.92
Minerals	−0.13	−2.35	1.66	1.52
Beverages and tobacco	0.09	0.28	4.43	4.52
Sugar	0.14	43.03	3.18	3.31
Other food products	0.10	0.09	4.37	4.46
Textiles apparel leather	0.45	−0.03	4.54	5.01
Petroleum coal products	−0.18	−0.53	3.78	3.59
Chemicals rubber plastic	0.07	−0.24	5.43	5.51
Metals	0.14	−0.72	4.84	5.00
Transport equipment and machinery	0.24	−0.48	3.84	4.09
Electronic Equipment	1.10	0.16	5.62	6.79
Utilities and construction	0.04	0.03	1.27	1.31
Transport and communication	0.13	0.13	9.30	9.45
Financial and business services	0.18	0.17	8.41	8.62
Recreation and other services	0.15	0.09	12.33	12.52
Public services	0.00	0.09	4.10	4.10

Source: Bank staff and IDS.

different, and we also see a strong increase in sugar exports to the EU. There is, understandably, some concern in the region about the impact of the changes in the EU sugar regime on selected Caribbean economies as the price of sugar exports to the EU received by Caribbean producers' declines as a result of the 2005 EU sugar regime reform and the end of the ACP Sugar Protocol. Yet these developments take place independent of the EPA and are subsumed in the reference equilibrium. Scenario CARIB5 indicates that under a full liberalization of EU sugar imports the Caribbean producers are no longer quantity constrained and can increase their exports to the EU substantially.

The changes in output are again slightly different when we introduce the changes in the EU sugar tariff, and not surprisingly this is particularly so for sugar cane and sugar beet which sees production expand by just over 20 percent, and sugar which sees production expand by over 40 percent. In comparison to the import side, there is little switch of exports to the EU. This result repeats the findings of our earlier study of a potential CARIFORUM EPA using an earlier version of the GLOBE model (See DfID Report chapter on Caribbean CGE model).

Turning to the service liberalization scenarios, experiment CARIB10 simulates the combined effect of a bilateral reduction in service trade barriers and a 10 percent total factor productivity increase in CARIFORUM non-public services sectors associated with an increased commercial presence of EU service providers in CARIFORUM markets. We have not been able to track down ex-ante studies of the potential impact of the EPA on productivity of service industries in CARIFORUM from which a sectorally disaggregated set of productivity shocks could be elicited, and hence the assumption of a uniform 10 percent total factor productivity (TFP) rise is ultimately arbitrary. However, indirect evidence from Eastern European transition economies that have opened their service sectors to EU competition strongly suggest that such gains are likely to be substantial (Arnold, Javorcik and Mattoo, 2007 and further studies cited therein; Fernandes, 2007). Experiments R1 and R2 reported in Appendix Tables A39–46 provide sensitivity analyses using alternative TFP shocks for comparison with the pure service productivity shock scenario CARIB6.

The key message which emerges from the service liberalization simulations, is that if there is to be a major source of welfare gains, then those welfare gains arise from the liberalization of investment and services trade. This can be seen with regard to the last two columns in each of the Tables below. In aggregate we see that the services liberalization alone leads to an absorption (welfare) gain of just under 5 percent, and this welfare gain is reflected in an increase in imports from both the United States and the EU15; as well as an increase in exports to both of these. This is then also reflected in an increase in output for all sectors, and an increase in employment of unskilled labor of just under 7 percent. These results reflect the discussion earlier in this report where we identified the importance of services for many of the CARIFORUM economies, and the dangers of trade diversion from the liberalization of goods trade alone.

Supplementary Experiments

Scenarios with Sales Tax Adjustment. In all simulations discussed so far, factor income tax rates except tax rates on unskilled labor adjust proportionally to balance government budgets. A comparison with Appendix Tables A23 to A30, which report the corresponding results under the alternative assumption of an endogenous sales tax adjustment, shows that the form of fiscal adjustment to tariff revenue shortfalls due to the EPA matters for the direction of the unskilled labor employment effects in the scenarios involving the reduction of CARIFORUM duties on EU imports, in particular scenarios CARIB2 to 5. Under the sales tax adjustment closure, indirect taxes on intermediate and final sales rise in the CARIFORUM region to compensate for the drop in tariff revenue on EU imports. This effect appears to affect domestic absorption and demand for the elastic factor unskilled labor more adversely than the required factor income tax rises under the alternative tax adjustment closure. Since the real wage for unskilled labor is fixed in terms of the consumer price index, the relative price of unskilled labor effectively rises in relation to the prices of capital and unskilled labor when domestic consumer prices rise ceteris paribus due to the indirect tax increases under the sales tax adjustment closure.

Scenarios with EU Budget Support Transfer to CARIFORUM.   For scenarios CARIB2 to 5 and 11, we have also simulated experiments in which the EU compensates the CARIFORUM region for tariff revenue shortfalls on EU imports after the implementation of the EPA tariff cuts in the form of a lump-sum government-to-government budget transfer. The results are reported in Appendix Tables A31 to A38. The size of the budget support transfer varies between 0.08 percent (CARIB2) and 0.31 percent (CARIB4) of benchmark CARIFORUM GDP. In this case, no significant domestic adjustments in factor income or sales taxes in the CARIFORUM region are required and the foreign transfer allows the CARIFORUM to sustain a larger trade balance deficit than in the reference equilibrium. Correspondingly, aggregate real imports, real consumption and domestic absorption rise stronger while aggregate real export effects are weaker compared to the respective scenarios without budget support transfers from the EU.

In these "aid for trade concessions" scenarios, the lump-sum transfer from the EU to CARIFORUM governments is just sufficient to offset tariff revenue losses while keeping real government expenditure and its composition unchanged. It would be desirable to consider additional genuine aid for trade scenarios in which further EU transfers are used to finance public investments in order to alleviate potential supply bottlenecks. However, in its present form, the GLOBE model is not suited to capture endogenous productivity effects of public investments. This limitation is addressed by using a dynamic CGE model (the SPAHD model), which is applied to the case of the Dominican Republic (see below).

Analysis of Further Trade Liberalization Options for CARIFORUM.   Table 6.9 and Appendix Tables A39 to A46 report the results of further experiments for comparison with the bilateral EPA tariff cut scenarios CARIB4 and CARIB5, namely (R3) a hypothetical CARIFORUM-U.S. partnership agreement *instead of the EPA* with the same final tariff rates on CARIFORUM-U.S. trade as in the EPA, (R4) a CARIFORUM-U.S. agreement as in R3 *in addition to the EPA tariff cuts* (as in CARIB4), (R5) the extension of the EPA import tariff cuts by CARIFORUM to all regions, and (R6) the complete elimination of all CARIFORUM tariffs on EU imports.[106]

It is evident from Appendix Tables A7 and A8 that in most traded commodity groups CARIFORUM's trade shares with the USA are substantially higher than the region's trade shares with the EU. Scenario R3 serves to compare the bilateral tariff reduction component of the EPA with a corresponding U.S.-CARIFORUM agreement with the same 2033 tariff schedule (that is, the USA eliminates all tariffs on CARIFORUM imports), while CARIFORUM applies the CARIB5 tariffs in Table 10 to U.S. imports while the EPA tariff cuts are not implemented.

The message from a comparison of the aggregate results in Table A39 with the corresponding CARIB5 results is that the CARIFORUM region would be substantially better off under a trade liberalization agreement with the USA than under the EPA. A glance at Appendix Table A41 confirms that this scenario entails noticeable diversion of trade with the EU.

Would the joint implementation of the R3 agreement with the United States and the EPA CARIB4 measures, which would simultaneously avoid diversion of U.S. trade under

---

106. The reported results assume the same factor income tax adjustment closure as in the main scenarios.

Table 6.9. Aggregate Results with Balanced Macro, Factor Tax Adjustment, Unemployed Unskilled Labor

Trade Policy Scenarios % Change on Reference Equilibrium	R1	R2	R3	R4	R5	R6
Absorption	2.44	7.11	0.47	0.46	0.17	0.05
Private Consumption	3.41	9.94	0.71	0.72	0.37	0.09
Import Demand	1.14	3.25	2.07	2.38	2.47	0.52
Export Supply	2.99	8.74	2.39	3.13	5.00	1.12
GDP	1.15	3.28	0.44	0.52	0.65	0.17
Unskilled Employment	3.18	9.11	1.17	1.39	1.79	0.45

Source: Bank staff and IDS.
Note: For sectoral results see Annex tables R13 to R19.

EPA and diversion of EU trade under a U.S. agreement, lead to higher gains for CARIFO-RUM than the sum of the gains from each scenario viewed in isolation? Scenario R4 addresses this question but does not confirm the conjecture that the two agreements considered here might be super-additive in this sense. The close resemblance of the aggregate results for R3 and R4 indicates that from a macro perspective EU trade diversion resulting from a U.S.-CARIFORUM agreement are of limited quantitative relevance. At the same time, the comparison of R4 with CARIB5 indirectly reconfirms our earlier suggestion that diversion of trade with the United States may be to a large extent accountable for the low welfare gains from tariff cuts under the EPA.

Scenario R5 combines the bilateral EPA tariff cuts with a unilateral extension of the 2033 CARIFORUM tariff schedule to CARIFORUM imports from *all* regions. On the one

Table 6.10. Experiments Description in the Jamaica model

SCENARIOS BASED ON:	Base 2008	SCENARIOS						
		JAM 1	JAM 2	JAM 3	JAM 4	JAM 5	JAM 6	JAM 7
Early tariffs under EPA		Yes						
Mid-term tariffs under EPA			Yes					
Final tariffs under EPA				Yes	Yes	Yes	Yes	Yes
Increase in world price of sugar					Yes		Yes	Yes
Services productivity increase						Yes	Yes	Yes
Unskilled wage fixed						Yes	Yes	Yes
Fixed rental on capital in services								Yes

Source: Bank staff and IDS.
Note: All scenarios with Balanced Macro Closure.

hand, from the perspective of CARIFORUM trade deviation effects are effectively elimi-nated, yet on the other hand the unilateral tariff reductions on imports of non-EU origin entail a substantial terms of trade deterioration on the order of negative 2.2 percent for CARIFORUM. As a result, scenario R5 yields considerably lower welfare gains for the region compared to scenarios R4 and R3 in which terms of trade effects remain small. Despite this strong adverse terms of trade effect, experiment R5 still yields a higher welfare gain than the pure EPA tariff cut scenarios CARIB4 and CARIB5.

Finally, scenario R6 contemplates a bilateral EPA tariff liberalization scenario with a complete elimination of CARIFORUM tariffs on EU imports[107] including the commodity groups in which CARIFORUM retains double-digit tariffs beyond 2033 according to the actual EPA tariff schedule in Table 6.3. The welfare gain in terms of aggregate real con-sumption or absorption rises only marginally in comparison to CARIB4. While the standard partial equilibrium cost-of-protection approach suggests that the welfare costs of a uni-form tariff rise with the square of the tariff rate, the preferential elimination of high tariffs is at the same time likely to generate high trade diversion costs and this counter-effect is clearly at work here. Moreover, this scenario is associated with a noticeably stronger terms-of-trade deterioration for CARIFORUM (−0.37 percent) than CARIB4 (−0.20 percent).

Assessing the Gains from Trade: A Dynamic Analysis for Jamaica

The key characteristics of the Jamaican Model are described in Technical Appendix D.

The Main Policy Scenarios

The simulations of various EPA scenarios are shown in Table 6.10. Simulations JAM-1 to JAM-3 impose the tariff schedules agreed to under the EPA. In each scenario, the changes in world prices facing Jamaica computed from the GLOBE model are assumed to apply to Jamaica, which include changes in effective world prices Jamaica receives due to elimina-tion of tariffs against Jamaica by the EU. Simulations JAM-4 to JAM-7 all start from sim-ulation JAM-3 and add additional effects. In JAM-4, Jamaica is assumed to have increased access to the EU protected market for sugar. JAM-5 assumes an increase in productivity of the services sectors, assumed to occur because of effective deep integration, and also spec-ifies a fixed real wage for unskilled labor, which implies that employment of unskilled labor can increase. JAM-6 and JAM-7 add increased access for sugar and JAM-7 adds the assumption that the EPA results in increased foreign investment so that the Jamaican cap-ital stock increases as well.

A number of variations on these experiments were run to explore sensitivity of the results to changes in parameters and closure rules. In particular, experiments were run to see if it mattered to the results whether the loss in tariff revenue was made up by increased direct taxes, which are assumed to be non-distorting or increased sales taxes, which are dis-torting. The results indicated little differential impact on the aggregate or structural results, so they are not shown here.

---

107. To maintain comparability with CARIB4, the EU still retains its sugar tariff in this scenario.

Table 6.11. Aggregate Results for Jamaica CGE Model (Percent change from Base value)

% Change from Base	Value Base 2008	JAM 1	JAM 2	JAM 3	JAM 4	JAM 5	JAM 6	JAM 7
Absorption	492.1	−0.1	−0.1	−−0.1	0.3	2.1	2.8	7.3
Consumption	295.9	−0.1	−0.2	−0.2	0.5	2.1	2.7	7.6
Investment	130.4					3.2	3.9	9.0
Government	65.8					0.4	0.5	2.3
Exports	147.6	−0.1	0.1	0.1	0.8	6.0	6.9	13.9
Imports	229.6	−0.2	−0.2	−0.2	1.3	3.6	5.2	9.7
Price indices								
Exchange rate	100.0	0.6	0.7	0.7	−0.5	0.2	−0.9	−0.5
Export Price Index	100.0	−0.8	−0.8	−0.8	0.8	−0.8	0.8	0.8
Import Price Index	100.0	−0.3	−0.3	−0.3	0.2	−0.3	0.2	0.2
Intl terms of Trade Index	100.0	−0.5	−0.5	−0.5	0.4	−0.5	0.4	0.4
Producer price index	100.0	0.0	0.0	0.0	0.4	−0.1	0.2	0.1
Consumer price index	100.0							
Agricultural terms of Trade	100.0	−0.5	−0.5	−0.5	0.6	−0.5	0.6	0.6
Investment/GDP ratio	31.8	0.1	0.0	0.0	−0.2	−0.1	−0.2	−0.5
Trade deficit/GDP ratio	20.0	0.2	0.2	0.2	−0.2	−0.4	−0.9	−1.8

Source: Bank staff and IDS.

The results for various macro aggregates and price indices are shown in Table 6.11, while Table 6.12 shows changes in aggregate trade by origin and destination. Table 6.18 shows change in aggregate factor employment (for simulations JAM-5 to JAM-7, where they change) and Table 6.14 shows sectoral production. The results from simulations JAM-1 to

Table 6.12. Aggregate Real Imports and Exports by Region

Imports	Base Value	Percent Change from Base Value						
		JAM-1	JAM-2	JAM-3	JAM-4	JAM-5	JAM-6	JAM-7
USA	98.9	0.2	−0.9	−1.0	0.5	2.7	4.4	8.8
EUN	26.7	−3.4	5.1	5.5	7.1	9.5	11.2	16.0
WRLD	104.1	0.2	-0.7	−0.8	0.7	3.0	4.6	9.0
TOTAL	229.6	−0.2	-0.1	−0.1	1.4	3.6	5.2	9.7
Exports								
USA	41.8	−0.1	0.1	0.1	-1.7	6.0	4.4	11.9
EUN	45.1	0.1	0.3	0.3	6.2	6.1	12.1	18.6
WRLD	60.8	−0.1	0.0	0.0	-1.4	5.9	4.7	11.7
TOTAL	147.6	−0.1	0.1	0.1	0.8	6.0	6.9	13.9

Source: Bank staff and IDS.

Table 6.13. Factor Employment

	Base Value	Percent Change from Base		
		JAM-5	JAM-6	JAM-7
Unskilled labor	65.8	4.0	5.4	11.3
Skilled labor	128.4	0.0	0.0	0.0
Capital	1,565.0	0.0	0.0	9.6

Source: Bank staff and IDS.

JAM-3 are consistent with analyses in a variety of counties of the impact of shallow integration under an EPA. The liberalization is asymmetric, with Jamaica offering more access to its markets than the EU reciprocates. In all three simulations, the result from the GLOBE model indicate a slight deterioration in the international terms of trade for Jamaica, with

Table 6.14. Gross Output by Sector, Jamaica CGE Model

% Change from Base	Base	JAM 1	JAM 2	JAM 3	JAM 4	JAM 5	JAM 6	JAM 7
Export Agriculture	17.4	0.20	0.22	0.22	10.04	2.66	12.53	17.61
Domestic Agriculture	18.0	−0.15	−0.35	−0.39	−0.67	1.13	1.35	7.19
Livestock	14.2	−0.07	−0.08	−0.11	0.01	2.62	2.82	8.56
Forestry and Fishing	5.1	0.00	−0.04	−0.20	−0.53	0.82	0.77	6.38
Mining	46.1	−0.11	−0.10	−0.10	0.02	−0.22	−0.08	−0.13
Sugar Cane and Beet	82.7	−0.08	−0.10	−0.12	0.06	2.60	2.84	8.56
Processed Sugar	6.5	0.08	0.51	0.54	65.57	0.81	65.00	65.77
Beverages and Tobacco	19.5	−0.02	−0.03	−0.02	−0.87	1.49	0.78	9.58
Textiles Clothing and Leather	9.4	−0.05	-0.12	−0.12	−0.28	3.17	3.06	8.61
Wood Products	5.8	0.05	0.17	0.17	0.64	2.22	3.01	7.92
Paper and Printing	5.4	0.15	0.07	0.07	0.52	1.69	2.28	7.55
Oil	24.1	0.80	0.83	0.83	−0.26	0.84	-0.14	3.31
Chemical Products	18.8	−0.26	−0.76	−0.77	−1.38	1.10	0.66	7.44
Non Metal Products	7.5	0.44	0.08	−0.01	-0.65	1.09	0.95	7.38
Domestic Machinery	1.7	−0.23	−1.75	−1.75	−3.45	0.35	−0.82	4.97
Machinery Export Processing	1.8	0.00	0.00	0.00	−0.11	0.00	−0.11	-0.05
Electricity Water	29.8	−0.02	−0.06	−0.06	1.65	2.53	4.34	9.95
Construction	106.7	−0.01	−0.01	−0.01	0.31	2.84	3.75	8.76
Commerce	175.2	0.12	0.20	0.21	−0.88	7.35	6.53	14.50
Transport	107.9	−0.11	−0.09	−0.09	−0.51	2.68	2.43	8.46
Finance and Insurance	34.1	−0.09	−0.12	−0.11	−0.11	0.31	0.42	7.32
Real estate and Business Services	41.9	0.05	0.15	0.17	−1.86	0.69	−0.89	5.75
Government Services	67.5	0.00	−0.01	−0.01	0.11	0.47	0.73	2.68
Other Services	45.3	−0.06	−0.16	−0.17	−0.04	1.69	1.92	6.08

Source: Bank staff and IDS.

world import prices rising relative to world export prices. In JAM-1, initial tariffs in Jamaica are hardly changed and the international price results actually lead to a decrease in imports from the EU. The result in all three simulations is trade diversion for Jamaica, with a slight decline in aggregate imports in all three and only a slight increase in aggregate exports in JAM-2 and JAM-3. The real exchange rate depreciates slightly (increases, since it is measured in local currency units per unit of foreign currency), indicating that the tariff regime modestly discriminated against exports. Aggregate welfare declines in all three simulations.

These results indicate no benefit to Jamaica from shallow integration alone in an EPA with the EU. More is needed to make the EPA development-friendly for Jamaica. Simulations JAM-4 to JAM-7 explore some possible sources of gains to Jamaica from an EPA. Simulation JAM-4 assumes only increased access to the protected EU market for Jamaican sugar exports. The results from the GLOBE model indicate that such increased access would yield an increase in the effective world price of sugar for Jamaica in the EU by 32 percent. The result in simulation JAM-4 is a slight gain in total absorption from the EPA, with an increase in aggregate exports and imports resulting from the improved international terms of trade (and a slight appreciation of the real exchange rate). Even though sugar exports are not a large share of total Jamaican exports, the dramatic price rise generates gains.

Simulation JAM-5 assumes a productivity increase in the "commerce" sector, which includes tourism, of 10 percent plus a fixed real wage of low skilled workers. The results are beneficial: aggregate absorption increases by 2.1 percent (Table 6.11) and employment of unskilled labor increases by 4.0 percent (Table 6.13). Aggregate exports and imports increase, mostly with the EU. Assuming that the productivity increase is linked to aspects of the EPA (elements of deep integration), then the EPA is clearly desirable.

Simulation JAM-6 adds the increase in sugar prices and JAM-7 adds, in addition, the assumption that the EPA is associated with increased investment in Jamaica, to the point where the profit rate stays at its initial value. The results are more beneficial. With the increase in sugar prices, absorption increases by 2.8 percent (Table 6.11). Employment of unskilled labor goes up by 5.4 percent, with synergy between gains from increased export revenue and employment. Simulation JAM-7 adds an open capital market, with increased foreign investment that keeps the profit rate at its base level. The result is an increase in the capital stock of 9.6 percent and increased employment of unskilled labor of 11.3 percent. Aggregate absorption increases by 7.3 percent.

The last three simulations, JAM-5 to JAM-7, all result in a significant increase in trade with all regions, although the largest increase is with the EU.

Trade Diversion and Trade Creation

In parallel with the sensitivity analysis done with the GLOBE CARIFORUM model, additional simulations were done with the single-country Jamaica model to explore the issue of trade diversion versus trade creation arising from different regional trade agreements. We compare a Jamaica-USA versus a Jamaica-EU trade agreement. The tariff cut in both cases is the assumed final tariff cut in the Jamaica-EU agreement. Essentially, for comparison, we assume that Jamaica achieves an identical agreement with the United States. We also consider comprehensive MFN import liberalization by Jamaica, which completely

Table 6.15. Trade Diversion Scenarios, Jamaica Model

	SCENARIOS			
SCENARIOS BASED ON:	JAM 5a	JAM 5b	JAM 5c	JAM 5d
Trade Agreement with EU or US or Jamaica MFN tariff cut	EU	US	EU-US	MFN
Final tariffs under EPA	Yes	Yes	Yes	Yes
Services productivity increase	Yes	Yes	Yes	Yes
Unskilled wage fixed	Yes	Yes	Yes	Yes

Source: Bank staff and IDS.
Note: All scenarios with Balanced Macro Closure, productivity increase in trade services, and fixed world prices.

eliminates trade diversion. These simulations start from the JAM5 scenario described in Table 6.10, except that they assume no change in world prices in order to control for terms-of-trade effects, including the price of sugar (effectively holding bilateral sugar tariffs fixed). They include an assumed productivity increase in trade services and a fixed real wage for unskilled labor. In these simulations, Jamaica is treated as a small country that cannot influence its terms of trade.

The macro results for the original JAM 5 is included in Table 6.16, imported from Table 6.11 and the new experiments JAM 5a to JAM 5d are shown in the remaining columns.

The original JAM 5 scenario also included a 10 percent increase in trade services productivity and the welfare effect of the EPA with the EU shows a modest 2.1 increase in absorption. Compared with the original JAM 5, JAM 5a shows an absorption increase of 2.3 percent. The source of the higher absorption change is due to the elimination of the terms of trade decline. Exports increase 6.2 percent rather than 2.1 percent as in JAM 5. The remaining comparisons of changes in trade agreement partners or MFN tariff reductions by Jamaica take JAM 5a as the reference point while experiments JAM 5b to 5d all have fixed world prices, including no change in the sugar price.

Table 6.16. Macro Results, Trade Diversion Scenarios, Jamaica Model

% Change from Base	JAM 5	JAM 5a	JAM 5b	JAM 5c	JAM 5d
GDP	2.7	2.8	2.9	3.0	3.2
Absorption	2.1	2.3	2.4	2.5	2.7
Exports	2.1	6.2	7.3	7.7	8.9
Imports	3.2	3.9	4.6	4.8	5.7
Exchange rate	0.4	−0.3	0.6	0.8	1.7
Unskilled labor	4.0	4.3	5.0	5.3	6.3

Source: Bank staff and IDS.

Table 6.17. Aggregate Real Imports and Exports by Region

Imports	Base 2000 Value $m	JAM 5	JAM 5a	JAM 5b	JAM 5c	JAM 5d
USA	98.9	2.7	1.9	12.2	10.4	5.9
EUN	26.7	9.5	17.6	−2.3	10.5	5.6
WRLD	104.1	3	2.4	−0.6	−1.7	5.5
TOTAL	229.6	3.6	4.0	4.7	4.9	5.7
Exports						
USA	41.8	6	6.2	7.3	7.6	8.7
EUN	45.1	6.1	6.2	7.5	7.9	9.2
WRLD	60.8	5.9	6.2	7.3	7.6	8.8
TOTAL	147.6	6	6.2	7.3	7.7	8.9

Source: Bank staff and IDS.

In welfare terms, as measured by the change in absorption, there is very little difference between the EU and the United States as partner in the trading agreement. However, the real exchange depreciates slightly in JAM 5b compared with JAM 5a, and both exports and imports increase more in the trading agreement with the United States. JAM 5c in which the trade agreement is between Jamaica and both the United States and the EU together, absorption increases slightly in comparison with JAM 5b and exports and imports increase slightly more as the real exchange rate depreciates slightly more.

Experiment JAM 5d in which Jamaica lowers all its import tariffs from the EU, the United States and the World by the same amount (a unilateral reduction in MFN tariffs), there is a sharp increase in absorption to 2.7 percent and a jump in the depreciation of the real exchange rate to 1.7 percent. The result is a strong increase in both exports and imports. The last row of Table 6.16 reports the change in the employment of unskilled labor, which is almost 50 percent greater in JAM 5d compared with JAM 5a. Changes in GDP between JAM 5a and JAM 5b are also shown in Table 6.16 and mirror the changes in absorption.

Behind the changes in aggregate exports and imports shown in Table 6.16 are the changes in the pattern of trade, summarized in Table 6.17.

In Table 6.17, the change in major partner countries lead to a large switch in source of imports when JAM 5a and JAM 5b are compared: imports from the United States increase from 1.9 percent in JAM 5a to 12.2 percent in JAM 5d. Imports from the EU change from an increase of 17.6 percent under JAM 5a to a decline of −2.3 percent under JAM 5b. In the combined EU-U.S. partnership, there is a strong and balanced increase in imports from both the EU and the United States of just over 10 percent.

The second half of Table 6.17 shows the impacts on exports. The message is that the direction of exports is little affected by the change in trading partnerships, since there is assumed to be no change in prices to Jamaica for its exports to different regions. The simulations focus on import liberalization. Under the MFN tariff cut shown in experiment 5d, there is a strong increase in imports from all trading partners, and an even stronger increase in exports to all trading partners.

In summary, the results of the simulations on choice of major trading partner and on a MFN unilateral tariff cut show that, in the context of the small country assumption of no changes in world prices, the MFN tariff cut dominates in welfare terms any of the FTA arrangements considered. Finally, lowering import tariffs on an MFN basis is the best option in the sense that it eliminates trade diversion.

An EPA or some kind of FTA or preferential trading agreement with a single partner (EU or USA) may benefit Jamaica, but it does lead to trade diversion and less benefit than could be achieved by lower MFN tariffs. An FTA can benefit Jamaica more if it results in increased market access to the trade partner, effectively raising the export prices received by Jamaica. The trade diversion effects of an FTA can always be ameliorated or eliminated by Jamaica through unilateral reduction of tariffs against other countries.

To summarize, the pattern of aggregate results for Jamaica is similar to those reported in Appendix Table A24 for the whole of CARIFORUM in the GLOBE model. A limited EPA that results only in lowering tariffs (shallow integration) does not increase welfare for the Caribbean region. This result arises from considerable trade diversion—a switch in imports from competitive sources such as the United States to the EU. The results from both the GLOBE and single-country models indicates that the trade diversion effects of an EPA/FTA can be eliminated by unilateral action on the part of the country, liberalizing trade on a MFN basis. In this case, market access gains from the FTA can be combined with general trade liberalization, resulting in the largest possible gains to the country. When we include the changes in the sugar regime, we see a similar pattern of aggregate changes, but with a small increase in aggregate absorption. The improvement in the terms of trade for sugar offset the trade diversion losses.

There is some concern in the region about the impact of the changes in the sugar regime on selected Caribbean economies. However, our simulations appear to indicate that the relaxation of the sugar regime still leads to increased sugar prices in the region. For those with preferential access, the price of sugar received by Caribbean producers may decline as a result of the change in the sugar regime, but the Caribbean producers are no longer quantity constrained and can increase their exports to the EU.

In comparison to the import side, there is little switch of exports to the EU. This result repeats the findings of our earlier study of a potential CARIFORUM EPA using an earlier version of the GLOBE model (See DfID Report chapter on Caribbean CGE model). The other key message which emerges from these results is that, if the EPA is to be development friendly, it must go beyond shallow integration. Significant welfare gains arise from the liberalization of investment and services trade, with increased productivity. These results corroborate the discussion earlier about the importance of services for many of the CARIFORUM economies, and the dangers of trade diversion from liberalization of only goods trade.

Aid for Trade, Growth, and Poverty: A Dynamic Analysis for the Dominican Republic

In the previous sections, two static, multi-sector models were used to assess the impact of the EU-CARIFORUM EPA on Caribbean countries. For the purpose at hand, however, these models suffer from two limitations: *a)* their static character does not allow a characterization of the transitional dynamics (in terms of growth, employment, and poverty) associated with the implementation of the EPA; and *b*) the lack of an explicit account of the role of public capital, and the externalities associated with some of its components (particularly infrastructure capital) does not allow a full understanding of the importance of an "aid for trade" program for these countries.[108]

In this Section a dynamic model is used to discuss both issues for the Dominican Republic.[109] Although the Dominican Republic is among the richest countries of the region, and therefore among those that are not necessarily in the best position to benefit from a large aid program to accompany the EPA, the model helps to illustrate (with perhaps lessons for other countries) the importance of complementing trade reforms with an increase in aid, in a context where implementation costs and infrastructure constraints are important, to enhance their effect on growth, employment and poverty.

The next subsection provides a brief discussion of the model. The baseline scenario for the period 2008–20 is then characterized and several policy experiments, involving changes in tariffs and in aid flows, are presented.

The SPAHD Model of the Dominican Republic: Brief Overview

The model used to analyze the impact of trade reform and aid programs in the Dominican Republic is a SPAHD framework built at the country's Ministry of the Economy, Planning, and Development. Unlike the models presented in the previous sections, SPAHD models are one-sector, one-household models. They do not therefore have the ability to address issues related to the sectoral impact of a trade agreement (as was done earlier) and its implications for income distribution. Accounting for these allocative effects is of course essential to provide a detailed assessment of the potential costs associated with factor movements across sectors, and thus on employment and poverty. In addition, the lack of disaggregation of trade flows by categories of goods and geographical regions precludes an analysis of the "trade diversion" effects associated with trade agreements with a particular partner or group of partners.

However, SPAHD models have other advantages. Being dynamic in nature, they allow the analyst to trace the aggregate effects of trade reforms (viewed as changes in average tariffs and possibly export prices) on growth, as well as employment and poverty. Moreover, they incorporate a detailed account of the composition of public investment and capital (disaggregated into infrastructure, education, and health), with infrastructure exerting positive externalities in the production of goods, health services, and education services—in addition to a "complementarity" effect on private investment.[110] They are therefore well suited to analyze the dynamic effects of an aid program involving an increase in public

---

108. The importance of access to infrastructure for trade performance is discussed in detail in Technical Appendix A.

109. The analysis in this section was conducted in close collaboration with staff from the Ministry of the Economy, Planning, and Development in the Dominican Republic, to whom the Team expresses its sincere gratitude.

110. The emphasis on public investment and the supply side in these models dwells on the more advanced class of IMMPA models, described in the collection of studies edited by Agénor, Izquierdo, and Jensen (2006).

investment—with the goal of alleviating the supply-side constraints that hamper the ability of producers to take advantage of new opportunities created by trade reforms.

In addition, the model incorporates a detailed account of interactions not only between growth and poverty (through a household survey), but also links between macroeconomic aggregates (including income and consumption per capita) and other human development (HD) indicators—namely, life expectancy, infant mortality, malnutrition, and access to safe water. These indicators, together with the literacy and poverty rates, are combined into a "composite human development index." Thus SPAHD models allow the analyst to assess not only the poverty effects of trade reform (again, viewed from a highly aggregate perspective), but more generally their impact on human development. Moreover, the model calculates a "composite HD index" by taking an unweighted geometric average of all these individual indicators—the literacy rate, life expectancy, access to safe water, as well as the inverse of the poverty rate, malnutrition prevalence, and infant mortality. Thus, a rise in the index indicates an improvement in human development. Technical Appendix F provides more details on the structure of SPAHD models.

Baseline Scenario

Tables A51 in Appendix and 6.18 below present the results of the baseline scenario for the period 2008–20 for the Dominican Republic. Table A51 provides data on macroeconomic indicators, whereas Table 6.18 below describes the evolution of human development indicators. The scenario is based on a number of assumptions—such as a constant population growth, no terms-of-trade effects for final goods (with export prices and prices of imports of final goods in foreign-currency terms growing at the same rate), constant effective tax rates, and fixed shares of public spending in GDP for maintenance, wages and salaries, investment (at 5 percent), and subsidies. The world price of oil is assumed to increase by 15 percent in 2008 and 5 percent a year after that. In addition, the average (effective) tariff rate on nonoil final imports, which is 5.3 percent in 2007, is kept constant for the period 2008–20. This figure represents a significant drop from 2005 (when it was 14.3 percent), because of the implementation of CAFTA-DR in 2006–07. Aid flows, which are small to begin with, are kept constant throughout at 0.2 percent of GDP and so is the share of domestic borrowing in GDP (0.5 percent).

In this scenario, the average growth rate of real GDP per capita, as well as real private consumption per capita, is about 4 percent. The unemployment rate drops gradually, from about 6.6 percent in 2008 to 5.1 percent in 2020. The current account deficit remains in the two-digit range throughout, but this is financed by large inflows of foreign direct investment and substantial government borrowing (which reflects a persistent fiscal deficit). The share of tax and nontax revenues in GDP, at about 15 percent, remains relatively low compared to countries at a similar level of development. With total expenditure varying between 22 and 23 percent, and with limited ability to borrow domestically, external debt increases sharply, from about 37 percent in 2008 to almost 72 percent in 2020. The sustained increase in real private consumption translates into a significant fall in poverty over time, from about 28 percent in 2008 to 13 percent in 2020. Other indicators of human development improve quite significantly as well, with infant mortality dropping from 22.8 in 2008 to 10.5 in 2020, and life expectancy increasing from 69 years in 2008 to 72 years in 2020. Overall, the composite HD index rises from 102 in 2008 to about 147 in 2020 (see Table 6.18).

Table 6.18. Dominican Republic Human Development Indicators, 2008–20 Baseline Scenario

| | Baseline Scenario | | | | | | | | | | | | |
| | Years | | | | | | | | | | | | |
	2008	2009	2010	2011	2012	2013	2014	2015	2016	2017	2018	2019	2020
Poverty rate (2003 = 63) *(% of population living under the poverty line)*													
IMMPA Method	27.9	26.6	25.4	23.9	22.5	21.1	19.7	18.5	17.3	16.3	15.0	13.9	12.9
Literacy rate *(% of educated labor in total population)*	22.2	22.4	22.7	23.0	23.3	23.6	23.9	24.3	24.7	25.1	25.5	26.0	26.4
Infant mortality (2004 = 27.4) *(Infant mortality rate per 1000 live births)*	22.8	21.7	20.6	19.4	18.3	17.2	16.1	15.1	14.0	13.1	12.2	11.3	10.5
Malnutrition (2002 = 5.3) *(Malnutrition prevalence, weight for age)*	5.0	4.8	4.6	4.5	4.4	4.2	4.1	4.0	3.8	3.7	3.6	3.5	3.4
Life expectancy (2004 = 67.8) *(Life expectancy at birth, years)*	68.9	69.2	69.5	69.8	70.1	70.4	70.7	71.0	71.3	71.6	71.8	72.1	72.3
Access to safe water (2002 = 93) *(Percentage of population with access to safe water)*	96.2	96.3	96.5	96.7	96.9	97.1	97.3	97.5	97.7	98.0	98.2	98.4	98.7
COMPOSITE MDG INDICATOR (2006 = 100) *(A rise denotes an improvement)*	102.1	104.6	107.2	110.3	113.5	117.0	120.6	124.3	128.3	132.4	137.0	141.7	146.7

Malnutrition prevalence is in % of children under 5.

Source: Bank staff and Government of Dominican Republic.

Policy Experiments

To illustrate the impact of trade reforms, accompanied or not by an aid-for-trade program, several experiments are performed with the model. All of them assume that the main provisions of the EPA can be implemented in 2008. In addition, they all involve a cut in tariffs imposed by the Dominican Republic, as well as an increase in export prices, with the latter reflecting the cut in tariffs on the country's exports to the EU. Calculations based on data on the composition of the Dominican Republic's external trade indicate that immediate implementation of the EPA leads to a permanent drop in the average tariff rate of about one percentage point, or equivalently, a permanent revenue loss of about 0.4 percent of GDP, in 2008 and beyond. This drop reflects a fall in duties on final imports originating not only from the EU but also products from other CARIFORUM countries, which also benefit from the cut in tariffs specified in the agreement.[111] This number is relatively small, because most of the country's external trade is with the United States, and a sizable cut in tariffs was implemented in the context of CAFTA-DR, as noted earlier.

Because most products exported by the Dominican Republic already enter duty free in the European Union, the reduction in EU tariffs is assumed to have only a marginal effect on the country's export prices; specifically, we assume that export prices (measured in foreign-currency terms) increase permanently by about 0.2 percentage points, starting in 2008.

Base Experiment: Tariff Loss Compensated by Higher Indirect Taxes

The first experiment assumes that the fall in tariff revenues is entirely offset by an immediate increase in indirect taxes. The impact of this policy on the economy is illustrated in Table 6.19 and Appendix Table A52 in terms of deviations from the baseline scenario. As can be expected, the effect on growth and unemployment is negligible, whereas both exports and nonoil imports increase slightly as a share of GDP. The increase in indirect taxes, however, raises the sales price of the composite good sold domestically; this reduces the purchasing power of income, leading to a drop in consumption (by about 0.2 percentage points) and a slight increase in poverty and infant mortality. Overall the composite HD index records a moderate but persistent deterioration (see Table 6.19).

Aid as a Temporary Compensation Scheme

The second experiment assumes that the fall in tariff revenues is initially offset by an increase in aid, with domestic taxation implemented subsequently. Specifically, the fall in tariff revenues is assumed to be compensated by an increase in foreign grants by the same amount, that is, 0.4 percentage points of GDP, for three years (2008 to 2010), and by an offsetting increase in the indirect tax rate starting in 2011, and kept constant after that.

The impact of this policy on the economy is illustrated in Table 6.20 and Appendix Table A53. The inflow of capital associated with the increase in aid leads (after a year) to a small real appreciation, which dampens the expansion of real exports and stimulates

---

111. Oil imports are not taxed in the Dominican Republic.

Table 6.19. Tariff Loss Compensated by Higher Indirect Taxes—Deviations from Baseline, 2008–20 (Dominican Republic Human Development Indicators)

	2008	2009	2010	2011	2012	2013	2014	2015	2016	2017	2018	2019	2020
Poverty rate (2003 = 63) *(% of population living under the poverty line)*													
IMMPA Method	0.07	0.06	0.05	0.06	0.05	0.09	0.06	0.05	0.12	0.07	0.06	0.06	0.07
Literacy rate *(% of educated labor in total population)*	0.00	0.00	0.00	0.00	0.00	0.00	0.00	0.00	−0.01	−0.01	−0.01	−0.01	−0.01
Infant mortality (2004 = 27.4) *(Infant mortality rate per 1000 live births)*	0.04	0.05	0.03	0.04	0.05	0.05	0.05	0.04	0.04	0.04	0.04	0.03	0.03
Malnutrition (2002 = 5.3) *(Malnutrition prevalence, weight for age)*	0.00	0.00	0.01	0.00	0.00	0.00	0.00	0.00	0.00	0.00	0.00	0.00	0.00
Life expectancy (2004 = 67.8) *(Life expectancy at birth, years)*	−0.01	−0.01	−0.01	−0.01	−0.01	−0.01	−0.01	−0.01	−0.01	−0.01	−0.01	−0.01	−0.01
Access to safe water (2002 = 93) *(Percentage of population with access to safe water)*	−0.01	−0.02	−0.01	−0.02	−0.02	−0.02	−0.02	−0.02	−0.02	−0.02	−0.02	−0.02	−0.01
COMPOSITE MDG INDICATOR (2006 = 100) *(A rise denotes an improvement)*	−0.08	−0.09	−0.11	−0.11	−0.11	−0.16	−0.15	−0.15	−0.24	−0.19	−0.19	−0.21	−0.24

Source: Bank staff and Government of Dominican Republic.

Note: Malnutrition prevalence is in % of children under 5.

Table 6.20. Aid as a Temporary Compensation Scheme—Deviations from Baseline, 2008–20 (Dominican Republic Human Development Indicators)

	2008	2009	2010	2011	2012	2013	2014	2015	2016	2017	2018	2019	2020
Poverty rate (2003 = 63) *(% of population living under the poverty line)*													
IMMPA Method	−0.09	−0.12	−0.18	0.01	0.02	0.06	0.04	0.05	0.12	0.07	0.09	0.06	0.07
Log-normal distribution	−0.06	−0.06	−0.13	0.03	0.04	0.05	0.05	0.06	0.07	0.06	0.06	0.06	0.05
Literacy rate *(% of educated labor in total population)*	0.00	0.00	0.00	0.00	0.00	0.00	0.00	0.00	0.00	0.00	0.00	0.00	0.00
Infant mortality (2004=27.4) *(Infant mortality rate per 1000 live births)*	−0.04	−0.05	−0.07	0.00	0.01	0.01	0.02	0.02	0.03	0.02	0.02	0.02	0.02
Malnutrition (2002=5.3) *(Malnutrition prevalence, weight for age)*	−0.02	−0.02	−0.01	0.01	0.01	0.00	0.00	0.00	0.00	0.00	0.00	0.00	0.00
Life expectancy (2004 = 67.8) *(Life expectancy at birth, years)*	0.01	0.01	0.02	0.00	0.00	0.00	0.01	0.01	0.01	0.01	0.01	0.01	0.01
Access to safe water (2002=93) *(Percentage of population with access to safe water)*	0.01	0.01	0.03	0.01	0.01	0.01	0.01	0.02	0.02	0.02	0.02	0.02	0.02
COMPOSITE MDG INDICATOR (2006 = 100) *(A rise denotes an improvement)*	0.15	0.19	0.24	0.02	0.01	0.06	0.06	0.09	0.19	0.14	0.18	0.15	0.19
International indicators													
External debt (% of GDP)	0.05	−0.05	−0.36	0.04	0.10	0.06	0.09	0.10	0.10	0.11	0.08	0.05	0.02
Interest payment on external public debt (% of GDP)	0.00	0.00	−0.01	0.00	0.00	0.00	0.01	0.01	0.01	0.01	0.01	0.00	0.00
Interest payment on external public debt (% of exports)	−0.01	−0.02	−0.04	0.02	0.00	0.01	0.01	0.01	0.02	0.01	0.02	0.03	0.03

Malnutrition prevalence is in % of children under 5.

Source: Bank staff and Government of Dominican Republic.

imports. The net effect is a deterioration of the trade balance during the initial phase of adjustment. Nevertheless, the current account improves slightly at first, due to the increase in aid flows. The real appreciation exerts a slight positive effect on output growth (due to the reduction in the domestic price of imported oil) and employment, but this effect is short lived. Poverty actually falls slightly during the first three years, but subsequently increases, because the increase in the indirect tax rate lowers real private consumption and reduces purchasing power (as discussed earlier).

Aid as a Joint Compensation-Promotion Scheme

In the next set of experiments, aid is assumed to not only compensate for the tariff loss during 2008–10, as in the previous case, but also to increase for four years, starting in 2009, by 2 percentage points of GDP, to finance public investment. The idea here is, as discussed elsewhere in this report, that the lack of public capital is a key constraint on the ability to capitalize on new trade opportunities, and that aid can play a critical role in alleviating these constraints.

In the first variant of this experiment, the allocation of public investment between infrastructure, education, and health, remains the same as in the baseline scenario; thus, only the level of public investment is affected. The results are illustrated in Tables A54 and 6.21 below. They indicate that the impact on growth is quite substantial—real GDP per capita increases at a rate of 2.4 percent in 2009 and about 1 percent in the subsequent 3 years.[112] This effect stems from both the externalities associated with public capital embedded in the model (see Box 5) and the reduction in the relative price of imported oil associated with the initial real appreciation. The expansion in labor demand leads to a significant drop in unemployment as well after 2009. However, the real appreciation associated with the inflow of aid translates within a year into a fall in the share of exports into GDP as well as a large increase in the share of total imports in GDP. As a result, the trade balance deteriorates quite significantly during the first few years of the adjustment process. Poverty falls throughout the simulation period (by more than one percentage point between 2010 and 2013), and the composite HD indicator improves eventually by about 4 percentage points (see Table 6.21 on the next page).

In the second variant of this experiment, the increase in aid is assumed to be allocated totally to an increase in public investment in infrastructure. As a result, the share of public investment allocated to infrastructure goes up temporarily (until 2012) from about 56 percent in the baseline to 68 percent in this scenario. The results are illustrated in Table 6.22 and Appendix Table A55. The implications for growth and trade flows are similar to those presented in the previous tables, but improvements in poverty and other HD indicators are less significant—the reason of course being that less spending on education and health implies less tangible results in terms of literacy, malnutrition, and infant mortality.

---

112. The results also show that the "growth dividend" tapers off over time. This, of course is very much because of the nature of the experiment. It could also be assumed that over time, as the increase in aid is removed, a tax reform or a reallocation of expenditure (from current spending to investment) is implemented to allow a sustained increase in public capital accumulation.

Table 6.21. Aid Increase Goes to Public Investment—Deviations from Baseline, 2008–20 (Dominican Republic Human Development Indicators)

	Years												
	2008	2009	2010	2011	2012	2013	2014	2015	2016	2017	2018	2019	2020
Poverty Rate (2003 = 63) (% of population living under the poverty line)													
IMMPA Method	−0.09	−0.84	−1.31	−1.39	−1.64	−1.04	−0.89	−0.64	−0.47	−0.56	−0.48	−0.33	−0.18
Literacy rate (% of educated labor in total population)	0.00	0.00	0.00	0.02	0.04	0.08	0.13	0.19	0.24	0.29	0.34	0.38	0.42
Infant mortality (2004 = 27.4) (Infant mortality rate per 1000 live births)	−0.04	−0.42	−0.92	−1.28	−1.62	−1.62	−1.49	−1.35	−1.22	−1.10	−0.99	−0.89	−0.81
Malnutrition (2002 = 5.3) (Malnutrition prevalence, weight for age)	−0.02	−0.01	−0.09	−0.15	−0.20	−0.26	−0.23	−0.21	−0.19	−0.18	−0.17	−0.16	−0.15
Life expectancy (2004 = 67.8) (Life expectancy at birth, years)	0.01	0.12	0.25	0.34	0.43	0.42	0.39	0.35	0.32	0.28	0.26	0.23	0.21
Access to safe water (2002 = 93) (Percentage of population with access to safe water)	0.01	0.19	0.25	0.28	0.33	0.20	0.20	0.18	0.15	0.13	0.11	0.09	0.07
COMPOSITE MDG INDICATOR (2006 = 100) (A rise denotes an improvement)	0.15	0.99	2.25	3.19	4.35	4.49	4.39	4.16	4.02	4.23	4.23	4.08	3.90

Malnutrition prevalence is in % of children under 5.

Source: Bank staff and Government of Dominican Republic.

Table 6.22. Aid Increase Goes to Public Infrastructure Investment—Deviations from Baseline, 2008–20 (Dominican Republic Human Development Indicators)

	2008	2009	2010	2011	2012	2013	2014	2015	2016	2017	2018	2019	2020
Poverty rate (2003 = 63) *(% of population living under the poverty line)*													
IMMPA Method	−0.09	−0.84	−1.31	−1.14	−1.08	−1.06	−0.81	−0.56	−0.40	−0.51	−0.44	−0.28	−0.15
Log-normal Distribution	−0.06	−0.78	−1.05	−0.99	−0.96	−0.86	−0.68	−0.60	−0.49	−0.40	−0.32	−0.24	−0.18
Literacy rate *(% of educated labor in total population)*	0.00	0.00	0.00	0.02	0.04	0.08	0.12	0.17	0.22	0.26	0.30	0.34	0.38
Infant mortality (2004=27.4) *(Infant mortality rate per 1000 live births)*	−0.04	−0.42	−0.92	−1.20	−1.37	−1.39	−1.31	−1.19	−1.07	−0.96	−0.87	−0.78	−0.71
Malnutrition (2002=5.3) *(Malnutrition prevalence, weight for age)*	−0.02	−0.01	−0.09	−0.16	−0.19	−0.21	−0.21	−0.18	−0.17	−0.16	−0.15	−0.14	−0.13
Life expectancy (2004 = 67.8) *(Life expectancy at birth, years)*	0.01	0.12	0.25	0.32	0.36	0.36	0.34	0.31	0.28	0.25	0.23	0.20	0.18
Access to safe water (2002=93) *(Percentage of population with access to safe water)*	0.01	0.19	0.25	0.24	0.23	0.21	0.17	0.15	0.13	0.11	0.09	0.08	0.06
COMPOSITE MDG INDICATOR (2006 = 100) *(A rise denotes an improvement)*	0.15	0.99	2.25	2.91	3.48	3.91	3.89	3.64	3.51	3.73	3.73	3.55	3.40

Malnutrition prevalence is in % of children under 5.

Source: Bank staff and Government of Dominican Republic.

Finally, as an alternative to this experiment, instead of assuming that aid increases for four years by 2 percentage points of GDP and decreases abruptly back to its baseline value, it is assumed that the reduction is gradual, after going up by 2 percentage points of GDP in 2009 and 2010, it drops to 1.5 percent in 2011, 1 percent in 2012, 0.6 percent in 2013, and back to baseline value after that. Results for both variants (fixed allocation shares of public investment, and the increase in aid allocated to infrastructure) are not reported here to save space, but they are qualitatively similar to those reported earlier—with the difference being that the impact on growth, unemployment, and trade flows is more persistent, as could be expected.

It is important to stress that the experiments reported above are illustrative in nature. Nevertheless, they provide a good sense of the potential benefits of an "aid for trade" program associated with a trade agreement—even for a middle-income country. Indeed, even as a compensation scheme, a temporary increase in aid can be helpful, to the extent that it mitigates the direct effect of changes in taxation on the cost of living and poverty. From both perspectives of welfare and political economy, this may be an important consideration to ensure the sustainability of trade reforms. Moreover, if external support can also be provided to finance increases in public investment aimed at alleviating supply bottlenecks, domestic producers may be better able to capitalize on new trade opportunities.

CHAPTER 7

From Diagnosis to Policy Recommendations

This chapter summarizes the five key policy recommendations emerging from the analysis of the report. Some of the proposed policy actions are short term actions that could trigger a virtuous process of growth and human development in the long term of global market integration, improvement of labor and capital productivity and creation of employment opportunities to strengthen the basis of human development. They represent a feasible and immediate set of actions that could bring vital gains in growth and well-being in Caribbean countries, and could thus save and improve millions of lives. They also have the advantage of not requiring extensive infrastructure for their delivery.

However, these short term policy actions alone will not translate into strong and sustained growth to achieve higher human development indicators in the Caribbean region. They will need to be complemented by investment strategies with longer timeframes in order to improve the supply of *public goods*, including transport infrastructure, energy services, and education and health services. Some of the proposed actions, in particular, investment in economic infrastructure will need to be financed in the first stage by *increased foreign aid*, coupled with adequate efforts to improve public sector management, *gradually mobilize domestic resources* and encourage a *greater involvement of the private sector*. The effectiveness of the recommended policy actions is conditional on the improvement of governance in Caribbean countries, which will avoid the wasting of resources. Maximizing Caribbean region's chances for success in achieving higher human development indicators will require improved *accountability, transparency,* and *effectiveness* in the use of public resources. This is essential for aid to be effective.

The findings of this chapter are the followings: (i) the Caribbean countries should reduce the macroeconomic and fiscal imbalances while investing in trade infrastructure to facilitate their integration in the global economy; (ii) the Caribbean countries should accelerate the implementation of national trade policy reforms and improve investment incentives; (iii) the region should adjust to the erosion of preference, accelerate the implementation of the CSME and the ongoing external trading agreements to reinforce their integration in the global economy, seize the new opportunities that the global economy offers; (iv) the region should develop a comprehensive trade strategy, which focuses on increased competitiveness and new areas of opportunities; (v) strengthen CARIFORUM's regional institutions with a focus on implementation.

Reducing Macroeconomic and Fiscal Imbalances, and Investing in Trade Infrastructure

Reducing the Current Macroeconomic and Fiscal Imbalances to Integrate the Global Economy

Caribbean countries have been experiencing macroeconomic and fiscal imbalances, which affect their competitiveness and integration. Integrating into the global economy would require reducing these imbalances. Appropriate policy responses will help reduce large fiscal and current account deficits and high indebtedness levels and debt overhang. In the short term, controlling the level of Government's expenditure should be a priority. In the medium term, accelerating reform to increase domestic revenue would be critical for a successful macroeconomic stabilization in the region. This could be done at the national level through the improvement of domestic policies. Yet, the long practice of inappropriate macroeconomic policies could be difficult to revert at the national level. A regional dimension of these policy responses could help the countries. Designing and implementing a macroeconomic convergence framework could help bring down the deficits and act as a *peer pressure mechanism*. This should be guided by a gradual approach which favors a gradual reduction of the deficits to avoid the social and poverty impact. The composition of expenditure reduction matters. Because of the incompressible nature of some of the expenditures (wages and salaries, and debt service), macroeconomic stability policies more often end up in drastic cuts in expenditure in infrastructure or social sectors, with adverse long-term effect on growth and human development. In the current context of global slowdown, the macroeconomic stability policy should be guided by the principle of *selectivity* by protecting expenditure in social sectors and in basic infrastructure.

Investing in Trade Infrastructure to Alleviate the Structural Constraints to Trading Both between Countries of the Region and between the Region and its International Trading Partners

Build and/or rehabilitate infrastructure, including roads, irrigation schemes, water and sanitation facilities, electricity distribution and ICT networks would help fill the Caribbean region's infrastructure gap and would facilitate increased economic activities and improved access by the population to social services. Many of the Caribbean countries (and notably the poorest in the region, such as Haiti and Guyana) remain ill equipped to take full advantage of new trade opportunities because of significant supply-side constraints. For instance, among the constraints that agriculture suffers from in Caribbean countries (in addition to limited and fragmented fertile land and relatively high labor costs) is an inadequate and costly transport infrastructure, which translates into high international transport costs for both inputs and outputs. These investments are needed to overcome bottlenecks in the realization of Caribbean region's growth potential and achieving higher human development indicators. To help to overcome the disadvantages faced by most Caribbean islands due to their small economic size and foster integration through increased intra-regional trade, there is a need for governments to foster the development of regional public goods in infrastructure, mainly regional transport links. Alleviating or eliminating infrastructure constraints, such as water shortages, electricity outages and difficult road access, would reduce production costs and favor the region's supply of exports. In terms of reducing poverty and improving human development, public infrastructure (electricity, roads, and sanitation) is linked to improvements in health and education outcomes. As discussed in Box 1, to the extent that core infrastructure exerts positive effects on health and education outcomes, improved access to infrastructure services can generate significant benefits for export activities in terms of a more productive/higher quality labor force.

Accelerating National Trade Policy Reforms and Improving Investment Incentives

Policy reforms should be accelerated in five major areas of weakness, including: (i) measures affecting imports; (ii) measures affecting exports; (iii) investment incentives; (iv) competition policy; and (v) trade policy formulation and implementation. Customs procedures and administration should be reinforced as well as the legal framework for businesses including taxation policy. The CARIFORUM countries would also need to create or strengthen incentive to promote investment. Trinidad and Tobago's incentive policy could serve as an example for the other CARIFORUM countries.

The success of trade reforms would require that the countries develop a comprehensive competition policy, which is currently missing in most of the CARIFORUM countries.

However, trade policy would not produce expected outcomes unless national institutions in charge of formulating trade policies, negotiating and implementing trade agreements are reinforced. The first step and perhaps the most important element of success of trade policy in the Caribbean is to reinforce the capacity of ministries of commerce and industry and trade related institutions to formulate trade policy, negotiate, and implement trade agreements. In this regards, donors should provide assistance in the context of the "Aid for trade" agenda. Technical assistance should be provided to help technical staff and policymakers of the Caribbean better understand the implications of trade agreements, design implementation action plans, and follow-up mechanisms.

Assessing the outcomes of trade reforms would require that data are available. Unfortunately, in many Caribbean countries trade data (in particular services data) are more often scarce, outdated or missing. Strengthening the capacity of national statistics departments to regularly produce and publish trade data should be a priority of a trade policy in the Caribbean countries. Donors should provide assistance in that area. The EPA offers a good opportunity and framework to design a comprehensive technical assistance to the Caribbean countries in trade data.

Adjusting to Preferences Erosion, Accelerating the Implementation of the CSME, and Using the EPA for Enhanced Competitiveness and Global Trade Integration

As this report indicates, the Caribbean region is facing three major trade developments, which will shape the region's trade environment over the next decades. First, trade preferences are eroding as a result of trade agreements (AGOA, CAFTA-DR, FTAs) that Caribbean's major trading partners (European Union and the United States) are concluding. Second, the region's competitors are increasing their global market share at the detriment of the Caribbean, reflecting the region's competitiveness problems. Third, the region is also redesigning the process of regional trade integration with the ongoing implementation of the Caribbean Single Market Economy (CSME).

The region has little leverage on the erosion of preferences and fierce competition from other developing countries. The question is therefore: what can be done at the countries and regional level to cope with the "new" trade environment and enhance the region's competiveness? What can the EPA bring to the competitiveness agenda?

The report argues that policy actions should center around three elements: (i) adjusting to the erosion of trade preferences; (ii) accelerating the implementation of the CSME agenda; and (iii) seizing the opportunities of the EPA.

Adjusting to the Erosion of Trade Preferences

For the past three decades, the Caribbean has pursued an external trade policy anchored on preferential access to the European and North American markets. However, the Caribbean is facing a situation where preferential access for traditional products is being eroded. Most notably, the reciprocity character of the EPA, which requires the Caribbean to reduce tariff and nontariff barriers on trade in goods, services, and the movement of capital with the EU, ends the preferences that the Caribbean countries had enjoyed over the past decades. However, the gradual approach of dismantlement of the preferences offers to the Caribbean the time to adjust to the new environment. In the *short term*, the Caribbean region would need to reinforce their competitiveness during the transition period. This requires the implementation of good macroeconomic policies, to support the basis of macroeconomic stability. Second, the region would need to address the short-term costs of the erosion of preferences in particular, the losses of Government's revenue following trade liberalization. Short-term compensatory measures should be explored to help losers (mainly exporters benefiting from preferences) to cope with revenue losses. The issue is the costs and the additional burden that these compensatory measures could imply for the Governments' revenues. Aid for trade could help alleviate the financial burden on the Governments' resources and thus encourage the liberalization reform process. In the *long term*, the focus should be on finding new niches of exports where the Caribbean countries have comparative advantages or segments of existing niches (see above).

Unilateral liberalization could be an option for individual Caribbean countries to integrate the world economy. However, given the similarities of the Caribbean countries and the common development agenda of these countries, regional integration should be used as a tool to integrate the world economy. This, in turn, implies advancing the CARIFORUM's regional integration agenda.

Accelerating the Implementation of the CSME to Make it the Cornerstone of Trade Integration and Economic Development of the Caribbean

The implementation of the CSME has been slow. While, the region has been successful at eliminating tariffs on goods originating in common market countries, CARICOM has still yet to be a single market economy. The CSME agenda has shown little results in the areas of harmonization of trade policies, sectoral development policies, and macroeconomic convergence (see Chapter 2). For the CSME to become the driver of integration and economic development of the region, CARICOM would need to accelerate the implementation of the main provisions of a single market economy. In the *short term (next two years)*, the focus should be on reducing tariff dispersion, advancing the free movement of labor, adopting a regional financial service and investment code, and establishing a regional stock exchange (Phase I of the CSME's implementation process). In the *medium term (next three to five years)*, the region would need to develop a common trade policy, which does not effectively exist and would be the backbone of a full and well-functioning single market. In the *long term*, the region should advance the harmonization of the regulatory regime and economic policies to complete the single economy and implement a CARICOM monetary union (Phase II of the CSME's implementation process).

Addressing the Economic Divergence among Member States to Advance Regional Integration

While the CARICOM Treaty rightly attributes special treatment to less developed countries in terms of their obligations under the Treaty, concrete policy actions are needed to reduce the disparities among member states. A US$250 million fund was launched in July 2008 with an initial $60 million towards its $250 million target.[113] While this initiative is laudable, past experiences within and outside the LAC region showed that development banks either national or regional have generally failed.

Using the EPA Framework to Reinforce Competitiveness

One of the main goals of the EPA is to promote competitiveness and development of Caribbean countries. Both the EU and CARIFORUM countries (Parties) acknowledge the importance of increasing the competitiveness of Caribbean economies, developing their capacity to access high quality markets and in view of their potential contribution to the sustainable development of the CARIFORUM States. But the EPA framework does not define a clear competitiveness strategy for the Caribbean. The challenge is for the Caribbean to use the relevant provisions of the EPA framework to reinforce competitiveness. The 25 years transitory period that the framework provides for full liberalization gives

---

113. The Fund, currently being held in an escrow account at the Caribbean Development Bank (CDB), will promote business development, among other areas. Member States would contribute $120 million of the Fund through a formula that would take into account size, per capita income and other minor indices. The remainder of the funds would come from contributions by development partners. Disadvantaged countries will be the main targets of the Fund and which could receive allocations from the Fund in the forms of loans, grants and interest subsidy grants.

time to the Caribbean to take policy actions to enhanced competitiveness including regulatory and legal reforms to improve doing business environment, controlling wages increases to match labor productivity, investing in infrastructure to reduce production costs. Some specific provisions of the EPA could be exploited to reinforce competitiveness and industrial development. The EPA framework excludes sensitive industrial sectors and contains an "infant industry clause" which allows CARIFORUM to reinstate tariffs in the future to protect growing industry and/or industries. There are also provisions on technical assistance towards developing the capacity to export successfully in EU markets. This was achieved with agreement on the Trade Partnership for Sustainable Development (Development Chapter) which includes support for infrastructure and the CARICOM Development vision. The Joint Declaration on Development Cooperation includes a commitment to channel EPA support through the CARICOM Development Fund.

The EPA also offers the opportunity for the Caribbean countries to improve the competitiveness of potentially *viable* production, including downstream processing, through innovation, training, promotion of linkages and other support activities, in agricultural and fisheries products, including both traditional and non traditional export sectors. Within the framework of European Community funding instruments, both Parties will decide on the programming of funds, in complementarity to the actions already funded, and with respect to the still available funds under the Special Framework of Assistance (SFA), to help the CARIFORUM banana industry to further adjust to the new challenges, including activities aimed at increasing the productivity and competitiveness in areas of viable production, the development of alternatives both within and outside the banana industry, addressing social impact arising from changes in the sector and for disaster mitigation.

Develop a Long-term Trade Strategy with a Focus on Increased Competitiveness and New Areas of Opportunities

Developing a Comprehensive Trade Strategy to Seize the New Opportunities

The current changing trading environment presents a challenge to the Caribbean region. However, it also offers the opportunity to the region to reposition itself in the global economy. The region would need to develop a full-fledged trade strategy to seize the new opportunities that the new trading environment offers. The strategy should focus on targeting sectors with high export and growth potential. Tourism is an area of opportunity. But traditional tourism has not created the dynamic linkages across sectors, and has thus not sustained high economic growth. Given the rapidly changing nature of global tourism demand, an area of new opportunities for CARIFORUM countries include adventure tourism, nature-based tourism, cultural, meetings and conferences, and community tourism.

But to seize these opportunities and promote the tourism industry, Caribbean countries will have to invest in infrastructure in the medium to long term. Building a public/private partnership would also support the promotion of tourism in Caribbean region. Knowledge management is crucial. In this regard, a long-term action is the creation of a

Tourism Satellite Account, a subset of the UN System of National Accounts. In the meantime, small surveys could provide a great deal of information on tourists and their likes/dislikes and establish baseline data on tourism economic, market and supply-side data. Short term policy actions also include: (i) the provision of detailed brochures describing the natural, cultural and historic resources of the Caribbean countries in order to inform potential tourists in a more accessible way; (ii) websites; and (iii) aggressive policy to attract high class tourists, mainly businessmen. If tourism is to become an engine of high and sustained growth in the Caribbean, stakeholders will need to address quality issues as matter of urgency. They will also need to protect The Caribbean's natural resources, cultural and historic patrimonies. Finally, the development of the tourism industry in the Caribbean region will also require building capacity. To this end, training should be a priority both for Caribbean countries, and given limited public resources, the private sector might be called on to support training programs.

Exploring Opportunities beyond the Tourism Sector

The long-term trade strategy would also require exploring opportunities in new areas such as high value financial services, banking, telecommunications, and maritime transport would be a critical step to expand the range of opportunities in services sector. The EPA provides a liberalization framework and advantages for the Caribbean in the service sector. The *asymmetric nature* of the liberalization process between CARIFORUM and the European Commission also gives the Caribbean countries leeway to prepare for the changing environment. It also gives them the opportunity to redeploy their service development strategy. However, the region would need to strengthen infrastructure for exports, and address the issues of their incentives regime most notably for small firms to be able to export services abroad.

More broadly, the region's efforts should focus on the following strategic directions: (i) expansion of value-added activities with a broader participation of the private sector; (ii) modernization of trade transaction system and concerted export strategy; and (iii) facilitation of sectoral development and provision of favorable investment climate. Priority should be given to the following actions. First, the Caribbean governments will need to invest in the production and marketing infrastructures of the sectors and in the technical and operational capacities of the private sector operators. Specific actions include among others, targeting the infrastructure for facilitating exports of services. Second, the governments' interventions should facilitate access to finance by exporters and traders through proper institutional arrangements. These could include revamping the Caribbean Export Development Agency (see paragraph 7.16 above). Third, the governments should also promote the dissemination of knowledge and information on markets and market standards. To this end, concrete policy actions include: (i) establishment of a market information system that will be accessible to producers and exporters; and (ii) establishment of a rural radio systems that will provide rural producers and traders with information on markets, access to resources such as services credit, input availability, niches for potential growth. Fourth, the effectiveness of a services business policy will also depend on the governments' capacity to attract and involve the private sector, so as to jointly design a services export-promotion policy.

*Improving the Investment Climate and the Business Environment to Reinforce
Complementarity between Private and Public Investment*

This is critical to ensure that the Caribbean governments exploit fully the potential of new
areas of opportunities. Accelerating the structural reform agenda would be a critical step
to reinforce private/public sectors' complementarity. While the governments have made
substantial progress in the implementation of their structural reform agenda, effectively
addressing the shortcomings in this area could considerably magnify the returns on public investment efforts, spur growth, and significantly contribute to the human development
goals. Speeding up the ongoing efforts aiming at improving the investment climate, including accelerating the regulatory reforms, and deepening the financial sector reforms are crucial if the Caribbean countries are to enhance their investment climate. Improving the
judicial and regulatory framework governing the private sector will require accelerating the
ongoing reforms including harmonizing the investment and business regulations, insurance, social security, and employment regulations between CARIFORUM member states.

Attract the private sector in sectors with high export and growth potential. This will
require that the Caribbean governments focus on addressing the issues related to the 5 I's:
investment, infrastructure, institutions, innovation, and inputs. These imply that the government make the investment necessary to improve the basic infrastructure; but also tackle
the institutional weaknesses, and facilitates the provision of inputs and market information to the benefit of the private agents.

Reinforcing CARIFORUM Regional Institutions with a Focus on Implementation

Perhaps one of the most critical weaknesses identified within the Caribbean regional and
international trade negotiations construct has been the endemic failure of the regions institutions to take advantage of the market access opportunities presented through either one-
way preferential arrangements or in more recent times, negotiated trade agreements with
international partners. In an effort to overcome this problem and to effectively coordinate
necessary activities that will emanate from the signing of the EPA, and indeed future agreements such as the CARICOM/Canada FTA, this report proposes a *Regional Implementation Mechanism* (RIM).

This structure can be placed within any of the existing regional governing institutions,
or be created as a separate entity. The proposed body can coordinate the regional objectives and activities with national bodies; which can mirror the regional structure. The entity
will be comprised of units charged with the following responsibilities.

- *Market Research Division.* This unit will undertake the analytical work required to
  identify niche markets (both existing and potential) in the EU for CARIFORUM
  exporters; the potential barriers to trade in each market area; identify the potential
  "winners" where market penetration will be most quickly gained; the costs associated and the necessary measures needed both nationally and regionally to engage
  these markets.
- *Legal Division.* This division will examine the legislative requirements to facilitate
  service providers and potential investors who may wish to transact business in the

EU; conduct negotiations with regard to facilitating entry and also examine the areas for mutual recognition agreements, among other variables.

- *Private Sector Division.* This unit would seek to develop the necessary cooperative relationships between the Caribbean private sector firms. In addition, this division would be the conduit through which private sector firms would be able to communicate their concerns and needs regarding barriers to the markets as well as potential investment opportunities available. These would then be translated into finite and concrete proposals to enhance the building of productive capacity in the country/region.
- *National Implementation Liaison Division.* This unit would coordinate the activities with the national implementation bodies in an effort to better facilitate use of funding, share knowledge, and allow the individual countries to raise their concerns and areas of interest.
- *The Project Fund Development Unit.* This unit would be responsible for the development of "sellable" projects in line with the prescribed format required by the EU, vetting of and assisting in the preparation of national projects, and lobbying of the EU on issues pertinent to ensuring a more viable framework for the disbursement of funds.

Implications for the Aid for Trade Agenda

Increasing the Volume and Predictability of Foreign Aid

The proposed policy agenda to accelerate trade integration and growth in the Caribbean region has important implications for the conduct of macroeconomic policy and the strategic focus of the development agenda in the Caribbean over the next decade. Macroeconomic management would be crucial to reduce the existing macroeconomic and fiscal imbalances if the Caribbean countries have to better integrate the global economy. The trade and growth strategy would also require investment in trade infrastructure to enable the Caribbean countries seize the opportunities of the global trade environment.

Given their limited resources, the Caribbean countries are unlikely to significantly increase their global trade penetration and thus achieve higher growth rates and reduce poverty without significant financing from donors. The growth experience over the past decades shows that even during period of good economic policies, global trade penetration was relatively low and economic growth rates were not sustained on a long term sustainable basis

The trade and growth strategy proposed here requires significant support from the international community. Foreign aid must play a major role in financing the strategy. More and predictable aid flows are needed to finance would be required to finance much needed trade infrastructures and help the CARIFORUM member states finance the proposed trade and growth strategy.

The proposed strategy requires that the Caribbean countries have in place an aggressive strategy of attracting foreign aid. However, a legitimate concern often expressed by the Caribbean Governments and more generally developing countries is that aid for trade may result in reduction in the volume of resources available for the developing countries.

In fact, the proposed strategy requires *additionality of resources* to finance Caribbean's development agenda. In this context, the donor community can play a positive role by ensuring that all resources available for Caribbean countries are allocated to the region. On the other hand, the government needs to increase domestic resources without frequent recourse to donors financing. Indeed, the issue of financing the proposed trade and growth is of *mutual accountability* (donors and Government of Caribbean countries).

A legitimate question that could be asked is to what extent the Caribbean economies can absorb huge inflows of foreign aid as this concerns the potential destabilizing macroeconomic effects associated with large inflows of foreign aid: real exchange rate appreciation (Dutch Disease) and disincentive effect on tax collection (moral hazard). Another concern is that increases in foreign aid may also lead to lower tax collection and reduce tax revenue (moral hazard effect).

Improving Macroeconomic Management to Prevent the Potential Destabilizing Macroeconomic Effects of Huge Flows of Foreign Aid

Good macroeconomic policies will be crucial for reducing the potential short-term Dutch Disease effects of increased foreign aid. This means that the Caribbean countries will have to continue implementing macro-stabilization programs to ensure that inflation, fiscal and current account deficits are under control. Moreover, effective management of aid flows is critical to ensure that their potential trade and growth-enhancing, poverty-reducing effects materialize. Improving *accountability, transparency,* and *efficiency* in the use of public resources is crucial to ensure that public investment translates into accumulation of capital and growth. Increasing efficiency of public investment in Caribbean countries is directly related to the ability of the government of Caribbean countries to improve governance. The implementation of the governance reforms (for example, in Haiti), together with procurement and public enterprise reforms, will help advance public finance reforms, and thereby improve economic governance. Decisive complementary actions to fight corruption, improve the rule of law, and advance judiciary reforms is also needed to decisively improve governance in the Caribbean region.

Appendix Tables

Table A1. Caribbean Economies, Real GDP Growth, 1997–2006

	1997	1998	1999	2000	2001	2002	2003	2004	2005	2006*	Average 1997–2000	Average 2001–2006	Average 1997–2006
Antigua and Barbuda	4.9	4.4	4.1	1.5	2.2	2.5	5.2	7.2	4.6	11.0	3.7	5.5	4.8
Bahamas	4.9	6.8	4.0	1.9	0.8	2.3	1.4	1.8	2.7	3.4	4.4	2.1	3.0
Barbados	4.6	6.2	0.5	2.3	-4.6	0.7	2.0	4.8	4.1	3.8	3.4	1.8	2.4
Belize	3.6	3.7	8.7	12.9	4.9	5.1	9.3	4.6	3.5	5.8	7.2	5.5	6.2
Dominica	2.2	3.2	0.6	0.6	-3.6	-4.2	2.2	6.3	3.3	4.0	1.7	1.3	1.5
Dominican Republic	8.1	8.3	6.1	7.9	2.3	5.0	-0.4	2.7	9.2	10.7	7.6	4.9	6.0
Grenada	4.3	8.2	7.0	7.0	-4.9	1.5	7.5	-7.4	13.2	7.0	6.6	2.8	4.3
Guyana	6.2	-1.7	3.8	-1.4	2.3	1.1	-0.7	1.6	-2.0	4.7	1.7	1.2	1.4
Haiti	2.7	2.2	2.7	0.9	-1.0	-0.3	0.4	-3.5	1.8	2.3	2.1	-0.1	0.8
Jamaica	-1.0	-1.2	1.0	0.7	1.5	1.1	2.3	1.0	1.4	2.5	-0.1	1.6	0.9
St. Kitts and Nevis	6.8	0.9	3.6	4.3	2.0	1.1	0.5	7.6	5.0	5.0	3.9	3.5	3.7
St. Lucia	0.6	6.4	2.4	-0.2	-5.1	3.0	4.1	5.6	7.7	7.0	2.3	3.7	3.2
St. Vincent and the Grenadines	3.5	5.2	4.4	1.8	1.0	3.7	3.2	6.2	1.5	4.0	3.7	3.3	3.5
Suriname	2.2	3.1	-2.4	4.0	5.9	1.9	6.1	7.7	5.6	5.8	1.7	5.5	4.0
Trinidad and Tobago	7.7	8.1	8.0	6.9	4.2	7.9	14.4	8.8	8.0	12.0	7.7	9.2	8.6
Average (All 15 countries)	4.1	4.3	3.6	3.4	0.5	2.2	3.8	3.7	4.6	5.9	3.9	3.5	3.6
Average OECS	3.7	4.7	3.7	2.5	-1.4	1.3	3.8	4.3	5.9	6.3	3.7	3.4	3.5
Average Non-OECS	4.3	3.9	3.6	4.0	1.8	2.8	3.9	3.3	3.8	5.7	4.0	3.6	3.7
Standard Deviation (All 15 countries)	2.5	3.2	3.0	3.8	3.6	2.7	4.1	4.5	3.7	3.1	3.1	3.6	3.4

Source: ECLAC database and Authors' calculations.

*Preliminary figures.

154

Table A2. Caribbean Economies, Inflation Rates, 1997–2006 (Variation in consumer prices, December–December)

	1997	1998	1999	2000	2001	2002	2003	2004	2005	2006*	Average 1997–2006	Average 2001–2006	Average 1997–2006
Antigua and Barbuda	0.3	3.4	1.1	-0.6	-0.4	2.5	1.8	2.8	2.5	3.4	1.1	2.1	1.7
Bahamas	0.6	1.9	1.4	1.0	2.9	1.9	2.4	1.9	1.2	2.3	1.2	2.1	1.7
Barbados	3.5	1.7	2.9	3.8	-0.3	0.9	0.3	4.3	7.4	5.6	3.0	3.0	3.0
Belize	-0.6	-0.8	-1.1	0.7	1.2	3.3	2.5	3.0	4.2	4.4	-0.5	3.1	1.7
Dominica	2.2	1.4	0.0	1.1	1.1	1.7	2.8	3.3	3.8	4.1	1.2	2.8	2.2
Dominican Republic	8.4	7.8	5.1	9.0	4.4	10.5	35.0	52.4	4.4	7.4	7.6	19.0	14.4
Grenada	0.9	1.2	1.1	3.4	2.5	-0.4	1.1	2.5	5.8	1.7	1.7	2.2	1.9
Guyana	4.2	4.7	8.7	5.8	1.5	6.0	5.0	5.5	8.2	4.2	5.9	5.1	5.4
Haiti	17	7.4	9.7	19.0	8.1	14.8	40.4	20.2	14.8	10.2	13.3	18.1	16.2
Jamaica	8.8	7.9	6.8	6.1	8.7	7.3	14.1	13.7	12.9	5.8	7.4	10.4	9.2
St. Kitts and Nevis	11.3	0.9	3.2	3.0	2.6	1.7	3.1	1.7	7.2	5.0	4.6	3.6	3.9
St. Lucia	1.6	3.6	6.1	0.4	0.0	1.4	0.5	3.5	5.2	-0.6	2.9	1.7	2.2
St. Vincent and the Grenadines	0.8	3.3	-1.8	1.4	-0.2	0.4	2.7	1.7	4.7	4.5	0.9	2.3	1.7
Suriname	18.3	22.9	112.9	76.1	4.6	28.4	14.0	9.3	15.8	4.7	57.6	12.8	30.7
Trinidad and Tobago	3.5	5.6	3.4	5.6	3.2	4.3	3.0	5.6	7.2	9.1	4.5	5.4	5.1
Average (All 15 countries)	**5.4**	**4.9**	**10.6**	**9.1**	**2.7**	**5.6**	**8.6**	**8.8**	**7.0**	**4.8**	**7.5**	**6.3**	**6.8**
Average OECS	2.9	2.3	1.6	1.5	0.9	1.2	2.0	2.6	4.9	3.0	2.1	2.4	2.3
Average Non-OECS	7.1	6.6	16.6	14.1	3.8	8.6	13.0	12.9	8.5	6.0	11.1	8.8	9.7
Standard Deviation (All 15 countries)	6.1	5.7	28.5	19.2	2.8	7.5	12.6	13.1	4.3	2.7	14.9	7.2	10.3

Source: ECLAC database and Authors' calculations.

*Preliminary figures

Table A3. Caribbean Economies, Merchandise Trade Balance in Percent of GDP, 1997–2006

	1997	1998	1999	2000	2001	2002	2003	2004	2005	2006	Average 1997–2000	Average 2001–2006	Average 1997–2006
Antigua and Barbuda	-47.7	-45.7	-48.5	-45.1	-39.1	-37.5	-40.8	-38.8	-39.3	-43.5	-46.8	-39.8	-42.6
Bahamas	-33.0	-32.8	-27.3	-26.6	-22.6	-20.5	-24.1	-23.8	-30.9	-31.0	-29.9	-25.5	-27.3
Barbados	-27.1	-27.2	-28.9	-29.1	-26.7	-29.1	-30.4	-34.4	-35.0	-30.8	-28.1	-31.1	-29.9
Belize	-12.5	-14.5	-16.2	-24.3	-24.4	-20.2	-20.9	-16.4	-20.8	-15.4	-16.9	-19.7	-18.6
Dominica	-20.4	-20.5	-25.1	-27.5	-26.8	-23.0	-24.3	-29.9	-34.1	-33.5	-23.4	-28.6	-26.5
Dominican Republic	-10.3	-13.0	-13.7	-16.0	-14.2	-14.7	-11.1	-9.0	-10.7	-12.2	-13.3	-12.0	-12.5
Grenada	-41.2	-38.7	-28.9	-33.5	-33.6	-34.2	-40.7	-46.5	-49.1	-42.8	-35.6	-41.2	-38.9
Guyana	-15.5	-5.1	-0.7	-9.0	-11.9	-10.8	-10.9	-17.6	-25.8	-27.6	-7.6	-17.4	-13.5
Haiti	-14.9	-13.9	-16.6	-20.6	-21.4	-24.7	-32.3	-29.4	-21.4	-20.9	-16.5	-25.0	-21.6
Jamaica	-14.7	-14.6	-15.3	-17.9	-19.9	-22.1	-23.5	-22.0	-25.3	-28.7	-15.6	-23.6	-20.4
St. Kitts and Nevis	-29.6	-30.1	-29.6	-36.8	-32.5	-32.6	-32.7	-29.6	-28.6	-30.2	-31.5	-31.0	-31.2
St. Vincent and the Grenadines	-36.8	-37.8	-38.6	-27.6	-31.7	-31.9	-35.8	-38.5	-38.5	-39.3	-35.2	-36.0	-35.7
St. Lucia	-35.6	-34.1	-36.3	-36.6	-31.8	-28.8	-37.9	-34.4	-38.0	-40.0	-35.7	-35.2	-35.4
Suriname	2.9	-5.2	-3.9	-1.7	-2.3	-5.5	-2.7	13.3	-7.8	5.4	-2.0	0.1	-0.8
Trinidad and Tobago	-3.1	-7.3	5.0	16.0	8.9	2.1	11.5	11.5	26.1	29.0	2.7	14.9	10.0
Average (All 15 countries)	-22.6	-22.7	-21.6	-22.4	-22.0	-22.2	-23.8	-23.0	-25.3	-24.1	-22.3	-23.4	-22.9
Average OECS	-35.2	-34.5	-34.5	-34.5	-32.6	-31.3	-35.4	-36.3	-37.9	-38.2	-34.7	-35.3	-35.0
Average Non-OECS	-14.2	-14.8	-13.1	-14.4	-14.9	-16.2	-16.0	-14.2	-16.8	-14.7	-14.1	-15.5	-14.9
Standard Deviation (All 15 countries)	14.6	13.3	14.8	15.4	12.8	11.2	15.0	17.3	17.9	19.6	14.5	15.6	15.2

Source: LDB and IMF Article IV Consultations, and Authors' calculations.

Table A4. Caribbean Economies. Current Account Balance, 1997–2006 (Percent of GDP)

	1997	1998	1999	2000	2001	2002	2003	2004	2005	2006*	Average 1997–2000	Average 2001–2006	Average 1997–2006
Antigua and Barbuda	-8.2	-7.5	-8.8	-9.8	-9.1	-15.3	-13.5	-10.2	-15.5	-20.2	-8.6	-14.0	-11.8
Bahamas	-12.0	-22.2	-4.2	-8.8	-11.6	-7.8	-8.6	-5.4	-13.9	-25.4	-11.8	-12.1	-12.0
Barbados	-2.2	-2.7	-6.0	-5.7	-4.3	-6.8	-6.3	-12.0	-12.8	-8.9	-4.2	-8.5	-6.8
Belize	-4.9	-8.7	-9.9	-19.4	-21.1	-17.8	-17.9	-14.8	-14.4	-2.5	-10.7	-8.8	-9.6
Dominica	-17.3	-8.9	-13.4	-22.1	-19.0	-17.8	-16.3	-21.7	-28.3	-19.4	-15.4	-20.4	-18.4
Dominican Republic	-1.1	-1.7	-2.0	-4.4	-3.0	-3.2	5.3	4.8	-1.4	-2.0	-2.3	0.1	-0.9
Grenada	-22.3	-23.9	-14.0	-21.5	-26.6	-30.8	-32.4	-13.4	-27.3	-23.9	-20.4	-25.7	-23.6
Guyana	-8.4	-15.4	-12.5	-17.2	-20.2	-16.5	-12.9	-9.2	-20.6	-21.3	-13.4	-16.8	-15.4
Haiti	-1.5	-1.0	-1.4	-3.0	-3.8	-2.8	-1.6	-1.5	1.3	0.0	-1.7	-1.4	-1.5
Jamaica	-4.4	-4.3	-2.8	-4.7	-9.3	-12.7	-9.4	-5.8	-10.4	-10.7	-4.1	-9.7	-7.5
St. Kitts and Nevis	-22.4	-16.1	-27.1	-20.1	-31.4	-35.5	-31.7	-22.3	-23.6	-28.4	-21.4	-28.8	-25.9
St. Lucia	-13.5	-9.4	-14.5	-13.8	-16.1	-15.4	-20.4	-13.0	-22.1	-32.2	-12.8	-19.9	-17.0
St. Vincent and the Grenadines	-28.5	-29.0	-22.0	-7.1	-10.9	-11.5	-20.8	-25.1	-25.6	-25.8	-21.7	-20.0	-20.6
Suriname	-7.3	-16.5	-3.8	-4.4	-17.5	-6.3	-12.6	-10.6	-9.7	6.6	-8.0	-4.2	-5.7
Trinidad and Tobago	-10.7	-10.6	0.4	6.7	4.7	0.8	8.8	12.8	18.2	18.3	-3.6	10.6	4.9
Average (All 15 countries)	-11.0	-11.9	-9.5	-10.4	-13.3	-13.3	-8.6	-9.8	-13.7	-13.1	-10.7	-12.0	-11.5
Average OECS	-18.7	-15.8	-16.6	-15.7	-18.9	-21.1	-22.5	-17.6	-23.7	-25.0	-16.7	-21.5	-19.6
Average Non-OECS	-5.8	-9.2	-4.7	-6.8	-9.6	-8.1	0.6	-4.6	-7.1	-5.1	-6.6	-5.7	-6.0
Standard Deviation (All 15 countries)	8.4	8.5	7.9	8.4	9.7	10.0	15.1	10.1	12.5	14.6	8.3	12.0	10.5

Source: ECLAC database and Authors' calculations.

*Preliminary figures.

157

Table A5. Caribbean Economies, Public Sector External Debt, 1997–2006 (Percent of GDP)

	1997	1998	1999	2000	2001	2002	2003	2004	2005	2006*	Average 1997–2000	Average 2001–2006	Average 1997–2006
Antigua and Barbuda	48.26	63.5	63.8	66.2	66.3	75.7	76.3	70.8	40.1	38.2	60.4	61.2	60.9
Bahamas	8.7	7.5	7.2	7.0	6.4	5.7	6.6	6.1	5.7	5.3	7.6	6.0	6.6
Barbados	15.9	14.3	15.7	19.8	26.7	27.2	24.8	23.7	25.6	23.2	16.4	25.2	21.7
Belize	—	33.4	34.6	51.6	56.2	69.9	83.2	86.5	87.3	80.7	39.9	77.3	64.8
Dominica	36.3	36.1	55.3	59.1	65.8	79.2	83.2	86.0	73.6	70.9	46.7	76.5	64.6
Dominican Republic	18.9	17.6	17.3	15.7	17.0	18.2	30.7	29.4	19.5	18.7	17.4	22.3	20.3
Grenada	28.9	29.7	30.2	33.9	39.0	64.2	62.5	75.4	80.5	78.6	30.7	66.7	52.3
Guyana	185.7	188.6	163.6	144.7	143.4	152.4	132.3	128.1	139.4	107.8	170.7	133.9	148.6
Haiti	28.0	29.4	28.4	31.9	33.9	38.3	46.5	37.6	32.1	29.9	29.4	36.4	33.6
Jamaica	48.2	42.7	39.1	42.8	51.1	51.3	51.2	58.1	55.3	56.6	43.2	53.9	49.6
St. Kitts and Nevis	39.0	43.2	49.8	49.2	62.9	74.3	86.4	75.1	62.8	61.5	45.3	70.5	60.4
St. Vincent and the Grenadines	30.3	31.8	48.5	47.8	49.1	74.1	75.6	80.3	77.1	50.1	39.6	67.7	56.5
St. Lucia	20.2	20.4	22.1	24.0	29.8	36.0	45.3	44.9	42.1	38.7	21.7	39.5	32.4
Suriname	—	—	33.4	37.5	47.5	34.9	30.3	26.3	23.3	23.2	35.5	30.9	32.1
Trinidad and Tobago	27.3	24.3	23.3	20.6	18.9	17.2	13.8	10.7	8.0	7.0	23.9	12.6	17.1
Average (All 15 countries)	41.2	41.6	42.1	43.5	47.6	54.6	56.6	55.9	51.5	46.0	42.1	52.0	48.1
Average OECS	33.8	37.5	44.9	46.7	52.2	67.2	71.5	72.1	62.7	56.3	40.7	63.7	54.5
Average Non-OECS	47.5	44.7	40.3	41.3	44.6	46.1	46.6	45.2	44.0	39.2	43.5	44.3	44.0
Standard Deviation (All 15 countries)	44.9	44.5	37.1	32.7	32.4	36.4	33.6	34.0	36.1	29.8	39.8	33.7	36.2

Source: ECLAC database and Bank staff's calculations.

Table A6. Caribbean Economies, Structure of Public Finance, 1997–2006 (Percent of GDP)

	1997	1998	1999	2000	2001	2002	2003	2004	2005	2006*	Average 1997–2000	Average 2001–2006	Average 1997–2006
Antigua and Barbuda													
Total income	27.7	29.2	21.9	21.7	19.2	21.7	21.5	24.6	46.0	24.8	25.1	26.3	25.8
Current income	—	—	19.7	17.8	18.7	20.1	20.8	21.4	21.0	22.5	18.8	20.8	20.3
Tax income	—	—	17.2	15.5	16.6	18.0	18.8	19.3	19.4	21.2	16.4	18.9	18.3
Capital income	—	—	2.1	3.9	0.5	0.2	0.1	1.0	0.8	0.2	3.0	0.5	1.1
Total expenditure	35.0	33.5	27.4	26.7	30.3	33.5	27.6	27.5	28.0	31.3	30.7	29.7	30.1
Current expenditure	—	—	25.2	24.6	25.6	28.4	24.4	25.0	24.0	23.9	24.9	25.2	25.1
Interest payment	—	—	4.0	4.7	4.4	4.9	3.8	4.9	3.8	3.6	4.4	4.2	4.3
Capital expenditure	—	—	2.1	2.1	4.7	5.2	3.2	2.5	4.0	7.4	2.1	4.5	3.9
Primary balance	—	—	-1.5	-0.3	-6.8	-6.9	-2.4	2.0	21.8	-2.9	-0.9**	0.8	0.4
Overall balance	-7.3	-4.3	-5.5	-5.0	-11.1	-11.8	-6.2	-3.0	18.0	-6.5	-5.5	-3.4	-4.3
Bahamas													
Total income	19.9	18.8	19.8	19.1	16.7	16.7	17.2	17.0	19.1	20.6	19.4	17.9	18.5
Current income	19.9	18.8	19.8	19.1	16.7	16.7	16.9	16.7	18.8	20.5	19.4	17.7	18.4
Tax income	17.3	17.0	18.1	17.1	15.0	15.1	15.1	15.1	16.8	18.4	17.4	15.9	16.5
Capital income	—	—	—	—	—	—	0.3	0.3	0.2	0.0	—	0.2	0.2
Total expenditure	20.9	19.7	19.8	18.6	19.5	19.4	19.5	19.4	20.9	21.8	19.8	20.1	20.0
Current expenditure	18.6	17.4	17.4	16.9	17.5	17.9	18.1	18.0	19.0	19.5	17.6	18.3	18.0
Interest payment	2.5	2.3	2.0	1.8	2.0	1.9	2.1	2.0	2.1	2.1	2.2	2.0	2.1
Capital expenditure	2.4	2.2	2.4	1.7	2.0	1.6	1.5	1.5	1.9	2.3	2.2	1.8	2.0
Primary balance	1.4	1.4	2.0	2.3	-0.8	-0.8	-0.3	-0.5	0.2	0.9	1.8	-0.2	0.6
Overall balance	-1.0	-0.9	0.0	0.5	-2.8	-2.7	-2.4	-2.5	-1.9	-1.1	-0.4	-2.2	-1.5

(Continued)

159

Table A.6. Caribbean Economies, Structure of Public Finance, 1997–2006 (Percent of GDP) *(Continued)*

	1997	1998	1999	2000	2001	2002	2003	2004	2005	2006*	Average 1997–2000	Average 2001–2006	Average 1997–2006
Barbados													
Total income	32.6	32.5	31.4	32.9	34.3	34.6	34.2	33.6	32.7	33.2	32.4	33.8	33.2
Current income	30.5	30.1	29.7	30.7	32.1	32.0	32.3	32.2	30.6	31.7	30.3	31.8	31.2
Tax income	—	—	—	—	—	—	—	—	—	—	—	—	—
Capital income	—	—	—	—	—	—	—	—	—	—	—	—	—
Total expenditure	33.5	33.3	33.8	34.4	37.8	40.9	37.2	35.9	36.8	34.7	33.8	37.2	35.8
Current expenditure	27.5	28.1	28.4	29.0	31.6	33.7	32.2	32.1	31.6	29.6	28.3	31.8	30.4
Interest payment	4.3	4.3	4.6	4.6	5.4	5.4	5.0	4.8	4.7	4.7	4.5	5.0	4.8
Capital expenditure	5.8	5.4	5.3	5.4	5.8	7.2	5.0	3.8	3.8	3.9	5.5	4.9	5.1
Primary balance	3.4	3.5	2.2	3.1	1.9	–1.0	2.0	2.6	0.5	3.2	3.1	1.5	2.1
Overall balance	–0.9	–0.8	–2.4	–1.5	–3.5	–6.4	–2.7	–2.2	–4.2	–1.5	–1.4	–3.4	–2.6
Belize													
Total income	24.0	26.0	29.5	26.1	27.8	30.4	22.8	24.3	23.9	24.6	26.4	25.6	25.9
Current income	22.0	21.9	23.0	20.4	26.3	28.9	21.6	21.6	23.0	23.2	21.8	24.1	23.2
Tax income	19.7	19.7	17.4	17.8	23.9	26.5	19.0	19.5	20.6	21.1	18.7	21.8	20.5
Capital income	2.0	4.1	6.4	5.7	0.7	0.2	0.9	1.3	0.3	0.4	4.6	0.6	2.2
Total expenditure	25.2	27.7	32.9	31.8	39.4	34.0	31.9	28.4	28.2	26.3	29.4	31.4	30.6
Current expenditure	19.3	19.2	19.9	17.9	30.7	26.9	20.0	20.3	24.1	22.4	19.1	24.1	22.1
Interest payment	1.9	1.8	2.1	2.5	10.1	6.3	4.0	3.9	6.7	5.7	2.1	6.1	4.5
Capital expenditure	5.9	8.5	13.1	14.0	8.7	7.2	11.9	8.1	4.1	4.0	10.4	7.3	8.6
Primary balance	0.6	0.1	–1.4	–3.2	–1.5	2.8	–5.0	–0.2	2.4	4.0	–1.0	0.4	–0.1
Overall balance	–1.3	–1.7	–3.5	–5.7	–11.6	–3.6	–9.0	–4.1	–4.3	–1.7	–3.1	–5.7	–4.7

Dominica

Total income	32.9	32.5	33.1	35.0	32.5	30.3	33.5	39.2	37.8	43.7	33.4	36.2	35.1
Current income	28.5	28.5	29.3	28.5	26.6	28.0	28.8	30.5	31.5	31.3	28.7	29.5	29.2
Tax income	23.7	24.2	24.9	24.1	22.6	23.5	25.3	26.6	36.9	28.8	24.2	27.3	26.1
Capital income	0.8	1.2	0.6	0.4	0.3	0.3	0.2	0.3	2.1	0.1	0.8	0.6	0.6
Total expenditure	35.9	37.4	41.0	46.2	43.3	36.0	38.5	40.9	36.4	37.8	40.1	38.8	39.3
Current expenditure	27.9	28.1	29.0	31.1	31.9	30.2	32.6	30.3	29.3	28.4	29.0	30.5	29.9
Interest payment	2.9	2.5	3.2	4.5	5.1	5.8	6.3	5.4	3.2	4.0	3.3	5.0	4.3
Capital expenditure	8.0	9.4	12.0	15.1	11.4	5.3	5.5	10.3	6.7	9.0	11.1	8.0	9.3
Primary balance	0.6	0.5	0.2	−2.5	−5.4	0.7	1.8	3.9	5.8	10.3	−0.3	2.9	1.6
Overall balance	−2.8	−5.7	−9.1	−11.2	−10.8	−5.1	−4.4	−1.5	2.6	6.3	−7.2	−2.2	−4.2

Dominica Republic

Total income	16.2	16.1	15.8	15.9	16.5	16.8	16.1	16.4	17.9	—	16.0	13.2	14.4
Current income	15.9	15.9	15.6	15.8	16.3	16.5	15.9	16.2	17.8	—	15.8	16.5	16.2
Tax income	15.1	15.2	14.9	14.9	15.7	15.7	14.8	15.1	16.8	—	15.0	15.6	15.4
Capital income	0.3	0.1	0.0	0.0	0.1	0.2	0.0	0.0	0.0	—	0.1	0.1	0.1
Total expenditure	17.5	16.5	17.4	15.6	17.6	18.5	19.6	19.5	19.3	—	16.8	18.9	17.9
Current expenditure	11.5	11.7	12.2	11.8	11.8	12.0	12.4	14.6	14.5	—	11.8	13.1	12.5
Interest payment	0.8	0.7	0.7	0.8	0.8	1.3	1.9	2.1	1.5	—	0.8	1.5	1.2
Capital expenditure	6.0	4.7	5.2	3.8	5.8	6.5	7.2	4.9	4.7	—	4.9	5.8	5.4
Primary balance	−0.8	−0.2	−1.1	−1.2	−1.5	−1.4	−3.3	−1.9	0.8	—	−0.8	−1.5	−1.2
Overall balance	−1.6	−1.0	−1.8	−2.1	−2.4	−2.7	−5.2	−4.0	−0.7	—	−1.6	−3.0	−2.4

(Continued)

Table A6. Caribbean Economies, Structure of Public Finance, 1997–2006 (Percent of GDP) (Continued)

	1997	1998	1999	2000	2001	2002	2003	2004	2005	2006*	Average 1997–2000	Average 2001–2006	Average 1997–2006
Grenada													
Total income	26.9	30.0	28.1	29.8	30.5	29.0	32.0	34.1	38.3	35.3	28.7	33.2	31.4
Current income	24.1	25.2	26.2	26.8	26.3	26.6	27.0	26.1	26.4	27.8	25.6	26.7	26.3
Tax income	22.0	22.2	22.7	23.9	23.6	23.8	24.9	24.3	25.3	25.9	22.7	24.6	23.9
Capital income	0.2	0.2	0.0	0.1	0.0	0.3	0.0	0.1	0.0	0.0	0.1	0.1	0.1
Total expenditure	33.1	33.1	31.6	33.3	39.1	48.0	36.8	35.0	34.2	42.4	32.8	39.3	36.7
Current expenditure	24.4	23.9	21.4	21.0	24.0	26.5	23.9	27.9	22.1	22.9	22.7	24.6	23.8
Interest payment	2.3	1.6	2.3	2.2	2.6	4.5	5.3	6.2	2.0	2.1	2.1	3.8	3.1
Capital expenditure	8.7	9.2	10.2	12.3	15.1	22.2	13.0	9.1	12.0	19.5	10.1	15.2	13.1
Primary balance	–0.3	1.3	4.8	6.0	2.3	–14.3	0.4	3.4	6.2	0.0	3.0	–0.3	1.0
Overall balance	–6.2	–3.1	–3.5	–3.2	–8.6	–19.0	–4.9	–2.9	4.1	–7.1	–4.0	–6.4	–5.4
Guyana													
Total income	34.5	33.3	33.8	37.0	37.0	40.5	37.3	39.5	41.3	44.0	34.7	39.9	37.8
Current income	31.9	30.7	29.8	31.8	31.1	32.2	31.5	33.0	34.0	35.0	31.1	32.8	32.1
Tax income	29.4	28.6	26.9	29.1	28.3	29.5	28.8	30.9	32.1	32.0	28.5	30.3	29.6
Capital income	2.6	2.6	4.0	5.2	6.0	0.0	0.0	0.0	0.0	0.0	3.6	1.0	2.0
Total expenditure	41.7	40.1	35.7	44.4	47.6	46.1	46.5	46.4	55.6	58.0	40.5	50.0	46.2
Current expenditure	26.3	28.0	25.7	31.3	35.3	34.8	34.5	32.1	34.3	33.0	27.8	34.0	31.5
Interest payment	—	—	—	—	8.8	7.7	6.2	4.9	4.4	3.0	—	5.8	5.8
Capital expenditure	15.4	12.1	10.0	13.2	12.4	11.4	12.0	14.3	21.3	23.0	12.7	15.7	14.5
Primary balance	—	—	—	—	–1.8	2.0	–3.0	–2.0	–9.2	4.0	—	–1.7	–1.0
Overall balance	–7.2	–6.8	–2.0	–7.4	–10.6	–5.7	–9.1	–6.9	–14.3	–13.0	–5.9	–9.9	–8.3

Haiti

Total income	10.1	9.6	9.2	8.2	7.8	8.3	9.1	8.9	13.1	13.5	9.3	10.1	9.8
Current income	8.9	8.5	9.1	8.0	7.4	8.2	8.9	8.9	9.7	10.0	8.6	8.9	8.8
Tax income	8.7	8.3	8.8	7.9	7.4	8.2	8.9	8.9	6.3	6.4	8.4	7.7	8.0
Capital income	—	—	—	—	—	—	—	—	—	—	—	—	—
Total expenditure	10.7	10.8	11.4	10.5	10.0	11.0	12.0	12.2	13.8	14.4	10.9	12.2	11.7
Current expenditure	9.4	8.8	9.3	8.1	8.2	9.0	9.2	9.6	9.6	9.6	8.9	9.2	9.1
Interest payment	0.7	0.7	0.8	0.5	0.3	0.1	0.2	0.7	0.7	0.8	0.7	0.5	0.6
Capital expenditure	1.3	2.0	2.1	2.4	1.8	2.0	2.7	2.6	4.1	5.3	2.0	3.1	2.6
Primary balance	0.1	−0.5	−1.4	−1.8	−1.9	−2.6	−2.7	−2.7	0.4	−1.2	−0.9	−1.8	−1.4
Overall balance	−0.6	−1.2	−2.2	−2.3	−2.2	−2.7	−2.9	−3.3	−0.6	−0.8	−1.6	−2.1	−1.9

Jamaica

Total income	24.8	25.8	29.2	29.1	27.0	28.6	31.7	32.0	30.9	32.2	27.2	30.4	29.1
Current income	24.4	25.3	27.0	28.1	25.7	26.7	30.1	30.1	29.3	31.5	26.2	28.9	27.8
Tax income	22.2	23.3	24.4	25.1	23.8	25.1	27.7	27.8	26.9	28.7	23.8	26.7	25.5
Capital income	0.2	0.2	1.9	0.5	0.7	1.6	1.5	1.1	1.4	0.5	0.7	1.1	1.0
Total expenditure	32.3	32.5	33.3	30.0	32.6	36.3	37.8	36.9	34.3	37.9	32.0	36.0	34.4
Current expenditure	27.0	29.5	30.0	27.6	29.9	34.4	36.6	34.8	31.8	34.3	28.5	33.6	31.6
Interest payment	9.2	12.0	13.4	12.4	13.4	15.1	18.6	17.2	14.6	14.9	11.8	15.6	14.1
Capital expenditure	4.9	2.6	2.9	2.7	2.7	1.9	1.2	2.1	2.6	3.6	3.3	2.4	2.7
Primary balance	1.7	5.4	9.4	11.5	7.8	7.4	12.5	12.2	11.1	12.2	7.0	10.5	9.1
Overall balance	−7.5	−6.7	−4.0	−0.9	−5.6	−7.8	−6.1	−4.9	−3.5	−5.6	−4.8	−5.6	−5.3

(Continued)

Table A6. Caribbean Economies, Structure of Public Finance, 1997–2006 (Percent of GDP) *(Continued)*

	1997	1998	1999	2000	2001	2002	2003	2004	2005	2006*	Average 1997–2000	Average 2001–2006	Average 1997–2006
St. Kitts and Nevis													
Total income	30.4	30.8	31.2	29.7	31.0	35.2	33.7	34.7	40.6	40.7	30.5	36.0	33.8
Current income	30.0	30.6	30.9	29.4	30.8	31.6	32.9	33.9	37.5	38.1	30.2	34.1	32.6
Tax income	22.2	22.6	22.6	21.8	21.9	22.4	23.9	26.2	29.7	29.0	22.3	25.5	24.2
Capital income	0.1	0.1	0.1	0.1	0.1	0.7	0.2	0.4	0.3	0.5	0.1	0.4	0.3
Total expenditure	34.1	37.2	36.8	38.3	37.4	51.8	41.9	42.6	43.9	42.7	36.6	43.4	40.7
Current expenditure	28.9	30.4	32.3	32.5	32.6	34.1	34.1	35.4	38.0	36.8	31.0	35.2	33.5
Interest payment	2.8	3.2	3.9	4.6	4.7	7.1	7.6	7.5	7.5	—	3.6	6.9	5.4
Capital expenditure	5.2	6.9	4.5	5.8	4.8	12.2	6.4	6.2	6.8	5.5	5.6	7.0	6.4
Primary balance	−0.8	−3.3	−1.7	−4.0	−1.7	−9.5	−0.6	−0.4	4.1	6.1	−2.5	−0.3	−1.2
Overall balance	−3.7	−6.5	−5.7	−8.6	−6.4	−16.6	−8.2	−7.9	−4.2	2.1	−6.1	−6.9	−6.6
St. Vincent and the Grenadines													
Total income	29.5	30.3	30.6	30.0	30.9	31.4	30.9	29.5	29.1	30.8	30.1	30.4	30.3
Current income	26.8	27.9	28.6	28.8	28.9	31.0	30.8	29.0	28.9	29.9	28.0	29.8	29.1
Tax income	—	—	—	—	—	27.7	26.4	25.9	26.4	27.5	—	26.8	26.8
Capital income	—	—	—	—	—	0.1	0.2	0.4	0.3	0.5	—	0.3	0.3
Total expenditure	32.4	33.6	32.3	30.3	33.2	33.4	34.1	32.4	34.5	34.6	32.2	33.7	33.1
Current expenditure	24.8	23.8	25.2	26.4	28.3	27.7	26.4	25.7	27.7	27.0	25.1	27.1	26.3
Interest payment	2.1	1.9	2.6	2.6	3.0	−1.6	−6.1	−9.7	−14.0	−7.0	2.3	−5.9	−2.6
Capital expenditure	4.6	9.8	7.1	3.9	5.0	5.9	7.9	7.0	7.3	7.9	6.4	6.8	6.6
Primary balance	−1.0	−1.4	0.9	2.3	0.6	0.7	−0.4	−0.5	−2.3	⋯	0.2	−0.4	−0.1
Overall balance	−1.5	−3.3	−1.7	−0.3	−2.4	−2.1	−2.7	−3.1	−5.4	−4.4	−1.7	−3.4	−2.7

St. Lucia													
Total income	25.4	27.2	29.1	28.2	26.6	26.2	25.7	25.3	24.3	25.8	27.5	25.7	26.4
Current income	24.1	24.7	25.5	26.1	25.4	23.5	23.1	25.0	24.2	25.6	25.1	24.5	24.7
Tax income	21.8	22.8	23.2	23.5	23.0	21.3	21.4	23.0	22.7	24.0	22.8	22.6	22.7
Capital income	0.1	0.2	0.2	0.1	0.1	1.1	0.4	0.0	0.0	0.0	0.2	0.3	0.2
Total expenditure	26.7	26.8	27.9	28.6	29.2	28.6	32.2	29.9	30.7	31.9	27.5	30.4	29.3
Current expenditure	20.4	19.8	19.5	30.3	21.9	21.4	23.2	22.8	20.8	21.9	22.5	22.0	22.2
Interest payment	0.9	1.2	1.4	1.5	2.0	2.5	0.8	-1.5	-1.3	-1.3	1.3	0.2	0.6
Capital expenditure	6.2	6.9	8.5	8.3	7.3	7.5	9.0	7.2	9.8	10.0	7.5	8.5	8.1
Primary balance	3.7	4.8	6.0	5.8	3.5	-0.1	-4.0	-1.8	-3.4	-3.0	5.1	-1.5	1.2
Overall balance	-1.2	0.5	0.5	-0.4	-2.6	-2.4	-6.5	-4.7	-6.3	-6.1	-0.2	-4.8	-2.9
Suriname													
Total income	33.7	36.0	23.7	27.2	37.1	26.6	27.9	27.9	28.9	29.1	30.2	29.6	29.8
Current income			21.1	25.3	34.1	25.5	26.5	26.5	27.1	28.6	23.2	28.1	26.8
Tax income			19.7	23.1	29.7	21.0	22.2	21.7	21.5	22.6	21.4	23.1	22.7
Capital income			—	—	13.9	9.1	9.2	10.3	11.4	—	—	10.8	10.8
Total expenditure	38.8	49.8	33.3	39.3	36.7	31.0	27.1	28.7	29.5	26.7	40.3	30.0	34.1
Current expenditure			26.5	37.0	31.0	28.0	24.1	24.8	24.6	23.0	31.8	25.9	27.4
Interest payment			0.4	0.6	2.0	2.3	2.0	1.7	1.9	1.8	0.5	2.0	1.6
Capital expenditure			5.7	2.3	5.0	2.9	2.7	3.8	4.9	2.8	4.0	3.7	3.8
Primary balance			-9.2	-11.6	2.3	-2.1	2.3	1.6	2.5	4.7	-10.4	1.9	-1.2
Overall balance	-5.2	-13.8	-9.6	-12.1	0.4	-4.4	0.7	-0.8	-0.6	2.4	-10.2	-0.4	-4.3
Trinidad and Tobago													
Total income	27.3	25.2	22.6	25.4	24.4	24.6	23.7	25.8	31.2	33.6	25.1	27.2	26.4
Current income	—	—	22.4	25.3	24.3	24.6	23.7	25.8	31.2	33.6	23.9	27.2	26.4
Tax income	—	—	15.7	14.9	15.5	21.6	22.2	24.3	29.3	32.1	15.3	24.2	22.0
Capital income	—	—	0.2	0.1	0.1	0.1	0.0	0.0	0.0	0.0	0.2	0.0	0.1

(Continued)

Table A6. Caribbean Economies, Structure of Public Finance, 1997–2006 (Percent of GDP) (Continued)

	1997	1998	1999	2000	2001	2002	2003	2004	2005	2006*	Average 1997–2000	Average 2001–2006	Average 1997–2006
Total expenditure	27.2	27.0	25.8	23.8	24.5	25.3	22.3	24.0	25.9	27.1	26.0	24.9	25.3
Current expenditure	24.1	24.8	24.6	21.4	22.9	24.1	21.2	21.9	23.0	23.2	23.7	22.7	23.1
Interest payment	—	—	5.5	4.7	4.0	4.3	3.5	3.0	2.7	2.2	5.1	3.3	3.7
Capital expenditure	3.1	2.2	1.2	2.4	1.6	1.2	1.1	2.0	2.9	4.0	2.2	2.1	2.2
Primary balance	1.0	0.3	2.3	6.3	4.0	3.7	4.9	4.9	7.9	8.7	2.5	5.7	4.4
Overall balance	0.1	−1.8	−3.2	1.6	−0.1	−0.6	1.4	1.9	5.3	6.5	−0.8	2.4	1.1
Average (All 15 countries)													
Total income	26.4	26.9	25.9	26.4	26.6	26.7	26.5	27.5	30.3	30.9	26.4	28.1	27.4
Total expenditure	29.7	30.6	29.4	30.1	31.9	32.9	31.0	30.6	31.5	33.4	29.9	31.9	31.1
Average OECS													
Total income	28.8	30.0	29.0	29.1	28.5	29.0	29.6	31.2	36.0	33.5	29.2	31.3	30.5
Total expenditure	32.9	33.6	32.8	33.9	35.4	38.6	35.2	34.7	34.6	36.8	33.3	35.9	34.8
Average Non—OECS													
Total income	24.8	24.8	23.9	24.5	25.4	25.2	24.4	25.0	26.6	28.9	24.5	25.9	25.4
Total expenditure	27.5	28.6	27.0	27.6	29.5	29.2	28.2	27.9	29.4	30.9	27.7	29.2	28.6
Standard Deviation (All 15 countries)													
Total income	7.3	7.7	7.4	8.1	9.0	8.8	8.6	9.2	9.9	9.1	7.6	9.1	8.5
Total expenditure	8.3	9.7	7.9	10.1	10.3	11.3	9.5	9.4	10.2	10.6	9.0	10.2	9.7

Source: ECLAC database and Bank staff's calculations.
*Preliminary estimates; **Average on 1999–2000.

Table A7. Regional Export Shares by Commodity: CARIFORUM Reference Equilibrium

Commodities	United States	Other NAFTA	South America	Central America	CARIFORUM	EU 15	EU 10	Other Europe and Transition	Asia	ROW	Sum
Vegetables fruit nuts	0.19	0.08	0.00	0.01	0.06	0.58	0.00	0.01	0.06	0.01	1.00
Sugar cane and sugar beet	0.02	0.34	0.02	0.08	0.26	0.08		0.07	0.13	0.01	1.00
Other agriculture	0.20	0.11	0.03	0.02	0.04	0.22	0.00	0.02	0.29	0.07	1.00
Forestry and fishing	0.60	0.12	0.00	0.00	0.02	0.12	0.00	0.01	0.11	0.01	1.00
Minerals	0.70	0.09	0.01	0.00	0.06	0.06	0.00	0.01	0.07	0.00	1.00
Beverages and tobacco	0.36	0.03	0.03	0.01	0.12	0.35	0.00	0.01	0.05	0.02	1.00
Sugar	0.38	0.01	0.00	0.00	0.01	0.59	0.00	0.00	0.01	0.00	1.00
Other food products	0.24	0.10	0.05	0.03	0.22	0.16	0.00	0.02	0.13	0.04	1.00
Textiles apparel leather	0.75	0.05	0.01	0.01	0.03	0.09	0.00	0.01	0.04	0.01	1.00
Petroleum coal products	0.31	0.04	0.07	0.13	0.24	0.13	0.00	0.00	0.02	0.06	1.00
Chemicals rubber plastic	0.41	0.11	0.05	0.02	0.07	0.17	0.00	0.01	0.14	0.02	1.00
Metals	0.19	0.24	0.03	0.01	0.04	0.30	0.00	0.09	0.10	0.01	1.00
Transport equipment and machinery	0.25	0.23	0.04	0.01	0.02	0.24	0.02	0.05	0.11	0.03	1.00
Electronic Equipment	0.07	0.19	0.05	0.01	0.01	0.26	0.01	0.01	0.36	0.02	1.00
Utilities and construction	0.03	0.06	0.04	0.00	0.00	0.44	0.02	0.09	0.26	0.05	1.00
Transport and communication	0.16	0.04	0.03	0.00	0.00	0.41	0.01	0.06	0.18	0.04	0.94
Financial and business services	0.10	0.06	0.03	0.00	0.00	0.48	0.02	0.05	0.21	0.05	1.00
Recreation and Other Services	0.16	0.05	0.03	0.00	0.00	0.45	0.02	0.06	0.18	0.05	1.00
Public services	0.28	0.03	0.04	0.00	0.00	0.26	0.01	0.03	0.13	0.22	1.00

Note: transport and communication shares add to 0.94 because they are calculated in domestic prices.

Table A8. Regional Import Shares by Commodity: CARIFORUM Reference Equilibrium

Commodities	United States	Other NAFTA	South America	Central America	CARIFORUM	EU 15	EU 10	Other Europe and Transition	Asia	ROW	Sum
Vegetables fruit nuts	0.40	0.17	0.09	0.05	0.09	0.09	0.00	0.00	0.09	0.02	1.00
Sugar cane and sugar beet	0.89	0.01	0.00		0.01	0.00	0.00	0.00	0.06	0.02	1.00
Other agriculture	0.70	0.08	0.09	0.01	0.03	0.03	0.00	0.00	0.05	0.02	1.00
Forestry and fishing	0.35	0.18	0.10	0.07	0.05	0.09	0.00	0.01	0.12	0.03	1.00
Minerals	0.03	0.26	0.45	0.00	0.05	0.01	0.00	0.05	0.01	0.14	1.00
Beverages and tobacco	0.16	0.07	0.04	0.02	0.30	0.37	0.01	0.01	0.03	0.01	1.00
Sugar	0.11	0.07	0.39	0.36	0.03	0.02	0.00	0.00	0.01	0.01	1.00
Other food products	0.38	0.09	0.12	0.02	0.09	0.16	0.00	0.02	0.10	0.01	1.00
Textiles apparel leather	0.49	0.09	0.06	0.04	0.03	0.08	0.00	0.00	0.19	0.01	1.00
Petroleum coal products	0.20	0.01	0.53	0.03	0.16	0.04	0.00	0.01	0.01	0.01	1.00
Chemicals rubber plastic	0.33	0.09	0.08	0.06	0.06	0.22	0.01	0.02	0.13	0.01	1.00
Metals	0.26	0.12	0.10	0.02	0.04	0.19	0.01	0.07	0.15	0.05	1.00
Transport equipment and machinery	0.24	0.12	0.02	0.02	0.01	0.24	0.01	0.02	0.31	0.01	1.00
Electronic Equipment	0.31	0.15	0.01	0.01	0.01	0.09	0.01	0.00	0.40	0.02	1.00
Utilities and construction	0.07	0.13	0.02	0.00	0.00	0.46	0.03	0.03	0.20	0.04	1.00
Transport and communication	0.13	0.04	0.02	0.01	0.01	0.41	0.02	0.06	0.23	0.07	1.00
Financial and business services	0.15	0.05	0.02	0.00	0.00	0.50	0.02	0.04	0.18	0.04	1.00
Recreation and public services	0.21	0.04	0.02	0.01	0.02	0.49	0.03	0.03	0.12	0.03	1.00
Public services	0.36	0.02	0.02	0.01	0.01	0.30	0.02	0.06	0.13	0.07	1.00

Source: World Bank staff and IDS.

Table A9. Private Consumption by Commodity CARIFORUM for GLOBE Model Experiments (Closure: Balanced Macro Closure, Factor Tax Adjustment, Unemployed Unskilled Labor)

Trade Policy Scenarios	CARIB 4	CARIB 5	CARIB 10	CARIB 11
% Change on Reference Equilibrium	Bilateral Tariff Reduction 2033	Bilateral Tariff Redux 2033 inc Sugar	Combined Service Liberalization	Goods and Services Liberalization
Vegetables fruit nuts	1.95	1.53	1.67	3.55
Sugar cane and sugar beet	-0.45	-0.83	2.50	2.02
Other agriculture	-0.49	-0.89	2.06	1.56
Forestry and fishing	-0.45	-0.88	1.44	0.97
Minerals	-0.43	-0.57	2.46	2.01
Beverages and tobacco	-0.01	0.29	3.80	3.79
Sugar	-0.16	16.47	2.63	2.46
Other food products	-0.07	0.05	3.79	3.71
Textiles apparel leather	0.05	0.24	3.57	3.62
Petroleum coal products	-0.06	-0.02	2.18	2.11
Chemicals rubber plastic	0.47	0.68	4.30	4.79
Metals	0.53	0.77	4.54	5.09
Transport equipment and machinery	0.79	1.17	3.68	4.50
Electronic Equipment	0.35	0.78	3.78	4.15
Utilities and construction	0.10	0.23	4.34	4.44
Transport and communication	0.00	0.11	11.07	11.07
Financial and business services	-0.04	0.09	11.09	11.05
Recreation and other services	0.05	0.09	13.23	13.29
Public services	0.00	0.14	4.57	4.57

Table A10. Total Exports by Sector CARIFORUM for GLOBE Model Experiments (Closure: Balanced Macro Closure, Factor Tax Adjustment, Unemployed Unskilled Labor)

Trade Policy Scenarios	CARIB 4	CARIB 5	CARIB 10	CARIB 11
% Change on Reference Equilibrium	Bilateral Tariff Reduction 2033	Bilateral Tariff Redux 2033 inc Sugar	Combined Service Liberalization	Goods and Services Liberalization
Vegetables fruit nuts	14.03	13.14	0.51	14.44
Sugar cane and sugar beet	1.49	17.40	2.35	3.84
Other agriculture	0.04	0.04	1.47	1.49
Forestry and fishing	−0.06	−0.56	0.87	0.80
Minerals	−0.10	−3.37	−0.49	−0.62
Beverages and tobacco	0.23	0.24	3.44	3.67
Sugar	0.32	89.77	1.70	2.01
Other food products	1.38	0.91	3.57	4.97
Textiles apparel leather	0.84	−0.08	3.62	4.49
Petroleum coal products	−0.12	−0.76	2.47	2.33
Chemicals rubber plastic	0.59	−0.14	5.05	5.67
Metals	0.80	−0.36	4.87	5.72
Transport equipment and machinery	1.06	0.02	3.55	4.66
Electronic Equipment	1.76	0.50	5.60	7.47
Utilities and construction	0.46	0.03	1.40	1.87
Transport and communication	0.35	0.05	10.63	11.03
Financial and business services	0.39	0.05	12.00	12.45
Recreation and other services	0.38	0.01	16.88	17.34
Public services	0.28	0.03	3.41	3.69

Source: World Bank staff and IDS.

Table A11. CARIFORUM Exports by Region of Destination for GLOBE Model Experiments (Closure: Balanced Macro Closure, Factor Tax Adjustment, Unemployed Unskilled Labor: United States)

Trade Policy Scenarios	CARIB 4	CARIB 5	CARIB 10	CARIB 11
% Change on Reference Equilibrium	Bilateral Tariff Reduction 2033	Bilateral Tariff Redux 2033 inc Sugar	Combined Service Liberalization	Goods and Services Liberalization
Vegetables fruit nuts	-2.59	-3.30	0.32	-2.38
Sugar cane and sugar beet	-0.56	10.83	1.36	0.78
Other agriculture	-0.04	-0.14	1.27	1.22
Forestry and fishing	-0.05	-0.51	0.72	0.66
Minerals	-0.10	-3.52	-0.79	-0.91
Beverages and tobacco	0.22	0.19	3.08	3.30
Sugar	0.30	3.73	1.64	1.94
Other food products	-0.05	-0.62	2.91	2.85
Textiles apparel leather	0.86	-0.07	3.51	4.40
Petroleum coal products	0.01	-0.78	1.53	1.53
Chemicals rubber plastic	0.70	-0.06	4.87	5.62
Metals	0.87	-0.29	4.81	5.74
Transport equipment and machinery	1.08	0.05	3.48	4.61
Electronic equipment	1.76	0.52	5.54	7.42
Utilities and construction	0.47	0.03	1.46	1.94
Transport and communication	0.36	0.04	10.89	11.30
Financial and business services	0.39	0.05	9.27	9.71
Recreation and other services	0.37	0.00	11.34	11.77
Public services	0.27	0.02	3.39	3.68

Source: World Bank staff and IDS.

Table A12. CARIFORUM Exports by Region of Destination for GLOBE model Experiments (Closure: Balanced Macro Closure, Factor Tax Adjustment, Unemployed Unskilled Labor: EU15)

Trade Policy Scenarios	CARIB 4	CARIB 5	CARIB 10	CARIB 11
% Change on Reference Equilibrium	Bilateral Tariff Reduction 2033	Bilateral Tariff Redux 2033 inc Sugar	Combined Service Liberalization	Goods and Services Liberalization
Vegetables fruit nuts	25.23	24.18	0.34	25.51
Sugar cane and sugar beet	22.99	32.84	1.34	24.63
Other agriculture	0.33	0.20	1.30	1.62
Forestry and fishing	−0.04	−0.64	0.87	0.82
Minerals	−0.06	−3.64	−0.84	−0.92
Beverages and tobacco	0.31	0.26	3.09	3.41
Sugar	0.34	128.68	1.67	2.00
Other food products	9.03	8.22	3.10	12.40
Textiles apparel leather	0.90	−0.11	3.54	4.47
Petroleum coal products	0.02	−0.80	1.54	1.55
Chemicals rubber plastic	0.74	−0.08	4.94	5.73
Metals	0.91	−0.30	4.84	5.81
Transport equipment and machinery	1.11	0.02	3.51	4.67
Electronic equipment	1.80	0.48	5.56	7.48
Utilities and construction	0.47	0.01	1.40	1.89
Transport and communication	0.37	0.03	10.89	11.31
Financial and business services	0.40	0.04	14.71	15.18
Recreation and other services	0.39	−0.01	22.99	23.48
Public services	0.29	0.00	3.39	3.69

Source: World Bank staff and IDS.

Table A13. Schematic Summary of Experiments: CARIFORUM Duties on EU Imports

GLOBE Commodities	Base	CARIB 1	CARIB 2	CARIB 3	CARIB 4	CARIB 5	CARIB 6	CARIB 7	CARIB 8	CARIB 9	CARIB 10	CARIB 11
Vegetables fruit nuts	23.15	23.15	18.23	15.55	15.21	15.21	23.15	15.21	23.15	23.15	23.15	15.21
Sugar cane and sugar beet	14.53	14.53	8.93	0.00	0.00	0.00	14.53	0.00	14.53	14.53	14.53	0.00
Other agriculture	9.77	9.77	4.85	2.26	1.76	1.76	9.77	1.76	9.77	9.77	9.77	1.76
Forestry and fishing	14.46	14.46	11.72	9.40	4.26	4.26	14.46	4.26	14.46	14.46	14.46	4.26
Minerals	4.88	4.88	2.98	0.87	0.00	0.00	4.88	0.00	4.88	4.88	4.88	0.00
Beverages and tobacco	14.58	14.58	14.54	14.53	14.53	14.53	14.58	14.53	14.58	14.58	14.58	14.53
Sugar	20.60	20.60	20.60	20.60	20.60	20.60	20.60	20.60	20.60	20.60	20.60	20.60
Other food products	17.32	17.32	16.74	15.45	14.59	14.59	17.32	14.59	17.32	17.32	17.32	14.59
Textiles apparel leather	9.77	9.77	8.16	4.66	4.49	4.49	9.77	4.49	9.77	9.77	9.77	4.49
Petroleum coal products	26.42	26.42	17.84	0.00	0.00	0.00	26.42	0.00	26.42	26.42	26.42	0.00
Chemicals rubber plastic	10.66	10.66	8.28	3.03	1.99	1.99	10.66	1.99	10.66	10.66	10.66	1.99
Metals	9.96	9.96	5.92	0.63	0.53	0.53	9.96	0.53	9.96	9.96	9.96	0.53
Transport equipment and machinery	7.13	7.13	5.56	0.69	0.63	0.63	7.13	0.63	7.13	7.13	7.13	0.63
Electronic Equipment	8.16	8.16	6.77	0.03	0.00	0.00	8.16	0.00	8.16	8.16	8.16	0.00
Utilities and construction	3.00	3.00	0.00	0.00	0.00	0.00	3.00	0.00	3.00	3.00	3.00	0.00
Transport and communication (3)	10.00	10.00	10.00	10.00	10.00	10.00	10.00	10.00	0.00	10.00	0.00	0.00
Financial and business services (3)	5.00	5.00	5.00	5.00	5.00	5.00	5.00	5.00	0.00	5.00	0.00	0.00
Recreation and other services (3)	5.00	5.00	5.00	5.00	5.00	5.00	5.00	5.00	0.00	5.00	0.00	0.00
Public services	0.00	0.00	0.00	0.00	0.00	0.00	0.00	0.00	0.00	0.00	0.00	0.00
Services productivity increases %												
Transport and communication	0.00	0.00	0.00	0.00	0.00	0.00	10.00	10.00	0.00	0.00	10.00	10.00
Financial and business services	0.00	0.00	0.00	0.00	0.00	0.00	10.00	10.00	0.00	0.00	10.00	10.00
Recreation and other services	0.00	0.00	0.00	0.00	0.00	0.00	10.00	10.00	0.00	0.00	10.00	10.00

Source: World Bank staff and IDS.

Notes

1. The 2001 EU tariff on sugar imports is a tariff equivalent estimated of the sugar tariff quota using the methodology in CEPII (2005). The sugar tariff equivalent for CARIFORUM imports into the EU for 2008 is reduced by 30% to reflect the ongoing CAP reforms between 2001 and 2008.

2. See description of simulations for treatment of CARIFORUM the EU tariff equivalents in the EPA.

3. The tariff equivalents were for the simulations where roughly estimated as a 30% reduction on the 2001 base resulting from intervening EU CAP reforms.

4. The productivity increase from additional investment used in the experiments is for illustrative purposes only.

Table A14. Schematic Summary of Experiments: EU Duties on CARIFORUM Imports

GLOBE commodities	Base	CARIB 1	CARIB 2	CARIB 3	CARIB 4	CARIB 5	CARIB 6	CARIB 7	CARIB 8	CARIB 9	CARIB 10	CARIB 11
Vegetables fruit nuts	30.47	0.00	0.00	0.00	0.00	0.00	30.47	0.00	30.47	30.47	30.47	0.00
Sugar cane and sugar beet	17.03	0.00	0.00	0.00	0.00	0.00	17.03	0.00	17.03	17.03	17.03	0.00
Other agriculture	0.00	0.00	0.00	0.00	0.00	0.00	0.00	0.00	0.00	0.00	0.00	0.00
Forestry and fishing	0.00	0.00	0.00	0.00	0.00	0.00	0.00	0.00	0.00	0.00	0.00	0.00
Minerals	0.00	0.00	0.00	0.00	0.00	0.00	0.00	0.00	0.00	0.00	0.00	0.00
Beverages and tobacco	0.00	0.00	0.00	0.00	0.00	0.00	0.00	0.00	0.00	0.00	0.00	0.00
Sugar (1)	114.54	114.54	114.54	114.54	114.54	0.00	114.54	114.54	114.54	114.54	114.54	114.54
Other food products	6.32	0.00	0.00	0.00	0.00	0.00	6.32	0.00	6.32	6.32	6.32	0.00
Textiles apparel leather	0.00	0.00	0.00	0.00	0.00	0.00	0.00	0.00	0.00	0.00	0.00	0.00
Petroleum coal products	0.00	0.00	0.00	0.00	0.00	0.00	0.00	0.00	0.00	0.00	0.00	0.00
Chemicals rubber plastic	0.00	0.00	0.00	0.00	0.00	0.00	0.00	0.00	0.00	0.00	0.00	0.00
Metals	0.00	0.00	0.00	0.00	0.00	0.00	0.00	0.00	0.00	0.00	0.00	0.00
Transport equipment and machinery	0.00	0.00	0.00	0.00	0.00	0.00	0.00	0.00	0.00	0.00	0.00	0.00
Electronic Equipment	0.00	0.00	0.00	0.00	0.00	0.00	0.00	0.00	0.00	0.00	0.00	0.00
Utilities and construction	0.00	0.00	0.00	0.00	0.00	0.00	0.00	0.00	0.00	0.00	0.00	0.00
Transport and communication (3)	0.00	0.00	0.00	0.00	0.00	0.00	0.00	0.00	0.00	0.00	0.00	0.00
Financial and business services (3)	5.00	5.00	5.00	5.00	5.00	5.00	5.00	5.00	5.00	0.00	0.00	0.00
Recreation and other services (3)	10.00	10.00	10.00	10.00	10.00	10.00	10.00	10.00	10.00	0.00	0.00	0.00
Public services	0.00	0.00	0.00	0.00	0.00	0.00	0.00	0.00	0.00	0.00	0.00	0.00

Source: World Bank staff and IDS.

Notes

1. The 2001 EU tariff on sugar imports is a tariff equivalent estimated of the sugar tariff quota using the methodology in CEPII (2005). The sugar tariff equivalent for CARIFORUM imports into the EU for 2008 is reduced by 30 percent to reflect the ongoing CAP reforms between 2001 and 2008.
2. See description of simulations for treatment of CARIFORUM the EU tariff equivalents in the EPA.
3. The tariff equivalents were for the simulations where roughly estimated as a 30 percent reduction on the 2001 base resulting from intervening EU CAP reforms.
4. The productivity increase from additional investment used in the experiments is for illustrative purposes only.

Table A15. Macro Results for GLOBE Model Experiments (Closure: Balanced Macro closure, Factor Tax Adjustment, Unemployed Unskilled Labor)

Trade Policy Scenarios	CARIB 1	CARIB 2	CARIB 3	CARIB 4	CARIB 5	CARIB 6	CARIB 7	CARIB 8	CARIB 9	CARIB 10	CARIB 11
% Change on Reference Equilibrium	Bilateral EU Tariff Elimination for CARIFORUM	Bilateral Tariff Reduction 2013	Bilateral Tariff Reduction 2023	Bilateral Tariff Reduction 2033	Tariff Redux 2033 inc Sugar	10% TFP Rise in CARIFORUM Services	CARIB 4 plus CARIB 6	CARIFORUM Service Barrier Reduction	EU Service Barrier Reduction	Combined Service Liberalization	Goods and Services Liberalization
Absorption	0.06	0.06	0.04	0.04	0.18	4.81	4.85	−0.01	0.16	4.98	5.02
Private Consumption	0.09	0.09	0.08	0.08	0.27	6.72	6.79	−0.02	0.23	6.96	7.04
Import Demand	0.11	0.20	0.38	0.40	0.84	2.22	2.63	0.09	0.29	2.61	3.02
Export Supply	−0.02	0.18	0.72	0.76	0.81	5.90	6.70	0.39	−0.02	6.29	7.09
GDP	0.03	0.05	0.10	0.11	0.15	2.24	2.35	0.06	0.08	2.38	2.49
Unskilled Labor Employment	0.08	0.14	0.28	0.29	0.41	6.21	6.52	0.15	0.23	6.62	6.92

Source: World Bank staff and IDS.

Table A 16. Gross Output by Sector CARIFORUM for GLOBE Model Experiments
(Closure: Balanced Macro closure, Factor Tax Adjustment, Unemployed Unskilled Labor)

Trade Policy Scenarios — % Change on Reference Equilibrium	CARIB 1 — EU Tariff Elimination for CARIFORUM	CARIB 2 — Bilateral Tariff Reduction 2013	CARIB 3 — Bilateral Tariff Reduction 2023	CARIB 4 — Bilateral Tariff Reduction 2033	CARIB 5 — Bilateral Tariff Redux 2033 inc Sugar	CARIB 6 — 10% TFP Rise in CARIFORUM Services	CARIB 7 — CARIB 4 plus CARIB 6	CARIB 8 — CARIFORUM Service Barrier Reduction	CARIB 9 — EU Service Barrier Reduction	CARIB 10 — Combined Service Liberalization	CARIB 11 — Goods and Services Liberalization
Vegetables fruit nuts	4.39	4.39	4.36	4.36	4.06	1.93	6.19	−0.08	0.14	1.98	6.24
Sugar cane and sugar beet	−0.04	0.02	0.15	0.16	21.90	3.94	4.09	0.10	−0.01	4.02	4.17
Other agriculture	−0.03	−0.01	0.04	0.04	1.32	3.81	3.84	0.01	0.08	3.90	3.93
Forestry and fishing	−0.11	−0.09	−0.07	−0.07	0.01	2.94	2.86	−0.02	0.08	2.99	2.92
Minerals	−0.96	−0.76	−0.17	−0.13	−2.35	1.69	1.54	0.53	−0.53	1.66	1.52
Beverages and tobacco	0.02	0.04	0.08	0.09	0.28	4.34	4.43	0.00	0.08	4.43	4.52
Sugar	−0.12	−0.05	0.12	0.14	43.03	3.16	3.29	0.09	−0.07	3.18	3.31
Other food products	0.11	0.12	0.10	0.10	0.09	4.27	4.36	−0.03	0.13	4.37	4.46
Textiles apparel leather	−0.09	0.05	0.42	0.45	−0.03	4.54	5.00	0.27	−0.25	4.54	5.01
Petroleum coal products	−0.17	−0.17	−0.19	−0.18	−0.53	3.69	3.49	0.09	0.01	3.78	3.59
Chemicals rubber plastic	−0.03	0.00	0.10	0.07	−0.24	5.34	5.42	0.31	−0.21	5.43	5.51
Metals	−0.19	−0.19	0.09	0.14	−0.72	4.80	4.97	0.52	−0.46	4.84	5.00

Transport equipment and machinery	-0.13	0.00	0.19	0.24	-0.48	3.85	4.11	0.43	-0.42	3.84	4.09
Electronic Equipment	-0.17	0.20	1.03	1.10	0.16	5.62	6.80	0.59	-0.57	5.62	6.79
Utilities and construction	0.00	0.00	0.04	0.04	0.03	1.22	1.27	0.03	0.01	1.27	1.31
Transport and communication	0.02	0.05	0.13	0.13	0.13	9.22	9.36	0.02	0.06	9.30	9.45
Financial and business services	0.01	0.05	0.18	0.18	0.17	8.07	8.27	-0.03	0.34	8.41	8.62
Recreation and other services	0.02	0.05	0.15	0.15	0.09	10.75	10.93	0.04	1.34	12.33	12.52
Public services	0.05	0.04	0.00	0.00	0.09	4.02	4.02	-0.02	0.10	4.10	4.10

Source: World Bank staff and IDS.

Table A17. Total Exports by Sector CARIFORUM for GLOBE Model Experiments (Closure: Balanced Macro closure, Factor Tax Adjustment, Unemployed Unskilled labor)

Trade Policy Scenarios % Change on Reference Equilibrium	CARIB 1 EU Tariff Elimination for CARIFORUM	CARIB 2 Bilateral Tariff Reduction 2013	CARIB 3 Bilateral Tariff Reduction 2023	CARIB 4 Bilateral Tariff Reduction 2033	CARIB 5 Bilateral Tariff Redux 2033 inc Sugar	CARIB 6 10% TFP Rise in CARIFORUM Services	CARIB 7 CARIB 4 plus CARIB 6	CARIB 8 CARIFORUM Service Barrier Reduction	CARIB 9 EU Service Barrier Reduction	CARIB 10 Combined Service Liberalization	CARIB 11 Goods and Services Liberalization
Vegetables fruit nuts	13.80	13.86	14.01	14.03	13.14	0.51	14.45	0.04	−0.04	0.51	14.44
Sugar cane and sugar beet	1.03	1.15	1.46	1.49	17.40	2.34	3.83	0.21	−0.18	2.35	3.84
Other agriculture	−0.34	−0.24	0.01	0.04	0.04	1.47	1.49	0.16	−0.16	1.47	1.49
Forestry and fishing	−0.28	−0.21	−0.07	−0.06	−0.56	0.89	0.82	0.07	−0.09	0.87	0.80
Minerals	−1.41	−1.08	−0.17	−0.10	−3.37	−0.37	−0.50	0.72	−0.80	−0.49	−0.62
Beverages and tobacco	−0.01	0.06	0.21	0.23	0.24	3.40	3.63	0.10	−0.05	3.44	3.67
Sugar	−0.26	−0.10	0.29	0.32	89.77	1.76	2.08	0.26	−0.31	1.70	2.01
Other food products	1.02	1.12	1.36	1.38	0.91	3.53	4.93	0.18	−0.13	3.57	4.97
Textiles apparel leather	−0.18	0.08	0.78	0.84	−0.08	3.72	4.59	0.48	−0.55	3.62	4.49
Petroleum coal products	−0.28	−0.24	−0.15	−0.12	−0.76	2.42	2.28	0.15	−0.10	2.47	2.33
Chemicals rubber plastic	−0.13	0.06	0.56	0.59	−0.14	5.03	5.65	0.50	−0.46	5.05	5.67

Metals	−0.25	−0.01	0.73	0.80	−0.36	4.88	5.74	0.67	−0.65	4.87	5.72
Transport equipment and machinery	−0.19	0.15	0.99	1.06	0.02	3.64	4.75	0.59	−0.64	3.55	4.66
Electronic Equipment	−0.23	0.30	1.66	1.76	0.50	5.65	7.53	0.77	−0.79	5.60	7.47
Utilities and construction	−0.09	0.05	0.43	0.46	0.03	1.43	1.90	0.22	−0.24	1.40	1.87
Transport and communication	−0.05	0.06	0.33	0.35	0.05	10.59	10.99	0.19	−0.15	10.63	11.03
Financial and business services	−0.06	0.06	0.37	0.39	0.05	10.10	10.54	0.16	1.56	12.00	12.45
Recreation and other services	−0.05	0.06	0.36	0.38	0.01	12.38	12.81	0.20	3.76	16.88	17.34
Public services	−0.02	0.05	0.26	0.28	0.03	3.40	3.68	0.17	−0.15	3.41	3.69

Source: World Bank staff and IDS.

Table A18. Total Imports by Sector CARIFORUM for GLOBE Model Experiments (Closure: Balanced Macro Closure, Factor Tax Adjustment Unemployed Unskilled Labor)

Trade Policy Scenarios % Change on Reference Equilibrium	CARIB 1 EU Tariff Elimination for CARIFORUM	CARIB 2 Bilateral Tariff Reduction 2013	CARIB 3 Bilateral Tariff Reduction 2023	CARIB 4 Bilateral Tariff Reduction 2033	CARIB 5 Bilateral Tariff Redux 2033 inc Sugar	CARIB 6 10% TFP Rise in CARIFORUM Services	CARIB 7 CARIB 4 plus CARIB 6	CARIB 8 CARIFORUM Service Barrier Reduction	CARIB 9 EU Service Barrier Reduction	CARIB 10 Combined Service Liberalization	CARIB 11 Goods and Services Liberalization
Vegetables fruit nuts	−0.09	0.05	−0.07	−0.07	0.52	2.80	2.72	−0.20	0.31	2.92	2.84
Sugar cane and sugar beet	0.32	0.28	0.15	0.12	14.16	3.32	3.45	−0.10	0.20	3.43	3.56
Other agriculture	0.40	0.45	0.29	0.29	2.25	4.06	4.37	−0.17	0.30	4.21	4.51
Forestry and fishing	0.17	0.27	0.25	0.53	1.27	3.42	3.96	−0.12	0.23	3.53	4.08
Minerals	0.49	0.37	0.05	0.05	1.14	4.54	4.60	−0.15	0.30	4.71	4.77
Beverages and tobacco	0.07	0.03	−0.11	−0.12	0.23	3.35	3.22	−0.13	0.22	3.45	3.33
Sugar	0.21	0.09	−0.25	−0.28	−7.23	3.44	3.15	−0.27	0.42	3.61	3.32
Other food products	0.13	0.08	−0.08	0.00	0.58	2.59	2.59	−0.27	0.39	2.72	2.71
Textiles apparel leather	0.12	0.12	0.05	0.04	0.55	2.85	2.89	−0.24	0.39	3.01	3.06
Petroleum coal products	0.14	0.24	0.49	0.48	0.84	3.83	4.32	−0.08	0.20	3.96	4.45
Chemicals rubber plastic	0.14	0.42	1.06	1.22	1.71	2.43	3.68	−0.17	0.31	2.58	3.83

Metals	0.03	0.52	1.12	1.13	1.28	1.59	2.74	−0.05	0.13	1.67	2.83
Transport equipment and machinery	0.07	0.19	0.65	0.64	0.98	1.62	2.28	−0.15	0.27	1.75	2.41
Electronic Equipment	0.07	0.06	0.22	0.21	0.53	1.80	2.01	−0.15	0.25	1.90	2.11
Utilities and construction	0.09	1.07	0.73	0.70	1.13	0.21	0.91	−0.19	0.27	0.29	1.00
Transport and communication	0.09	0.01	−0.21	−0.23	0.15	1.75	1.51	2.52	0.29	4.62	4.38
Financial and business services	0.08	0.02	−0.16	−0.17	0.20	0.83	0.65	1.33	0.26	2.44	2.26
Recreation and other services	0.09	0.01	−0.22	−0.24	0.14	2.04	1.79	1.40	0.25	3.73	3.47
Public services	0.10	0.00	−0.27	−0.29	0.09	2.16	1.86	−0.20	0.30	2.26	1.97

Source: World Bank staff and IDS.

Table A19. CARIFORUM Imports by Region of Origin for GLOBE Model Experiments (Closure: Balanced Macro Closure, Factor Tax Adjustment, Unemployed Unskilled Labor: United States)

Trade Policy Scenarios	CARIB 1	CARIB 2	CARIB 3	CARIB 4	CARIB 5	CARIB 6	CARIB 7	CARIB 8	CARIB 9	CARIB 10	CARIB 11
% Change on Reference Equilibrium	EU Tariff Elimination for CARIFORUM	Bilateral Tariff Reduction 2013	Bilateral Tariff Reduction 2023	Bilateral Tariff Reduction 2033	Bilateral Tariff Redux 2033 inc Sugar	10% TFP Rise in CARIFORUM Services	CARIB 4 plus CARIB 6	CARIFORUM Service Barrier Reduction	EU Service Barrier Reduction	Combined Service Liberalization	Goods and Services Liberalization
Vegetables fruit nuts	0.15	−0.09	−0.43	−0.46	0.20	2.80	2.32	−0.21	0.32	2.92	2.44
Sugar cane and sugar beet	0.33	0.26	0.09	0.07	13.80	3.28	3.35	−0.10	0.20	3.39	3.46
Other agriculture	0.40	0.23	−0.04	−0.08	1.86	3.99	3.91	−0.17	0.30	4.13	4.05
Forestry and fishing	0.17	0.04	−0.17	−0.36	0.36	3.10	2.73	−0.11	0.22	3.21	2.84
Minerals	0.63	0.39	−0.15	−0.21	1.40	5.29	5.09	−0.21	0.39	5.50	5.29
Beverages and tobacco	0.08	0.01	−0.16	−0.18	0.12	2.64	2.46	−0.15	0.24	2.74	2.56
Sugar	0.22	0.09	−0.27	−0.30	−7.13	3.42	3.11	−0.28	0.43	3.59	3.28
Other food products	0.17	0.00	−0.44	−0.53	0.07	2.31	1.76	−0.29	0.40	2.43	1.88
Textiles apparel leather	0.13	−0.11	−0.70	−0.74	−0.19	2.73	1.96	−0.25	0.41	2.89	2.13
Petroleum coal products	0.18	−0.02	−0.52	−0.54	−0.01	3.60	3.05	−0.10	0.22	3.73	3.17
Chemicals rubber plastic	0.14	−0.38	−1.63	−1.86	−1.34	2.17	0.27	−0.20	0.33	2.31	0.41

Metals	0.04	−0.81	−2.13	−2.16	−1.95	1.41	−0.77	−0.07	0.15	1.50	−0.69
Transport equipment and machinery	0.07	−0.52	−2.37	−2.41	−2.07	1.57	−0.87	−0.15	0.27	1.70	−0.75
Electronic equipment	0.07	−0.22	−1.55	−1.57	−1.23	1.76	0.16	−0.16	0.25	1.86	0.26
Utilities and construction	0.09	−0.56	−0.90	−0.92	−0.50	0.21	−0.72	−0.20	0.28	0.30	−0.63
Transport and communication	0.09	0.01	−0.21	−0.22	0.15	1.65	1.42	−1.86	0.29	0.06	−0.17
Financial and business services	0.07	0.02	−0.15	−0.16	0.19	0.79	0.62	−1.17	0.26	−0.14	−0.30
Recreation and other services	0.09	0.01	−0.22	−0.24	0.14	1.78	1.53	−1.18	0.28	0.87	0.62
Public services	0.10	0.00	−0.26	−0.28	0.10	2.14	1.85	−0.20	0.30	2.24	1.95

Source: World Bank staff and IDS.

Table A20. **CARIFORUM Imports by Region of Origin for GLOBE Model Experiments (Closure: Balanced Macro Closure, Factor Tax Adjustment, Unemployed Unskilled Labor: EU15)**

Trade Policy Scenarios % Change on Reference Equilibrium	CARIB 1 EU Tariff Elimination for CARIFORUM	CARIB 2 Bilateral Tariff Reduction 2013	CARIB 3 Bilateral Tariff Reduction 2023	CARIB 4 Bilateral Tariff Reduction 2033	CARIB 5 Bilateral Tariff Redux 2033 inc Sugar	CARIB 6 10% TFP Rise in CARIFORUM Services	CARIB 7 CARIB 4 plus CARIB 6	CARIB 8 CARIFORUM Service Barrier Reduction	CARIB 9 EU Service Barrier Reduction	CARIB 10 Combined Service Liberalization	CARIB 11 Goods and Services Liberalization
Vegetables fruit nuts	0.15	4.10	6.15	6.43	7.18	2.82	9.42	−0.21	0.32	2.94	9.55
Sugar cane and sugar beet	0.37	7.30	20.19	20.16	34.44	3.64	24.53	−0.12	0.23	3.76	24.67
Other agriculture	0.42	7.36	10.55	11.89	14.28	4.14	16.52	−0.18	0.32	4.29	16.68
Forestry and fishing	0.19	2.39	4.22	8.92	9.79	3.36	12.58	−0.13	0.24	3.48	12.71
Minerals	0.64	6.58	13.41	16.59	18.57	5.24	22.70	−0.22	0.40	5.43	22.93
Beverages and tobacco	0.08	0.03	−0.14	−0.16	0.29	2.62	2.46	−0.15	0.24	2.72	2.55
Sugar	0.22	0.08	−0.29	−0.32	−5.82	3.37	3.04	−0.28	0.43	3.53	3.20
Other food products	0.19	0.71	1.84	2.83	3.68	2.43	5.33	−0.31	0.42	2.55	5.45
Textiles apparel leather	0.13	2.63	8.32	8.60	9.29	2.76	11.59	−0.26	0.42	2.93	11.78
Petroleum coal products	0.19	7.95	28.41	28.39	29.11	3.66	33.07	−0.11	0.23	3.78	33.23
Chemicals rubber plastic	0.15	3.28	10.72	12.35	13.03	2.17	14.78	−0.21	0.34	2.31	14.94

Metals	0.05	6.28	15.23	15.42	15.77	1.40	17.04	−0.08	0.16	1.49	17.14
Transport equipment and machinery	0.07	2.30	9.75	9.84	10.33	1.59	11.59	−0.16	0.28	1.72	11.73
Electronic equipment	0.08	2.69	17.14	17.18	17.72	1.78	19.27	−0.17	0.26	1.88	19.38
Utilities and construction	0.09	2.77	2.42	2.39	2.85	0.20	2.59	−0.20	0.27	0.29	2.68
Transport and communication	0.09	0.01	−0.22	−0.24	0.17	1.65	1.41	8.46	0.29	10.58	10.31
Financial and business services	0.08	0.01	−0.16	−0.18	0.21	0.79	0.60	3.75	0.26	4.85	4.65
Recreation and other services	0.09	0.01	−0.24	−0.26	0.15	1.78	1.52	3.74	0.27	5.89	5.62
Public services	0.10	0.00	−0.28	−0.30	0.10	2.14	1.84	−0.21	0.30	2.24	1.94

Source: World Bank staff and IDS.

Table A21. CARIFORUM Exports by Region of Destination for GLOBE Model Experiments (Closure: Balanced Macro Closure, Factor Tax Adjustment, Unemployed Unskilled Labor: United States)

Trade Policy Scenarios % Change on Reference Equilibrium	CARIB 1 EU Tariff Elimination for CARIFORUM	CARIB 2 Bilateral Tariff Reduction 2013	CARIB 3 Bilateral Tariff Reduction 2023	CARIB 4 Bilateral Tariff Reduction 2033	CARIB 5 Bilateral Tariff Redux 2033 inc Sugar	CARIB 6 10% TFP Rise in CARIFORUM Services	CARIB 7 CARIB 4 plus CARIB 6	CARIB 8 CARIFORUM Service Barrier Reduction	CARIB 9 EU Service Barrier Reduction	CARIB 10 Combined Service Liberalization	CARIB 11 Goods and Services Liberalization
Vegetables fruit nuts	-2.79	-2.73	-2.61	-2.59	-3.30	0.33	-2.37	0.04	-0.05	0.32	-2.38
Sugar cane and sugar beet	-1.11	-0.96	-0.59	-0.56	10.83	1.38	0.80	0.25	-0.26	1.36	0.78
Other agriculture	-0.43	-0.33	-0.07	-0.04	-0.14	1.28	1.22	0.17	-0.16	1.27	1.22
Forestry and fishing	-0.25	-0.19	-0.06	-0.05	-0.51	0.74	0.68	0.07	-0.08	0.72	0.66
Minerals	-1.48	-1.13	-0.17	-0.10	-3.52	-0.66	-0.78	0.74	-0.84	-0.79	-0.91
Beverages and tobacco	-0.05	0.03	0.20	0.22	0.19	3.05	3.27	0.11	-0.08	3.08	3.30
Sugar	-0.25	-0.11	0.27	0.30	3.73	1.71	2.01	0.25	-0.30	1.64	1.94
Other food products	-0.54	-0.41	-0.08	-0.05	-0.62	2.91	2.85	0.24	-0.22	2.91	2.85
Textiles apparel leather	-0.19	0.08	0.80	0.86	-0.07	3.62	4.51	0.49	-0.57	3.51	4.40
Petroleum coal products	-0.33	-0.24	-0.02	0.01	-0.78	1.51	1.51	0.18	-0.16	1.53	1.53
Chemicals rubber plastic	-0.14	0.08	0.67	0.70	-0.06	4.86	5.61	0.51	-0.48	4.87	5.62

Metals	−0.25	0.02	0.80	0.87	−0.29	4.82	5.75	0.67	−0.65	4.81	5.74
Transport equipment and machinery	−0.19	0.15	1.01	1.08	0.05	3.57	4.70	0.58	−0.64	3.48	4.61
Electronic equipment	−0.23	0.30	1.67	1.76	0.52	5.60	7.49	0.76	−0.78	5.54	7.42
Utilities and construction	−0.09	0.05	0.44	0.47	0.03	1.49	1.97	0.23	−0.25	1.46	1.94
Transport and communication	−0.05	0.06	0.34	0.36	0.04	10.85	11.25	0.20	−0.16	10.89	11.30
Financial and business services	−0.06	0.06	0.36	0.39	0.05	10.10	10.54	0.16	−0.92	9.27	9.71
Recreation and other services	−0.05	0.06	0.35	0.37	0.00	12.33	12.76	0.20	−1.12	11.34	11.77
Public services	−0.02	0.05	0.26	0.27	0.02	3.38	3.67	0.17	−0.15	3.39	3.68

Source: World Bank staff and IDS.

Table A22. CARIFORUM Exports by Region of Destination for GLOBE Model Experiments (Closure: Balanced Macro Closure, Factor Tax Adjustment, Unemployed Unskilled Labor: EU15)

Trade Policy Scenarios	CARIB 1	CARIB 2	CARIB 3	CARIB 4	CARIB 5	CARIB 6	CARIB 7	CARIB 8	CARIB 9	CARIB 10	CARIB 11
% Change on Reference Equilibrium	EU Tariff Elimination for CARIFORUM	Bilateral Tariff Reduction 2013	Bilateral Tariff Reduction 2023	Bilateral Tariff Reduction 2033	Bilateral Tariff Redux 2033 inc Sugar	10% TFP Rise in CARIFORUM Services	CARIB 4 plus CARIB 6	CARIFORUM Service Barrier Reduction	EU Service Barrier Reduction	Combined Service Liberalization	Goods and Services Liberalization
Vegetables fruit nuts	24.93	25.01	25.20	25.23	24.18	0.35	25.53	0.05	−0.06	0.34	25.51
Sugar cane and sugar beet	22.28	22.47	22.95	22.99	32.84	1.35	24.65	0.26	−0.26	1.34	24.63
Other agriculture	−0.10	0.01	0.30	0.33	0.20	1.31	1.63	0.18	−0.17	1.30	1.62
Forestry and fishing	−0.31	−0.23	−0.05	−0.04	−0.64	0.90	0.85	0.09	−0.11	0.87	0.82
Minerals	−1.53	−1.16	−0.14	−0.06	−3.64	−0.71	−0.79	0.78	−0.87	−0.84	−0.92
Beverages and tobacco	0.03	0.10	0.29	0.31	0.26	3.06	3.38	0.12	−0.08	3.09	3.41
Sugar	−0.26	−0.10	0.30	0.34	128.68	1.74	2.07	0.26	−0.31	1.67	2.00
Other food products	8.42	8.58	8.99	9.03	8.22	3.10	12.39	0.26	−0.24	3.10	12.40
Textiles apparel leather	−0.19	0.09	0.84	0.90	−0.11	3.64	4.58	0.50	−0.58	3.54	4.47
Petroleum coal products	−0.33	−0.24	0.00	0.02	−0.80	1.52	1.54	0.19	−0.16	1.54	1.55
Chemicals rubber plastic	−0.14	0.09	0.70	0.74	−0.08	4.93	5.72	0.53	−0.50	4.94	5.73

Metals	−0.26	0.02	0.84	0.91	−0.30	4.85	5.83	0.68	−0.66	4.84	5.81
	−0.20	0.16	1.04	1.11	0.02	3.59	4.76	0.59	−0.65	3.51	4.67
Transport equipment and machinery											
Electronic equipment	−0.24	0.30	1.71	1.80	0.48	5.62	7.54	0.77	−0.79	5.56	7.48
Utilities and construction	−0.09	0.05	0.44	0.47	0.01	1.43	1.92	0.23	−0.25	1.40	1.89
Transport and communication	−0.05	0.06	0.35	0.37	0.03	10.84	11.26	0.21	−0.16	10.89	11.31
Financial and business services	−0.06	0.06	0.38	0.40	0.04	10.10	10.55	0.16	4.02	14.71	15.18
Recreation and other services	−0.05	0.06	0.37	0.39	−0.01	12.37	12.82	0.21	9.19	22.99	23.48
Public services	−0.02	0.06	0.27	0.29	0.00	3.38	3.68	0.17	−0.15	3.39	3.69

Source: World Bank staff and IDS.

Tables for Sales Tax Adjustment Seenarrios

Table A23. Macro Results for GLOBE Model Experiments (Closure: Balanced Macro Closure, Sales Tax Adjustment, Unemployed Unskilled Labor)

Trade Policy Scenarios / % Change on Reference Equilibrium	CARIB 1 — EU Tariff Elimination for CARIFORUM	CARIB 2 — Bilateral Tariff Reduction 2013	CARIB 3 — Bilateral Tariff Reduction 2023	CARIB 4 — Bilateral Tariff Reduction 2033	CARIB 5 — Bilateral Tariff Redux 2033 inc Sugar	CARIB 6 — 10% TFP Rise in CARIFORUM Services	CARIB 7 — CARIB 4 plus CARIB 6	CARIB 8 — CARIFORUM Service Barrier Reduction	CARIB 9 — EU Service Barrier Reduction	CARIB 10 — Combined Service Liberalization	CARIB 11 — Goods and Services Liberalization
Absorption	0.06	0.01	−0.13	−0.14	−0.01	4.85	4.70	−0.09	0.16	4.92	4.77
Import Demand	0.11	0.16	0.24	0.25	0.68	2.25	2.50	0.02	0.28	2.56	2.81
Export Supply	−0.03	0.09	0.38	0.40	0.42	5.97	6.38	0.23	−0.03	6.18	6.59
GDP	0.02	−0.01	−0.10	−0.11	−0.08	2.28	2.16	−0.04	0.07	2.31	2.19
Unskilled Labor Employment	0.07	−0.02	−0.28	−0.29	−0.20	6.33	6.01	−0.11	0.21	6.43	6.11

Source: World Bank staff and IDS.

Table A24. Gross Output by Sector CARIFORUM for GLOBE Model Experiments (Closure: Balanced Macro Closure, Sales Tax Adjustment, Unemployed Unskilled Labor)

Trade Policy Scenarios % Change on Reference Equilibrium	CARIB 1 EU Tariff Elimination for CARIFORUM	CARIB 2 Bilateral Tariff Reduction 2013	CARIB 3 Bilateral Tariff Reduction 2023	CARIB 4 Bilateral Tariff Reduction 2033	CARIB 5 Bilateral Tariff Redux 2033 inc Sugar	CARIB 6 10% TFP Rise in CARIFORUM Services	CARIB 7 CARIB 4 plus CARIB 6	CARIB 8 CARIFORUM Service Barrier Reduction	CARIB 9 EU Service Barrier Reduction	CARIB 10 Combined Service Liberalization	CARIB 11 Goods and Services Liberalization
Vegetables fruit nuts	4.38	4.25	3.87	3.85	3.52	2.02	5.78	−0.32	0.13	1.84	5.59
Sugar cane and sugar beet	−0.05	−0.08	−0.21	−0.21	21.52	4.01	3.78	−0.07	−0.02	3.90	3.67
Other agriculture	−0.04	−0.13	−0.38	−0.39	0.87	3.89	3.48	−0.18	0.07	3.77	3.36
Forestry and fishing	−0.11	−0.12	−0.18	−0.19	−0.12	2.96	2.76	−0.08	0.08	2.96	2.76
Minerals	−0.96	−0.76	−0.16	−0.12	−2.35	1.69	1.58	0.53	−0.53	1.68	1.56
Beverages & tobacco.	−0.01	−0.24	−0.92	−0.96	−0.84	4.55	3.54	−0.48	0.06	4.10	3.11
Sugar	−0.13	−0.12	−0.13	−0.12	42.77	3.21	3.07	−0.03	−0.07	3.10	2.97
Other food products	0.10	−0.03	−0.42	−0.45	−0.49	4.37	3.90	−0.27	0.11	4.21	3.74
Textiles apparel leather	−0.10	−0.06	0.00	0.01	−0.50	4.62	4.63	0.07	−0.26	4.41	4.41
Petroleum coal products	−0.18	−0.24	−0.43	−0.43	−0.79	3.73	3.29	−0.02	0.00	3.71	3.26
Chemicals rubber plastic	−0.04	−0.12	−0.31	−0.36	−0.70	5.42	5.04	0.11	−0.22	5.29	4.91

(Continued)

Table A24. Gross Output by Sector CARIFORUM for GLOBE Model Experiments (Closure: Balanced Macro Closure, Sales Tax Adjustment, Unemployed Unskilled Labor) (*Continued*)

Trade Policy Scenarios	CARIB 1	CARIB 2	CARIB 3	CARIB 4	CARIB 5	CARIB 6	CARIB 7	CARIB 8	CARIB 9	CARIB 10	CARIB 11
% Change on Reference Equilibrium	EU Tariff Elimination for CARIFORUM	Bilateral Tariff Reduction 2013	Bilateral Tariff Reduction 2023	Bilateral Tariff Reduction 2033	Bilateral Tariff Redux 2033 inc Sugar	10% TFP Rise in CARIFORUM Services	CARIB 4 plus CARIB 6	CARIFORUM Service Barrier Reduction	EU Service Barrier Reduction	Combined Service Liberalization	Goods and Services Liberalization
Metals	−0.20	−0.31	−0.34	−0.31	−1.19	4.89	4.58	0.31	−0.48	4.70	4.38
Transport eq. and machinery	−0.14	−0.12	−0.23	−0.20	−0.94	3.93	3.73	0.23	−0.43	3.70	3.49
Electronic eq.	−0.19	0.02	0.36	0.40	−0.57	5.76	6.19	0.28	−0.59	5.39	5.83
Utilities and construction	−0.01	−0.02	−0.04	−0.04	−0.06	1.24	1.20	−0.01	0.01	1.24	1.20
Transport & comm.	0.01	−0.03	−0.15	−0.16	−0.18	9.28	9.10	−0.11	0.05	9.21	9.03
Financial & business services	0.00	−0.02	−0.11	−0.11	−0.15	8.12	8.01	−0.16	0.33	8.32	8.20
Recreation and other services	0.01	0.01	0.00	0.00	−0.08	10.78	10.79	−0.03	1.33	12.28	12.30
Public services	0.05	0.02	−0.08	−0.09	0.00	4.04	3.94	−0.06	0.10	4.07	3.98

Source: World Bank staff and IDS.

Table A25. Total Exports by Sector CARIFORUM for GLOBE Model Experiments (Closure: Balanced Macro Closure, Sales Tax Adjustment, Unemployed Unskilled Labor)

Trade Policy Scenarios / % Change on Reference Equilibrium	CARIB 1 EU Tariff Elimination for CARIFORUM	CARIB 2 Bilateral Tariff Reduction 2013	CARIB 3 Bilateral Tariff Reduction 2023	CARIB 4 Bilateral Tariff Reduction 2033	CARIB 5 Bilateral Tariff Redux 2033 inc Sugar	CARIB 6 10% TFP Rise in CARIFORUM Services	CARIB 7 CARIB 4 plus CARIB 6	CARIB 8 CARIFORUM Service Barrier Reduction	CARIB 9 EU Service Barrier Reduction	CARIB 10 Combined Service Liberalization	CARIB 11 Goods and Services Liberalization
Vegetables fruit nuts	13.79	13.77	13.69	13.70	12.80	0.57	14.20	−0.11	−0.04	0.42	14.03
Sugar cane and sugar beet	1.02	1.09	1.24	1.26	17.17	2.38	3.65	0.10	−0.19	2.29	3.55
Other agriculture	−0.35	−0.30	−0.18	−0.17	−0.17	1.50	1.34	0.07	−0.16	1.41	1.24
Forestry and fishing	−0.28	−0.21	−0.06	−0.05	−0.55	0.89	0.84	0.07	−0.09	0.87	0.83
Minerals	−1.41	−1.02	0.06	0.14	−3.12	−0.42	−0.26	0.83	−0.79	−0.40	−0.24
Beverages and tobacco	−0.03	−0.17	−0.57	−0.59	−0.63	3.55	2.94	−0.28	−0.07	3.18	2.57
Sugar	−0.26	−0.15	0.14	0.17	89.57	1.79	1.96	0.18	−0.31	1.65	1.82
Other food products	1.00	0.98	0.87	0.86	0.36	3.63	4.51	−0.06	−0.15	3.41	4.29
Textiles apparel leather	−0.19	−0.04	0.35	0.39	−0.55	3.80	4.21	0.28	−0.56	3.48	3.88
Petroleum coal products	−0.29	−0.28	−0.29	−0.28	−0.91	2.45	2.16	0.08	−0.10	2.43	2.14
Chemicals rubber plastic	−0.14	−0.06	0.14	0.14	−0.60	5.12	5.26	0.30	−0.47	4.91	5.05

(Continued)

Table A25. Total Exports by Sector CARIFORUM for GLOBE Model Experiments (Closure: Balanced Macro Closure, Sales Tax Adjustment, Unemployed Unskilled Labor) (*Continued*)

Trade Policy Scenarios	CARIB 1	CARIB 2	CARIB 3	CARIB 4	CARIB 5	CARIB 6	CARIB 7	CARIB 8	CARIB 9	CARIB 10	CARIB 11
% Change on Reference Equilibrium	EU Tariff Elimination for CARIFORUM	Bilateral Tariff Reduction 2013	Bilateral Tariff Reduction 2023	Bilateral Tariff Reduction 2033	Bilateral Tariff Redux 2033 inc Sugar	10% TFP Rise in CARIFORUM Services	CARIB 4 plus CARIB 6	CARIFORUM Service Barrier Reduction	EU Service Barrier Reduction	Combined Service Liberalization	Goods and Services Liberalization
Metals	−0.26	−0.13	0.31	0.36	−0.83	4.97	5.36	0.47	−0.66	4.73	5.12
Transport equipment and machinery	−0.21	0.02	0.52	0.56	−0.50	3.73	4.32	0.36	−0.66	3.40	3.98
Electronic Equipment	−0.25	0.09	0.94	0.99	−0.30	5.80	6.87	0.42	−0.81	5.35	6.41
Utilities and construction	−0.09	0.01	0.31	0.34	−0.10	1.45	1.79	0.17	−0.25	1.36	1.70
Transport and communication	−0.05	−0.02	0.07	0.08	−0.24	10.65	10.74	0.07	−0.16	10.54	10.62
Financial and business services	−0.06	−0.01	0.14	0.15	−0.21	10.15	10.32	0.05	1.55	11.92	12.09
Recreation and other services	−0.05	0.02	0.22	0.23	−0.15	12.41	12.68	0.14	3.76	16.82	17.11
Public services	−0.03	0.02	0.13	0.14	−0.11	3.42	3.57	0.11	−0.15	3.36	3.51

Source: World Bank staff and IDS.

Table A26. Total Imports by Sector CARIFORUM for GLOBE Model Experiments (Closure: Balanced Macro Closure, Sales Tax Adjustment, Unemployed Unskilled Labor)

Trade Policy Scenarios	CARIB 1	CARIB 2	CARIB 3	CARIB 4	CARIB 5	CARIB 6	CARIB 7	CARIB 8	CARIB 9	CARIB 10	CARIB 11
% Change on Reference Equilibrium	EU Tariff Elimination for CARIFORUM	Bilateral Tariff Reduction 2013	Bilateral Tariff Reduction 2023	Bilateral Tariff Reduction 2033	Bilateral Tariff Redux 2033 inc Sugar	10% TFP Rise in CARIFORUM Services	CARIB 4 plus CARIB 6	CARIFORUM Service Barrier Reduction	EU Service Barrier Reduction	Combined Service Liberalization	Goods and Services Liberalization
Vegetables fruit nuts	−0.10	−0.08	−0.55	−0.57	−0.01	2.90	2.30	−0.43	0.30	2.77	2.18
Sugar cane and sugar beet	0.32	0.20	−0.15	−0.18	13.85	3.38	3.18	−0.24	0.19	3.33	3.13
Other agriculture	0.39	0.34	−0.11	−0.12	1.80	4.14	4.01	−0.36	0.29	4.08	3.94
Forestry and fishing	0.17	0.22	0.06	0.33	1.06	3.46	3.79	−0.21	0.23	3.47	3.80
Minerals	0.48	0.26	−0.36	−0.38	0.68	4.63	4.21	−0.34	0.29	4.57	4.16
Beverages and tobacco	0.05	−0.19	−0.89	−0.94	−0.64	3.51	2.54	−0.50	0.20	3.20	2.24
Sugar	0.20	0.01	−0.51	−0.55	−7.49	3.50	2.92	−0.39	0.41	3.52	2.95
Other food products	0.13	0.02	−0.32	−0.25	0.31	2.64	2.38	−0.39	0.38	2.64	2.38
Textiles apparel leather	0.12	0.08	−0.08	−0.10	0.40	2.87	2.77	−0.30	0.39	2.97	2.87
Petroleum coal products	0.13	0.16	0.22	0.19	0.55	3.88	4.08	−0.21	0.19	3.87	4.07
Chemicals rubber plastic	0.13	0.38	0.91	1.07	1.55	2.46	3.56	−0.24	0.30	2.53	3.63

(Continued)

Table A26. Total Imports by Sector CARIFORUM for GLOBE Model Experiments (Closure: Balanced Macro Closure, Sales Tax Adjustment, Unemployed Unskilled Labor) (*Continued*)

Trade Policy Scenarios / % Change on Reference Equilibrium	CARIB 1 EU Tariff Elimination for CARIFORUM	CARIB 2 Bilateral Tariff Reduction 2013	CARIB 3 Bilateral Tariff Reduction 2023	CARIB 4 Bilateral Tariff Reduction 2033	CARIB 5 Bilateral Tariff Redux 2033 inc Sugar	CARIB 6 10% TFP Rise in CARIFORUM Services	CARIB 7 CARIB 4 plus CARIB 6	CARIB 8 CARIFORUM Service Barrier Reduction	CARIB 9 EU Service Barrier Reduction	CARIB 10 Combined Service Liberalization	CARIB 11 Goods and Services Liberalization
Metals	0.03	0.47	0.95	0.95	1.09	1.62	2.59	−0.13	0.12	1.61	2.59
Transport equipment and machinery	0.07	0.17	0.59	0.59	0.93	1.63	2.23	−0.17	0.27	1.73	2.33
Electronic Equipment	0.07	0.03	0.12	0.10	0.42	1.82	1.92	−0.20	0.24	1.87	1.97
Utilities and construction	0.09	1.07	0.74	0.72	1.14	0.21	0.92	−0.19	0.27	0.30	1.02
Transport and communication	0.09	−0.02	−0.33	−0.35	0.01	1.77	1.41	2.46	0.28	4.58	4.21
Financial and business services	0.07	−0.03	−0.32	−0.35	0.01	0.86	0.51	1.25	0.25	2.39	2.03
Recreation and other services	0.09	−0.01	−0.29	−0.31	0.07	2.05	1.73	1.36	0.25	3.71	3.39
Public services	0.10	0.01	−0.25	−0.27	0.11	2.16	1.88	−0.20	0.30	2.27	1.98

Source: World Bank staff and IDS.

Table A27. CARIFORUM Imports by Region of Origin for GLOBE Model Experiments (Closure: Balanced Macro Closure, Sales Tax Adjustment, Unemployed Unskilled Labor: United States of America)

Trade Policy Scenarios	CARIB 1	CARIB 2	CARIB 3	CARIB 4	CARIB 5	CARIB 6	CARIB 7	CARIB 8	CARIB 9	CARIB 10	CARIB 11
% Change on Reference Equilibrium	EU Tariff Elimination for CARIFORUM	Bilateral Tariff Reduction 2013	Bilateral Tariff Reduction 2023	Bilateral Tariff Reduction 2033	Bilateral Tariff Redux 2033 inc Sugar	10% TFP Rise in CARIFORUM Services	CARIB 4 plus CARIB 6	CARIFORUM Service Barrier Reduction	EU Service Barrier Reduction	Combined Service Liberalization	Goods and Services Liberalization
Vegetables fruit nuts	0.13	−0.22	−0.89	−0.95	−0.31	2.90	1.92	−0.43	0.31	2.77	1.80
Sugar cane and sugar beet	0.32	0.18	−0.20	−0.23	13.49	3.34	3.09	−0.24	0.19	3.29	3.04
Other agriculture	0.39	0.12	−0.43	−0.49	1.42	4.07	3.55	−0.35	0.29	4.01	3.49
Forestry and fishing	0.17	−0.01	−0.35	−0.54	0.16	3.14	2.57	−0.20	0.21	3.15	2.58
Minerals	0.62	0.25	−0.64	−0.72	0.85	5.39	4.62	−0.44	0.38	5.33	4.56
Beverages and tobacco	0.06	−0.16	−0.79	−0.83	−0.57	2.77	1.92	−0.45	0.23	2.54	1.70
Sugar	0.21	0.02	−0.53	−0.57	−7.39	3.47	2.88	−0.40	0.43	3.51	2.91
Other food products	0.17	−0.05	−0.64	−0.74	−0.16	2.35	1.59	−0.38	0.39	2.36	1.61
Textiles apparel leather	0.12	−0.14	−0.82	−0.87	−0.32	2.75	1.86	−0.31	0.41	2.86	1.96
Petroleum coal products	0.18	−0.09	−0.78	−0.80	−0.29	3.65	2.82	−0.23	0.22	3.64	2.81
Chemicals rubber plastic	0.14	−0.41	−1.75	−1.98	−1.46	2.19	0.17	−0.25	0.33	2.27	0.25

(Continued)

Table A27. CARIFORUM Imports by Region of Origin for GLOBE Model Experiments (Closure: Balanced Macro Closure, Sales Tax Adjustment, Unemployed Unskilled Labor: United States of America) (*Continued*)

Trade Policy Scenarios / % Change on Reference Equilibrium	CARIB 1 EU Tariff Elimination for CARIFORUM	CARIB 2 Bilateral Tariff Reduction 2013	CARIB 3 Bilateral Tariff Reduction 2023	CARIB 4 Bilateral Tariff Reduction 2033	CARIB 5 Bilateral Tariff Redux 2033 inc Sugar	CARIB 6 10% TFP Rise in CARIFORUM Services	CARIB 7 CARIB 4 plus CARIB 6	CARIB 8 CARIFORUM Service Barrier Reduction	CARIB 9 EU Service Barrier Reduction	CARIB 10 Combined Service Liberalization	CARIB 11 Goods and Services Liberalization
Metals	0.04	−0.86	−2.28	−2.32	−2.12	1.44	−0.91	−0.14	0.15	1.45	−0.90
Transport equipment and machinery	0.07	−0.53	−2.42	−2.46	−2.12	1.58	−0.92	−0.17	0.26	1.68	−0.81
Electronic equipment	0.07	−0.25	−1.65	−1.67	−1.34	1.78	0.08	−0.20	0.25	1.83	0.13
Utilities and construction	0.09	−0.55	−0.88	−0.91	−0.48	0.20	−0.71	−0.19	0.28	0.30	−0.61
Transport and communication	0.09	−0.02	−0.33	−0.35	0.02	1.68	1.32	−1.91	0.28	0.02	−0.33
Financial and business services	0.07	−0.03	−0.32	−0.34	0.01	0.82	0.48	−1.25	0.25	−0.19	−0.53
Recreation and other services	0.09	−0.01	−0.29	−0.31	0.07	1.79	1.48	−1.21	0.27	0.85	0.54
Public services	0.10	0.01	−0.25	−0.27	0.11	2.14	1.86	−0.20	0.30	2.24	1.97

Source: World Bank staff and IDS.

Table A28. CARIFORUM Imports by Region of Origin for GLOBE Model Experiments (Closure: Balanced Macro Closure, Sales Tax Adjustment, Unemployed Unskilled Labor: EU15)

Trade Policy Scenarios / % Change on Reference Equilibrium	CARIB 1 EU Tariff Elimination for CARIFORUM	CARIB 2 Bilateral Tariff Reduction 2013	CARIB 3 Bilateral Tariff Reduction 2023	CARIB 4 Bilateral Tariff Reduction 2033	CARIB 5 Bilateral Tariff Redux 2033 inc Sugar	CARIB 6 10% TFP Rise in CARIFORUM Services	CARIB 7 CARIB 4 plus CARIB 6	CARIB 8 CARIFORUM Service Barrier Reduction	CARIB 9 EU Service Barrier Reduction	CARIB 10 Combined Service Liberalization	CARIB 11 Goods and Services Liberalization
Vegetables fruit nuts	0.13	3.96	5.65	5.91	6.63	2.91	8.99	−0.44	0.31	2.79	8.86
Sugar cane and sugar beet	0.36	7.21	19.80	19.75	34.02	3.70	24.17	−0.27	0.22	3.65	24.11
Other agriculture	0.41	7.24	10.11	11.42	13.77	4.22	16.11	−0.37	0.31	4.15	16.03
Forestry and fishing	0.18	2.34	4.02	8.71	9.56	3.40	12.39	−0.22	0.23	3.42	12.41
Minerals	0.62	6.44	12.86	16.00	17.93	5.34	22.17	−0.45	0.39	5.27	22.08
Beverages and tobacco	0.06	−0.14	−0.76	−0.81	−0.41	2.75	1.92	−0.45	0.22	2.52	1.70
Sugar	0.21	0.01	−0.54	−0.59	−6.08	3.42	2.81	−0.40	0.42	3.45	2.84
Other food products	0.18	0.65	1.62	2.61	3.43	2.47	5.14	−0.41	0.42	2.49	5.16
Textiles apparel leather	0.13	2.59	8.19	8.47	9.14	2.79	11.48	−0.32	0.42	2.89	11.60
Petroleum coal products	0.18	7.87	28.07	28.04	28.63	3.71	32.76	−0.23	0.21	3.69	32.74
Chemicals rubber plastic	0.14	3.25	10.59	12.21	12.86	2.20	14.67	−0.26	0.33	2.27	14.76

(Continued)

Table A28. CARIFORUM Imports by Region of Origin for GLOBE Model Experiments (Closure: Balanced Macro Closure, Sales Tax Adjustment, Unemployed Unskilled Labor: EU15) *(Continued)*

Trade Policy Scenarios	CARIB 1	CARIB 2	CARIB 3	CARIB 4	CARIB 5	CARIB 6	CARIB 7	CARIB 8	CARIB 9	CARIB 10	CARIB 11
% Change on Reference Equilibrium	EU Tariff Elimination for CARIFORUM	Bilateral Tariff Reduction 2013	Bilateral Tariff Reduction 2023	Bilateral Tariff Reduction 2033	Bilateral Tariff Redux 2033 inc Sugar	10% TFP Rise in CARIFORUM Services	CARIB 4 plus CARIB 6	CARIFORUM Service Barrier Reduction	EU Service Barrier Reduction	Combined Service Liberalization	Goods and Services Liberalization
Metals	0.04	6.23	15.06	15.23	15.56	1.43	16.89	−0.15	0.15	1.44	16.89
Transport equipment and machinery	0.07	2.29	9.70	9.79	10.26	1.60	11.54	−0.18	0.28	1.70	11.66
Electronic equipment	0.07	2.66	17.02	17.06	17.59	1.80	19.17	−0.22	0.26	1.85	19.22
Utilities and construction	0.09	2.77	2.43	2.40	2.86	0.20	2.61	−0.19	0.27	0.29	2.70
Transport and communication	0.09	−0.02	−0.34	−0.36	0.02	1.68	1.31	8.40	0.28	10.54	10.14
Financial and business services	0.07	−0.03	−0.33	−0.35	0.03	0.82	0.46	3.67	0.26	4.79	4.42
Recreation and other services	0.09	−0.01	−0.30	−0.32	0.09	1.79	1.47	3.71	0.27	5.87	5.53
Public services	0.00	−0.24	−0.89	−0.94	−0.01	−1.30	−1.97	−0.36	0.39	−1.24	−1.90

Source: World Bank staff and IDS.

Table A29. CARIFORUM Exports by Region of Destination for GLOBE Model Experiments (Closure: Balanced Macro Closure, Sales Tax Adjustment, Unemployed Unskilled Labor: United States of America)

Trade Policy Scenarios % Change on Reference Equilibrium	CARIB 1 EU Tariff Elimination for CARIFORUM	CARIB 2 Bilateral Tariff Reduction 2013	CARIB 3 Bilateral Tariff Reduction 2023	CARIB 4 Bilateral Tariff Reduction 2033	CARIB 5 Bilateral Tariff Redux 2033 inc Sugar	CARIB 6 10% TFP Rise in CARIFORUM Services	CARIB 7 CARIB 4 plus CARIB 6	CARIB 8 CARIFORUM Service Barrier Reduction	CARIB 9 EU Service Barrier Reduction	CARIB 10 Combined Service Liberalization	CARIB 11 Goods and Services Liberalization
Vegetables fruit nuts	-2.79	-2.80	-2.84	-2.84	-3.55	0.38	-2.55	-0.08	-0.06	0.25	-2.67
Sugar cane and sugar beet	-1.11	-1.00	-0.73	-0.70	10.73	1.40	0.70	0.19	-0.26	1.32	0.62
Other agriculture	-0.43	-0.38	-0.24	-0.23	-0.33	1.32	1.09	0.08	-0.17	1.23	1.00
Forestry and fishing	-0.25	-0.19	-0.05	-0.04	-0.50	0.74	0.71	0.07	-0.08	0.73	0.69
Minerals	-1.48	-1.06	0.10	0.18	-3.24	-0.71	-0.51	0.87	-0.83	-0.70	-0.49
Beverages and tobacco	-0.06	-0.17	-0.50	-0.52	-0.59	3.19	2.66	-0.22	-0.10	2.85	2.32
Sugar	-0.26	-0.15	0.13	0.15	3.64	1.74	1.89	0.18	-0.31	1.60	1.75
Other food products	-0.55	-0.53	-0.51	-0.50	-1.09	2.99	2.48	0.03	-0.23	2.78	2.27
Textiles apparel leather	-0.20	-0.04	0.37	0.42	-0.54	3.70	4.13	0.29	-0.58	3.38	3.80
Petroleum coal products	-0.33	-0.26	-0.10	-0.08	-0.86	1.53	1.45	0.14	-0.16	1.50	1.43
Chemicals rubber plastic	-0.15	-0.04	0.25	0.26	-0.52	4.95	5.23	0.31	-0.49	4.73	5.01

(Continued)

Table A29. CARIFORUM Exports by Region of Destination for GLOBE Model Experiments (Closure: Balanced Macro Closure, Sales Tax Adjustment, Unemployed Unskilled Labor: United States of America) (Continued)

Trade Policy Scenarios / % Change on Reference Equilibrium	CARIB 1 EU Tariff Elimination for CARIFORUM	CARIB 2 Bilateral Tariff Reduction 2013	CARIB 3 Bilateral Tariff Reduction 2023	CARIB 4 Bilateral Tariff Reduction 2033	CARIB 5 Bilateral Tariff Redux 2033 inc Sugar	CARIB 6 10% TFP Rise in CARIFORUM Services	CARIB 7 CARIB 4 plus CARIB 6	CARIB 8 CARIFORUM Service Barrier Reduction	CARIB 9 EU Service Barrier Reduction	CARIB 10 Combined Service Liberalization	CARIB 11 Goods and Services Liberalization
Metals	−0.26	−0.10	0.39	0.44	−0.75	4.91	5.38	0.47	−0.66	4.67	5.14
Transport equipment and machinery	−0.20	0.03	0.54	0.59	−0.46	3.66	4.28	0.36	−0.65	3.33	3.94
Electronic equipment	−0.25	0.09	0.95	1.00	−0.28	5.75	6.82	0.42	−0.80	5.30	6.37
Utilities and construction	−0.10	0.01	0.32	0.34	−0.10	1.51	1.86	0.17	−0.25	1.42	1.77
Transport and communication	−0.05	−0.02	0.07	0.08	−0.25	10.91	10.99	0.07	−0.16	10.80	10.88
Financial and business services	−0.06	−0.01	0.14	0.15	−0.20	10.15	10.32	0.05	−0.92	9.19	9.36
Recreation and other services	−0.05	0.02	0.21	0.23	−0.15	12.36	12.63	0.14	−1.12	11.29	11.56
Public services	−0.03	0.02	0.13	0.14	−0.12	3.41	3.56	0.11	−0.15	3.35	3.50

Source: World Bank staff and IDS.

Table A30. CARIFORUM Exports by Region of Destination for GLOBE Model Experiments (Closure: Balanced Macro Closure, Sales Tax Adjustment, Unemployed Unskilled Labor: EU15)

Trade Policy Scenarios % Change on Reference Equilibrium	CARIB 1 EU Tariff Elimination for CARIFORUM	CARIB 2 Bilateral Tariff Reduction 2013	CARIB 3 Bilateral Tariff Reduction 2023	CARIB 4 Bilateral Tariff Reduction 2033	CARIB 5 Bilateral Tariff Redux 2033 inc Sugar	CARIB 6 10% TFP Rise in CARIFORUM Services	CARIB 7 CARIB 4 plus CARIB 6	CARIB 8 CARIFORUM Service Barrier Reduction	CARIB 9 EU Service Barrier Reduction	CARIB 10 Combined Service Liberalization	CARIB 11 Goods and Services Liberalization
Vegetables fruit nuts	24.92	24.92	24.87	24.88	23.82	0.41	25.28	−0.08	−0.07	0.26	25.10
Sugar cane and sugar beet	22.28	22.43	22.78	22.82	32.70	1.38	24.53	0.19	−0.27	1.30	24.43
Other agriculture	−0.11	−0.04	0.12	0.13	0.00	1.34	1.49	0.09	−0.18	1.25	1.40
Forestry and fishing	−0.31	−0.23	−0.04	−0.02	−0.63	0.89	0.87	0.09	−0.11	0.88	0.86
Minerals	−1.53	−1.09	0.14	0.23	−3.41	−0.76	−0.51	0.91	−0.87	−0.74	−0.50
Beverages and tobacco	0.01	−0.10	−0.42	−0.44	−0.54	3.20	2.75	−0.22	−0.10	2.86	2.42
Sugar	−0.27	−0.15	0.15	0.18	128.44	1.77	1.95	0.19	−0.32	1.63	1.81
Other food products	8.40	8.44	8.48	8.50	7.67	3.19	11.97	0.04	−0.25	2.96	11.72
Textiles apparel leather	−0.20	−0.03	0.41	0.45	−0.59	3.73	4.20	0.30	−0.59	3.40	3.86
Petroleum coal products	−0.34	−0.26	−0.09	−0.06	−0.90	1.54	1.48	0.15	−0.16	1.52	1.45
Chemicals rubber plastic	−0.15	−0.03	0.28	0.30	−0.54	5.02	5.33	0.32	−0.51	4.80	5.11

(Continued)

Table A30. CARIFORUM Exports by Region of Destination for GLOBE Model Experiments (Closure: Balanced Macro Closure, Sales Tax Adjustment, Unemployed Unskilled Labor: EU15) (Continued)

Trade Policy Scenarios % Change on Reference Equilibrium	CARIB 1 EU Tariff Elimination for CARIFORUM	CARIB 2 Bilateral Tariff Reduction 2013	CARIB 3 Bilateral Tariff Reduction 2023	CARIB 4 Bilateral Tariff Reduction 2033	CARIB 5 Bilateral Tariff Redux 2033 inc Sugar	CARIB 6 10% TFP Rise in CARIFORUM Services	CARIB 7 CARIB 4 plus CARIB 6	CARIB 8 CARIFORUM Service Barrier Reduction	CARIB 9 EU Service Barrier Reduction	CARIB 10 Combined Service Liberalization	CARIB 11 Goods and Services Liberalization
Metals	−0.27	−0.09	0.42	0.47	−0.76	4.94	5.45	0.48	−0.67	4.70	5.21
Transport equipment and machinery	−0.21	0.03	0.57	0.62	−0.50	3.69	4.34	0.37	−0.66	3.35	4.00
Electronic equipment	−0.26	0.10	0.98	1.04	−0.32	5.76	6.88	0.43	−0.81	5.32	6.42
Utilities and construction	−0.09	0.02	0.33	0.35	−0.12	1.45	1.81	0.17	−0.25	1.37	1.72
Transport and communication	−0.05	−0.01	0.08	0.09	−0.27	10.90	11.00	0.08	−0.17	10.79	10.89
Financial and business services	−0.06	0.00	0.15	0.16	−0.22	10.14	10.33	0.05	4.01	14.63	14.82
Recreation and other services	−0.05	0.02	0.23	0.24	−0.17	12.40	12.68	0.14	9.18	22.93	23.24
Public services	0.00	0.00	0.01	0.02	−0.03	0.02	0.04	0.00	0.00	0.02	0.04

Source: World Bank staff and IDS.

Tables For EU Budget Support Scenarios

Table A31. Macro Results for GLOBE Model Experiments (Closure: Balanced Macro closure, EU Budget Transfer, Unemployed Unskilled Labor)					
Trade Policy Scenarios	CARIB 2	CARIB 3	CARIB 4	CARIB 5	CARIB 11
% Change on Reference Equilibrium	Bilateral Tariff Reduction 2013	Bilateral Tariff Reduction 2023	Bilateral Tariff Reduction 2033	Bilateral Tariff Redux 2033 incl. Sugar	Goods and Services Liberalization
Absorption	0.13	0.31	0.32	0.44	5.43
Private Consumption	0.18	0.44	0.46	0.63	7.60
Import Demand	0.30	0.80	0.83	1.26	3.63
Export Supply	0.01	0.10	0.11	0.14	6.20
GDP	0.04	0.09	0.10	0.13	2.50
Unskilled Labor Employment	0.12	0.27	0.29	0.37	6.96

Source: World Bank staff and IDS.

Table A32. CARIFORUM Imports by Region of Origin for GLOBE Model Experiments (Closure: Balanced Macro Closure, EU Budget Support Transfer, Unemployed Unskilled Labor: United States)

Trade Policy Scenarios	CARIB 2	CARIB 3	CARIB 4	CARIB 5	CARIB 11
% Change on Reference Equilibrium	Bilateral Tariff Reduction 2013	Bilateral Tariff Reduction 2023	Bilateral Tariff Reduction 2033	Bilateral Tariff Redux 2033 incl. Sugar	Goods and Services Liberalization
Vegetables fruit nuts	0.03	0.05	0.04	0.67	3.17
Sugar cane and sugar beet	0.34	0.41	0.40	14.04	3.95
Other agriculture	0.35	0.43	0.41	2.32	4.77
Forestry and fishing	0.13	0.18	0.01	0.72	3.37
Minerals	0.53	0.42	0.39	1.96	6.16
Beverages and tobacco	0.09	0.16	0.17	0.42	3.07
Sugar	0.26	0.39	0.39	−6.44	4.26
Other food products	0.17	0.20	0.13	0.72	2.82
Textiles apparel leather	0.05	−0.10	−0.12	0.43	3.01
Petroleum coal products	0.06	−0.20	−0.20	0.30	3.65
Chemicals rubber plastic	−0.26	−1.18	−1.38	−0.87	1.08
Metals	−0.77	−1.96	−1.98	−1.78	−0.43
Transport equipment and machinery	−0.43	−2.04	−2.06	−1.73	−0.26
Electronic equipment	−0.13	−1.19	−1.19	−0.86	0.80
Utilities and construction	−0.46	−0.52	−0.53	−0.10	−0.09
Transport and communication	0.13	0.24	0.25	0.61	0.48
Financial and business services	0.11	0.23	0.23	0.58	0.25
Recreation and other services	0.14	0.28	0.28	0.66	1.34
Public services	0.14	0.24	0.25	0.62	2.68

Source: World Bank staff and IDS.

Table A33. CARIFORUM Imports by Region of Origin for GLOBE Model Experiments (Closure: Balanced Macro Closure, EU Budget Support Transfer, Unemployed Unskilled Labor: EU15)

Trade Policy Scenarios	CARIB 2	CARIB 3	CARIB 4	CARIB 5	CARIB 11
% Change on Reference Equilibrium	Bilateral Tariff Reduction 2013	Bilateral Tariff Reduction 2023	Bilateral Tariff Reduction 2033	Bilateral Tariff Redux 2033 incl. Sugar	Goods and Services Liberalization
Vegetables fruit nuts	4.22	6.66	6.97	7.69	10.33
Sugar cane and sugar beet	7.40	20.62	20.61	34.77	25.34
Other agriculture	7.49	11.10	12.47	14.81	17.53
Forestry and fishing	2.50	4.63	9.37	10.22	13.35
Minerals	6.74	14.08	17.31	19.24	23.98
Beverages and tobacco	0.11	0.18	0.18	0.58	3.07
Sugar	0.25	0.37	0.37	−5.13	4.18
Other food products	0.89	2.53	3.56	4.39	6.48
Textiles apparel leather	2.79	8.99	9.31	9.99	12.77
Petroleum coal products	8.03	28.80	28.80	29.39	33.81
Chemicals rubber plastic	3.41	11.24	12.90	13.55	15.72
Metals	6.33	15.45	15.64	15.97	17.46
Transport equipment and machinery	2.40	10.15	10.26	10.74	12.31
Electronic equipment	2.80	17.60	17.66	18.19	20.06
Utilities and construction	2.87	2.80	2.79	3.25	3.23
Transport and communication	0.13	0.23	0.23	0.62	11.03
Financial and business services	0.11	0.22	0.22	0.60	5.24
Recreation and other services	0.14	0.27	0.27	0.68	6.39
Public services	0.13	0.23	0.24	0.64	2.68

Source: World Bank Staff and IDS.

Table A34. Gross Output by Sector CARIFORUM for GLOBE Model Experiments (Closure: Balanced Macro Closure, EU Budget Support Transfer, Unemployed Unskilled Labor)

Trade Policy Scenarios	CARIB 2	CARIB 3	CARIB 4	CARIB 5	CARIB 11
% Change on Reference Equilibrium	Bilateral Tariff Reduction 2013	Bilateral Tariff Reduction 2023	Bilateral Tariff Reduction 2033	Bilateral Tariff Redux 2033 incl. Sugar	Goods and Services Liberalization
Vegetables fruit nuts	4.43	4.54	4.55	4.21	6.54
Sugar cane and sugar beet	0.00	0.12	0.13	21.66	4.16
Other agriculture	0.01	0.16	0.17	1.41	4.14
Forestry and fishing	−0.04	0.12	0.13	0.20	3.20
Minerals	−1.01	−1.09	−1.09	−3.28	0.22
Beverages and tobacco	0.04	0.14	0.15	0.27	4.68
Sugar	−0.07	0.07	0.08	42.58	3.27
Other food products	0.16	0.31	0.31	0.27	4.80
Textiles apparel leather	−0.05	0.07	0.08	−0.42	4.53
Petroleum coal products	−0.19	−0.24	−0.22	−0.58	3.55
Chemicals rubber plastic	−0.11	−0.27	−0.32	−0.66	4.99
Metals	−0.40	−0.70	−0.69	−1.57	3.86
Transport equipment and machinery	−0.19	−0.49	−0.48	−1.21	3.13
Electronic equipment	−0.05	0.10	0.13	−0.84	5.47
Utilities and construction	−0.01	0.03	0.03	0.01	1.30
Transport and communication	0.07	0.22	0.23	0.21	9.62
Financial and business services	0.06	0.20	0.21	0.18	8.68
Recreation and other services	0.08	0.24	0.25	0.17	12.66
Public services	0.10	0.24	0.25	0.34	4.47

Source: World Bank Staff and IDS.

Table A35. Total Exports by Sector CARIFORUM for GLOBE Model Experiments (Closure: Balanced Macro Closure, EU Budget Support Transfer, Unemployed Unskilled Labor)

Trade Policy Scenarios	CARIB 2	CARIB 3	CARIB 4	CARIB 5	CARIB 11
% Change on Reference Equilibrium	Bilateral Tariff Reduction 2013	Bilateral Tariff Reduction 2023	Bilateral Tariff Reduction 2033	Bilateral Tariff Redux 2033 incl. Sugar	Goods and Services Liberalization
Vegetables fruit nuts	13.82	13.89	13.91	13.01	14.30
Sugar cane and sugar beet	1.07	1.15	1.17	16.89	3.43
Other agriculture	−0.31	−0.24	−0.22	−0.24	1.15
Forestry and fishing	−0.23	−0.14	−0.14	−0.64	0.69
Minerals	−1.43	−1.50	−1.50	−4.69	−2.48
Beverages and tobacco	0.01	0.08	0.09	0.04	3.53
Sugar	−0.22	−0.13	−0.11	88.63	1.43
Other food products	1.05	1.14	1.15	0.65	4.69
Textiles apparel leather	−0.14	−0.02	0.01	−0.93	3.36
Petroleum coal products	−0.30	−0.35	−0.34	−0.97	2.06
Chemicals rubber plastic	−0.15	−0.19	−0.20	−0.94	4.59
Metals	−0.30	−0.33	−0.31	−1.48	4.18
Transport equipment and machinery	−0.12	−0.02	0.01	−1.05	3.22
Electronic Equipment	−0.05	0.41	0.44	−0.85	5.65
Utilities and construction	−0.05	0.05	0.07	−0.37	1.34
Transport and communication	−0.01	0.09	0.10	−0.22	10.67
Financial and business services	−0.02	0.08	0.09	−0.27	12.00
Recreation and other services	−0.01	0.11	0.12	−0.27	16.91
Public services	0.01	0.10	0.11	−0.14	3.47

Source: World Bank Staff and IDS.

Table A36. CARIFORUM Exports by Region of Destination for GLOBE Model Experiments (Closure: Balanced Macro Closure, EU Budget Support Transfer, Unemployed Unskilled Labor: United States)

Trade Policy Scenarios	CARIB 2	CARIB 3	CARIB 4	CARIB 5	CARIB 11
% Change on Reference Equilibrium	Bilateral Tariff Reduction 2013	Bilateral Tariff Reduction 2023	Bilateral Tariff Reduction 2033	Bilateral Tariff Redux 2033 incl. Sugar	Goods and Services Liberalization
Vegetables fruit nuts	−2.76	−2.71	−2.70	−3.41	−2.51
Sugar cane and sugar beet	−1.07	−1.01	−0.99	10.25	0.21
Other agriculture	−0.40	−0.33	−0.32	−0.42	0.86
Forestry and fishing	−0.21	−0.13	−0.13	−0.59	0.56
Minerals	−1.49	−1.57	−1.56	−4.90	−2.86
Beverages and tobacco	−0.03	0.03	0.04	−0.04	3.10
Sugar	−0.22	−0.14	−0.12	3.14	1.38
Other food products	−0.50	−0.42	−0.41	−1.00	2.39
Textiles apparel leather	−0.14	−0.02	0.01	−0.94	3.25
Petroleum coal products	−0.31	−0.30	−0.29	−1.06	1.14
Chemicals rubber plastic	−0.13	−0.11	−0.11	−0.89	4.50
Metals	−0.27	−0.26	−0.24	−1.41	4.19
Transport equipment and machinery	−0.11	0.01	0.04	−1.00	3.19
Electronic equipment	−0.04	0.41	0.45	−0.82	5.61
Utilities and construction	−0.06	0.05	0.06	−0.38	1.39
Transport and communication	−0.01	0.09	0.10	−0.22	10.94
Financial and business services	−0.02	0.07	0.08	−0.27	9.27
Recreation and other services	−0.01	0.10	0.11	−0.26	11.38
Public services	0.01	0.10	0.11	−0.15	3.45

Source: World Bank Staff and IDS.

Table A37. **CARIFORUM Exports by Region of Destination for GLOBE Model Experiments (Closure: Balanced Macro Closure, EU Budget Support Transfer, Unemployed Unskilled Labor: EU15)**

Trade Policy Scenarios	CARIB 2	CARIB 3	CARIB 4	CARIB 5	CARIB 11
% Change on Reference Equilibrium	Bilateral Tariff Reduction 2013	Bilateral Tariff Reduction 2023	Bilateral Tariff Reduction 2033	Bilateral Tariff Redux 2033 incl. Sugar	Goods and Services Liberalization
Vegetables fruit nuts	24.97	25.04	25.06	24.00	25.32
Sugar cane and sugar beet	22.33	22.42	22.44	32.12	23.90
Other agriculture	−0.07	0.02	0.03	−0.12	1.23
Forestry and fishing	−0.26	−0.16	−0.15	−0.75	0.67
Minerals	−1.54	−1.60	−1.59	−5.14	−2.98
Beverages and tobacco	0.04	0.10	0.12	0.01	3.19
Sugar	−0.22	−0.13	−0.11	127.29	1.40
Other food products	8.46	8.57	8.59	7.76	11.83
Textiles apparel leather	−0.14	0.00	0.02	−1.00	3.28
Petroleum coal products	−0.32	−0.30	−0.29	−1.11	1.14
Chemicals rubber plastic	−0.13	−0.10	−0.10	−0.93	4.58
Metals	−0.27	−0.24	−0.22	−1.44	4.24
Transport equipment and machinery	−0.11	0.02	0.05	−1.07	3.22
Electronic equipment	−0.04	0.43	0.47	−0.88	5.64
Utilities and construction	−0.05	0.06	0.07	−0.39	1.35
Transport and communication	−0.01	0.10	0.11	−0.25	10.93
Financial and business services	−0.02	0.08	0.09	−0.29	14.71
Recreation and other services	−0.01	0.11	0.12	−0.29	23.03
Public services	0.01	0.10	0.11	−0.18	3.46

Source: World Bank Staff and IDS.

Table A38. Private Consumption by Sector CARIFORUM for GLOBE Model Experiments (Closure: Balanced Macro Closure, EU Budget Support Transfer, Unemployed Unskilled Labor)

Trade Policy Scenarios	CARIB 2	CARIB 3	CARIB 4	CARIB 5	CARIB 11
% Change on Reference Equilibrium	Bilateral Tariff Reduction 2013	Bilateral Tariff Reduction 2023	Bilateral Tariff Reduction 2033	Bilateral Tariff Redux 2033 incl. Sugar	Goods and Services Liberalization
Vegetables fruit nuts	2.17	2.31	2.32	1.86	4.11
Sugar cane and sugar beet	−0.15	0.06	0.08	−0.28	2.76
Other agriculture	−0.15	0.04	0.06	−0.33	2.30
Forestry and fishing	−0.14	0.06	0.09	−0.33	1.69
Minerals	−0.05	0.19	0.21	0.09	2.89
Beverages and tobacco	0.05	0.14	0.15	0.36	4.09
Sugar	0.01	0.19	0.21	16.76	2.97
Other food products	0.12	0.30	0.33	0.42	4.31
Textiles apparel leather	0.18	0.48	0.50	0.67	4.25
Petroleum coal products	0.11	0.52	0.53	0.55	2.95
Chemicals rubber plastic	0.30	0.86	0.95	1.14	5.46
Metals	0.43	1.06	1.08	1.31	5.87
Transport equipment and machinery	0.42	1.39	1.41	1.77	5.38
Electronic equipment	0.30	1.00	1.01	1.42	5.08
Utilities and construction	0.19	0.50	0.52	0.64	5.05
Transport and communication	0.13	0.32	0.33	0.43	11.58
Financial and business services	0.14	0.32	0.33	0.45	11.62
Recreation and other services	0.13	0.32	0.33	0.37	13.72
Public services	0.15	0.35	0.37	0.50	5.08

Source: World Bank Staff and IDS.

Tables For Supplementary Scenarios R1 To R6

Table A39. Aggregate Results with Balanced Macro, Factor Tax Adjustment, Unemployed Unskilled Labor

Trade Policy Scenarios	R 1	R 2	R 3	R 4	R 5	R 6
% Change on Reference Equilibrium	5% TFP Rise in CARIFORUM Services	15% TFP Rise in CARIFORUM Services	US-CARIFORUM Agreement	EPA and US-CARIFORUM	EPA and Reduction of CARIFORUM MFN Duties	EPA with zero CARIFORUM Duties
Absorption	2.44	7.11	0.47	0.46	0.17	0.05
Private Consumption	3.41	9.94	0.71	0.72	0.37	0.09
Import Demand	1.14	3.25	2.07	2.38	2.47	0.52
Export Supply	2.99	8.74	2.39	3.13	5.00	1.12
GDP	1.15	3.28	0.44	0.52	0.65	0.17
Unskilled Employment	3.18	9.11	1.17	1.39	1.79	0.45

Source: World Bank Staff and IDS.

Table A40. CARIFORUM Imports by Region of Origin for GLOBE Model Experiments (Closure: Balanced Macro Closure, Factor Tax Adjustment, Unemployed Unskilled Labor: United States)

% Change on Reference Equilibrium	R 1 5% TFP Rise in CARIFORUM Services	R 2 15% TFP Rise in CARIFORUM Services	R 3 US-CARIFORUM Agreement	R 4 EPA and US-CARIFORUM	R 5 EPA and Reduction of CARIFORUM MFN Duties	R 6 EPA with zero CARIFORUM Duties
Vegetables fruit nuts	1.44	4.09	7.36	6.77	5.00	−1.21
Sugar cane and sugar beet	1.68	4.82	29.19	28.93	23.83	−0.11
Other agriculture	2.04	5.86	5.06	4.61	0.96	−0.38
Forestry and fishing	1.59	4.53	8.69	8.17	4.38	−0.65
Minerals	2.67	7.86	24.30	23.35	10.41	−0.45
Beverages and tobacco	1.36	3.86	8.45	8.21	5.22	−1.30
Sugar	1.76	5.01	−0.81	−1.27	−1.12	−0.87
Other food products	1.19	3.37	2.31	1.65	−0.69	−1.99
Textiles apparel leather	1.40	3.97	11.92	11.04	5.25	−1.36
Petroleum coal products	1.84	5.30	17.70	16.90	10.92	−0.64
Chemicals rubber plastic	1.11	3.16	12.23	10.09	4.32	−2.45
Metals	0.72	2.07	16.89	14.42	8.42	−2.36
Transport equipment and machinery	0.80	2.30	16.22	13.47	1.95	−2.76
Electronic equipment	0.90	2.57	10.30	8.58	−1.16	−1.72
Utilities and construction	0.10	0.32	0.21	−0.76	−3.42	−1.12
Transport and communication	0.85	2.41	0.56	0.29	−1.69	−0.39
Financial and business services	0.41	1.13	0.65	0.44	−1.23	−0.29
Recreation and other services	0.92	2.59	0.49	0.19	−1.83	−0.42
Public services	1.10	3.11	0.34	0.01	−2.12	−0.47

Source: World Bank Staff and IDS.

Table A41. CARIFORUM Imports by Region of Origin for GLOBE Model Experiments (Closure: Balanced Macro Closure, Factor Tax Adjustment, Unemployed Unskilled Labor: EU15)

Trade Policy Scenarios % Change on Reference Equilibrium	R 1 5% TFP Rise in CARIFORUM Services	R 2 15% TFP Rise in CARIFORUM Services	R 3 US-CARIFORUM Agreement	R 4 EPA and US-CARIFORUM	R 5 EPA and Reduction of CARIFORUM MFN Duties	R 6 EPA with zero CARIFORUM Duties
Vegetables fruit nuts	1.45	4.11	−0.82	5.46	3.72	21.75
Sugar cane and sugar beet	1.86	5.36	−6.07	12.51	7.33	19.91
Other agriculture	2.11	6.08	−0.31	11.14	7.17	14.49
Forestry and fishing	1.73	4.92	0.51	9.33	5.18	13.00
Minerals	2.64	7.78	0.15	16.10	4.14	16.26
Beverages and tobacco	1.35	3.83	−0.05	−0.25	−2.97	6.92
Sugar	1.73	4.93	−0.97	−1.45	−1.31	28.89
Other food products	1.25	3.55	0.34	3.05	0.60	23.03
Textiles apparel leather	1.42	4.03	−3.04	5.25	−0.26	16.96
Petroleum coal products	1.86	5.38	−1.36	26.47	19.91	28.24
Chemicals rubber plastic	1.12	3.17	−1.37	10.75	4.98	15.36
Metals	0.72	2.06	−2.52	12.56	6.73	16.29
Transport equipment and machinery	0.81	2.33	−2.68	6.93	−3.95	10.73
Electronic equipment	0.91	2.60	−2.52	14.23	4.01	16.99
Utilities and construction	0.10	0.31	0.22	2.57	−0.07	2.19
Transport and communication	0.85	2.41	0.57	0.29	−1.69	−0.41
Financial and business services	0.41	1.13	0.66	0.44	−1.22	−0.31
Recreation and other services	0.92	2.60	0.50	0.20	−1.82	−0.44
Public services	1.10	3.12	0.36	0.01	−2.11	−0.48

Source: World Bank Staff and IDS.

Table A42. Gross Output by Sector CARIFORUM for GLOBE Model Experiments (Closure: Balanced Macro Closure, Factor Tax Adjustment, Unemployed Unskilled Labor)

Trade Policy Scenarios	R 1	R 2	R 3	R 4	R 5	R 6
% Change on Reference Equilibrium	5% TFP Rise in CARIFORUM Services	15% TFP Rise in CARIFORUM Services	US-CARIFORUM Agreement	EPA and US-CARIFORUM	EPA and Reduction of CARIFORUM MFN Duties	EPA with zero CARIFORUM Duties
Vegetables fruit nuts	1.01	2.76	0.19	0.16	4.51	4.33
Sugar cane and sugar beet	2.03	5.74	4.80	5.03	1.55	0.19
Other agriculture	1.97	5.53	0.96	1.05	0.45	−0.03
Forestry and fishing	1.52	4.25	1.69	1.76	0.45	−0.10
Minerals	0.90	2.39	−1.60	−0.86	2.32	0.38
Beverages and tobacco	2.23	6.35	0.42	0.49	0.40	0.19
Sugar	1.63	4.59	8.39	8.71	1.97	0.21
Other food products	2.21	6.21	0.52	0.52	0.29	−0.10
Textiles apparel leather	2.33	6.63	6.90	7.50	2.60	0.65
Petroleum coal products	1.89	5.40	−0.61	−0.63	0.05	−0.09
Chemicals rubber plastic	2.73	7.83	0.12	0.19	1.96	0.21
Metals	2.46	7.04	−0.93	−0.67	3.36	0.54
Transport equipment and machinery	1.97	5.64	−0.68	−0.37	2.20	0.58
Electronic equipment	2.87	8.25	−0.42	0.75	7.04	1.66
Utilities and construction	0.63	1.80	0.14	0.19	0.43	0.06
Transport and communication	4.64	13.74	0.35	0.46	0.94	0.18
Financial and business services	4.07	12.00	0.44	0.61	1.32	0.25
Recreation and other services	5.38	16.10	0.14	0.27	1.02	0.20
Public services	2.06	5.88	0.20	0.16	−0.14	−0.02

Source: World Bank Staff and IDS.

Table A43. Total Exports by Sector CARIFORUM for GLOBE Model Experiments (Closure: Balanced Macro Closure, Factor Tax Adjustment, Unemployed Unskilled Labor)

Trade Policy Scenarios	R 1	R 2	R 3	R 4	R 5	R 6
% Change on Reference Equilibrium	5% TFP Rise in CARIFORUM Services	15% TFP Rise in CARIFORUM Services	US-CARIFORUM Agreement	EPA and US-CARIFORUM	EPA and Reduction of CARIFORUM MFN Duties	EPA with zero CARIFORUM Duties
Vegetables fruit nuts	0.29	0.68	−0.12	0.05	15.18	14.13
Sugar cane and sugar beet	1.22	3.36	1.63	2.08	2.73	1.68
Other agriculture	0.79	2.06	0.91	1.27	2.26	0.19
Forestry and fishing	0.48	1.25	0.75	0.97	1.45	0.02
Minerals	−0.14	−0.67	−2.04	−0.88	6.06	0.61
Beverages and tobacco	1.75	4.96	0.28	0.50	0.72	0.33
Sugar	0.93	2.52	17.91	18.56	3.66	0.58
Other food products	1.83	5.11	0.59	0.92	1.18	1.32
Textiles apparel leather	1.91	5.42	15.35	16.48	6.14	1.31
Petroleum coal products	1.25	3.53	−0.69	−0.55	1.65	0.02
Chemicals rubber plastic	2.57	7.37	0.16	0.80	5.15	0.97
Metals	2.50	7.15	−0.63	0.31	7.31	1.37
Transport equipment and machinery	1.86	5.32	−0.10	1.05	7.80	1.61
Electronic Equipment	2.89	8.30	0.10	1.94	12.39	2.48
Utilities and construction	0.73	2.08	−0.03	0.48	3.39	0.68
Transport and communication	5.31	15.85	−0.01	0.36	2.62	0.55
Financial and business services	5.07	15.11	0.01	0.43	2.85	0.60
Recreation and other services	6.17	18.62	−0.19	0.20	2.66	0.57
Public services	1.74	4.96	−0.07	0.20	1.91	0.44

Source: World Bank Staff and IDS.

Table A44. CARIFORUM Exports by Region of Destination for GLOBE Model Experiments (Closure: Balanced Macro Closure, Factor Tax Adjustment, Unemployed Unskilled Labor: United States)

Trade Policy Scenarios	R 1	R 2	R 3	R 4	R 5	R 6
% Change on Reference Equilibrium	5% TFP Rise in CARIFORUM Services	15% TFP Rise in CARIFORUM Services	US-CARIFORUM Agreement	EPA and US-CARIFORUM	EPA and Reduction of CARIFORUM MFN Duties	EPA with zero CARIFORUM Duties
Vegetables fruit nuts	0.19	0.42	0.18	0.35	−1.07	−2.49
Sugar cane and sugar beet	0.74	1.93	3.31	3.85	3.60	−0.30
Other agriculture	0.69	1.79	5.16	5.54	2.40	0.12
Forestry and fishing	0.40	1.03	0.69	0.89	1.45	0.03
Minerals	−0.29	−1.10	−2.09	−0.86	6.84	0.65
Beverages and tobacco	1.57	4.44	0.54	0.79	1.94	0.45
Sugar	0.90	2.45	54.47	55.30	3.81	0.55
Other food products	1.52	4.18	2.48	2.94	3.79	0.22
Textiles apparel leather	1.86	5.28	20.36	21.56	6.63	1.35
Petroleum coal products	0.79	2.17	−0.14	0.16	3.26	0.18
Chemicals rubber plastic	2.49	7.12	0.70	1.46	5.81	1.12
Metals	2.47	7.07	−0.52	0.49	7.59	1.44
Transport equipment and machinery	1.83	5.23	0.16	1.32	7.88	1.62
Electronic equipment	2.87	8.22	0.14	1.99	12.54	2.48
Utilities and construction	0.77	2.18	−0.01	0.51	3.55	0.69
Transport and communication	5.44	16.24	0.01	0.38	2.69	0.56
Financial and business services	5.07	15.11	0.03	0.44	2.86	0.59
Recreation and other services	6.15	18.55	−0.18	0.21	2.66	0.56
Public services	1.74	4.94	−0.06	0.21	1.92	0.43

Source: World Bank Staff and IDS.

Table A45. CARIFORUM Exports by Region of Destination for GLOBE Model Experiments (Closure: Balanced Macro Closure, Factor Tax Adjustment, Unemployed Unskilled Labor: EU15)

Trade Policy Scenarios	R 1	R 2	R 3	R 4	R 5	R 6
% Change on Reference Equilibrium	5% TFP Rise in CARIFORUM Services	15% TFP Rise in CARIFORUM Services	US-CARIFORUM Agreement	EPA and US-CARIFORUM	EPA and Reduction of CARIFORUM MFN Duties	EPA with zero CARIFORUM Duties
Vegetables fruit nuts	1.45	4.11	−0.82	0.08	3.72	21.75
Sugar cane and sugar beet	1.86	5.36	−6.07	3.91	7.33	19.91
Other agriculture	2.11	6.08	−0.31	0.22	7.17	14.49
Forestry and fishing	1.73	4.92	0.51	1.08	5.18	13.00
Minerals	2.64	7.78	0.15	−0.89	4.14	16.26
Beverages and tobacco	1.35	3.83	−0.05	0.41	−2.97	6.92
Sugar	1.73	4.93	−0.97	0.02	−1.31	28.89
Other food products	1.25	3.55	0.34	0.43	0.60	23.03
Textiles apparel leather	1.42	4.03	−3.04	1.46	−0.26	16.96
Petroleum coal products	1.86	5.38	−1.36	−0.14	19.91	28.24
Chemicals rubber plastic	1.12	3.17	−1.37	0.73	4.98	15.36
Metals	0.72	2.06	−2.52	0.51	6.73	16.29
Transport equipment and machinery	0.81	2.33	−2.68	1.07	−3.95	10.73
Electronic equipment	0.91	2.60	−2.52	2.02	4.01	16.99
Utilities and construction	0.10	0.31	0.22	0.49	−0.07	2.19
Transport and communication	0.85	2.41	0.57	0.37	−1.69	−0.41
Financial and business services	0.41	1.13	0.66	0.43	−1.22	−0.31
Recreation and other services	0.92	2.60	0.50	0.20	−1.82	−0.44
Public services	1.10	3.12	0.36	0.20	−2.11	−0.48

Source: World Bank Staff and IDS.

Table A46. Private Consumption by Sector CARIFORUM for GLOBE Model Experiments (Closure: Balanced Macro Closure, Factor Tax Adjustment, Unemployed Unskilled Labor)

Trade Policy Scenarios	R 1	R 2	R 3	R 4	R 5	R 6
% Change on Reference Equilibrium	5% TFP Rise in CARIFORUM Services	15% TFP Rise in CARIFORUM Services	US-CARIFORUM Agreement	EPA and US-CARIFORUM	EPA and Reduction of CARIFORUM MFN Duties	EPA with zero CARIFORUM Duties
Vegetables fruit nuts	0.86	2.28	0.59	0.47	1.49	2.04
Sugar cane and sugar beet	1.27	3.44	0.31	0.14	−1.00	−0.54
Other agriculture	1.05	2.83	0.38	0.17	−1.00	−0.59
Forestry and fishing	0.75	1.97	0.09	−0.10	−0.92	−0.56
Minerals	1.24	3.39	0.36	0.12	−0.03	−0.61
Beverages and tobacco	1.92	5.42	0.57	0.54	0.45	0.42
Sugar	1.36	3.74	3.64	3.59	−0.59	−0.15
Other food products	1.91	5.35	0.50	0.41	−0.84	0.17
Textiles apparel leather	1.81	5.10	3.26	3.28	1.62	0.09
Petroleum coal products	1.10	3.00	1.65	1.68	2.97	−0.27
Chemicals rubber plastic	2.16	6.12	1.16	1.59	1.62	0.51
Metals	2.28	6.45	1.34	1.81	2.10	0.44
Transport equipment and machinery	1.85	5.21	1.92	2.62	4.80	0.70
Electronic equipment	1.89	5.33	1.78	2.05	3.20	0.15
Utilities and construction	2.19	6.21	0.50	0.56	0.45	0.03
Transport and communication	5.40	16.01	0.17	0.13	−0.05	−0.03
Financial and business services	5.32	15.79	0.13	0.04	−0.42	−0.11
Recreation and other services	6.08	18.23	0.08	0.08	0.14	0.02
Public services	2.31	6.56	0.28	0.23	−0.16	−0.04

Source: World Bank Staff and IDS.

Tables for Jamaica Model

Table A47. Structural Shares by Commodity: Jamaica Base 2000

Commodities	VAshr	PRDshr	EMPshr	EXPshr	EXP-OUTshr	IMPshr	IMP-DEMshr
Export Agriculture	1.2	1.9	1.8	2.2	18.6	0.3	5.0
Domestic Agriculture	3.3	2.0	4.4	0.6	4.9	2.3	25.3
Livestock	0.9	1.6	1.4	0.0	0.0	0.1	1.4
Forestry and Fishing	0.4	0.6	0.5	0.2	5.3	2.0	51.6
Mining	4.3	5.2	1.5	23.3	74.7	0.4	7.6
Sugar Cane and Beet	2.6	9.3	1.9	1.7	3.0	6.2	17.1
Processed Sugar	0.2	0.7	0.4	1.8	40.4	0.7	35.0
Beverages and Tobacco	2.9	2.2	0.8	1.8	13.9	0.8	12.2
Textiles Clothing and Leather	0.1	1.1	0.3	0.0	0.6	1.1	22.5
Wood Products	0.2	0.6	0.4	0.0	1.0	0.5	19.0
Paper and Printing	0.3	0.6	0.4	0.0	0.9	2.0	48.5
Oil	0.8	2.7	0.3	1.0	5.8	12.8	56.5
Chemical Products	0.7	2.1	0.3	2.0	16.0	8.5	57.2
Non Metal Products	0.7	0.8	0.4	0.1	2.2	1.8	36.6
Domestic machinery	0.0	0.2	0.0			34.3	98.0
Exported machinery	0.1	0.2	0.1	1.2	100.0		
Imported machinery						0.7	100.0
Electricity Water	3.7	3.3	1.6	0.0	0.1		
Construction	10.5	12.0	11.9				
Commerce	20.1	19.6	12.9	50.8	42.8	1.7	3.7
Transport	12.8	12.1	12.1	9.2	12.6		
Finance and Insurance	6.0	3.8	3.2	1.3	5.5	3.7	20.9
Real estate and Business Services	6.5	4.7	6.8	2.4	8.5	19.8	54.3
Government Services	13.8	7.6	24.8				
Other Services	7.8	5.1	11.6	0.3	1.0	0.2	1.1
TOTAL-1	100.0	100.0	100.0	100.0	16.5	100.0	24.6
TAGR	5.8	6.1	8.2	3.0	8.0	4.6	19.2
TNAGR	94.2	93.9	91.8	97.0	17.1	95.4	25.0
TOTAL-2	100.0	100.0	100.0	100.0	16.5	100.0	24.6

Source: World Bank Jamaica SAM 2000.

Table A48. Regional Export Shares by Commodity: Jamaica Base 2000

Commodities	United States	European Union	Rest of the World	$m 2000 TOTAL Exports
Export Agriculture	14.9	35.9	49.2	3.2
Domestic Agriculture	62.7	13.9	23.4	0.9
Livestock	26.1		73.9	0.0
Forestry and Fishing	71.4	23.2	5.4	0.3
Mining	21.7	32.9	45.4	34.4
Sugar Cane and Beet	42.2	9.0	48.7	2.4
Processed Sugar	0.0	99.9	0.1	2.6
Beverages and Tobacco	36.9	22.2	40.9	2.7
Textiles Clothing and Leather	53.4	15.7	30.9	0.1
Wood Products	91.0	0.2	8.7	0.1
Paper and Printing	8.6	5.5	86.0	0.0
Oil	71.8		28.2	1.4
Chemical Products	62.8	1.4	35.8	3.0
Non Metal Products	47.0	0.3	52.7	0.2
Domestic machinery	65.9	6.9	27.2	1.8
Exported machinery	28.3	30.5	41.2	0.0
Imported machinery	28.3	30.5	41.2	75.0
Electricity Water	28.3	30.5	41.2	13.6
Construction	28.3	30.5	41.2	1.9
Commerce	28.3	30.5	41.2	3.6
Transport	28.3	30.5	41.2	0.5
TOTAL	28.3	30.5	41.2	147.6

Source: World Bank Jamaica SAM 2000.

Table A49. Regional Import Shares by Commodity: Jamaica Base 2000

Commodities	United States	European Union	Rest of the World	$m 2000 TOTAL Exports
Export Agriculture	44.2	9.9	45.9	0.6
Domestic Agriculture	57.9	8.1	34.0	5.2
Livestock	30.2	0.2	69.6	0.2
Forestry and Fishing	22.3	4.4	73.2	4.7
Mining	9.2	11.4	79.4	0.9
Sugar Cane and Beet	48.9	9.2	41.9	14.3
Processed Sugar	22.8	3.4	73.8	1.6
Beverages and Tobacco	17.8	22.7	59.5	1.9
Textiles Clothing and Leather	57.4	4.3	38.3	2.5
Wood Products	31.8	2.6	65.7	1.2
Paper and Printing	43.1	5.1	51.8	4.6
Oil	27.5	4.8	67.8	29.5
Chemical Products	52.2	13.1	34.7	19.6
Non Metal Products	27.7	14.4	57.9	4.0
Domestic machinery	47.6	15.4	37.0	78.8
Exported machinery	47.6	15.4	37.0	1.6
Imported machinery	43.1	11.6	45.3	3.8
Electricity Water	43.1	11.6	45.3	8.5
Construction	43.1	11.6	45.3	45.6
Commerce	43.1	11.6	45.3	0.5
TOTAL	43.0	11.6	45.3	229.6

Source: World Bank Jamaica SAM 2000.

Table A50. Factor Shares within Sector: Jamaica Base 2000

Activities	Unskilled Labor	Skilled Labor	Capital	Total Share
Export Agriculture	57.9	24.4	17.7	100
Domestic Agriculture	54.4	19.9	25.7	100
Livestock	32.2	55.9	12	100
Forestry and Fishing	38.1	27.9	34.1	100
Mining	4.8	14.8	80.4	100
Sugar Cane and Beet	9.4	31.3	59.3	100
Processed Sugar	30.6	59.6	9.9	100
Beverages and Tobacco	3	12.7	84.3	100
Textiles Clothing and Leather	34.3	62.1	3.5	100
Wood Products	27.5	65.8	6.7	100
Paper and Printing	5.3	66.8	27.9	100
Oil	8.4	13.7	77.8	100
Chemical Products	2.5	25.3	72.1	100
Non Metal Products	7.9	24.9	67.1	100
Domestic Machinery	28	67.4	4.6	100
Machinery Export Processing	28	67.4	4.6	100
Electricity Water	3.5	20.4	76.1	100
Construction	33.9	29	37.1	100
Commerce	14.1	21.5	64.4	100
Transport	17	35.4	47.6	100
Finance and Insurance	3.7	26.2	70.1	100
Real estate and Business Services	18.5	39.8	41.7	100
Government Services	18.3	81.1	0.6	100
Other Services	29.2	53.4	17.5	100
TOTAL	18.8	36.7	44.5	100

Source: World Bank Jamaica SAM 2000.

Tables for Dominican Republic Model

Table A51. Dominican Republic Human Development Indicators, 2007–20, Baseline Scenario (Efficiency parameter: 0.6)

	Years													
	2007	2008	2009	2010	2011	2012	2013	2014	2015	2016	2017	2018	2019	2020
Real GDP per capita at market prices (% change)	−2.8	1.5	3.2	3.4	3.9	4.0	4.1	4.2	4.3	4.4	4.4	4.4	4.4	4.4
Poverty rate														
IMMPA Method	28.5	27.9	26.6	25.4	23.9	22.5	21.1	19.7	18.5	17.3	16.3	15.0	13.9	12.9
Log-normal distribution	26.3	25.8	24.7	23.6	22.4	21.2	20.0	18.9	17.7	16.6	15.5	14.5	13.5	12.5
External Sector (% of GDP)														
Trade balance	−13.8	−14.1	−14.0	−14.0	−13.8	−13.8	−13.8	−13.8	−13.9	−14.0	−13.9	−13.9	−13.9	−13.9
Current account	−10.0	−10.3	−10.4	−10.5	−10.5	−10.6	−10.7	−10.9	−11.2	−11.4	−11.5	−11.8	−11.9	−12.1
Capital account	10.4	10.7	10.9	11.1	11.2	11.4	11.6	11.7	11.9	12.1	12.2	12.4	12.6	12.7
Change in net foreign assets	0.3	0.1	0.4	0.4	0.5	0.5	0.5	0.5	0.6	0.6	0.6	0.6	0.6	0.6
Government Sector (% of GDP)														
Total resources (including grants)	16.4	16.5	16.4	16.5	16.4	16.4	16.4	16.4	16.4	16.4	16.4	16.4	16.4	16.4
Total tax revenues	15.2	15.3	15.3	15.3	15.2	15.2	−15.2	15.2	15.2	15.2	15.2	15.2	15.2	15.2
Domestic taxes	13.1	13.2	13.2	13.2	13.2	13.2	13.2	13.2	13.2	13.2	13.2	13.2	13.2	13.2
Indirect taxes on imports	2.1	2.1	2.1	2.1	2.1	2.1	2.1	2.1	2.1	2.0	2.0	2.0	2.0	2.0
Total nontax revenues	1.0	1.0	1.0	1.0	1.0	1.0	1.0	1.0	1.0	1.0	1.0	1.0	1.0	1.0
Foreign aid (grants)	0.1	0.2	0.2	0.2	0.2	0.2	0.2	0.2	0.2	0.2	0.2	0.2	0.2	0.2
Total expenditure	21.8	22.0	22.1	22.2	22.3	22.4	22.5	22.6	22.8	22.9	22.9	23.0	23.1	23.2
Spending on goods and services (total)	6.2	6.2	6.2	6.2	6.2	6.2	6.1	6.1	6.1	6.1	6.1	6.1	6.1	6.1
Maintenance expenditure	0.7	0.7	0.7	0.7	0.7	0.7	0.7	0.7	0.7	0.7	0.7	0.7	0.7	0.7
Other expenditures on goods and services	5.6	5.6	5.5	5.5	5.5	5.5	5.5	5.5	5.5	5.5	5.5	5.4	5.4	5.4

(Continued)

Table A51. Dominican Republic Human Development Indicators, 2007–20, Baseline Scenario (Efficiency parameter: 0.6) *(Continued)*

	Years													
	2007	2008	2009	2010	2011	2012	2013	2014	2015	2016	2017	2018	2019	2020
Wages and salaries	4.3	4.3	4.3	4.3	4.3	4.3	4.3	4.3	4.3	4.3	4.3	4.3	4.3	4.3
Investment	5.0	5.0	5.0	5.0	5.0	5.0	5.0	5.0	5.0	5.0	5.0	5.0	5.0	5.0
Interest payments	4.6	4.8	4.9	5.1	5.2	5.3	5.4	5.6	5.7	5.8	5.9	5.9	6.0	6.1
Overall fiscal balance including grants (cash basis)	−5.4	−5.5	−5.7	−5.8	−5.9	−6.0	−6.1	−6.2	−6.3	−6.5	−6.5	−6.6	−6.7	−6.8
Domestic borrowing	0.5	0.5	0.5	0.5	0.5	0.5	0.5	0.5	0.5	0.5	0.5	0.5	0.5	0.5
Foreign financing	4.9	5.0	5.2	5.3	5.4	5.5	5.6	5.7	5.8	6.0	6.0	6.1	6.2	6.3
Prices and Real Exchange Rate														
Composite good price (after indirect taxes, % change)	−0.8	−0.5	−1.3	−1.7	−1.7	−2.0	−2.1	−2.2	−2.4	−2.3	−2.3	−2.4	−2.4	−2.4
Nominal exchange rate (% change)	−1.2	0.8	0.1	−0.4	−1.3	−1.5	−1.7	−1.8	−2.1	−2.1	−2.2	−2.2	−2.3	−2.4
Real exchange rate (% change)	−0.4	1.3	1.4	1.2	0.4	0.6	0.5	0.4	0.4	0.2	0.2	0.1	0.1	0.1
Memorandum items														
Educated labor (in % of population)	22.0	22.2	22.4	22.7	23.0	23.3	23.6	23.9	24.3	24.7	25.1	25.5	26.0	26.4
Private investment (% of GDP)	13.6	13.3	13.1	13.0	12.9	12.9	12.9	12.8	12.9	12.9	12.9	12.9	12.9	12.9
Public investment (% of total public expenditure)	23.1	22.8	22.7	22.5	22.4	22.3	22.2	22.1	22.1	22.0	21.9	21.8	21.8	21.7
Health (% of public investment)	6.1	6.1	6.1	6.1	6.1	6.1	6.1	6.1	6.1	6.1	6.1	6.1	6.1	6.1
Infrastructure (% of public investment)	56.2	56.2	56.2	56.2	56.2	56.2	56.2	56.2	56.2	56.2	56.2	56.2	56.2	56.2
Education (% of public investment)	7.2	7.2	7.2	7.2	7.2	7.2	7.2	7.2	7.2	7.2	7.2	7.2	7.2	7.2
Other (% of public investment)	30.5	30.5	30.5	30.5	30.5	30.5	30.5	30.5	30.5	30.5	30.5	30.5	30.5	30.5
Aid (% of total public investment)	2.9	3.0	3.1	3.2	3.2	3.2	3.2	3.2	3.2	3.2	3.2	3.2	3.2	3.2

Table A52. Tariff Loss Compensated by Higher Indirect Taxes—Deviations from Baseline, 2008–20

	Years												
	2008	2009	2010	2011	2012	2013	2014	2015	2016	2017	2018	2019	2020
Real Sector (in billions of current DR$)													
Total supply of goods and services	(0.0)	(0.0)	(0.0)	(0.1)	(0.1)	(0.1)	(0.1)	(0.1)	(0.1)	(0.1)	(0.1)	(0.1)	(0.1)
Gross domestic product at factor cost	(0.0)	(0.1)	(0.0)	(0.1)	(0.1)	(0.1)	(0.1)	(0.1)	(0.1)	(0.1)	(0.1)	(0.1)	(0.1)
Imports of goods and NFS (inclusive of tariffs)	0.0	(0.0)	(0.0)	(0.1)	(0.1)	(0.1)	(0.1)	(0.1)	(0.1)	(0.1)	(0.1)	(0.1)	(0.1)
Total expenditure on goods and services	(0.2)	(0.2)	(0.3)	(0.2)	(0.2)	(0.2)	(0.2)	(0.2)	(0.2)	(0.2)	(0.2)	(0.2)	(0.2)
Total consumption	(0.2)	(0.2)	(0.3)	(0.2)	(0.2)	(0.2)	(0.2)	(0.2)	(0.2)	(0.2)	(0.2)	(0.2)	(0.2)
Private consumption	(0.2)	(0.2)	(0.4)	(0.2)	(0.2)	(0.2)	(0.2)	(0.2)	(0.2)	(0.2)	(0.2)	(0.2)	(0.2)
Public spending on goods and services	(0.2)	(0.2)	(0.2)	(0.2)	(0.2)	(0.2)	(0.2)	(0.2)	(0.2)	(0.2)	(0.2)	(0.2)	(0.2)
Total investment	(0.2)	(0.3)	(0.2)	(0.3)	(0.3)	(0.3)	(0.3)	(0.3)	(0.3)	(0.2)	(0.2)	(0.2)	(0.2)
Private investment	(0.2)	(0.3)	(0.3)	(0.3)	(0.3)	(0.3)	(0.3)	(0.3)	(0.3)	(0.2)	(0.2)	(0.2)	(0.2)
Public investment	(0.2)	(0.3)	(0.2)	(0.2)	(0.3)	(0.3)	(0.3)	(0.3)	(0.3)	(0.2)	(0.2)	(0.2)	(0.2)
Exports of goods and NFS	(0.1)	(0.2)	(0.1)	(0.2)	(0.2)	(0.2)	(0.2)	(0.3)	(0.3)	(0.2)	(0.2)	(0.2)	(0.2)
Gross domestic product at market prices	(0.0)	(0.1)	0.3	(0.1)	(0.1)	(0.1)	(0.1)	(0.1)	(0.1)	(0.1)	(0.1)	(0.0)	(0.0)
Disposable income	(0.0)	(0.0)	0.0	(0.0)	(0.0)	(0.0)	(0.0)	(0.0)	(0.0)	(0.0)	(0.0)	(0.0)	(0.0)
Poverty rate													
IMMPA Method	0.07	0.06	0.05	0.06	0.05	0.09	0.06	0.05	0.12	0.07	0.06	0.06	0.07
External Sector (% of GDP)													
Current account	0.0	(0.0)	0.1	0.0	0.0	0.0	0.0	0.0	0.0	0.0	0.0	0.0	0.0
Trade balance	0.0	(0.0)	0.1	(0.0)	(0.0)	(0.0)	(0.0)	(0.0)	(0.0)	(0.0)	(0.0)	(0.0)	(0.0)
Exports of goods and NFS	0.2	0.2	0.1	0.2	0.2	0.2	0.2	0.2	0.2	0.2	0.2	0.2	0.2
Imports of goods and NFS	0.2	0.2	(0.0)	0.2	0.2	0.2	0.2	0.2	0.2	0.2	0.2	0.2	0.2
Private unrequited transfers	0.0	0.1	(0.0)	0.1	0.1	0.1	0.1	0.1	0.1	0.1	0.1	0.1	0.1

(Continued)

Table A52. Tariff Loss Compensated by Higher Indirect Taxes—Deviations from Baseline, 2008–20 (*Continued*)

	Years												
	2008	2009	2010	2011	2012	2013	2014	2015	2016	2017	2018	2019	2020
Income (net)	(0.0)	(0.0)	0.0	(0.0)	(0.0)	(0.0)	(0.0)	(0.0)	(0.0)	(0.0)	(0.0)	(0.0)	(0.0)
Public	(0.0)	(0.0)	0.0	(0.0)	(0.0)	(0.0)	(0.0)	(0.0)	(0.0)	(0.0)	(0.0)	(0.0)	(0.0)
Private	(0.0)	(0.0)	0.0	(0.0)	(0.0)	(0.0)	(0.0)	(0.0)	(0.0)	(0.0)	(0.0)	(0.0)	(0.0)
Aid, total	0.0	0.0	0.0	0.0	0.0	0.0	0.0	0.0	0.0	0.0	0.0	0.0	0.0
Other current account flows (net)	0.0	0.0	(0.0)	0.0	0.0	0.0	0.0	0.0	0.0	0.0	0.0	0.0	0.0
Capital account	(0.0)	0.0	(0.0)	(0.0)	(0.0)	(0.0)	(0.0)	(0.0)	(0.0)	(0.0)	(0.0)	(0.0)	(0.0)
Foreign direct investment	(0.0)	0.0	(0.0)	(0.0)	(0.0)	(0.0)	(0.0)	(0.0)	(0.0)	(0.0)	(0.0)	(0.0)	(0.0)
Public borrowing	(0.0)	(0.0)	0.0	0.0	0.0	0.0	0.0	0.0	0.0	0.0	0.0	0.0	0.0
Other capital inflows	0.0	0.0	(0.0)	0.0	0.0	0.0	0.0	0.0	0.0	0.0	0.0	0.0	0.0
Government Sector (% of GDP)													
Total resources (including grants)	0.0	0.0	(0.0)	0.0	0.0	0.0	0.0	0.0	0.0	0.0	0.0	0.0	0.0
Total tax revenues	0.0	0.0	(0.0)	0.0	0.0	0.0	0.0	0.0	0.0	0.0	0.0	0.0	0.0
Domestic taxes	0.4	0.4	0.4	0.4	0.4	0.4	0.4	0.4	0.4	0.4	0.4	0.4	0.4
Direct taxes	0.0	0.0	(0.0)	0.0	0.0	0.0	0.0	0.0	0.0	0.0	0.0	0.0	0.0
Indirect taxes	0.4	0.4	0.4	0.4	0.4	0.4	0.4	0.4	0.4	0.4	0.4	0.4	0.4
Indirect taxes on imports	(0.4)	(0.4)	(0.4)	(0.4)	(0.4)	(0.4)	(0.4)	(0.4)	(0.4)	(0.4)	(0.4)	(0.4)	(0.4)
Total nontax revenues	(0.0)	(0.0)	(0.0)	0.0	0.0	0.0	0.0	0.0	0.0	0.0	0.0	0.0	0.0
Foreign aid (grants)	0.0	0.0	(0.0)	0.0	0.0	0.0	0.0	0.0	0.0	0.0	0.0	0.0	0.0
Total expenditure	(0.0)	0.0	(0.0)	0.0	0.0	0.0	0.0	0.0	0.0	0.0	0.0	0.0	0.0
Spending on goods and services (total)	(0.0)	0.0	(0.0)	0.0	0.0	0.0	0.0	0.0	0.0	0.0	0.0	0.0	0.0
Maintenance expenditure	0.0	0.0	(0.0)	0.0	0.0	0.0	0.0	0.0	0.0	0.0	0.0	0.0	0.0
Other expenditures on goods and services	(0.0)	0.0	(0.0)	0.0	0.0	0.0	0.0	0.0	0.0	0.0	0.0	0.0	0.0
Wages and salaries	(0.0)	(0.0)	(0.0)	0.0	0.0	0.0	0.0	0.0	0.0	0.0	0.0	0.0	(0.0)

Investment	(0.0)	(0.0)	(0.0)	0.0	0.0	0.0	0.0	(0.0)	(0.0)	(0.0)
Interest payments	0.0	0.0	0.0	0.0	0.0	0.0	0.0	0.0	0.0	0.0
Domestic debt	0.0	0.0	0.0	0.0	0.0	0.0	0.0	0.0	0.0	0.0
Foreign debt	0.0	0.0	0.0	0.0	0.0	0.0	0.0	0.0	0.0	0.0
Subsidies	(0.0)	(0.0)	(0.0)	0.0	0.0	0.0	(0.0)	(0.0)	(0.0)	(0.0)
Overall fiscal balance including grants (cash basis)	0.0	0.0	0.0	(0.0)	(0.0)	0.0	0.0	0.0	0.0	0.0
Total financing	(0.0)	0.0	0.0	0.0	0.0	0.0	(0.0)	(0.0)	(0.0)	(0.0)
Domestic borrowing	(0.0)	(0.0)	0.0	0.0	0.0	0.0	(0.0)	(0.0)	(0.0)	(0.0)
Foreign financing	(0.0)	(0.0)	0.0	0.0	0.0	0.0	(0.0)	(0.0)	(0.0)	(0.0)
Real exchange rate (% change)	0.1	0.1	(0.3)	0.4	(0.0)	0.0	(0.0)	0.0	0.0	0.0
Memorandum items										
Real GDP per capita at factor cost (% change)	(0.2)	(0.1)	0.2	(0.1)	(0.0)	0.0	0.0	0.0	0.0	0.0
Real GDP per capita at market prices (% change)	(0.2)	(0.1)	0.2	(0.1)	(0.0)	0.0	0.0	0.0	0.0	0.0
Real disposable income per capita (% change)	(0.2)	(0.0)	(0.1)	0.1	(0.0)	(0.0)	(0.0)	0.0	0.0	0.0
Private savings rate (% of GDP)	0.0	0.0	0.0	0.0	0.0	0.0	0.0	0.0	0.0	0.0
Real private consumption per capita (% change)	(0.2)	(0.0)	(0.1)	0.1	(0.0)	(0.0)	(0.0)	0.0	0.0	0.0
Unemployment	0.0	0.0	0.0	0.0	0.0	0.0	0.0	0.0	0.0	0.0
Private investment (% of GDP)	(0.0)	(0.0)	(0.0)	(0.0)	(0.0)	(0.0)	(0.0)	0.0	0.0	0.0
Private investment (% of total investment)	0.0	(0.0)	(0.0)	(0.0)	(0.0)	(0.0)	(0.0)	0.0	0.0	0.0
Public investment (% of total public expenditure)	(0.0)	(0.0)	0.0	(0.0)	(0.0)	(0.0)	(0.0)	(0.0)	(0.0)	(0.0)
Health (% of public investment)	—	—	—	—	—	—	—	—	—	—
Infrastructure (% of public investment)	—	—	—	—	—	—	—	—	—	—
Education (% of public investment)	—	—	—	—	—	—	—	—	—	—
Other (% of public investment)	—	—	—	—	—	—	—	—	—	—

(Continued)

Table A52. Tariff Loss Compensated by Higher Indirect Taxes—Deviations from Baseline, 2008–20 (*Continued*)

	Years												
	2008	2009	2010	2011	2012	2013	2014	2015	2016	2017	2018	2019	2020
Domestic debt (% of GDP)	0.0	0.0	(0.0)	0.0	0.0	0.0	0.0	0.0	0.0	0.0	0.0	0.0	0.0
External debt (% of GDP)	0.1	0.1	(0.1)	0.2	0.2	0.2	0.2	0.2	0.2	0.1	0.1	0.1	0.1
Interest payment on external public debt (% of exports)	(0.0)	(0.0)	(0.0)	(0.0)	(0.0)	(0.0)	(0.0)	(0.0)	(0.0)	(0.0)	(0.0)	(0.0)	(0.0)
Degree of openness (total trade in % of GDP)	0.3	0.4	0.1	0.4	0.4	0.4	0.4	0.4	0.4	0.4	0.4	0.4	0.4
Educated labor (in % of population)	—	(0.0)	(0.0)	(0.0)	(0.0)	(0.0)	(0.0)	(0.0)	(0.0)	(0.0)	(0.0)	(0.0)	(0.0)

Note: The real exchange rate is defined as the growth rate of nominal exchange rate plus the growth rate of the import price index minus the growth rate of composite good price after indirect taxes.

Table A53. Aid as a Temporary Compensation Scheme—Deviations from Baseline, 2008–20

	Years												
	2008	2009	2010	2011	2012	2013	2014	2015	2016	2017	2018	2019	2020
Real Sector (in billions of current DR$)													
Total supply of goods and services	0.3	0.4	0.5	0.2	0.1	0.0	0.0	(0.0)	(0.0)	(0.1)	(0.0)	(0.1)	(0.1)
Gross domestic product at factor cost	0.1	0.1	0.2	0.0	(0.0)	0.0	(0.0)	(0.0)	(0.0)	(0.0)	(0.0)	(0.0)	(0.0)
Imports of goods and NFS (inclusive of tariffs	0.8	1.0	1.1	0.6	0.4	0.1	0.0	(0.0)	(0.1)	(0.1)	(0.1)	(0.1)	(0.1)
Total expenditure on goods and services	0.3	0.4	0.4	0.1	0.1	(0.1)	(0.2)	(0.2)	(0.2)	(0.2)	(0.2)	(0.2)	(0.2)
Total consumption	0.5	0.6	0.5	0.1	0.1	(0.1)	(0.2)	(0.2)	(0.2)	(0.2)	(0.2)	(0.2)	(0.2)
Private consumption	0.5	0.6	0.5	0.1	0.1	(0.1)	(0.2)	(0.2)	(0.2)	(0.2)	(0.2)	(0.2)	(0.2)
Public spending on goods and services	0.2	0.2	0.3	0.2	0.4	(0.1)	(0.2)	(0.2)	(0.2)	(0.1)	(0.2)	(0.2)	(0.2)
Total investment	0.2	0.3	0.4	0.3	0.5	0.1	(0.0)	(0.1)	(0.2)	(0.1)	(0.2)	(0.2)	(0.2)
Private investment	0.2	0.3	0.4	0.3	0.5	0.2	0.1	(0.1)	(0.2)	(0.1)	(0.2)	(0.2)	(0.2)
Public investment	0.2	0.2	0.3	0.3	0.4	(0.1)	(0.2)	(0.2)	(0.3)	(0.1)	(0.3)	(0.3)	(0.3)
Exports of goods and NFS	0.0	0.1	0.2	0.1	(0.0)	(0.1)	(0.1)	(0.2)	(0.2)	(0.2)	(0.2)	(0.2)	(0.2)
Gross domestic product at market prices	(0.3)	(0.3)	0.0	(0.2)	(0.2)	0.0	0.0	(0.0)	(0.0)	(0.0)	(0.0)	(0.0)	(0.1)
Disposable income	0.1	0.1	0.2	0.0	(0.0)	0.0	0.0	0.0	(0.0)	(0.0)	(0.0)	(0.0)	(0.0)
Poverty rate													
IMMPA Method	(0.09)	(0.12)	(0.18)	0.01	0.02	0.06	0.04	0.05	0.12	0.07	0.09	0.06	0.07
External Sector (% of GDP)													
Current account	0.1	0.1	0.2	(0.2)	(0.2)	(0.0)	(0.0)	(0.0)	(0.0)	(0.1)	(0.0)	(0.0)	(0.0)
Trade balance	(0.3)	(0.4)	(0.2)	(0.2)	(0.3)	(0.1)	(0.0)	(0.0)	(0.0)	(0.1)	(0.0)	(0.0)	(0.0)
Exports of goods and NFS	0.2	0.1	0.1	0.1	0.0	0.1	0.2	0.2	0.2	0.2	0.2	0.2	0.2
Imports of goods and NFS	0.5	0.5	0.3	0.2	0.3	0.2	0.2	0.2	0.2	0.2	0.2	0.2	0.2
Private unrequited transfers	0.0	0.0	0.0	0.0	0.0	0.0	0.0	0.0	0.1	0.1	0.1	0.1	0.1
Income (net)	(0.0)	(0.0)	0.0	(0.0)	(0.0)	(0.0)	(0.0)	(0.0)	(0.0)	(0.0)	(0.0)	(0.0)	(0.0)

(*Continued*)

Table A53. Aid as a Temporary Compensation Scheme—Deviations from Baseline, 2008–20 (Continued)

	Years												
	2008	2009	2010	2011	2012	2013	2014	2015	2016	2017	2018	2019	2020
Public	(0.0)	0.0	0.0	0.0	(0.0)	(0.0)	(0.0)	(0.0)	(0.0)	(0.0)	(0.0)	(0.0)	(0.0)
Private	(0.0)	(0.0)	0.0	(0.0)	(0.0)	(0.0)	(0.0)	(0.0)	(0.0)	(0.0)	(0.0)	(0.0)	(0.0)
Aid, total	0.4	0.4	0.4	0.0	0.0	0.0	0.0	0.0	0.0	0.0	0.0	0.0	0.0
Other current account flows (net)	0.0	0.0	(0.0)	0.0	0.0	0.0	0.0	0.0	0.0	0.0	0.0	0.0	0.0
Capital account	(0.0)	(0.0)	(0.1)	0.0	0.1	0.0	0.0	0.0	0.0	0.0	0.0	0.0	0.0
Foreign direct investment	0.0	0.0	(0.0)	0.0	0.0	0.0	0.0	0.0	0.0	0.0	0.0	0.0	0.0
Public borrowing	(0.0)	(0.1)	(0.1)	0.0	0.1	(0.0)	(0.0)	(0.0)	(0.0)	0.0	(0.0)	(0.0)	(0.0)
Other capital inflows	0.0	0.0	(0.0)	0.0	0.0	0.0	0.0	0.0	0.0	0.0	0.0	0.0	0.0
Government Sector (% of GDP)													
Total resources (including grants)	0.0	0.1	0.0	0.1	0.1	0.0	0.0	0.0	0.0	0.0	0.0	0.0	0.0
Total tax revenues	(0.4)	(0.4)	(0.4)	0.0	0.0	0.0	0.0	0.0	0.0	0.0	0.0	0.0	0.0
Domestic taxes	0.0	0.0	0.0	0.4	0.4	0.4	0.4	0.4	0.4	0.4	0.4	0.4	0.4
Direct taxes	0.0	0.0	0.0	0.0	0.0	0.0	0.0	0.0	0.0	0.0	0.0	0.0	0.0
Indirect taxes	0.0	0.0	0.0	0.4	0.4	0.4	0.4	0.4	0.4	0.4	0.4	0.4	0.4
Indirect taxes on imports	(0.4)	(0.4)	(0.4)	(0.4)	(0.4)	(0.4)	(0.4)	(0.4)	(0.4)	(0.4)	(0.4)	(0.4)	(0.4)
Total nontax revenues	0.0	0.0	0.0	0.0	0.0	0.0	0.0	0.0	0.0	0.0	0.0	0.0	0.0
Foreign aid (grants)	0.4	0.4	0.4	0.0	0.1	0.0	0.0	0.0	0.0	0.0	0.0	0.0	0.0
Total expenditure	0.0	0.0	(0.0)	0.1	0.1	0.0	0.0	0.0	0.0	0.0	0.0	0.0	0.0
Spending on goods and services (total)	0.0	(0.0)	(0.0)	0.0	0.0	0.0	0.0	0.0	0.0	0.0	0.0	0.0	0.0
Maintenance expenditure	0.0	0.0	(0.0)	0.0	0.0	0.0	0.0	0.0	0.0	0.0	0.0	0.0	0.0
Other expenditures on goods and services	(0.0)	(0.0)	(0.0)	0.0	0.0	0.0	0.0	0.0	0.0	0.0	0.0	0.0	(0.0)
Wages and salaries	0.0	0.0	(0.0)	0.0	0.0	0.0	0.0	0.0	0.0	0.0	0.0	0.0	(0.0)
Investment	0.0	0.0	(0.0)	0.0	0.0	0.0	0.0	0.0	0.0	0.0	0.0	0.0	(0.0)

	1	2	3	4	5	6	7	8	9	10	11	12
Interest payments	0.0	0.0	(0.0)	0.0	0.0	0.0	0.0	0.0	0.0	0.0	0.0	0.0
Domestic debt	0.0	0.0	(0.0)	0.0	0.0	0.0	0.0	0.0	0.0	0.0	0.0	0.0
Foreign debt	0.0	(0.0)	(0.0)	(0.0)	0.0	0.0	0.0	0.0	0.0	0.0	0.0	0.0
Subsidies	0.0	0.0	(0.0)	0.0	0.0	0.0	0.0	0.0	0.0	0.0	0.0	(0.0)
Overall fiscal balance including grants (cash basis)	0.0	0.1	0.1	(0.0)	(0.0)	0.0	0.0	0.0	0.0	(0.0)	0.0	0.0
Total financing	(0.0)	(0.1)	(0.1)	0.0	0.0	(0.0)	0.0	(0.0)	0.0	(0.0)	(0.0)	(0.0)
Domestic borrowing	0.0	0.0	0.0	0.0	0.0	0.0	0.0	(0.0)	0.0	(0.0)	(0.0)	(0.0)
Foreign financing	(0.0)	(0.1)	(0.1)	0.0	0.1	(0.0)	0.0	(0.0)	0.0	(0.0)	(0.0)	(0.0)
Real exchange rate (% change)	0.4	(0.1)	(0.4)	0.2	0.2	0.1	0.0	0.0	0.0	(0.0)	(0.0)	0.0
Memorandum items												
Real GDP per capita at factor cost (% change)	0.2	0.0	0.2	(0.5)	(0.0)	(0.0)	0.0	(0.0)	0.0	(0.0)	0.0	0.0
Real GDP per capita at market prices (% change)	0.2	0.0	0.2	(0.5)	(0.0)	(0.0)	0.0	(0.0)	0.0	(0.0)	0.0	0.0
Real disposable income per capita (% change)	0.5	0.0	(0.1)	(0.4)	(0.1)	(0.2)	0.0	(0.0)	0.0	(0.0)	0.0	0.0
Private savings rate (% of GDP)	0.1	0.1	0.0	0.0	0.0	0.0	0.0	0.0	0.0	0.0	0.0	0.0
Real private consumption per capita (% change)	0.6	0.0	(0.1)	(0.4)	(0.1)	(0.2)	0.0	(0.0)	0.0	(0.0)	0.0	0.0
Unemployment	(0.0)	(0.0)	(0.0)	0.0	0.0	0.0	0.0	0.0	0.0	(0.0)	0.0	0.0
Private investment (% of GDP)	0.0	0.0	0.0	0.0	0.1	0.0	0.0	0.0	0.0	0.0	0.0	0.0
Private investment (% of total investment)	0.0	0.0	0.0	0.0	0.0	0.1	0.1	0.0	0.0	0.0	0.0	0.0
Public investment (% of total public expenditure)	(0.0)	(0.0)	0.0	0.0	0.0	(0.0)	0.0	(0.0)	0.0	(0.0)	(0.0)	(0.0)
Health (% of public investment)	—	—	—	—	—	—	—	—	—	—	—	—
Infrastructure (% of public investment)	—	—	—	—	—	—	—	—	—	—	—	—
Education (% of public investment)	—	—	—	—	—	—	—	—	—	—	—	—
Other (% of public investment)	—	—	—	—	—	—	—	—	—	—	—	—

(Continued)

233

Table A53. Aid as a Temporary Compensation Scheme—Deviations from Baseline, 2008–20 (*Continued*)

	Years												
	2008	2009	2010	2011	2012	2013	2014	2015	2016	2017	2018	2019	2020
Domestic debt (% of GDP)	0.1	0.1	(0.0)	0.0	0.0	(0.0)	(0.0)	0.0	0.0	0.0	0.0	0.0	0.0
External debt (% of GDP)	0.1	(0.1)	(0.4)	(0.0)	0.1	0.1	0.1	0.1	0.1	0.1	0.1	0.1	0.0
Interest payment on external public debt (% of exports)	(0.0)	(0.0)	(0.0)	(0.0)	(0.0)	(0.0)	(0.0)	(0.0)	(0.0)	(0.0)	(0.0)	(0.0)	(0.0)
Degree of openness (total trade in % of GDP)	0.6	0.6	0.3	0.3	0.4	0.4	0.4	0.4	0.4	0.4	0.4	0.4	0.4
Educated labor (in % of population)	—	0.0	0.0	0.0	0.0	0.0	0.0	0.0	0.0	0.0	0.0	0.0	0.0

Note: The real exchange rate is defined as the growth rate of nominal exchange rate plus the growth rate of the import price index minus the growth rate of composite good price after indirect taxes.

Table A54. Aid Increase Goes to Public Infrastructure Investment—Deviations from Baseline, 2008–20

	Years												
	2008	2009	2010	2011	2012	2013	2014	2015	2016	2017	2018	2019	2020
Real Sector (in billions of current DR$)													
Total supply of goods and services	0.3	2.0	3.2	3.8	4.4	3.4	3.0	2.7	2.5	2.2	2.0	1.8	1.6
Gross domestic product at factor cost	0.1	0.4	1.5	2.3	3.2	3.6	3.4	3.2	3.1	2.9	2.7	2.5	2.2
Imports of goods and NFS (inclusive of tariffs)	0.8	5.1	6.3	6.5	6.7	3.0	2.3	1.7	1.4	1.2	1.0	0.8	0.6
Total expenditure on goods and services	0.3	2.6	3.5	4.1	4.7	3.0	2.8	2.3	2.0	1.7	1.5	1.2	1.0
Total consumption	0.5	1.8	2.7	3.1	3.5	2.8	2.4	2.0	1.7	1.5	1.2	1.0	0.8
Private consumption	0.5	1.8	2.7	3.1	3.4	2.7	2.3	1.9	1.6	1.4	1.2	0.9	0.7
Public spending on goods and services	0.2	2.0	2.9	4.1	4.7	3.8	4.1	3.3	2.8	2.6	2.1	1.8	1.5
Total investment	0.2	13.7	14.8	16.8	17.9	5.4	5.8	4.7	3.8	3.2	2.6	2.1	1.6
Private investment	0.2	2.5	3.5	5.6	6.9	6.1	6.7	5.5	4.4	3.7	3.0	2.4	1.9
Public investment	0.2	43.1	44.3	45.8	46.3	3.4	3.5	2.7	2.2	2.0	1.6	1.3	1.0
Exports of goods and NFS	0.0	0.6	1.4	2.0	2.7	2.7	2.5	2.2	2.0	1.7	1.5	1.2	1.0
Gross domestic product at market prices	(0.3)	0.9	2.0	2.8	4.0	3.7	3.9	3.8	3.5	3.3	3.0	2.7	2.4
Disposable income	0.1	0.3	1.3	2.1	2.9	3.4	3.2	3.1	2.9	2.8	2.6	2.4	2.2
Poverty rate													
IMMPA Method	(0.09)	(0.84)	(1.31)	(1.39)	(1.64)	(1.04)	(0.89)	(0.64)	(0.47)	(0.56)	(0.48)	(0.33)	(0.18)
External Sector (% of GDP)													
Current account	0.1	0.8	0.7	0.3	0.5	(0.2)	(0.1)	0.1	0.2	0.1	0.1	0.1	0.1
Trade balance	(0.3)	(1.4)	(1.5)	(1.5)	(1.2)	(0.2)	0.0	0.2	0.2	0.1	0.1	0.1	0.1
Exports of goods and NFS	0.2	(1.1)	(1.2)	(1.2)	(1.2)	(0.0)	(0.0)	0.1	0.2	0.1	0.2	0.2	0.2
Imports of goods and NFS	0.5	0.3	0.3	0.3	0.1	0.1	(0.0)	(0.1)	(0.1)	0.0	0.1	0.1	0.1
Private unrequited transfers	0.0	(0.4)	(0.6)	(0.6)	(0.7)	(0.3)	(0.3)	(0.2)	(0.2)	(0.2)	(0.1)	(0.1)	(0.1)
Income (net)	(0.0)	0.3	0.4	0.4	0.5	0.2	0.2	0.2	0.1	0.1	0.1	0.1	0.0

(Continued)

Table A54. Aid Increase Goes to Public Investment—Deviations from Baseline, 2008–20 (Continued)

	Years												
	2008	2009	2010	2011	2012	2013	2014	2015	2016	2017	2018	2019	2020
Public	(0.0)	0.1	0.1	0.1	0.1	0.1	0.1	0.0	0.0	0.0	0.0	0.0	0.0
Private	(0.0)	0.2	0.3	0.3	0.3	0.1	0.1	0.1	0.1	0.1	0.1	0.1	0.0
Aid, total	0.4	2.4	2.4	2.0	2.0	0.0	0.0	0.0	0.0	0.0	0.0	0.0	0.0
Other current account flows (net)	0.0	(0.0)	(0.0)	(0.0)	(0.0)	(0.0)	(0.0)	(0.0)	(0.0)	(0.0)	(0.0)	(0.0)	(0.0)
Capital account	(0.0)	(0.3)	(0.5)	(0.4)	(0.5)	(0.3)	(0.2)	(0.2)	(0.2)	(0.1)	(0.1)	(0.1)	(0.1)
Foreign direct investment	0.0	(0.0)	(0.1)	(0.1)	(0.2)	(0.2)	(0.2)	(0.2)	(0.2)	(0.1)	(0.1)	(0.1)	(0.1)
Public borrowing	(0.0)	(0.2)	(0.3)	(0.2)	(0.3)	(0.1)	0.0	0.0	0.0	0.0	0.0	0.0	0.0
Other capital inflows	0.0	(0.0)	(0.0)	(0.0)	(0.0)	(0.0)	(0.0)	(0.0)	(0.0)	(0.0)	(0.0)	(0.0)	(0.0)
Government Sector (% of GDP)													
Total resources (including grants)	0.0	2.1	2.1	2.1	2.0	(0.0)	(0.0)	(0.1)	(0.1)	(0.0)	(0.0)	(0.0)	(0.0)
Total tax revenues	(0.4)	(0.3)	(0.3)	0.1	0.1	(0.0)	(0.1)	(0.1)	(0.1)	(0.1)	(0.1)	(0.1)	(0.0)
Domestic taxes	0.0	0.1	0.1	0.5	0.5	0.4	0.4	0.3	0.3	0.3	0.3	0.4	0.4
Direct taxes	0.0	(0.0)	(0.0)	(0.0)	(0.0)	(0.0)	(0.0)	(0.0)	(0.0)	(0.0)	(0.0)	(0.0)	(0.0)
Indirect taxes	0.0	0.1	0.1	0.5	0.5	0.4	0.4	0.4	0.4	0.4	0.4	0.4	0.4
Indirect taxes on imports	(0.4)	(0.4)	(0.4)	(0.4)	(0.4)	(0.4)	(0.4)	(0.4)	(0.4)	(0.4)	(0.4)	(0.4)	(0.4)
Total nontax revenues	0.0	(0.0)	(0.0)	0.0	0.0	0.0	0.0	0.0	0.0	0.0	0.0	0.0	0.0
Foreign aid (grants)	0.4	2.4	2.4	2.0	2.0	0.0	0.0	0.0	0.0	0.0	0.0	0.0	0.0
Total expenditure	0.0	1.9	1.8	1.9	1.8	(0.1)	(0.0)	(0.1)	(0.1)	(0.0)	(0.0)	(0.0)	(0.0)
Spending on goods and services (total)	0.0	(0.0)	(0.0)	0.0	0.0	0.0	0.1	0.0	0.0	0.0	0.0	0.0	0.0
Maintenance expenditure	0.0	(0.0)	(0.0)	(0.0)	0.0	0.0	0.0	0.0	0.0	0.0	0.0	0.0	0.0
Other expenditures on goods and services	(0.0)	(0.0)	(0.0)	0.0	(0.0)	0.0	0.0	0.0	0.0	0.0	0.0	0.0	0.0
Wages and salaries	0.0	(0.0)	(0.0)	0.0	0.0	0.0	0.0	0.0	0.0	0.0	0.0	0.0	0.0
Investment	0.0	2.0	2.0	2.0	2.0	0.0	0.0	0.0	0.0	0.0	0.0	0.0	0.0

Interest payments	0.0	(0.1)	(0.2)	(0.2)	(0.2)	(0.2)	(0.1)	(0.1)	(0.1)	(0.1)	(0.1)	(0.1)	(0.0)
Domestic debt	0.0	(0.0)	(0.1)	(0.1)	(0.1)	(0.1)	(0.1)	(0.1)	(0.1)	(0.1)	(0.1)	(0.1)	(0.0)
Foreign debt	0.0	(0.1)	(0.1)	(0.1)	(0.1)	(0.1)	(0.1)	(0.0)	(0.0)	(0.0)	(0.0)	(0.0)	(0.0)
Subsidies	0.0	(0.0)	(0.0)	0.0	0.0	0.0	0.0	0.0	0.0	0.0	0.0	0.0	0.0
Overall fiscal balance including grants (cash basis)	0.0	0.2	0.3	0.2	0.3	0.1	0.0	0.0	0.0	0.0	0.0	0.0	0.0
Total financing	(0.0)	(0.2)	(0.3)	(0.2)	(0.3)	(0.1)	0.0	0.0	0.0	0.0	0.0	0.0	0.0
Domestic borrowing	0.0	(0.0)	(0.0)	0.0	0.0	0.0	0.0	0.0	0.0	0.0	0.0	0.0	0.0
Foreign financing	(0.0)	(0.2)	(0.3)	(0.2)	(0.3)	(0.1)	0.0	0.0	0.0	0.0	0.0	0.0	0.0
Real exchange rate (% change)	0.4	(1.7)	(0.3)	0.3	0.0	1.6	0.2	0.1	0.0	0.0	0.0	0.0	0.0
Memorandum items													
Real GDP per capita at factor cost (% change)	0.2	2.4	0.9	0.5	0.8	(1.7)	(0.1)	(0.4)	(0.4)	(0.3)	(0.3)	(0.3)	(0.3)
Real GDP per capita at market prices (% change)	0.2	2.3	0.9	0.5	0.8	(1.6)	(0.1)	(0.4)	(0.4)	(0.3)	(0.3)	(0.3)	(0.3)
Real disposable income per capita (% hange)	0.5	1.3	0.9	0.4	0.4	(0.7)	(0.4)	(0.5)	(0.3)	(0.2)	(0.2)	(0.2)	(0.2)
Private savings rate (% of GDP)	0.1	(0.1)	(0.1)	(0.1)	(0.2)	(0.0)	(0.1)	(0.1)	(0.1)	(0.1)	(0.1)	(0.0)	(0.0)
Real private consumption per capita (% change)	0.6	1.3	0.9	0.4	0.4	(0.7)	(0.4)	(0.5)	(0.3)	(0.2)	(0.2)	(0.2)	(0.2)
Unemployment	(0.0)	(0.1)	(0.2)	(0.3)	(0.4)	(0.5)	(0.4)	(0.3)	(0.2)	(0.2)	(0.2)	(0.1)	(0.1)
Private investment (% of GDP)	0.0	0.0	0.0	0.2	0.3	0.4	0.5	0.4	0.3	0.2	0.2	0.1	0.1
Private investment (% of total investment)	0.0	(7.2)	(7.1)	(6.9)	(6.7)	0.5	0.6	0.5	0.4	0.3	0.3	0.2	0.2
Public investment (% of total public expenditure)	(0.0)	6.5	6.6	6.6	6.6	0.2	0.2	0.1	0.1	0.0	0.0	0.0	0.0
Health (% of public investment)	—	—	—	—	—	—	—	—	—	—	—	—	—
Infrastructure (% of public investment)	—	—	—	—	—	—	—	—	—	—	—	—	—
Education (% of public investment)	—	—	—	—	—	—	—	—	—	—	—	—	—
Other (% of public investment)	—	—	—	—	—	—	—	—	—	—	—	—	—

(Continued)

Table A54. Aid Increase Goes to Public Infrastructure Investment—Deviations from Baseline, 2008–20 (*Continued*)

							Years						
	2008	2009	2010	2011	2012	2013	2014	2015	2016	2017	2018	2019	2020
Domestic debt (% of GDP)	0.1	(0.2)	(0.3)	(0.5)	(0.7)	(0.6)	(0.6)	(0.6)	(0.5)	(0.4)	(0.4)	(0.3)	(0.3)
External debt (% of GDP)	0.1	(1.6)	(2.3)	(2.5)	(3.0)	(1.4)	(1.2)	(1.0)	(0.8)	(0.6)	(0.4)	(0.2)	0.0
Interest payment on external public debt (% of exports)	(0.0)	(0.0)	(0.1)	(0.1)	(0.2)	(0.2)	(0.1)	(0.1)	(0.1)	(0.1)	(0.1)	(0.1)	(0.0)
Degree of openness (total trade in % of GDP)	0.6	(0.8)	(0.8)	(1.0)	(1.1)	0.1	(0.1)	(0.0)	0.1	0.2	0.3	0.3	0.4
Educated labor (in % of population)	—	0.0	0.0	0.0	0.0	0.1	0.1	0.2	0.2	0.3	0.3	0.4	0.4

Note: The real exchange rate is defined as the growth rate of nominal exchange rate plus the growth rate of the import price index minus the growth rate of composite good price after indirect taxes.

238

Table A55. Aid Increase Goes to Public Infrastructure Investment—Deviations from Baseline, 2008–20

	Years												
	2008	2009	2010	2011	2012	2013	2014	2015	2016	2017	2018	2019	2020
Real Sector (in billions of current DR$)													
Total supply of goods and services	0.3	2.0	3.1	3.5	4.1	3.0	2.6	2.4	2.2	2.0	1.8	1.7	1.5
Gross domestic product at factor cost	0.1	0.4	1.3	2.0	2.7	3.0	2.9	2.8	2.8	2.6	2.5	2.3	2.1
Imports of goods and NFS (inclusive of tariffs	0.8	5.1	6.3	6.3	6.6	2.9	2.2	1.6	1.2	1.0	0.8	0.5	0.3
Total expenditure on goods and services	0.3	2.6	3.4	3.9	4.4	2.7	2.5	2.1	1.8	1.6	1.3	1.0	0.8
Total consumption	0.5	1.8	2.6	2.8	3.3	2.5	2.1	1.7	1.4	1.2	1.0	0.8	0.5
Private consumption	0.5	1.8	2.6	2.8	3.2	2.4	2.0	1.6	1.3	1.1	0.9	0.7	0.5
Public spending on goods and services	0.2	2.0	2.7	3.7	4.6	3.8	4.1	3.5	3.1	2.8	2.4	2.0	1.7
Total investment	0.2	13.7	14.7	16.1	17.5	5.2	5.8	5.3	4.7	4.2	3.5	3.0	2.4
Private investment	0.2	2.5	3.3	4.9	6.4	6.1	6.9	6.4	5.6	5.1	4.3	3.6	3.0
Public investment	0.2	43.1	44.1	45.0	45.9	3.1	3.1	2.5	2.1	1.9	1.5	1.2	0.9
Exports of goods and NFS	0.0	0.6	1.4	1.9	2.5	2.4	2.2	1.9	1.7	1.4	1.2	0.9	0.7
Gross domestic product at market prices	(0.3)	0.9	1.8	2.6	3.5	3.1	3.5	3.6	3.5	3.3	3.1	2.8	2.6
Disposable income	0.1	0.3	1.1	1.7	2.4	2.8	2.8	2.7	2.7	2.6	2.4	2.3	2.1
Poverty rate													
IMMPA Method	(0.09)	(0.84)	(1.28)	(1.31)	(1.52)	(0.93)	(0.84)	(0.62)	(0.47)	(0.55)	(0.47)	(0.30)	(0.15)
External Sector (% of GDP)													
Current account	0.1	0.8	0.7	0.4	0.5	(0.3)	(0.0)	0.1	0.1	0.1	0.1	0.1	0.1
Trade balance	(0.3)	(1.4)	(1.5)	(1.4)	(1.3)	(0.2)	0.0	0.1	0.2	0.1	0.1	0.1	0.1
Exports of goods and NFS	0.2	(1.1)	(1.2)	(1.2)	(1.2)	(0.1)	(0.1)	(0.0)	0.0	0.0	0.1	0.1	0.1
Imports of goods and NFS	0.5	0.3	0.3	0.1	0.0	0.1	(0.1)	(0.2)	(0.2)	(0.1)	(0.1)	(0.0)	0.0
Private unrequited transfers	0.0	(0.4)	(0.6)	(0.6)	(0.7)	(0.3)	(0.3)	(0.2)	(0.2)	(0.2)	(0.1)	(0.1)	(0.1)
Income (net)	(0.0)	0.3	0.4	0.4	0.5	0.2	0.2	0.2	0.1	0.1	0.1	0.1	0.0

(Continued)

Table A55. Aid Increase Goes to Public Infrastructure Investment—Deviations from Baseline, 2008–20 (*Continued*)

	Years												
	2008	2009	2010	2011	2012	2013	2014	2015	2016	2017	2018	2019	2020
Public	(0.0)	0.1	0.1	0.1	0.1	0.1	0.1	0.0	0.0	0.0	0.0	0.0	(0.0)
Private	(0.0)	0.2	0.3	0.3	0.3	0.1	0.1	0.1	0.1	0.1	0.1	0.1	0.0
Aid, total	0.4	2.4	2.4	2.0	2.0	0.0	0.0	0.0	0.0	0.0	0.0	0.0	0.0
Other current account flows (net)	0.0	(0.0)	(0.0)	(0.0)	(0.0)	(0.0)	(0.0)	(0.0)	(0.0)	(0.0)	(0.0)	(0.0)	(0.0)
Capital account	(0.0)	(0.3)	(0.5)	(0.5)	(0.5)	(0.2)	(0.2)	(0.2)	(0.2)	(0.1)	(0.1)	(0.1)	(0.1)
Foreign direct investment	0.0	(0.0)	(0.1)	(0.2)	(0.2)	(0.2)	(0.2)	(0.2)	(0.2)	(0.2)	(0.2)	(0.1)	(0.1)
Public borrowing	(0.0)	(0.2)	(0.3)	(0.3)	(0.3)	(0.0)	(0.0)	0.0	0.0	0.0	0.0	0.0	0.0
Other capital inflows	0.0	(0.0)	(0.0)	(0.0)	(0.0)	(0.0)	(0.0)	(0.0)	(0.0)	(0.0)	(0.0)	(0.0)	(0.0)
Government Sector (% of GDP)													
Total resources (including grants)	0.0	2.1	2.1	2.1	2.0	0.0	(0.0)	(0.1)	(0.1)	(0.1)	(0.0)	(0.0)	(0.0)
Total tax revenues	(0.4)	(0.3)	(0.3)	0.1	0.1	(0.0)	(0.1)	(0.1)	(0.1)	(0.1)	(0.1)	(0.1)	(0.1)
Domestic taxes	0.0	0.1	0.1	0.5	0.5	0.4	0.4	0.3	0.3	0.3	0.3	0.3	0.4
Direct taxes	0.0	(0.0)	(0.0)	(0.0)	(0.0)	(0.0)	(0.0)	(0.0)	(0.0)	(0.0)	(0.0)	(0.0)	(0.0)
Indirect taxes	0.0	0.1	0.1	0.5	0.5	0.4	0.4	0.4	0.4	0.4	0.4	0.4	0.4
Indirect taxes on imports	(0.4)	(0.4)	(0.4)	(0.4)	(0.4)	(0.4)	(0.4)	(0.4)	(0.4)	(0.4)	(0.4)	(0.4)	(0.4)
Total nontax revenues	0.0	(0.0)	(0.0)	(0.0)	(0.0)	0.0	0.0	0.0	0.0	0.0	0.0	0.0	0.0
Foreign aid (grants)	0.4	2.4	2.4	2.0	2.0	0.0	0.0	0.0	0.0	0.0	0.0	0.0	0.0
Total expenditure	0.0	1.9	1.8	1.8	1.8	(0.0)	(0.0)	(0.1)	(0.1)	(0.0)	(0.0)	(0.0)	0.0
Spending on goods and services (total)	0.0	(0.0)	(0.0)	0.0	0.0	0.1	0.1	0.1	0.1	0.1	0.1	0.0	0.0
Maintenance expenditure	0.0	(0.0)	0.0	0.0	0.0	0.0	0.1	0.1	0.1	0.1	0.1	0.0	0.0
Other expenditures on goods and services	(0.0)	(0.0)	(0.0)	(0.0)	(0.0)	0.0	0.0	0.0	0.0	0.0	0.0	0.0	(0.0)
Wages and salaries	0.0	(0.0)	(0.0)	(0.0)	(0.0)	0.0	0.0	0.0	0.0	0.0	0.0	0.0	0.0

Investment	0.0	2.0	2.0	2.0	2.0	2.0	0.0	0.0	0.0	0.0	0.0	0.0
	0.0											
Interest payments	0.0	(0.1)	(0.2)	(0.2)	(0.2)	(0.2)	(0.2)	(0.1)	(0.1)	(0.1)	(0.1)	(0.1)
												(0.0)
Domestic debt	0.0	(0.0)	(0.1)	(0.1)	(0.1)	(0.1)	(0.1)	(0.1)	(0.0)	(0.0)	(0.0)	(0.1)
												(0.0)
Foreign debt	0.0	(0.1)	(0.1)	(0.1)	(0.1)	(0.1)	(0.1)	(0.0)	(0.0)	(0.0)	(0.0)	(0.1)
												(0.0)
Subsidies	0.0	(0.0)	(0.0)	(0.0)	(0.0)	(0.0)	(0.0)	(0.0)	0.0	0.0	0.0	0.0
												0.0
Overall fiscal balance including grants (cash basis)	0.0	0.2	0.3	0.3	0.3	0.3	0.0	0.2	0.0	0.0	0.0	(0.0)
												(0.0)
Total financing	(0.0)	(0.2)	(0.3)	(0.3)	(0.3)	(0.3)	(0.0)	0.0	0.0	0.0	0.0	0.0
												0.0
Domestic borrowing	0.0	(0.0)	(0.0)	(0.0)	(0.0)	(0.0)	0.0	0.0	0.0	0.0	0.0	0.0
												0.0
Foreign financing	(0.0)	(0.2)	(0.3)	(0.3)	(0.3)	(0.3)	(0.0)	0.0	0.0	0.0	0.0	0.0
												0.0
Real exchange rate (% change)	0.4	(1.7)	0.4	0.1	0.1	0.3	1.6	0.2	0.0	0.0	0.0	(0.0)
												(0.0)
Memorandum items												
Real GDP per capita at factor cost (% change)	0.2	2.4	0.8	0.4	0.4	0.7	(1.7)	(0.0)	(0.2)	(0.3)	(0.3)	(0.3)
												(0.3)
Real GDP per capita at market prices (% change)	0.2	2.3	0.8	0.4	0.4	0.7	(1.7)	(0.0)	(0.2)	(0.3)	(0.3)	(0.3)
												(0.3)
Real disposable income per capita (% change)	0.5	1.3	0.8	0.2	0.2	0.4	(0.8)	(0.4)	(0.4)	(0.3)	(0.2)	(0.2)
												(0.2)
Private savings rate (% of GDP)	0.1	(0.1)	(0.1)	(0.1)	(0.1)	(0.2)	(0.0)	(0.1)	(0.1)	(0.1)	(0.1)	(0.1)
												(0.1)
Real private consumption per capita (% change)	0.6	1.3	0.8	0.2	0.2	0.4	(0.8)	(0.4)	(0.4)	(0.3)	(0.2)	(0.2)
												(0.2)
Unemployment	(0.0)	(0.1)	(0.1)	(0.1)	(0.1)	(0.2)	(0.2)	(0.1)	(0.1)	(0.1)	(0.1)	(0.1)
												(0.1)
Private investment (% of GDP)	0.0	0.0	0.0	0.2	0.3	0.4	0.5	0.5	0.4	0.4	0.4	0.3
												0.3
Private investment (% of total investment)	0.0	(7.2)	(7.1)	(6.9)	(6.9)	(6.8)	0.6	0.7	0.7	0.6	0.5	0.5
												0.4
Public investment (% of total public expenditure)	(0.0)	6.5	6.6	6.6	6.6	6.6	0.1	0.1	0.1	0.1	0.1	0.0
												(0.0)
Health (% of public investment)	—	(1.7)	(1.7)	(1.7)	(1.7)	(1.7)	—	—	—	—	—	—
Infrastructure (% of public investment)	—	12.5	12.5	12.5	12.5	12.5	—	—	—	—	—	—
Education (% of public investment)	—	(2.0)	(2.0)	(2.0)	(2.0)	(2.0)	—	—	—	—	—	—
Other (% of public investment)	—	(8.7)	(8.7)	(8.7)	(8.7)	(8.7)	—	—	—	—	—	—

(Continued)

Table A55. Aid Increase Goes to Public Infrastructure Investment—Deviations from Baseline, 2008–20 (*Continued*)

	Years												
	2008	2009	2010	2011	2012	2013	2014	2015	2016	2017	2018	2019	2020
Domestic debt (% of GDP)	0.1	(0.2)	(0.3)	(0.4)	(0.6)	(0.5)	(0.5)	(0.5)	(0.5)	(0.4)	(0.4)	(0.3)	(0.3)
External debt (% of GDP)	0.1	(1.6)	(2.3)	(2.6)	(3.0)	(1.4)	(1.1)	(0.9)	(0.7)	(0.5)	(0.2)	(0.0)	0.2
Interest payment on external public debt (% of exports)	(0.0)	(0.0)	(0.1)	(0.1)	(0.2)	(0.2)	(0.1)	(0.1)	(0.1)	(0.1)	(0.0)	(0.0)	(0.0)
Degree of openness (total trade in % of GDP)	0.6	(0.8)	(0.9)	(1.1)	(1.2)	(0.0)	(0.2)	(0.2)	(0.1)	(0.1)	0.0	0.1	0.2
Educated labor (in % of population)	—	0.0	0.0	0.0	0.0	0.0	0.0	0.0	0.1	0.1	0.1	0.1	0.1

Note: The real exchange rate is defined as the growth rate of nominal exchange rate plus the growth rate of the import price index minus the growth rate of composite good price after indirect taxes.

Table A56. Aid Sustained Longer to Public Investment—Deviations from Baseline, 2008–20

	Years													
	2007	2008	2009	2010	2011	2012	2013	2014	2015	2016	2017	2018	2019	2020
Real Sector (in billions of current DR$)														
Total supply of goods and services	—	0.3	2.0	3.2	3.4	3.4	3.2	2.7	2.4	2.2	2.0	1.8	1.6	1.4
Gross domestic product at factor cost	—	0.1	0.4	1.5	2.3	2.8	3.0	3.0	2.9	2.7	2.5	2.4	2.2	2.0
Imports of goods and NFS (inclusive of tariffs)	—	0.8	5.1	6.3	5.5	4.5	3.4	2.2	1.6	1.3	1.1	0.9	0.7	0.6
Total expenditure on goods and services	—	0.3	2.6	3.5	3.6	3.4	3.0	2.4	2.1	1.8	1.5	1.3	1.1	0.8
Total consumption	—	0.5	1.8	2.7	2.8	2.8	2.6	2.1	1.7	1.5	1.3	1.1	0.9	0.7
Private consumption	—	0.5	1.8	2.7	2.8	2.7	2.5	2.1	1.7	1.4	1.2	1.0	0.8	0.7
Public spending on goods and services	—	0.2	2.0	2.9	3.6	3.8	3.8	3.4	2.9	2.5	2.3	1.9	1.6	1.3
Total investment	—	0.2	13.7	14.8	13.3	11.0	8.2	4.8	4.2	3.3	2.8	2.2	1.8	1.4
Private investment	—	0.2	2.5	3.5	5.1	5.9	6.0	5.6	4.9	3.9	3.3	2.6	2.1	1.6
Public investment	—	0.2	43.1	44.3	34.8	24.3	13.7	2.9	2.4	1.9	1.8	1.4	1.1	0.9
Exports of goods and NFS	—	0.0	0.6	1.4	1.9	2.2	2.3	2.2	2.0	1.8	1.5	1.3	1.1	0.9
Gross domestic product at market prices	—	(0.3)	0.9	2.0	2.5	3.2	3.4	3.3	3.3	3.1	2.9	2.6	2.4	2.1
Disposable income	—	0.1	0.3	1.3	2.0	2.6	2.8	2.9	2.7	2.6	2.4	2.3	2.1	1.9
Poverty rate														
IMMPA Method	—	(0.09)	(0.84)	(1.31)	(1.14)	(1.08)	(1.06)	(0.81)	(0.56)	(0.40)	(0.51)	(0.44)	(0.28)	(0.15)
Log-normal distribution	—	(0.06)	(0.78)	(1.05)	(0.99)	(0.96)	(0.86)	(0.68)	(0.60)	(0.49)	(0.40)	(0.32)	(0.24)	(0.18)
External Sector (% of GDP)														
Current account	—	0.1	0.8	0.7	0.2	0.1	0.1	(0.1)	0.1	0.1	0.0	0.1	0.1	0.0
Trade balance	—	(0.3)	(1.4)	(1.5)	(1.2)	(0.8)	(0.4)	(0.0)	0.1	0.2	0.1	0.1	0.1	0.1
Exports of goods and NFS	—	0.2	(1.1)	(1.2)	(0.9)	(0.6)	(0.3)	0.0	0.1	0.2	0.1	0.2	0.2	0.2
Imports of goods and NFS	—	0.5	0.3	0.3	0.3	0.1	0.1	0.0	(0.0)	0.1	0.1	0.1	0.1	0.2
Private unrequited transfers	—	0.0	(0.4)	(0.6)	(0.5)	(0.4)	(0.3)	(0.2)	(0.2)	(0.2)	(0.1)	(0.1)	(0.1)	(0.1)

(Continued)

Table A56. Aid Sustained Longer to Public Investment—Deviations from Baseline, 2008–20 (Continued)

	Years													
	2007	2008	2009	2010	2011	2012	2013	2014	2015	2016	2017	2018	2019	2020
Income (net)	—	(0.0)	0.3	0.4	0.3	0.3	0.2	0.2	0.1	0.1	0.1	0.1	0.0	0.0
Public	—	(0.0)	0.1	0.1	0.1	0.1	0.1	0.1	0.0	0.0	0.0	0.0	0.0	(0.0)
Private	—	(0.0)	0.2	0.3	0.3	0.2	0.2	0.1	0.1	0.1	0.1	0.1	0.0	0.0
Aid, total	—	0.4	2.4	2.4	1.5	1.0	0.5	0.0	0.0	0.0	0.0	0.0	0.0	0.0
Other current account flows (net)	—	0.0	(0.0)	(0.0)	(0.0)	(0.0)	(0.0)	(0.0)	(0.0)	(0.0)	(0.0)	(0.0)	(0.0)	(0.0)
Capital account	—	(0.0)	(0.3)	(0.5)	(0.4)	(0.3)	(0.3)	(0.2)	(0.2)	(0.2)	(0.1)	(0.1)	(0.1)	(0.1)
Foreign direct investment	—	0.0	(0.0)	(0.1)	(0.1)	(0.2)	(0.2)	(0.1)	(0.1)	(0.1)	(0.1)	(0.1)	(0.1)	(0.1)
Public borrowing	—	(0.0)	(0.2)	(0.3)	(0.2)	(0.1)	(0.1)	0.0	0.0	(0.0)	0.0	0.0	0.0	0.0
Other capital inflows	—	0.0	(0.0)	(0.0)	(0.0)	(0.0)	(0.0)	(0.0)	(0.0)	(0.0)	(0.0)	(0.0)	(0.0)	(0.0)
Government Sector (% of GDP)														
Total resources (including grants)	—	0.0	2.1	2.1	1.6	1.0	0.5	(0.0)	(0.1)	(0.1)	(0.1)	(0.0)	(0.0)	(0.0)
Total tax revenues	—	(0.4)	(0.3)	(0.3)	0.1	0.0	(0.0)	(0.0)	(0.1)	(0.1)	(0.1)	(0.1)	(0.1)	(0.0)
Domestic taxes	—	0.0	0.1	0.1	0.5	0.4	0.4	0.4	0.3	0.3	0.3	0.4	0.4	0.4
Direct taxes	—	0.0	(0.0)	(0.0)	(0.0)	(0.0)	(0.0)	(0.0)	(0.0)	(0.0)	(0.0)	(0.0)	(0.0)	(0.0)
Indirect taxes	—	0.0	0.1	0.1	0.5	0.5	0.4	0.4	0.4	0.4	0.4	0.4	0.4	0.4
Indirect taxes on imports	—	(0.4)	(0.4)	(0.4)	(0.4)	(0.4)	(0.4)	(0.4)	(0.4)	(0.4)	(0.4)	(0.4)	(0.4)	(0.4)
Total nontax revenues	—	0.0	(0.0)	(0.0)	0.0	0.0	0.0	0.0	0.0	0.0	0.0	0.0	0.0	0.0
Foreign aid (grants)	—	0.4	2.4	2.4	1.5	1.0	0.5	0.0	0.0	0.0	0.0	0.0	0.0	0.0
Total expenditure	—	0.0	1.9	1.8	1.4	0.9	0.4	(0.0)	(0.1)	(0.1)	(0.0)	(0.0)	(0.0)	(0.0)
Spending on goods and services (total)	—	0.0	(0.0)	(0.0)	0.0	0.0	0.0	0.1	0.0	0.0	0.0	0.0	0.0	0.0
Maintenance expenditure	—	0.0	(0.0)	(0.0)	0.0	0.0	0.0	0.0	0.0	0.0	0.0	0.0	0.0	0.0
Other expenditures on goods and services	—	(0.0)	(0.0)	(0.0)	0.0	0.0	0.0	0.0	0.0	0.0	0.0	0.0	0.0	0.0
Wages and salaries	—	0.0	(0.0)	(0.0)	0.0	0.0	0.0	0.0	0.0	0.0	0.0	0.0	0.0	(0.0)

Investment	—	0.0	2.0	2.0	1.5	1.0	0.5	0.0	0.0	0.0	0.0	0.0	(0.0)
Interest payments	—	0.0	(0.1)	(0.1)	(0.1)	(0.1)	(0.2)	(0.1)	(0.1)	(0.1)	(0.1)	(0.1)	(0.0)
Domestic debt	—	0.0	(0.0)	(0.1)	(0.1)	(0.1)	(0.1)	(0.1)	(0.1)	(0.1)	(0.1)	(0.0)	(0.0)
Foreign debt	—	0.0	(0.1)	(0.1)	(0.1)	(0.1)	(0.1)	(0.1)	(0.0)	(0.0)	(0.0)	(0.0)	(0.0)
Subsidies	—	0.0	(0.0)	(0.0)	0.0	0.0	0.0	0.0	0.0	0.0	0.0	0.0	(0.0)
Overall fiscal balance including grants (cash basis)	—	0.0	0.2	0.3	0.2	0.1	0.1	0.0	0.0	0.0	0.0	0.0	(0.0)
Total financing	—	(0.0)	(0.2)	(0.3)	(0.2)	(0.1)	(0.1)	(0.0)	(0.0)	(0.0)	0.0	0.0	0.0
Domestic borrowing	—	0.0	(0.0)	(0.0)	0.0	0.0	0.0	0.0	0.0	0.0	0.0	0.0	0.0
Foreign financing	—	(0.0)	(0.2)	(0.3)	(0.2)	(0.1)	(0.1)	(0.0)	(0.0)	(0.0)	0.0	0.0	0.0
Prices and Real Exchange Rate													
GDP at factor cost deflator (% change)	—	—	—	—	—	—	—	—	—	—	—	—	—
Composite good price (after indirect taxes, % change)	—	(0.5)	(1.0)	0.2	0.6	0.6	0.5	0.4	0.3	0.1	0.0	0.0	0.0
Nominal exchange rate (% change)	—	(0.0)	(2.8)	(0.2)	1.3	1.0	0.9	0.8	0.2	0.1	0.0	0.0	0.0
Real exchange rate (% change)	—	0.4	(1.7)	(0.3)	0.7	0.5	0.4	0.4	(0.0)	0.1	0.0	0.0	0.0
Memorandum items													
Real GDP per capita at factor cost (% change)	—	0.2	2.4	0.9	(0.1)	0.0	(0.3)	(0.6)	(0.2)	(0.4)	(0.3)	(0.3)	(0.3)
Real GDP per capita at market prices (% change)	—	0.2	2.3	0.9	(0.1)	0.0	(0.3)	(0.6)	(0.2)	(0.3)	(0.3)	(0.3)	(0.2)
Real disposable income per capita (% change)	—	0.5	1.3	0.9	0.1	(0.1)	(0.2)	(0.4)	(0.4)	(0.3)	(0.2)	(0.2)	(0.2)
Private savings rate (% of GDP)	—	0.1	(0.1)	(0.1)	(0.1)	(0.1)	(0.1)	(0.1)	(0.1)	(0.1)	(0.1)	(0.0)	(0.0)
Real private consumption per capita (% change)	—	0.6	1.3	0.9	0.1	0.1	(0.2)	(0.4)	(0.4)	(0.3)	(0.2)	(0.2)	(0.2)
Unemployment	—	(0.0)	(0.1)	(0.2)	(0.3)	(0.4)	(0.4)	(0.3)	(0.3)	(0.2)	(0.2)	(0.1)	(0.1)
Private investment (% of GDP)	—	0.0	0.0	0.0	0.2	0.3	0.4	0.4	0.3	0.2	0.2	0.1	0.1
Private investment (% of total investment)	—	0.0	(7.2)	(7.1)	(5.3)	(3.4)	(1.4)	0.5	0.5	0.4	0.3	0.2	0.1

(Continued)

Table A56. Aid Sustained Longer to Public Investment—Deviations from Baseline, 2008–20 (*Continued*)

	Years													
	2007	2008	2009	2010	2011	2012	2013	2014	2015	2016	2017	2018	2019	2020
Public investment (% of total public expenditure)	—	(0.0)	6.5	6.6	5.1	3.5	1.9	0.1	0.1	0.1	0.1	0.0	0.0	0.0
Health (% of public investment)	—	—	—	—	—	—	—	—	—	—	—	—	—	—
Infrastructure (% of public investment)	—	—	—	—	—	—	—	—	—	—	—	—	—	—
Education (% of public investment)	—	—	—	—	—	—	—	—	—	—	—	—	—	—
Other (% of public investment)	—	—	—	—	—	—	—	—	—	—	—	—	—	—
Domestic debt (% of GDP)	—	0.1	(0.2)	(0.3)	(0.4)	(0.5)	(0.5)	(0.5)	(0.5)	(0.4)	(0.4)	(0.3)	(0.3)	(0.2)
External debt (% of GDP)	—	0.1	1.6	2.3	2.1	1.9	1.6	1.0	0.9	0.7	0.4	0.2	0.1	0.1
Interest payment on external public debt (% of exports)	—	(0.0)	(0.0)	(0.1)	(0.1)	(0.1)	(0.1)	(0.1)	(0.1)	(0.1)	(0.1)	(0.1)	(0.0)	(0.0)
Degree of openness (total trade in % of GDP)	—	0.6	(0.8)	(0.8)	(0.6)	(0.5)	(0.2)	0.0	0.0	0.1	0.2	0.3	0.3	0.4
Educated labor (in % of population)	—	—	0.0	0.0	0.0	0.0	0.1	0.1	0.2	0.2	0.3	0.3	0.3	0.4
Net foreign assets (in months of imports)	—	(0.0)	0.0	0.0	0.0	(0.0)	(0.0)	(0.0)	0.0	0.0	0.0	0.0	(0.0)	(0.0)
Oil Price (2005 = 100)	—	—	—	—	—	—	—	—	—	—	—	—	—	—

Note: The real exchange rate is defined as the growth rate of nominal exchange rate plus the growth rate of the import price index minus the growth rate of composite good price after indirect taxes.

Table A57. Aid Sustained Longer to Public Infrastructure Investment—Deviations from Baseline, 2008–20

							Years							
	2007	2008	2009	2010	2011	2012	2013	2014	2015	2016	2017	2018	2019	2020
Real Sector (in billions of current DR$)														
Total supply of goods and services	—	0.3	2.0	3.1	3.2	3.1	2.9	2.5	2.2	2.0	1.8	1.7	1.5	1.3
Gross domestic product at factor cost	—	0.1	0.4	1.3	1.9	2.3	2.6	2.6	2.6	2.5	2.4	2.2	2.1	1.9
Imports of goods and NFS (inclusive of tariffs)	—	0.8	5.1	6.3	5.5	4.5	3.4	2.1	1.5	1.2	0.9	0.7	0.5	0.4
Total expenditure on goods and services	—	0.3	2.6	3.4	3.4	3.2	2.8	2.3	1.9	1.7	1.4	1.2	0.9	0.7
Total consumption	—	0.5	1.8	2.6	2.6	2.6	2.3	1.9	1.5	1.3	1.1	0.9	0.7	0.5
Private consumption	—	0.5	1.8	2.6	2.6	2.5	2.2	1.8	1.4	1.2	1.0	0.8	0.6	0.4
Public spending on goods and services	—	0.2	2.0	2.7	3.5	3.8	3.9	3.5	3.2	2.7	2.5	2.1	1.8	1.5
Total investment	—	0.2	13.7	14.7	13.0	10.9	8.3	5.2	4.8	4.2	3.7	3.1	2.6	2.1
Private investment	—	0.2	2.5	3.3	4.7	5.7	6.3	6.2	5.8	5.1	4.5	3.8	3.2	2.6
Public investment	—	0.2	43.1	44.1	34.4	24.1	13.5	2.7	2.3	1.9	1.7	1.3	1.0	0.8
Exports of goods and NFS	—	0.0	0.6	1.4	1.8	2.1	2.1	1.9	1.7	1.5	1.3	1.1	0.8	0.6
Gross domestic product at market prices	—	(0.3)	0.9	1.8	2.2	2.7	3.0	3.0	3.2	3.1	2.9	2.7	2.5	2.3
Disposable income	—	0.1	0.3	1.1	1.7	2.1	2.4	2.5	2.5	2.4	2.3	2.2	2.0	1.9
Poverty rate														
IMMPA Method	—	(0.09)	(0.84)	(1.28)	(1.05)	(1.05)	(0.97)	(0.76)	(0.54)	(0.40)	(0.51)	(0.42)	(0.26)	(0.13)
Log-normal distribution	—	(0.06)	(0.78)	(1.01)	(0.94)	(0.90)	(0.80)	(0.64)	(0.57)	(0.48)	(0.39)	(0.31)	(0.23)	(0.17)
External Sector (% of GDP)														
Current account	—	0.1	0.8	0.7	0.2	0.1	0.0	(0.1)	0.0	0.1	0.0	0.1	0.0	0.0
Trade balance	—	(0.3)	(1.4)	(1.5)	(1.2)	(0.8)	(0.4)	(0.0)	0.1	0.1	0.1	0.1	0.1	0.0
Exports of goods and NFS	—	0.2	(1.1)	(1.2)	(1.0)	(0.7)	(0.4)	(0.1)	(0.0)	0.0	0.0	0.1	0.1	0.1
Imports of goods and NFS	—	0.5	0.3	0.3	0.2	0.1	0.0	(0.0)	(0.1)	(0.1)	(0.0)	(0.0)	0.0	0.1
Private unrequited transfers	—	0.0	(0.4)	(0.6)	(0.5)	(0.4)	(0.3)	(0.2)	(0.2)	(0.2)	(0.1)	(0.1)	(0.1)	(0.1)

(Continued)

Table A57. Aid Sustained Longer to Public Infrastructure Investment—Deviations from Baseline, 2008–20 (*Continued*)

	Years													
	2007	2008	2009	2010	2011	2012	2013	2014	2015	2016	2017	2018	2019	2020
Income (net)	—	(0.0)	0.3	0.4	0.4	0.3	0.2	0.2	0.1	0.1	0.1	0.1	0.0	0.0
Public	—	(0.0)	0.1	0.1	0.1	0.1	0.1	0.0	0.0	0.0	0.0	0.0	(0.0)	(0.0)
Private	—	(0.0)	0.2	0.3	0.3	0.2	0.2	0.1	0.1	0.1	0.1	0.1	0.0	0.0
Aid, total	—	0.4	2.4	2.4	1.5	1.0	0.5	0.0	0.0	0.0	0.0	0.0	0.0	0.0
Other current account flows (net)	—	0.0	(0.0)	(0.0)	(0.0)	(0.0)	(0.0)	(0.0)	(0.0)	(0.0)	(0.0)	(0.0)	(0.0)	(0.0)
Capital account	—	(0.0)	(0.3)	(0.5)	(0.4)	(0.3)	(0.2)	(0.1)	(0.1)	(0.1)	(0.1)	(0.1)	(0.0)	(0.0)
Foreign direct investment	—	0.0	(0.0)	(0.1)	(0.1)	(0.1)	(0.1)	(0.1)	(0.1)	(0.1)	(0.1)	(0.1)	(0.0)	(0.1)
Public borrowing	—	(0.0)	(0.2)	(0.3)	(0.2)	(0.1)	(0.1)	0.0	0.0	0.0	0.0	0.0	0.0	0.1
Other capital inflows	—	0.0	(0.0)	(0.0)	(0.0)	(0.0)	(0.0)	(0.0)	(0.0)	(0.0)	(0.0)	(0.0)	(0.0)	(0.0)
Government Sector (% of GDP)														
Total resources (including grants)	—	0.0	2.1	2.1	1.6	1.0	0.5	(0.0)	(0.1)	(0.1)	(0.1)	(0.1)	(0.0)	(0.0)
Total tax revenues	—	(0.4)	(0.3)	(0.3)	0.1	0.0	(0.0)	(0.0)	(0.1)	(0.1)	(0.1)	(0.1)	(0.1)	(0.0)
Domestic taxes	—	0.0	0.1	0.1	0.5	0.4	0.4	0.4	0.3	0.3	0.3	0.3	0.4	0.4
Direct taxes	—	0.0	(0.0)	(0.0)	(0.0)	(0.0)	(0.0)	(0.0)	(0.0)	(0.0)	(0.0)	(0.0)	(0.0)	(0.0)
Indirect taxes	—	0.0	0.1	0.1	0.5	0.5	0.4	0.4	0.4	0.4	0.4	0.4	0.4	0.4
Indirect taxes on imports	—	(0.4)	(0.4)	(0.4)	(0.4)	(0.4)	(0.4)	(0.4)	(0.4)	(0.4)	(0.4)	(0.4)	(0.4)	(0.4)
Total nontax revenues	—	0.0	(0.0)	(0.0)	0.0	0.0	0.0	0.0	0.0	0.0	0.0	0.0	0.0	0.0
Foreign aid (grants)	—	0.4	2.4	2.4	1.5	1.0	0.5	0.0	0.0	0.0	0.0	0.0	0.0	0.0
Total expenditure	—	0.0	1.9	1.8	1.4	0.9	0.4	(0.0)	(0.1)	(0.1)	(0.0)	(0.0)	(0.0)	0.0
Spending on goods and services (total)	—	0.0	(0.0)	(0.0)	0.0	0.0	0.1	0.1	0.1	0.1	0.1	0.0	0.0	0.0
Maintenance expenditure	—	0.0	(0.0)	(0.0)	0.0	0.0	0.0	0.1	0.1	0.0	0.0	0.0	0.0	0.0
Other expenditures on goods and services	—	(0.0)	(0.0)	(0.0)	0.0	0.0	0.0	0.0	0.0	0.0	0.0	0.0	0.0	0.0
Wages and salaries	—	0.0	(0.0)	(0.0)	0.0	0.0	0.0	0.0	0.0	0.0	0.0	0.0	0.0	0.0

Investment	—	0.0	2.0	2.0	1.5	1.0	0.5	0.0	0.0	0.0	0.0	0.0	0.0	0.0
Interest payments	—	0.0	(0.1)	(0.2)	(0.2)	(0.2)	(0.2)	(0.1)	(0.1)	(0.1)	(0.1)	(0.1)	(0.0)	(0.0)
Domestic debt	—	0.0	(0.0)	(0.1)	(0.1)	(0.1)	(0.1)	(0.1)	(0.1)	(0.1)	(0.1)	(0.1)	(0.1)	(0.0)
Foreign debt	—	0.0	(0.1)	(0.1)	(0.1)	(0.1)	(0.1)	(0.0)	(0.0)	(0.0)	(0.0)	(0.0)	(0.0)	(0.0)
Subsidies	—	0.0	(0.0)	(0.0)	0.0	0.0	0.0	0.0	0.0	0.0	0.0	0.0	0.0	0.0
Overall fiscal balance including grants (cash basis)	—	0.0	0.2	0.3	0.2	0.1	0.1	(0.0)	(0.0)	(0.0)	(0.0)	(0.0)	(0.0)	(0.0)
Total financing	—	(0.0)	(0.2)	(0.3)	(0.2)	(0.1)	(0.1)	0.0	0.0	0.0	0.0	0.0	0.0	0.0
Domestic borrowing	—	0.0	(0.0)	(0.0)	0.0	0.0	0.0	0.0	0.0	0.0	0.0	0.0	0.0	0.0
Foreign financing	—	(0.0)	(0.2)	(0.3)	(0.2)	(0.1)	(0.1)	0.0	0.0	0.0	0.0	0.0	0.0	0.1
Prices and Real Exchange Rate														
GDP at factor cost deflator (% change)	—	—	—	—	—	—	—	—	—	—	—	—	—	—
Composite good price (after indirect taxes, % change)	—	(0.5)	(1.0)	0.1	0.6	0.5	0.5	0.5	0.3	0.2	0.1	0.1	0.1	0.0
Nominal exchange rate (% change)	—	(0.0)	(2.8)	(0.4)	1.1	1.0	1.0	1.0	0.4	0.2	0.1	0.1	0.0	0.0
Real exchange rate (% change)	—	0.4	(1.7)	(0.4)	0.5	0.5	0.5	0.5	0.0	0.0	0.0	0.0	(0.0)	(0.0)
Memorandum items														
Real GDP per capita at factor cost (% change)	—	0.2	2.4	0.8	(0.2)	(0.0)	(0.3)	(0.5)	(0.2)	(0.3)	(0.3)	(0.3)	(0.3)	(0.3)
Real GDP per capita at market prices (% change)	—	0.2	2.3	0.8	(0.2)	(0.0)	(0.3)	(0.5)	(0.1)	(0.3)	(0.3)	(0.3)	(0.3)	(0.3)
Real disposable income per capita (% change)	—	0.5	1.3	0.8	(0.0)	(0.1)	(0.3)	(0.4)	(0.4)	(0.3)	(0.2)	(0.2)	(0.2)	(0.2)
Private savings rate (% of GDP)	—	0.1	(0.1)	(0.1)	(0.1)	(0.1)	(0.1)	(0.1)	(0.1)	(0.1)	(0.1)	(0.1)	(0.1)	(0.1)
Real private consumption per capita (% change)	—	0.6	1.3	0.8	(0.0)	(0.1)	(0.3)	(0.4)	(0.4)	(0.2)	(0.2)	(0.2)	(0.2)	(0.2)
Unemployment	—	(0.0)	(0.1)	(0.1)	(0.1)	(0.1)	(0.1)	(0.1)	(0.1)	(0.1)	(0.1)	(0.1)	(0.1)	(0.1)
Private investment (% of GDP)	—	0.0	0.0	0.0	0.2	0.3	0.4	0.5	0.5	0.4	0.4	0.3	0.3	0.2
Private investment (% of total investment)	—	0.0	(7.2)	(7.1)	(5.3)	(3.3)	(1.3)	0.7	0.7	0.6	0.5	0.5	0.4	0.4

(Continued)

Table A57. Aid Sustained Longer to Public Infrastructure Investment—Deviations from Baseline, 2008–20 (*Continued*)

	Years													
	2007	2008	2009	2010	2011	2012	2013	2014	2015	2016	2017	2018	2019	2020
Public investment (% of total public expenditure)	—	(0.0)	6.5	6.6	5.1	3.5	1.8	0.1	0.1	0.1	0.0	0.0	0.0	(0.0)
Health (% of public investment)	—	—	(1.7)	(1.7)	(1.4)	(1.0)	(0.6)	—	—	—	—	—	—	—
Infrastructure (% of public investment)	—	—	12.5	12.5	10.1	7.3	4.0	—	—	—	—	—	—	—
Education (% of public investment)	—	—	(2.0)	(2.0)	(1.7)	(1.2)	(0.6)	—	—	—	—	—	—	—
Other (% of public investment)	—	—	(8.7)	(8.7)	(7.0)	(5.1)	(2.8)	—	—	—	—	—	—	—
Domestic debt (% of GDP)	—	0.1	(0.2)	(0.3)	(0.4)	(0.4)	(0.5)	(0.5)	(0.5)	(0.4)	(0.4)	(0.3)	(0.3)	(0.3)
External debt (% of GDP)	—	0.1	(1.6)	(2.3)	(2.1)	(1.9)	(1.5)	(0.9)	(0.8)	(0.5)	(0.3)	(0.1)	0.1	0.3
Interest payment on external public debt (% of exports)	—	(0.0)	(0.0)	(0.1)	(0.1)	(0.1)	(0.1)	(0.1)	(0.1)	(0.1)	(0.0)	(0.0)	(0.0)	0.0
Degree of openness (total trade in % of GDP)	—	0.6	(0.8)	(0.9)	(0.7)	(0.6)	(0.4)	(0.1)	(0.2)	(0.1)	0.0	0.1	0.2	0.2
Educated labor (in % of population)	—	—	0.0	0.0	0.0	0.0	0.0	0.0	0.0	0.0	0.1	0.1	0.1	0.1
Net foreign assets (in months of imports)	—	(0.0)	0.0	0.0	(0.0)	(0.0)	(0.0)	(0.0)	0.0	0.0	0.0	0.0	0.0	0.0
Oil Price (2005 = 100)	—	—	—	—	—	—	—	—	—	—	—	—	—	—

Note: The real exchange rate is defined as the growth rate of nominal exchange rate plus the growth rate of the import price index minus the growth rate of composite good price after indirect taxes.

Technical Appendixes

Infrastructure, Trade, and Growth—Evidence and Implications for Trade Reform in the Caribbean

This Technical Appendix examines the evidence pertaining to the links between infrastructure, trade performance, and growth, and discusses the policy implications of this literature for the design of trade reforms in Caribbean countries. It begins with a review of the various types of externalities associated with core infrastructure, including those associated with health and education outcomes.[114] It then considers how access (or lack thereof) to infrastructure services affects the gains from trade by considering its impact on production costs, the quality of the labor force, and adjustment costs to tariff reform. The last part draws both general and specific lessons for trade reform in the Caribbean. Three issues specific to the region are identified: the disparity in initial infrastructure assets among countries, the need to develop regional public goods to foster regional integration, and the need to cope with infrastructure vulnerability.

Externalities Associated with Infrastructure

Much recent evidence supports the view that core infrastructure plays an important role in the growth process. Calderón and Servén (2004), for instance, in a study covering a large sample of countries over the period 1960–2000, found that growth is positively affected by the stock of infrastructure assets. Along the same line, Loayza, Fajnzylber, and Calderón (2004) found that infrastructure (measured by the number of telephone lines per capita)

---

114. Core public infrastructure refers to energy (namely, electricity), transportation (roads, railways, etc.), telecommunications, and water and sanitation (including irrigation in rural areas).

has a positive and significant effect on growth in Latin America and the Caribbean.[115] For the poorest countries, where infrastructure is scarce and basic networks have not been completed, growth effects tend to be even more dramatic.

Conventional Effects

Infrastructure, particularly when it is publicly provided, is usually viewed as promoting growth through two main channels. First, if production inputs are gross complements (as is normally the case), it tends to increase the marginal productivity of private inputs, thereby lowering production costs. For instance, a study by the African Development Bank suggests that transport and energy costs, at 16 and 35 percent respectively, represent by far the largest share of firms' indirect costs in Sub-Saharan Africa. A large fraction of these costs is the result of the poor quality of basic infrastructure. Because of inadequate transport facilities and unreliable supply of electricity, in particular, firms often incur additional costs in the form of more expensive transportation means and onerous energy back-up systems.[116] These additional expenses are particularly damaging for small firms, due to size effects; only a small fraction of small firms are typically able to purchase generators to alleviate a chronic lack of access to government-provided electricity. As a result, profit margins tend to be thin and to discourage production.

Second, (public) infrastructure can exert a positive effect on growth through its impact on private capital formation. As noted earlier, infrastructure increases the marginal productivity of production inputs; in so doing, it raises the perceived rate of return on, and may increase the demand for, physical capital by the private sector. For instance, the rate of return to building a factory is likely to be much higher if the country has already invested in power generation, transportation, and telecommunications. This growth-enhancing, complementarity effect has been well documented in the empirical literature on private investment in developing countries, despite the fact that the flow of public investment itself can mitigate it through crowding-out effects.[117]

New Channels

In addition to these conventional effects, core public infrastructure may spur growth through a variety of other channels.[118] First, by facilitating the reallocation of capital across sectors following from shocks to relative prices (for example, an increase in the relative price of tradables, which would draw resources away from the nontradables sector), public infrastructure may reduce the magnitude of adjustment costs associated with increases in private capital formation. An expansion in the road network may not only reduce congestion and facilitate the shipment of goods across the country (thereby reducing unit production

---

115. Neither one of these studies, however, accounts for the government budget constraint in their estimation, as do for instance Bose, Haque, and Osborn (2007).

116. Firms that do not undertake these additional investments may still incur costs in the form of lost production resulting from equipment breakdowns.

117. See Agénor (2004), Chapter 2.

118. See Agénor and Moreno-Dodson (2007) for a review of the recent literature.

costs, as noted earlier) but it may also reduce the cost of building a new plant or the transportation of heavy equipment for installation to a new location for future production.

Second, the durability of private capital may be significantly improved by improving the availability, and quality, of core public infrastructure. Reliable power grids and well-maintained roads, tend to reduce the need for the private sector to spend on maintenance of its own stock of physical capital (for instance, the trucks that are used to move goods across the country). For instance, Gyamfi and Ruan (1996, p. 5) have estimated that for Latin America and the Caribbean, each dollar not spent on road maintenance leads to a $3.0 increase in vehicle operating costs as a result of poor road conditions. Better roads, by reducing the rate of depreciation of private capital, may raise the rate of return on physical assets, thereby stimulating private investment and growth.

Third, core infrastructure (most importantly, electricity, roads, and sanitation) may have a significant impact on health and education outcomes—particularly in countries where, to begin with, infrastructure assets are low. Access to clean energy for cooking and better transport (particularly in rural areas) may contribute significantly to better health.[119] Studies have also found that access to clean water and sanitation has a significant effect on the incidence of malaria, and more generally on child mortality. In the cross-section regressions for developing countries reported by McGuire (2006) for instance, average years of female schooling have a statistically significant impact on under-five mortality rates.

Infrastructure may also have a significant effect on education outcomes. Studies have shown that the quality of education tends to improve with better transportation networks in rural areas, whereas attendance rates for girls tend to increase with access to sanitation in schools. Electricity allows for more studying and access to technology, such as computers, which enhance the quality of human capital. Schools that lack access to basic water supply and sanitation services tend to have a higher incidence of illnesses among their students.

In turn, poor health is an important underlying factor for low school enrollment, absenteeism (often the result of respiratory infections, as noted by Bundy and others (2005)), poor classroom performance, and early school dropout. Inadequate nutrition, which often takes the form of deficiencies in micronutrients, also reduces the ability to learn. At the same time, studies have found that higher education levels can improve health; where mothers are better educated, infant mortality rates are lower, and attendance rates in school tend to be higher (See Wagstaff and Claeson (2005)). Thus, the impact of infrastructure on health and education outcomes can be magnified through interactions between health and education themselves.[120]

119. According to the 2006 *World Development Report* of the World Bank, the dramatic drop in the maternal mortality ratio observed in recent years in Malaysia and Sri Lanka (from 2,136 in 1930 to 24 in 1996 in Sri Lanka, and from 1,085 in 1933 to 19 in 1997 in Malaysia) was due not only to a sharp increase in medical workers in rural and disadvantaged communities, but also to improved communication and transportation services—which helped to reduce geographic barriers.

120. The large effect of government investment in education and total expenditures in education on growth identified by Bose, Haque, and Osborn (2007) for instance may therefore be the (indirect) result of higher spending on infrastructure and health.

The Gains from Trade and Access to Infrastructure

From the perspective of external trade performance (as opposed to growth *per se*), improved access to infrastructure is critical for most developing countries who intend to reap the benefits from trade. There are three specific channels through which infrastructure can impinge on trade performance: through transportation costs, the quality of the labor force, and adjustment costs to tariff cuts.

Infrastructure Constraints, Production Costs, and Exports

From the perspective of international trade, the reduction in production costs that improved infrastructure may lead to is the most direct effect. Eliminating infrastructure constraints, such as water shortages, electricity outages and difficult road access, can facilitate the process of shifting private resources to more productive sectors, for instance from nontradables to tradables, or from agriculture to services and manufacturing. In addition, by facilitating movement of people and goods, improved infrastructure can lead in the medium term to higher investments in the rural sector and greater agricultural diversification, by raising expected rates of return. Farmers must be able to obtain inputs at reasonable costs, and also to sell their outputs at remunerative prices. Transportation costs, in particular, are crucial for them to decide whether or not to engage in certain activities.

Several studies have documented the importance of good infrastructure for trade and export performance. In a study conducted in the late 1990s, the African Development Bank found that freight charges on exports of the poor countries of the region to the United States, as a proportion of CIF value, are on average 20 percent higher than for comparable products from other low-income countries. More recently, Yoshino (2007) found that poor quality of public infrastructure—measured in terms of the average numbers of days per year for which firms experience disruptions in electricity—has an adverse effect on exports in sub-Saharan Africa. In Rwanda, farmers receive only 20 percent of the price of their coffee as it is loaded onto ships in Monbasa; the other 80 percent disappear into the costs of poor roads (as well as red tape) between Rwanda and Kenya. High domestic and international transport costs have also been identified as a key impediment to export growth in South Africa (see Naudé and Matthee (2007)).

Regarding Latin America and the Caribbean, a study by the Inter-American Development Bank suggests that for many countries of the region shipping costs (which depend significantly on port efficiency) may be a greater barrier to U.S. markets than import tariffs (see Micco and Pérez (2002)). Moreover, a comparative study by Dollar and others (2006) of four countries in Latin America (Brazil, Honduras, Nicaragua, and Peru) and four Asian countries (Bangladesh, China, India, and Pakistan) found that inadequate access to core infrastructure services is one of the key factors that explains the more rapid pace of international trade integration in the latter group of countries.

A possible mechanism through which infrastructure may affect positively exports is through foreign direct investment (FDI); for Latin America in particular, there is indeed evidence suggesting that FDI flows are positively related to the availability of infrastructure services (as measured by the number of telephone lines per capita; see Nunes, Oscategui, and Peschiera (2006).

Infrastructure, Labor Force Quality, and Trade Opportunities

Another way through which infrastructure may enhance trade performance relates to its external effects on human capital. To the extent that, as discussed earlier, core infrastructure exerts positive effects on health and education outcomes, improved access to infrastructure services can generate significant benefits for export activities in terms of a more productive/higher quality labor force.

Moreover, if infrastructure capital enhances the degree of complementarity between skilled labor and physical capital, it will also increase private incentives to invest in the accumulation of knowledge. This may in turn create new opportunities for trade (by opening up new areas of specialization) and economic growth.

Trade Liberalization and Infrastructure: Mitigating Adjustment Costs

When tariffs are reduced, import-competing firms must reduce their production in the face of new competition, causing some of their workers to become redundant and their capital to lie idle for a period. In addition, firms may incur adjustment costs as resources are moved from one sector to another. These intersectoral movements result from the fact that liberalization is typically preceded by (or associated with) a significant depreciation of the real exchange rate, which provides producers with an incentive to shift resources toward the tradable goods sector.[121] Thus, adjustment costs can be defined as frictions that prevent firms from adjusting their labor force and capital stock fully and instantaneously in response to the change in relative prices associated with trade reform.[122]

In addition, the shift in resources toward the tradable goods sector stimulates investment in that sector and depresses capital formation in the nontradable goods sector. To the extent that capital goods are imported (as is often the case in developing countries), a real depreciation may also lower investment, by raising the cost of these goods; at the same time, the real cost of imported intermediate inputs also falls—thereby stimulating the demand for these goods and possibly private investment.[123]

If the net effect on investment is positive, access to infrastructure may reduce the incidence of adjustment costs associated with increases in private capital formation. Poor infrastructure, particularly in low-income countries, may be an important cause for these costs.[124] By implication, an expansion in the road network may not only reduce congestion on highways and facilitate the shipment of goods across regions (thereby reducing unit production costs, as noted earlier) but also reduce expenses associated with the construction of a new factory or the transportation of heavy equipment for installation to a new,

---

121. See Li (2004) for a review of the recent evidence.

122. They include therefore costs associated with the sale, purchase or productive implementation of capital goods, over and above the price of these goods. Such costs are associated with, for instance, searching for, and deciding upon, the proper type of equipment needed for a particular purpose, scrapping obsolete machines, installing the new capital stock, and reorganizing and training the workforce.

123. As argued by Amiti and Konings (2007) in a study of Indonesia's recent experience with tariff reductions, the fall in the cost of imported intermediate inputs may also raise productivity via learning, variety, and quality effects, thereby stimulating further output growth.

124. Other factors, such as underdeveloped or poorly functioning capital markets, may of course be equally (if not more) important in some countries.

remote production site. Similarly, shifting capital from the nontradable sector (say, cash crops in rural areas) to the traded sector (say, export crops) can be made easier by the existence of public assets such as wells, which facilitate irrigation, and rural roads, which allow faster shipment to ports and foreign markets.

In sum, following an adjustment in tariffs, improved access to infrastructure may reduce adjustment costs by facilitating the reallocation of capital from the nontradable to the tradable sector. Moreover, by lowering not only production costs (at a given level of the stock of capital) but also adjustment costs related to investment, improved provision of infrastructure services will tend to raise expected rates of return and therefore stimulate private capital formation.[125] At the same time, by enhancing the ability of the private sector to respond to price signals, lower adjustment costs may be accompanied by efficiency gains, which may translate into permanent growth effects.

Implications for Trade Reform in the Caribbean

To assess the implications of the foregoing discussion for the trade agenda of Caribbean countries, it is best to draw first the general policy lessons, and then reflect on the specific context of Caribbean countries.

General Lessons

Harnessing trade for growth and poverty reduction creates new pressures to strengthen competitiveness and to "connect" more effectively with global markets. How to respond to these pressures is a critical issue for the Caribbean, where most countries are highly trade dependent and have endorsed economic strategies that hinge significantly on the expansion of exports.

The foregoing discussion suggests that the positive externalities associated with improved access to core infrastructure may be substantial in Caribbean countries and must be accounted for in the design of trade reforms aimed at fostering growth and reducing poverty. Many of these countries (and notably the poorest in the region, such as Haiti and Guyana) remain ill equipped to take full advantage of new trade opportunities because of significant supply-side constraints. The costs of trade are often higher in the region compared with many other developing countries because of (in addition to institutional weaknesses and inefficient regulatory structures) sizable gaps in physical infrastructure. These costs reduce the region's capacity to compete in global markets, and diminish the gains from trade, investment and technological innovation. Firm-level surveys have indeed identified infrastructure constraints as a significant factor affecting export development (World Bank 2005).

For instance, among the constraints that agriculture suffers from in Caribbean countries (in addition to limited and fragmented fertile land and relatively high labor costs) is an inadequate and costly transport infrastructure, which translates into high international

---

125. In that sense, there is again a complementarity effect between public infrastructure and private investment, but this time it operates through overall adjustment costs, rather than solely through the direct rate of return on private capital.

transport costs for both inputs and outputs.[126] To overcome these constraints and seize new opportunities (discussed in Chapter 4) requires improving the ability to reach markets, both domestic and international, through an improved transport network, as well as improvement in water resource management and irrigation systems. Indeed, the real challenge facing farmers in some of the Caribbean countries may not be in producing for export markets, but whether access to transportation services will be sufficient to market effectively what is produced. Governments need to upgrade rural roads and invest in port facilities to enable farmers to access markets. Put differently, improved market access without the capacity and transportation to sell is not sufficient; the gains from trade liberalization are conditional on an environment that—in addition to facilitating investment in new areas of activity—allows labor, capital, and physical assets to be redeployed across sectors.

Similarly, to the extent that the production of health services is constrained by the lack of availability of infrastructure (lack of electricity to run hospitals and refrigerate vaccines, lack of roads to allow easy access to hospitals and clinics, etc.), a strategy designed to expand trade and spur growth through an increase in the quality of human capital may need to incorporate a large, front-loaded increase in public spending on core infrastructure. Size matters here not only because infrastructure investments are often lumpy in nature, but also because the network externalities associated with infrastructure, which translate into strong increasing returns (at least initially) in the productivity of public capital, tend to "kick in" only after the stock of infrastructure assets itself has reached a certain threshold.[127]

Thus, for many countries of the region, reaping the benefits of greater openness will require that complementary reforms and policies be implemented prior to, and in conjunction with, trade reform. Seen in this context, supporting trade adjustment and integration in the Caribbean will also require a shift toward more efficient transfer/assistance mechanisms with support directed at priority areas defined in national development plans and strategies. Put differently, if only from the perspective of the impact of infrastructure on trade performance, there is a strong case for an "aid for trade" strategy, as discussed in Technical Appendix B. Failure to provide assistance will hamper the ability of Caribbean countries to respond to the opportunities that trade liberalization and integration can bring. At the same time, it must be recognized that although regional and global trade integration are key determinants for long-run growth and poverty reduction for all countries in the region, there are important differences among them that need to be considered in designing an "aid for trade" agenda for each individual country.

Some Specific Considerations

In addition to these general considerations, there are specific constraints that Caribbean countries are faced with. These relate to heterogeneity in initial levels of income and infrastructure assets among countries of the region, the need for regional public goods imposed by small size, and the need to cope with infrastructure vulnerability.

---

126. Caribbean agricultural products, such as rice and sugar, are bulky commodities, whereas others, such as fresh fruits, vegetables, and meats, are highly perishable items, which require different transportation requirements. Modern commercial agriculture is also input-intensive, using a broad range of products from fertilizers to feed additives. These inputs require a wide variety of transportation services as well.

127. See Agénor (2006) for a more detailed discussion.

Large Disparities across Countries.   There are large disparities across Caribbean countries in terms of income per capita and access to infrastructure (see Chapter 1). At higher levels of income, households typically demand more "luxury" goods and services, many of which are not produced in the region. Thus, large initial income disparities, by themselves, may act as a constraint on intra-regional trade. In turn, this would reduce the benefits of infrastructure investments aimed at fostering regional integration. From a dynamic perspective, however, global integration may help to alleviate this impediment to trade, by helping poorer countries grow faster and eventually "catch up" with the richer ones. Regarding initial access to infrastructure, there are also large differences across Caribbean countries (see Chapter 1). Without improved access to infrastructure, the poorest countries of the region will not only be unable to compete effectively on international markets, they will also find it difficult to reap the benefits from intra-regional integration.

The Need for Regional Public Goods in Infrastructure.   To help to overcome the disadvantages faced by most Caribbean islands due to their small economic size and foster integration through increased intra-regional trade, there is a need for governments to foster the development of regional transport links. This is all the more important in view of the fact that prospects for public-private partnerships (PPPs) in infrastructure investment appear limited for the region—particularly for the poorest ones.[128]

Developing regional public goods in infrastructure to foster trade, especially for small island economies, requires a high degree of sub-regional cooperation and coordination. This is particularly important in transport infrastructure, given that transportation remains a critical factor of production and the fact that network building is often critical to reap the full benefits of infrastructure. But this is also the case in other areas, such as electricity. Improving the reliability of electricity supply in OECS countries, for instance, given the technical nature of the issue and the limited capacity of member country governments, may require a regional approach similar to ECTEL (World Bank 2005).[129] Similar arguments can be made in the context of telecommunications.[130]

Caribbean countries already have experience with regional arrangements. Some have developed new mechanisms and institutions for exploiting economies of scale in designing and implementing regional programs and projects (see Chapter 2). In the present case, regional institutions can play a vital role in identifying key infrastructure projects and in coordinating donors and countries across the region. There is therefore considerable scope to build upon and expand regional approaches, particularly as regards policy coordination, priority setting, and improved financing in the area of infrastructure. A possible option would be to develop a regional program similar to the Initiative for the Integration of Regional Infrastructure in South America (IIRSA), which supports the development and

---

128. For LAC as a whole, Fay and Morrison (2005) estimate that the value of LAC infrastructure with private participation dropped to $16 billion in 2003, down from a peak of $71 billion in 1998. By total project value, 93% of private investment in LAC infrastructure over 1990–2003 went to just 6 countries (Argentina, Brazil, Chile, Colombia, Peru and Mexico), and mostly into telecommunications and energy.

129. A regional approach may also offer the possibility of depoliticizing pricing issues and improving regulatory harmonization in critical utility services.

130. See Escobari, Rodriguez, and Rabkin (2005) for an overview of the role of ICT in Caribbean economic potential.

integration of an energy, transport, and telecommunications infrastructure program that covers 12 countries spanning two different regional trading blocs, or the more recent Infrastructure Consortium for Africa, which is jointly supported by African countries, the European Commission, G-8 countries, and key multilateral institutions.[131] In addition, regional initiatives cannot be designed or implemented in isolation from national and even local policies. Regional programs are a complement, not a substitute, for national programs.

The Need to Cope with Infrastructure Vulnerability.   The Caribbean region is highly susceptible to natural disasters such as hurricanes, landslides, and earthquakes. In a study of the impact of damage and losses in 6 Caribbean countries (Bahamas, Cayman Islands, Dominican Republic, Grenada, Haiti, and Jamaica) associated with hurricanes during 2004, ECLAC estimated that 76 percent of the total impact was constituted by actual physical damage to assets, both private (houses and businesses) and public (roads and bridges, utilities, schools, hospitals and clinics). By themselves, damage and losses to infrastructure and utilities (such as electricity, water and sanitation, and transport) represented 15.6 percent. For Grenada alone, the total loss represented 19.6 percent to core infrastructure assets, education and health systems.[132] This loss of assets translated into a sizable loss in terms of annual flows as well, due to disruptions in activity.

Each time a natural disaster occurs, scarce resources must be redirected to rebuilding damaged infrastructure assets, investing in new ones to help the development of the region's economic base. With growing risks of more violent weather in the next 10 to 50 years due to climate change, the scope for large losses in physical assets may increase dramatically—with consequent pressure on public finances.[133] This in turn, may increase macroeconomic instability and real exchange rate volatility, thereby distorting critical signals in relative prices for producers. Thus, to the extent that trade performance depends on macroeconomic stability, Caribbean countries must improve their ability to cope with infrastructure vulnerability. Not only must the region take appropriate measures to improve warning systems and prevention, but the contingent liabilities associated with these losses must be accounted for in designing fiscal policy. The possibility that these contingent liabilities may, should they materialize, lead to a sharp increase in taxation is a possible reason why private investors (both domestic and foreign) remain reluctant to engage in potentially high-return export activities. Put differently, the mere possibility that taxes may have to increase in order to help rebuild infrastructure assets may act as a strong deterrent to private investment. This adverse impact may be magnified in the presence of irreversibility effects.

---

131. See http://www.iirsa.org/ and http://www.icafrica.org/. See also Fujimura (2004) for a discussion of the experience of Asian countries with cross-border transport infrastructure, particularly the Greater Mekong Sub-region.

132. In Grenada, total damage and losses (inflicted mostly by Hurricane Ivan) amounted to more than twice the size of GDP in the previous year. In the Cayman Islands, damage and losses exceeded by more than one third the country's estimated GDP of the previous year.

133. An examination by the World Bank (2005) of the post-hurricane spending patterns during the 1990s in OECS countries undertaken in recent Public expenditure reviews reveals that there has been a tendency for subsequent increases in capital spending to be permanent rather than temporary—thereby exacerbating pressures on fiscal deficits and public debt. Weaknesses in the formulation and implementation of public investment programs appear to have been at the heart of the problem.

Aid for Trade—Rationale and Implications for Trade Reform in Caribbean Countries

This Technical Appendix reviews various arguments that have been offered to justify "aid for trade" programs for developing economies and examines their relevance and application in the current context of Caribbean countries. The first section reviews arguments centered on aid as a "compensatory scheme," designed to alleviate the adverse effects of trade liberalization. In that context, the evidence on the impact of trade reforms on tax revenues, and possible adverse effects of revenue losses on public expenditure, is also examined. The second section examines the role of aid as a "promotion scheme", designed to help countries benefit fully from greater trade integration. The third section discusses the relevance and implications of these various arguments for trade policy in Caribbean countries, particularly for some of the poorer countries in the region, where lack of public infrastructure remains a serious impediment to reaping the benefits from trade reform in terms of higher growth and poverty reduction.

"Aid for Trade" as a Compensatory Scheme

In general, arguments in favor of an "aid for trade" agenda center around five dimensions: (i) assistance to offset adjustment costs, such as fiscal support to help countries make the transition from tariffs to other sources of revenue; (ii) technical assistance; (iii) capacity building, including support for trade facilitation; (iv) institutional reform; and (v) investments in trade-related infrastructure.[134] In what follows, we adopt a more convenient analytical

---

134. As noted by (Stiglitz and Charlton, 2006, p. 8), until recently the existing aid for trade approach was to provide modest amount of aid on an *ad hoc* basis—primarily to cope with specific bottlenecks, or to support participation in WTO negotiations.

approach, which consists of grouping these arguments under two headers: aid for trade as a "compensatory scheme"; and aid for trade as a "promotion scheme." This section focuses on the first group of arguments, which can in turn be grouped into two main rationales: mitigating revenue-induced cuts in productive expenditure, and mitigating adjustment and implementation costs.

Mitigating Revenue-induced Cuts in Productive Expenditure

Tariff revenues are a key source of government income relative to the value-added tax and sales taxes in developing countries, particularly the small, low-income ones. Given the heavy dependence of these countries on trade taxes and the limited ability to raise revenues from other sources—in some cases as a result of a large informal sector and high rates of tax evasion—a key issue in this context, therefore, is the extent to which trade reform leads to a reduction in revenues, and what these revenue losses impose on the spending side of the budget.

Trade Reform and Tax Revenues. A reduction in tariffs, unaccompanied by compensatory fiscal measures may lead to reduced government revenue in the short run. Over time, however, to the extent that lower tariffs lead to increased imports (that is, an expansion of the tax base) trade reform may increase government revenue. Higher revenues may also result from the fact that greater openness to trade leads over time to higher collection efficiency for other taxes, such as VAT (Aizenman and Jinjarak (2006)). In addition, if offsetting revenue measures (in the form of temporary higher taxes on other items, for instance), or reductions in spending are taken in parallel to cuts in tariffs, the adverse short-run effect may be mitigated.[135]

More generally, although trade liberalization may lead to a fall in revenue in the short term, some trade liberalization measures (such as the replacement of quotas by tariffs) can be implemented without significant declines in revenue. Lifting quantitative restrictions may even lead to an increase in revenue if the newly liberalized categories of imports increase and are subject to tariffs. Moreover, in countries where the foreign exchange market is being liberalized at the same time, and the official exchange rate depreciates significantly as a result, the increase in the domestic-currency price of imports may be large enough to lead to higher revenue, even with falling tariff rates (Agénor 2004, Chapter 14).

Nevertheless, concerns about adverse revenue effects often figure prominently among explanations of a slow pace of trade liberalization (Ebrill, Stotsky, and Gropp 1999). In countries where the share of trade taxes in total revenues is large, trade barriers have often been gradually dismantled due to fiscal constraints. The extent to which total tax revenue fall depends, of course, on what alternative tax bases the government can rely on following a cut in tariffs; but switching to other sources of revenues may entail not only (temporary) switching costs, but also a permanently higher administrative burden—which may be all

---

135. There are a number of other channels through which trade openness can affect budget balances; see Combes and Saadi (2006) for a discussion. Using cross-country regression analysis, they find that trade policy (as opposed to "natural" openness) tends to improve budget balances; however, they provide only a static analysis.

the more important in countries with a large informal sector.[136] If so, then a cut in tariffs is unlikely to be revenue neutral.

The recent experience of developing countries suggests indeed that trade reforms have often been accompanied by revenue losses. In a well publicized study dwelling on data for 111 countries over 25 years, Baunsgaard and Keen (2005) found that high-income countries were able to recover from other sources the revenues that they had lost during previous episodes of trade liberalization. However, for middle-income countries, recovery was on average in the order of 45–60 cents for each dollar of lost trade tax revenue; and for low-income countries (which are those most dependent on trade tax revenues, as noted earlier), recovery was, at best, no more than about 30 cents of each lost dollar. They also found no evidence that the presence of a value-added tax had, in itself, made it easier to cope with the revenue effects of trade liberalization.[137]

Revenue Losses and Spending Cuts. A fall in revenues associated with a reduction in tariffs may force governments to implement concomitant cuts in expenditure in the short term. If these cuts take the form of reductions in social expenditure, they will have a direct effect on poverty, thereby mitigating the welfare gains from trade—at least in the short term. There is some empirical evidence suggesting that this has indeed been the case in some countries (Winters, McCulloch, and McKay 2004).

There is also evidence to suggest that the loss of revenue has led not only to cuts in current spending but at times to significant cuts in public investment, most notably in infrastructure (see Atolia (2007)). Given the importance of the externalities associated with public infrastructure (as discussed in Technical Appendix A), a sustained loss in tariff revenue may have an adverse effect on growth, which may offset the benefits of greater openness. Moreover, the positive effect of public capital on the marginal productivity of private inputs may hold not only for infrastructure but also for other components of public capital—such as in education and health, which may both affect the productivity of labor. Thus, cuts in productive expenditure in general may be particularly damaging to growth.[138]

The Role of Aid. Developing countries rely on tariffs as a source of revenue far more than do developed countries largely because tariffs are an administratively efficient way of raising revenues. To the extent that trade liberalization may reduce tariff revenue, that replacing lost tariff revenue with other sources may take time and may have high associated costs, and that revenue losses may have an adverse effect on productive public expenditure, tariff reforms may need to be accompanied by a temporary increase in aid. This will

---

136. For instance, Emran and Stiglitz (2004) have shown that in developing countries with an informal sector in which, say, a VAT cannot be imposed, it is desirable to retain some trade taxes, e.g. to tax imports at a higher rate than domestic production.

137. By contrast, Agbeyegbe, Stotsky, and WoldeMariam (2006), using panel data for 22 countries in Sub-Saharan Africa over 1980-96, found evidence that the relationship between trade liberalization and tax revenue is sensitive to the measure used to proxy trade liberalization.

138. Other components of public spending, related for instance to the enforcement of property rights and maintenance of public order, could also increase productivity and exert a positive effect on private investment and growth, despite the fact that they may not be considered as being directly "productive."

provide "breathing space" for governments to implement measures aimed at strengthening the domestic tax system (by reducing tax collection costs, fighting tax evasion, etc.) and other reforms on the expenditure side (such as improving the efficiency of public spending).[139]

Mitigating Adjustment Costs and Implementation Costs

As noted in Technical Appendix A, the relative price adjustments that accompany (or precede) trade liberalization often entail large intersectoral movements in resources; firms may incur sizable adjustment costs as a result of these movements. While it may take some time for the gains from trade to materialize (as they often depend on reform in other areas, as discussed elsewhere in this Report), adjustment costs tend to be "paid" upfront.

For some countries, these adjustment costs (which include not only higher rates of unemployment in import-competing sectors but also pressures on the balance of payments and fiscal accounts) may be particularly significant. Even by spreading adjustment costs over a relatively long implementation period (say, 10 to 15 years), some countries may have limited capacity to bear them.[140]

There are also costs associated with the implementation of the regulatory reforms that are part of trade agreements.[141] While tariff reductions are relatively easy to implement, regulatory changes (customs reform, intellectual property rights, and sanitary and phytosanitary measures) may impose a burden that may be very large (at least in the short term) compared to the benefits that countries may receive from new market access opportunities. For instance, these regulatory changes may require higher expenditure on system design and drafting of legislation, capital expenditure on buildings and equipment, personnel training, as well as improvements in administration and enforcement capability. For some of the poorest countries, the extent of reform of administrative systems that is required to meet agreed standards may be overwhelming.

Thus, although implementation costs are hard to quantify, there is a risk that changes in the regulatory environment that are mandated by trade agreements draw money away from development budgets (and possibly from more productive uses), as pointed out by Stiglitz and Charlton (2006) in a broader context. The role of aid in this context is not only to facilitate job creation in areas most adversely affected by trade liberalization, or to help those who have lost their jobs obtain alternative employment (as is commonly argued), but also to mitigate the risk that the implementation of the regulatory agreements that are required as part of trade arrangements may lead to "resource diversion."

---

139. Note also that aid may also affect incentives to control public spending and collect taxes. An increase in aid may lead to a decline in public savings through lower tax revenues, as governments reduce their tax collection effort. Alternatively, as documented by Chatterjee, Giuliano, and Kaya (2007), increases in aid may translate into a shift in the composition of government spending away from investment and toward consumption. In turn, reduced incentives to mobilize domestic resources, or shifts away from productive spending, may mitigate the benefits of sustained increases in aid for economic growth and welfare.

140. Labor mobility costs can slow adjustment to trade liberalization significantly; see Artuc et al. (2008) for some illustrative simulation results.

141. A case in point is the EPA recently signed between Caribbean countries and the European Union, as discussed later.

"Aid for Trade" as a Promotion Scheme

In addition to being viewed as a "compensatory" mechanism, aid may be designed to help countries realize the full benefits of new market opportunities. In that perspective, the first argument is that aid may help countries invest in infrastructure (both at the national and regional levels) so as to alleviate supply-side constraints. The second is that it may help to support capacity building and strengthen the institutional environment. The third is that it may help to support structural reforms that are complementary to trade reforms, such as labor market reforms.

Facilitating Domestic Investment in Infrastructure and the Provision of Regional Public Goods

As emphasized elsewhere in this Report, market access on its own is not sufficient to bring the benefits of trade; in many cases, countries are unable to take significant advantage of new trading opportunities because their supply capacity and competitiveness are limited. In particular, as discussed in Technical Appendix A, poor transport infrastructure can prevent local farmers from accessing domestic markets and international ports; poor storage facilities can increase inventory costs; and inadequate energy and water supplies can disrupt production or increase costs. Some countries need to invest in the necessary exporting infrastructure (e.g. efficient ports, adequate roads, reliable electricity and communications) to stimulate private investment in productive capacity. Thus, by supporting domestic infrastructure investment, aid for trade programs may foster the ability of the private sector to take advantage of changes in competitiveness and more generally enhance its role in promoting development.

In addition, as also noted in Technical Appendix A, aid for trade is particularly important for regional public goods in infrastructure. Coordination failures often create a gap in the optimal provision of these goods. In addition, for regions where countries are relatively small (as is the case in the Caribbean), size is an important incentive for governments to pool resources for the provision of efficient, cost-effective common services (CARICOM (2007, p. 77)). Regional investments supported by foreign grants may generate therefore potentially large returns.

Supporting Capacity Building and Institutional Reform

When implementing trade reforms, capacity building and institutional reforms are essential in a range of areas. As noted earlier, strengthening tax administration and enforcement capability is essential in the medium term to mitigate the impact of tariff reductions on revenues. In addition, countries often lack the necessary technology and knowledge to meet product standards prevailing in high value markets (sanitary measures, technical barriers, certification, and so forth). Assistance to build supply capacity may involve fostering the development of a favorable business climate to help private sector enterprises capitalize on new trade opportunities and identifying infrastructure bottlenecks. In turn, this may entail removing the obstacles that ineffective institutions place on the ability of firms with high export potential to grow—by developing for instance more effective customs authorities, more accountable policing, and more efficient port authorities.[142] To benefit fully from trade liberalization, developing countries may also need to strengthen regional institutions. A well-designed aid for trade program, which avoids the "diversion risk" alluded to above, may promote all these objectives.

Financing Complementary Structural Reforms

To achieve their full impact, trade reforms often need to be accompanied by complementary structural reforms. It is well recognized, for instance, that there is a need to invest in educational programs to enhance competitiveness and support diversification, by allowing workers (particularly those who lose their jobs in import-competing industries) to "retool" and adjust their skills to those required in the expanding sectors. More generally, there is good evidence suggesting that trade liberalization has stronger effects when labor markets are more flexible (see Technical Appendix C).

As noted elsewhere in this Report, however, the need for complementary reforms may involve not only the labor market but also the financial sector. In countries with underdeveloped financial sectors, inadequate access to finance—whether to finance short-term capital needs or physical investment—is a major factor inhibiting exports. Difficulties in assessing the creditworthiness of (and the value of collateral pledged by) small exporting firms, in particular, may constrain access to formal sector loans, with an adverse effect on employment and poverty. Again, a well-designed aid for trade program may help to alleviate these constraints.

Implications for Trade Reform in the Caribbean

As discussed in Chapter 1, since 2000 many countries in the Caribbean have been grappling with difficult fiscal and public debt situations.[143] At the same time, some of these countries rely quite heavily on trade taxes as a source of current revenue. Taxes on international trade account for only 7 percent of current revenues for Trinidad and Tobago and 9 percent for Barbados; both countries derive a larger share of revenues from corporate, consumption, and income taxes. By contrast, the six Eastern Caribbean States (the Bahamas, Belize, the Dominican Republic, Jamaica, and Suriname) all depend on trade taxes for more than 25 percent of current government revenue. The Bahamas, Dominica, and St. Vincent rely on such taxes for more than 40 percent of their current tax revenues (Schott 2001, Chapter 2).

Relevance of "Aid for Trade" Arguments

It is well recognized that, given the current fiscal imbalances and high levels of indebtedness, many countries in the region will need to embark on a sustained process of fiscal

---

142. Institutional capacity can affect trade costs if customs procedures, inspections, and certifying bodies are run inefficiently.

143. In Antigua and Barbuda for instance, public debt in 2003 accounted for 142 percent of GDP; in the same year, this ratio reached 171 percent in St Kitts and Nevis, and 150 percent in Jamaica (with an interest bill of about 16 percent of GDP).

adjustment and public sector reform (see, for instance, Kufa, Pellechio, and Rizavi (2005) and the World Bank (2005) for Eastern Caribbean countries). For the issue at hand, large deficits and high ratios of public debt act as major constraints on the ability of most countries of the region to cut tariffs. Indeed, in an analysis of the fiscal effects of tariff reduction for the Caribbean Community, Peters (2005) concluded that Caribbean countries are likely to experience short-run revenue shortfall as a consequence of trade liberalization. Indications are that the shortfall could be as much as a 45 per cent decline in customs duties. In order to mitigate this substantial effect, Peters argues for the need to strengthen ongoing efforts at fiscal reform, paying particular attention to lowering tax exemptions, enhancing indirect tax systems (by implementing a broad based tax such as the VAT), improving tax collection and administration (with regard in particular to the personal income tax), and more generally modifying the tax structure to reduce dependence on trade taxes for fiscal receipts and create fiscal space for a reduction in tariffs.

However, developing non trade-based, fiscal revenue structures which are broad based and capable of generating revenues on a sustainable basis is likely to take significant time. Thus, to avoid possible adverse effects of revenue losses on productive government spending (as noted earlier), temporary financing in the form of increased aid may be necessary to increase incentives to implement (and sustain) trade reform.

The second argument often used to justify "aid for trade" as a Compensatory Scheme applies with equal force to the current context of Caribbean countries. The Economic Partnership Agreement (EPA) recently completed between the European Union and the CARIFORUM Group EPA contains explicit provisions related to compliance with, and adoption of, international technical, health, and quality standards pertaining to food production and marketing (agricultural goods, fish and fish products, etc.).[144] Compliance with these (at times very demanding) standards will impose a significant burden on governments in the region; to avoid the "diversion risk" alluded to earlier, a "aid for trade" program is likely to be essential. This need is well recognized in the EPA.[145]

Other arguments that view aid for trade as a promotion scheme are also relevant for Caribbean countries. As noted elsewhere in this Report, as well as in Technical Appendix A, significant supply-side and institutional constraints prevent a number of Caribbean countries from taking full advantage of new trade opportunities. The ability of many countries to compete in world markets is undermined by the absence or inadequacy of infrastructure services (such as roads and ports), a weak institutional environment (including modern and efficient customs), or simply knowledge about export market opportunities and how to access them. Furthermore, although trade reforms may be necessary to stimulate increases in productivity and output, reaping the full benefits of these reforms may require complementary reforms. This is one of the main messages, for instance, of a recent review of CARICOM's performance by the Inter-American Development Bank (2005). Thus, there is a strong case for increased assistance to Caribbean countries, in the form of

144. The EPA, negotiated in individual regional groupings, replaces the Cotonou Agreement signed between the EU and ACP countries from January 1, 2008. The agreement also indicates that the EU will assist CARIFORUM States in establishing harmonized intra-regional sanitary and phytosanitary (SPS) standards.
145. The EPA also includes provisions to provide technical assistance for tax reforms aimed at reducing CARIFORUM States' reliance on trade taxes.

grants or loans (with disbursements perhaps over a 4–5 year horizon), to cover a wide range of needs—from investments in infrastructure (at both the domestic and regional levels), to capacity building and institutional reform, and support for complementary reforms—to alleviate key obstacles to trade expansion.

The EPA recently concluded with the European Union recognizes these needs. In Part I, Article 8 states that development co-operation shall be primarily focused on the following areas:

(i) The provision of technical assistance to build human, legal and institutional capacity in the CARIFORUM States so as to facilitate their ability to comply with the commitments set out in the Agreement;

(ii) The provision of assistance for capacity and institution building for fiscal reform in order to strengthen tax administration and improve the collection of tax revenues with a view to shifting dependence from tariffs to other forms of indirect taxation;[146]

(iii) The provision of support measures aimed at promoting private sector and enterprise development, in particular small economic operators, and enhancing the international competitiveness of CARIFORUM firms and diversification of the CARIFORUM economies;

(iv) Diversification of CARIFORUM exports of goods and services through new investment and the development of new sectors;

(v) Support for the development of infrastructure in CARIFORUM States necessary for the conduct of trade.

Some Specific Issues for Caribbean Countries

However, although there are a number of arguments in favor of a comprehensive aid for trade program for Caribbean countries, there are several issues that need to be explored in this context. The first relates to a possible "additionality" problem. The second refers to the mechanism through which aid should be delivered and monitored. The third relates to the possibility that large increases in aid may translate into Dutch disease effects. Finally, the fourth relates to the possibility that aid may remain highly volatile, hampering the ability of Caribbean countries from designing medium-term investment programs.

Should Caribbean Countries Worry about an "Additionality" Problem?   Although there seems to be convergence regarding the benefits of an aid for trade program for Caribbean countries, it is important to ensure that this translates into the allocation of *additional resources* to support trade. In the EPA concluded with the European Union, for instance, no specific mechanism for new aid is projected. The risk is that aid allocated to promote trade may substitute for other allocations of aid, some with potentially higher return in terms of growth and welfare—such as education and health. This new "aid additionality" problem needs to be carefully monitored.[147]

---

146. In Part II, the Agreement also recognizes that there may be a need for flexibility, regarding the phased elimination of customs duties; depending on progress toward necessary fiscal reforms.

147. The problem of "aid additionality" was first raised in studies of the HIPC initiative and basically consists in a tradeoff between debt reduction and new aid. Here, it is viewed essentially as a "crowding out" problem.

How Should Aid be Delivered and Monitored?   The experience with "aid for trade" programs under the Doha round suggests that there is a need to improve coherence and coordination of action among donors. The multiplicity of actors (international organizations and individual counties) may create problems of coherence and consistency (to the extent that priorities are determined independently), efficiency in management, as well as cost and development effectiveness. These donors, in particular bilaterals and non-specialized international organizations, have been criticized for appearing to determine their priorities independently of each other. Moreover, donors have often proved unable to coordinate their efforts with national development strategies. This may explain why trade-related assistance has a mixed record on country ownership.

The Integrated Framework for Trade-Related Technical Assistance (IF) is a complementary mechanism upon which to build an expanded aid for trade program for the Caribbean.[148] The IF is intended to ensure that aid for trade corresponds to country priorities and focuses on poverty reduction. From that perspective, it is important to view aid for trade not only as a mechanism for transfers to compensate for losses but also as a development tool, designed to ensure that the root causes of weak supply response and lagging export performance are addressed.

However, ensuring that trade is adequately integrated into broader development and poverty reduction strategies remains actually a challenge in the region. For the poorest countries in the Caribbean, for which the international community makes external assistance conditional on the elaboration of an explicit Poverty Reduction Strategy (PRS), it is essential to enhance their ability to bring trade needs into the PRS process. Doing so would allow these countries to generate additional resources, to address infrastructure constraints, the lack of human capital, and so on. In that sense, aid for trade would involve helping Caribbean countries to design and implement a trade agenda as part of a donor-supported, broader national development strategy. Countries could then decide whether to use resources allocated to trade reform either for specific projects identified within the prioritized list of trade-capacity building needs, or for direct budget support (in case of loss of fiscal revenue).[149] A review of existing PRSPs in the region, however, indicates that trade reforms have received limited consideration.

For the richer countries in the Caribbean, donors should also ensure that "aid for trade" assistance is linked with broader development programs, and complements or strengthens a country's own plans, budgets, and structures. However, monitoring is more difficult in the case of these countries because they are not, in a sense, "required" to develop an explicit development strategy.

Regarding the form that aid should take, it is clear that for the poorest and least creditworthy countries in the Caribbean, direct grants to governments (in the form of additional

---

148. The IF brings together multilateral agencies (the IMF, ITC, UNCTAD, UNDP, WTO, and the World Bank) and bilateral and multilateral donors to assist poor countries in integrating trade into national development plans and Poverty Reduction Strategies, and providing coordinated delivery of trade-related technical assistance.

149. In practice, however, a key problem is to distinguish between infrastructure projects that are conducive to development in general, and those that have a direct effect on trade; in the words of Stiglitz and Charlton (2006, p. 6), "When you are building a road, how close does it have to be to the port to become and aid for trade project?" This has important implications for the *allocation* of aid, to the extent that trade-offs may emerge regarding the effect of various components on growth and poverty.

contributions from ODA budgets) will continue to be the primary means of addressing development needs—particularly for lumpy investments in infrastructure, education, and health. Richer countries of the region, however, have limited access to ODA grant resources and concessional lending. Non-concessional lending (through multilateral institutions, in particular) and equity investment will therefore be key in addressing the region's trade-related capacity and infrastructure needs. From that perspective, aid-for-trade grants may be viewed as providing crucial "seed money" for larger infrastructure programs and other supply-side interventions (such as the creation of lending institutions to finance export-oriented investments) that require non-concessional financing or "blending" with donor assistance.[150]

Should Caribbean Countries Worry about Dutch Disease Effects?   Assuming that there is no additionality problem, and that aid for trade translates into a sizable increase in aid flows, an important question that Caribbean countries may need to consider is whether an increase in these flows may have unintended negative consequences for trade—through a Dutch disease effect. The argument, essentially, is that if aid is at least partially spent on nontraded goods, it may put upward pressure on domestic prices and lead to a real exchange rate appreciation. In turn, a real appreciation may induce a reallocation of labor toward the nontraded goods sector, thereby raising real wages in terms of the price of tradables. The resulting deterioration in competitiveness may lead to a decline in export performance, unsustainable current account deficits, and an adverse effect on growth.

The international evidence does suggest that aid may lead to real exchange rate appreciation, and thereby reduce international competitiveness, in the short run. However, if aid raises public investment in infrastructure, then the longer-run effect on the real exchange rate may turn out to be positive (that is, a real depreciation).[151] The reason, of course, is the supply-side effects that are associated with an increase in core infrastructure services (see Technical Appendix A). Put differently, once dynamic considerations are taken into account, the Dutch "disease" does not have to be a terminal illness; longer-run, supply-side effects may eventually outweigh short-term, adverse demand-side effects on the real exchange rate. It is therefore important for Caribbean countries to ensure that aid is properly allocated to investment. Ensuring that adequate attention is paid to other, non-price aspects of competitiveness (such as product standards) is also important.

Should Caribbean Countries worry about Aid Volatility?   Finally, a possible concern for trade reform in Caribbean countries relates to aid volatility. This is a general issue associated with aid, as documented in a number of recent studies.[152] Of course, by their very nature, some

---

150. For richer countries of the region, with some existing industrial capacity, donors should devote greater attention to the private sector, and attempt to implement programs which act as catalysts and facilitators for enterprises to establish themselves, grow, adopt technology, acquire finance, and reach international markets.

151. See Agénor and Yilmaz (2008) for a more detailed discussion.

152. Studies by Bulir and Hamann (2006) and Hudson and Mosley (2006) have found that the volatility of aid is much larger than the volatility of domestic tax revenues, with coefficients of variation in the range of 40–60 percent of mean aid flows. Both studies also found that aid volatility has actually increased since the late 1990s, as does Kharas (2007) for a large group of aid recipients. See Agénor and Aizenman (2007) for a more detailed discussion.

types of aid (such as emergency aid or, to a lower extent, program aid) should indeed exhibit a high degree of volatility. By contrast, project aid should be relatively stable, given that it is designed to promote (directly or indirectly) investment in physical and human capital. Volatility in that category of aid could make it difficult for recipient governments to formulate medium-term investment programs to spur growth. In the specific context of Caribbean countries (especially among the poorest ones), it is therefore important to ensure any aid-for-trade initiative that involves a sizable increase in spending on trade-related infrastructure makes aid flows predictable over the medium term, to secure sustained commitment in the region.

Employment and Poverty Effects of Trade Reforms—Evidence and Policy Lessons for the Caribbean

T his Appendix provides an overview of the recent evidence on the impact of trade reforms on employment and poverty in developing countries, with a particular focus on the experience of Caribbean countries. It begins with an analytical review of the different channels through which the structure of the labor market conditions the impact of trade reform on employment and poverty. It considers next the evidence on these channels. Following a brief review of the features of the labor market and the extent of poverty in the Caribbean, it then draws policy lessons for the current trade reform agenda in the region, in particular the complementarities between trade liberalization, labor market reforms, and policies aimed at enhancing the ability of the poor to take advantage of potentially beneficial changes.

Trade, the Labor Market, and Poverty: Analytical Overview

The structure of the labor market is critical to understand how trade openness and trade liberalization affect wages, employment, and poverty. This section begins with a discussion of how the structure of the labor market conditions the effects of trade reform on wages and employment. It then considers more generally how trade reforms may affect poverty.

Trade Reform and the Labor Market

In conventional trade theory, movements of labor (and other production inputs) across sectors are what allow countries to reap the benefits of trade openness. In classical trade models, the gains from trade are generated by moving resources, including labor, toward sectors in which a country has a comparative advantage, itself resulting from relative differences across countries in either technology (as in the Ricardian model) or factor endowments (as in the Heckscher-Ohlin model). Beyond these longer-run effects, however, conventional trade theory usually ignores the role that labor market structure and rigidities may play in transmitting the impact of trade reforms to wages and employment. The argument is often that the level of employment is a macroeconomic issue, and that the effects of trade policy should be judged primarily in terms of its impact on efficiency.

However, both theory and empirical evidence suggest that the links between trade reforms and the functioning of the labor market are important, both in the short and the long term. For instance, whether or not a real devaluation associated with a drop in tariffs leads to a reduction in a country's current account deficit depends to a significant extent on how much real wages are flexible downward. More generally, labor market distortions may affect the productivity of all categories of workers, skilled and unskilled, thereby affecting the incomes of all types of households and their response to trade-induced changes in relative prices. Moreover, labor market regulations may reduce the elasticity of employment with respect to wages, thereby impeding the adjustment process to trade reforms. For instance, in a study of India based on industry-level data disaggregated by states, Hasan and others (2007) found a positive impact of trade liberalization on (the absolute values of) labor demand elasticities in the manufacturing sector. The magnitudes of these elasticities were found to be negatively related to protection levels and to be larger in size for those states with more flexible labor regulations.

Oslington (2005) provides a useful analytical framework for understanding the links between trade and unemployment. In his analysis unemployment is introduced through a particular type of labor market rigidity—a wage floor that applies to all types of labor but binds only for unskilled labor. The role and impact of unemployment is identified by considering the effects of opening trade with an otherwise identical economy without a wage floor. A number of important results are derived from his analysis; for instance, although a wage floor is a source of comparative advantage, trade based on this advantage may not generate significant gains—it may actually *increase* unemployment. Of more direct importance for developing countries (and the Caribbean region in particular), the analysis also shows that there will always be gains from opening up trade with countries with *higher* wage floors (as is the case in industrial countries); and relative abundance of the factor on which the floor binds may magnify the gains from liberalization, if as a result of greater openness to trade the good that uses the unemployed factor relatively intensely is exported.

Although Oslington's analysis is static in nature and does not consider sources of unemployment other than a purely exogenous wage floor, it illustrates well how the structure of the labor market may affect the gains from trade reform. More complex dynamic studies, with endogenous relative wages and imperfect labor mobility across sectors—due, for instance, to locational preferences or high relocation costs—largely corroborate this main insight. In Agénor and Aizenman (1996), for instance, the direction of the long-run effects of tariff reform on the labor market depends crucially on the characteristics of the migration process across sectors and the wage formation mechanism. In addition, fixed labor supply in the export sector has important consequences for the short-run effects of trade liberalization on unemployment: if labor is imperfectly mobile across sectors, the conventional transmission mechanism of trade reform is altered, because the reallocation of resources in response to relative price signals can only take place over time.[153]

The foregoing discussion suggests therefore that, if only from the perspective of evaluating the long-run gains from trade reform, understanding the role of the labor market structure is important—particularly in developing countries, where the labor market is often characterized by structural rigidities stemming from government intervention (Agénor 2006). Critical considerations in this context are the effects of trade liberalization on the demand for labor and the elasticity of labor supply, both in the short and the longer run. Also important is the impact of trade reform on private investment. Whether this impact is positive will depend in part on all the policies that determine how effectively input markets function—in particular the labor market. The impact of trade reform on capital accumulation will thus depend not only upon the effectiveness of other policies directly affecting investment (such as policies toward domestic and foreign investment and market competition) that often accompany these reforms, but also on complementary labor market policies.

The emphasis on labor market structure in the context of trade reform is well supported by the evidence by Chang and others (2005), who suggest that the effect of trade liberalization on growth is magnified by a high degree of labor market flexibility, and by Dennis (2006), who suggests that the welfare gain from trade reforms under flexible factor markets can be as much as six times greater than the gain realized under rigid ones.

Linkages between Trade Reform and Poverty

In line with Winters (2002) and Winters, McCulloch, and McKay (2004), trade liberalization can be viewed as affecting poverty through five main channels: economic growth; wages and employment (or, more generally, the labor market); changes in relative prices; exposure to volatility; and the government budget. It is important to emphasize at the outset that these channels are not independent; the extent to which exposure to volatility matters, for instance, depends on the nature of the jobs that are created and destroyed during the adjustment process. Nevertheless, a taxonomic approach is retained here for analytical convenience. In what follows these various channels are reviewed, with a more detailed focus on the role of the labor market.

Economic Growth.   Endogenous growth theory suggests that trade reform can foster growth through various effects—most notably through productivity effects, as a result of increased import competition or by allowing the domestic economy to get access to partner countries' stock of knowledge through its imports of capital goods. As documented by Winters (2004), in practice there remains much controversy as to the magnitude of the effect of trade reform on growth. Lee and others (2004), for instance, found that trade

---

153. Another study that also finds that trade reform may have adverse effects on the labor market is Batra and Beladi (1999). In that study, the condition for unemployment to emerge depends solely on the endogeneity of labor supply and on whether the production of importables is more labor-intensive than the production of exportables.

openness has a small positive effect on growth.[154] Moreover, the evidence also suggests that the productivity effects of trade reform can be limited if necessary complementary policies, such as the provision of public infrastructure services, are absent, or if the initial stock of human capital is insufficient.[155]

More importantly for the issue at stake, the immediate effect of an increase in productivity could be to reduce production inputs while at the same time it raises output. The net effect on employment will then depend on the relative sizes of the output and productivity shocks and will be influenced by factors such as the flexibility of the labor market, as discussed next. Thus, although in the longer run trade opportunities can have a major impact in creating more productive and higher paying jobs (thereby creating new opportunities for the poor), in the short term it may well have an adverse effect on employment and poverty.

Wages and Employment.   To the extent that they affect wages and employment (as discussed earlier), trade reforms may also have sizable effects on poverty. In most countries, some (if not the majority) of the poor rely on the sale of labor for the bulk of their income. Thus, to the extent that the poor generate a sizable share of their income from unskilled wage employment, standard Heckscher-Ohlin trade theory suggests that in relatively unskilled-labor-abundant countries trade liberalization should boost employment and reduce poverty.[156]At the same time, however, trade reform may raise poverty levels in the short term if it leads to a (transitional) increase in unskilled unemployment in import-substituting industries. This effect may be exacerbated if these industries (or more generally those producing nontradable goods) rely primarily on unskilled labor, whereas the production of exportables draws mainly on the semi-skilled. In such conditions, the poor will suffer most from transitional unemployment.

Of course, unless poverty is measured on an income basis, being unemployed and being poor are not the same thing. An unemployed worker who receives no benefits can maintain consumption unchanged by running down his or her liquid assets. Almost by definition, however, the poor have limited accumulated assets to rely on if they become unemployed; this suggests that the correlation between unemployment and poverty should be positive.

However, there are also a number of reasons why the correlation could actually be negative. If trade liberalization leads to an increase in employment (particularly for unskilled workers) in labor-intensive industries, where wages are low, the share of the "working poor" (that is, workers who earn less than the national or international poverty line) in total employment may rise significantly. Thus, a trade-off between unemployment reduction

154. The most robust measure of openness in their study is the parallel market premium, which captures not only trade openness per se but also reflects many other economic and policy distortions. They conclude therefore that what appears to be conducive to growth is openness in a broad sense (related to the overall economic, policy, and institutional environment), rather than openness to trade by itself.

155. See Sharma, Jayasuriya, and Oczkowski (2000) for the case of Nepal and Technical Appendix A for a more general discussion of the role of infrastructure constraints.

156. However, if trade liberalization is accompanied by skill-biased technological change, the demand for skilled labor may increase whereas the demand for unskilled labor may fall—sufficiently so perhaps to increase unskilled employment and poverty.

and poverty alleviation may emerge: to the extent that the higher growth rates of output and job creation that are associated with trade reform require a significant drop in real wages in some sectors, the deterioration in living standards may lead to higher poverty. This trade-off may be particularly steep if the expansion in employment is skewed toward low-paying jobs.[157]

Changes in Relative Prices.   Trade reform may also affect poverty through changes in the relative price of final goods, particularly of imported products. If the majority of the poor are self-employed, then this channel may be more important that the labor market channel discussed earlier, as noted by Winters (2002). To the extent, for instance, that trade liberalization is accompanied by a depreciation of the exchange rate, it may lead to an increase in the cost of the consumption—which in turn may increase poverty in urban areas.[158]

More generally, the extent to which price changes associated with trade reforms affect the poor depends on *a*) how much of any (trade-induced) price change gets passed through to the poor; and *b*) their consumption (and production) patterns. Regarding the first issue, the extent of transmission depends on a number of factors, including transport costs and other costs of distribution; the extent of competition between traders; the quality of infrastructure; and domestic taxes and regulations.[159] With monopolistic markets, for instance, changes in the domestic price of importables and exportables may respond little to trade reforms.[160]

Regarding the second, the extent to which households are able to respond to the price changes that reach them, among important factors are access to credit and adequate infrastructure services.[161] Households may be unable to respond to favorable trade-induced price movements (for instance, in the price of an agricultural product), because poor access to transport infrastructure makes it impossible to reach urban markets and seaports. Moreover, because poorer households often have limited access to credit, they tend to be less able to respond to price signals than richer households (because they are unable to finance working capital needs prior to the sale of output).

Exposure to Volatility.   To the extent that trade reforms lead to greater exposure to, say, terms-of-trade shocks, or fluctuations in activity in trade partner countries, they may

---

157. See Agénor (2004*a*) for a more detailed discussion of potential trade-offs between unemployment and poverty.

158. Episodes of trade reform have usually been preceded by, or associated with, a significant depreciation of the real exchange rate. See Li (2004) for a review.

159. In many low-income countries in sub-Saharan Africa, high transport costs resulting from poor infrastructure prevent some households (particularly those in rural areas) from expanding trade in response to changes in relative prices at the border. Yoshino (2007) found that poor quality of infrastructure—measured in terms of the average numbers of days per year for which firms experience disruptions in electricity—has an adverse effect on exports in sub-Saharan Africa.

160. As emphasized by Winters (2002) and Winters, McCulloch, and McKay (2004), equally (if not more) important than price changes is whether markets exist at all; trade reform can both create and destroy markets. The disappearance of a market can have a severe adverse effect on poverty, whereas the creation of markets for previously untraded or unavailable goods can be very beneficial.

161. In practice, estimating the price changes appropriate to each household (that is, the correct price deflator) is fraught with difficulties, but is an essential step to making poverty assessments.

also lead to greater volatility in domestic income. The poor are likely to be particularly vulnerable to such volatility, because their inherently precarious condition and lack of collateral constrain their ability to access credit markets. The lack of insurance makes it therefore more difficult for the poor to cope with negative shocks, compared with the non-poor. In turn, the inability to get protection against adverse movements in income implies that consumption smoothing is unfeasible and recourse to sub-optimal strategies (such as taking children out of school or reducing spending on health) is inevitable—with adverse long-run consequences on poverty.

Government Budget.   As discussed in Technical Appendix A, trade reforms may be accompanied (at least in the short run) by declines in tariff revenues. Thus, even if trade reform is beneficial to the poor in the long run, poverty may be adversely affected in the short term if, following a cut in tariffs, a binding budget constraint forces the government to cut spending (possibly through a reduction in transfers to low-income families or a reduction in employment in the civil service) or to raise indirect taxes (which may raise the cost of living for the poor).

Such adverse effects on poverty are not, of course, inevitable and depend very much on the composition of fiscal adjustment and the broader policy context. For instance, increasing direct taxes—if feasible—to close a financing gap should not have much impact on the poor. At the same time, however, the possibility of adverse effects brings to the fore the possible need for an aid compensation package (as discussed in Technical Appendix B) during the transition phase of a trade reform.

The Impact of Trade Reform on Employment and Poverty: Recent Evidence

There is by now a substantial literature investigating the links between trade reform and labor market outcomes, in terms of both wages and employment; Matusz and Tarr (1999) and Hoekman and Winters (2005) provide a comprehensive review. A common finding is that much of the shorter run impact of trade reform involves a reallocation of labor or changes in wages *within* sectors. This reflects a pattern of expansion of more productive firms—especially export-oriented firms or suppliers to exporters—and contraction and adjustment of less productive firms in sectors that become exposed to greater import competition. Wage responses to trade reforms are generally greater than employment effects. Wacziarg and Wallack (2004) also found that the effects of liberalization on intersectoral shifts in labor differ significantly across countries, in a way related to the scope and depth of reforms, but that overall effects are relatively small in magnitude.

However, some of the evidence does seem to suggest that trade liberalization may be associated with significant reductions in employment in the short run, particularly in sub-Saharan Africa in recent years.[162] Moreover, the empirical literature has focused almost

---

162. See for instance Fosu and Mold (2008) for a discussion of several episodes in Sub-Saharan Africa and McIntyre (2005) for an analysis of the potential impact of the East African Community customs union on Kenya.

exclusively on the (formal) manufacturing sector—despite the importance, in many developing countries, of agriculture and service industries as a source of employment.[163] Overall, therefore, as pointed out by (Winters, McCulloch, and McKay (2004, 2004, p. 102)), "... there is too little evidence to form a general view on manufacturing employment, and still less on whether similar points apply to agriculture or services, or indeed outside the formal sector."

The impact of trade reform on poverty has also been the subject of an extensive literature, which has been reviewed by Hertel and Reimer (2004) and Winters, McCulloch, and McKay (2004)). The first study provides an overview of the research aimed at assessing the survey-based, disaggregated household and firm level effects of trade policies. It finds that the earnings-side effects dominate the consumption-side effects of trade reform, and that from the perspective of the poor—and in line with the discussion in the previous section— it is the market for unskilled labor that is most important. The poverty effects of trade policy often hinge crucially on how much of the increased demand for labor in one part of the economy is transmitted to other sectors by way of increased wages or employment.

A recent study that uses household surveys to analyze the impact of trade reform on poverty is Gasiorek and Chwiejczak (2007), which focuses on Dominica, St.Kitts and Nevis, and St. Lucia.[164] The methodology involves using survey data on household expenditures to estimate changes in the cost of living relative to reference poverty bundle that arise in responses to simulated price changes of key consumption items. They examine changes in the cost of living for different deciles of the per capita expenditure distribution, and for the poor and non-poor, and identify which types of households are more likely to gain or lose from the simulated price changes. Their results indicate, first, that there are strong relationships between certain household characteristics and the probability of being poor. In Dominica, households with better educated heads are less likely to be poor, as are female headed households. Households with higher dependency ratios are much more likely to be poor, as are households with larger proportions of unemployed members. Households with better educated heads are less likely to be poor; rural households are more likely to be poor and households with more dependants and fewer workers are generally more likely to be poor.

More importantly for the issue at hand, they conduct two experiments: a change in prices arising from a reduction in tariffs on EU imports, and change in prices resulting from the same liberalization of tariffs—but coupled with the introduction of a revenue neutral consumption tax. In almost all cases, these shocks result in falls in the average cost of living.[165] In order to assess the *real* reductions in the cost of living, the reduction in household-specific cost of living is compared to a reference standard—calculated as the cost of the consumption bundle used for setting the poverty line in each country. This analysis indicates that for St. Kitts and Nevis, and for St.Lucia, there are real income gains

---

163. Another drawback of many of these studies is that they rely on intersectoral or inter-firm variations to identify employment effects and so do not capture general equilibrium interactions. It is well-known that such indirect effect can dominate direct effects, particularly in the longer run.

164. For another recent application, see Justino, Litchfield, and Pham (2008) on trade reform and poverty in Vietnam.

165. The exception is for St. Lucia, where they find a very slight increase, 0.14 percent, in total annual expenditure in the presence of the revenue neutral sales tax.

across the whole distribution, whereas for Dominica, it tends to be the poorer deciles which experience the real increase in living standards. Although households in the lower deciles gain on average by proportionately more than the reduction in the poverty line, poverty headcounts may rise. This is because either the gain is not sufficient to lift a poor household above the poverty line, or the loss of a non-poor household pushes it below the poverty line. In Dominica, the headcount poverty rate does indeed rise by as much as 2.31 percentage points. St Kitts experiences smaller increases, Nevis relatively little change under each simulation, whereas St Lucia sees poverty headcount rates falling under most scenarios.

Winters, McCulloch, and McKay (2004) survey a broader variety of research methodologies aimed at examining the impact of trade reform on poverty, including simulation studies based on computable general equilibrium models. These studies often reveal short-term negligible impacts, at least at the aggregate level. This result is not very surprising; given that most of them are conducted in a static framework where the allocation of production factors among households is fixed and full employment is assumed. In this context, the sole effect of trade liberalization is obtained through a variation in factor and consumer prices. In order to capture the long-term factor accumulation and growth effects, which are likely to be much stronger, a dynamic approach is required. Moreover, it is necessary to take into consideration not only initial factor endowments and their accumulation over time, but also the functioning of factor markets themselves, especially labor market distortions.[166]

Finally, as noted earlier, some studies have found that trade liberalization is accompanied by an increase in unemployment in the short run. However, these studies do not answer the question of whether those laid off following trade liberalization are disproportionately poor, or equivalently that the loss of employment is an important cause of a temporary increase in poverty (Winters, McCulloch, and McKay 2004, p. 102). There is very little evidence on whether transitional unemployment is disproportionately concentrated among the poor—although the experience of some sub-Saharan African countries, as documented by Fosu and Mold (2008), would seem to corroborate that view.

Implications for Trade Reform in Caribbean Countries

Structure of the Labor Market in the Caribbean

Available information on the structure of the labor market in Caribbean countries remains sketchy. Some recent data are reported by the Inter-American Development Bank (2003), Downes (2006), the ILO (2006), Cortázar (2007), and the Caribbean Labor Market Information System (CLMIS).[167] The picture that emerges is that the labor market in these

---

166. See, for instance, Agénor and Aizenman (1996). Taylor and Arnim (2006) provide a critical discussion of computable general equilibrium models of trade, regarding notably the treatment of the labor market.

167. The CLMIS is an initiative of the ILO and the United States Department of Labor to provide technical assistance and funding for building and enhancing the capacity for the production and use of labor market information in countries of the English-speaking Caribbean and Suriname. See http://www.ilo.org/public/english/region/ampro/cinterfor/dbase/clmis.htm.

Table A58. Labor Force that has Migrated to OECD Countries and the USA by Level of Schooling, 2000 (Percent)

| Country | Level of Schooling | | | | | |
| | Primary | | Secondary | | Tertiary | |
	OECD	USA	OECD	USA	OECD	USA
Antigua and Barbuda	6	5	36	29	71	63
Bahamas	2	2	12	10	36	36
Barbados	10	4	24	20	61	46
Belize	6	3	49	58	51	51
Dominica	8	6	61	53	59	47
Grenada	10	5	70	60	67	55
Guyana	14	6	34	30	86	77
Jamaica	8	4	30	27	83	76
St. Kitts and Nevis	10	7	37	29	72	63
St. Lucia	3	2	32	33	36	25
St. Vincent and the Grenadines	6	3	53	50	57	42
Suriname	18	—	44	—	90	—
Trinidad and Tobago	6	3	21	17	78	68

Source: OECD 2003.

countries suffers from a number of imperfections and distortions. These distortions include large and expanding government sectors, distinct wage-setting mechanisms for the public and private sectors, labor regulations that raise the cost of hiring and firing workers, fragmentation of the sub-regional labor market, and inadequate labor market information.

Challenges include youth unemployment, the mismatch between the educational system and the needs of the labor market, the creation of jobs, low levels of productivity coupled with relatively high wages, sustained emigration flows of skilled labor from the region. For instance, in 2000 the rates of migration for tertiary level educated individuals ranged from 36 percent in the Bahamas and St Lucia to 90 percent in Suriname (Table A58). For OECS countries alone, between 64 and 78 percent of the labor force with tertiary level education migrated to the OECD member countries over the period 1965 to 2000 (Downes and Lewis 2008, p. 81). In fact, as of 2000, close to half of all people who were born in the Caribbean countries and who are in the labor force had emigrated (Ozden (2008)). Although this "brain drain" has generated some substantial benefits (in terms of sizable remittance flows to families at home, in particular) it also constrains the ability of many countries in the region to reap the benefits from trade reforms.

Table A59, taken from Downes and others (2003), summarizes the main characteristics of labor market regulations in English-Speaking Caribbean countries during the 1990s, whereas Table A60, taken from Bussolo and Medvedev (2007), provides more detailed information about Jamaica. They both indicate that these regulations are pervasive and significantly tighter compared to OECD countries. Firing costs, in particular, are about twice as high in the region, compared to industrial countries. Nevertheless, English-speaking

Table A59. Characteristics of Labor Market Regulation for the English Speaking Caribbean in the 1990s

	Bahamas	Barbados	Belize	Guyana	Jamaica	Trinidad/Tobago
Period of prior notice	Half to one month	Negotiable	Half to one month	Half month	2 to 12 weeks	2 months
Payment for Dismissal with Just Cause	0	0	0	0	0	0
Payment for Dismissal without Just Cause	Negotiable collectively	2 $1/2$ weeks for service between 1 to 10 years; 3 weeks for service between 10 and 20 years; 3 $1/2$ weeks for more than 20 years	1 week's pay per year of service after 5 years of service	Negotiable collectively		$1/2$ times period of service for 1 to 4 years of service; $3/4$ times period of service for more than 5 years
Payment for Dismissal for Economic Reason	Negotiable collectively	2 $1/2$ weeks for service between 1 to 10 years; 3 weeks for service between 10 and 20 years; 3 $1/2$ weeks for more than 20 years	1 week's pay per year after 5 years of service	Negotiable collectively		$1/2$ times period of service for 1 to 4 years of service; $3/4$ times period of service for more than 5 years
Limit to Payment for Dismissal	No	Maximum limit to monthly salary	Maximum of 42 weeks	No		No
Compensation for Termination by Worker	None	None	For 10 years of service, $1/4$ times the number of years of service	None	None	None
Unemployment Insurance	No	Yes	No	No	No	No
Probationary Period	3 months to 1 year	Negotiable	2 weeks	None	3 months	Negotiable

Duration of Temporary Contracts	Without restrictions	Without restrictions	Without restrictions	Without restrictions	Without restrictions	Without restrictions, but in practice it is 6 months
Maximum Workday (hrs/wk)	48	40	45	48		
Charges for Added Hours	50	50	50	50		
Charges for Night Work	Nothing if ordinary work day	Nothing	Nothing if ordinary work day	Nothing if ordinary work day		
Charges for Work on Holidays (%)	100 for Sundays; 150 for holidays	100	Nothing if ordinary work day	100		

Source: Downes and others (2003).

Table A60. Jamaica: Indicators of Labor Market Rigidity

Indicator	Jamaica	Region	OECD
Difficulty of Hiring Index	11.0	40.5	30.1
Rigidity of Hours Index	0.0	50.9	49.6
Difficulty of Firing Index	20.0	29.5	27.4
Rigidity of Employment			
Hiring cost (% of salary)	11.5	15.9	20.7
Firing costs (weeks of wages)	60.2	62.9	35.1
Collective relation Index	22.6	46.5	46.2
Social Security Index	16.8	57.8	73.9

Source: Bussolo and Medvedev (2007).

Notes: Four areas are subject to statutory regulation in all countries: employment, social security, industrial relations and occupational health and safety. Doing Business focuses on the regulation of employment. The *rigidity of employment index* (in italics in the table) is the average of three sub-indices: a *difficulty of hiring index,* a *rigidity of hours index* and a *difficulty of firing index.* All the sub-indices have several components, and all take values between 0 and 100, with higher values indicating more rigid regulation. The *hiring cost* indicator measures all social security payments and payroll taxes associated with hiring an employee. The cost is expressed as a percentage of the worker's salary. The *firing cost indicator* measures the cost of advance notice requirements, severance payments and penal-ties due when dismissing a redundant worker, expressed in weekly wages. In Botero and others (2004), the *Collective relation index* combines information from two sub-areas of the collective action laws: (i) the power granted by the law to labor unions and (ii) the laws governing collective disputes. The sub-index of labor union power measures the power of labor unions over working conditions. The second sub-index measures protection of employees engaged in collective disputes. Higher values of the index are associated to higher workers' protection. The *Social security index* considers coverage and generos-ity of pensions, sickness and healthcare insurance, and unemployment.

Caribbean countries appear to have less stringent job security regulations than Latin American countries (IADB 2003, p. 215). Moreover, most countries of the region have a large informal sector, where labor regulations are not enforced. According to estimates by Gasparini and Tornarolli (2007, Table 3.2), informal employment as a share of total employment rep-resented 51.3 in the Dominican Republic in 2004, 82.1 percent in Haiti in 2001, and 57.6 percent in Jamaica in 2002. In Saint Lucia, the share of informal employment was 30.5 percent in 2000 (Downes 2006, Table 6).

Most countries in the region are also characterized by persistently high rates of open unemployment, ranging in recent years from 8 percent in Antigua and Barbuda to 19 percent in St Lucia and Grenada (Downes and Lewis (2008, p. 78)), and pervasive disguised unemployment in the informal sector. As show in Table A61, Bahamas, Barbados, Belize, Jamaica, and Suriname recorded double digit, or nearly double digit, unemployment rates on average during the period 2002–06. Youth unemployment, in particular, is a major issue in many countries of the region and is related to the growing concern about increases in crime and violence.[168] There is some indication that real wages have grown faster than

---

168. See, for instance, World Bank (2006) on Jamaica.

Table A61. Caribbean: Unemployment Rates in Selected Countries 2002–06 (Percent)

	2002	2003	2004	2005	2006*	Average 2002–06
Bahamas	9.1	10.8	10.2	10.2	7.6	9.6
Barbados	10.3	11.0	9.8	9.1	8.7	9.8
Belize	10.0	12.9	11.6	11.0	9.4	11.0
Jamaica	14.2	11.4	11.7	11.3	10.3	11.8
Suriname	10.0	7.0	8.4	11.2	12.1	9.7
Trinidad and Tobago	10.4	10.5	8.4	8.0	6.2	8.7
Average	10.7	10.6	10.0	10.1	9.0	

Source: ECLAC Data and Bank staff's calculations.
*Preliminary.

labor productivity in the OECS countries, with an adverse impact on the competitiveness of the sub-region (World Bank 2005, Chapter 6). At the same time, however, Downes and others (2003) found that for Barbados, Jamaica, and Trinidad and Tobago, selected labor market regulations (the minimum wage, contributions to the national insurance system, and severance payments) have had a limited impact on employment; rather, the main reason for the increase in unemployment in these countries appears to have been weak economic growth.[169]

Poverty in the Caribbean

Progress toward reducing poverty has been overall relatively slow and remains uneven in the region. Haiti and Suriname are at the high end of the spectrum of poverty incidence with an estimated 65 percent and 63 percent, respectively, of their populations below the absolute international poverty line (US$1 a day). In OECS countries, poverty rates range from 16 percent in Saint Kitts and Nevis to almost 40 percent in Dominica (Table A62). In Belize, Dominica, Grenada, Guyana, St. Kitts and Nevis, and St. Vincent and the Grenadines, relative poverty rates remain in the 30–40 percent range, whereas in Anguilla and the British Virgin Islands, and St. Lucia, it remains in the 20–30 percent range. For Barbados and Trinidad and Tobago, poverty rates remain in the 10–20 percent range, with about 14 percent and 21 percent, respectively.

Jamaica experienced a large decline in poverty between the early 1990s and the early 2000s. As shown in Table A62, the absolute poverty rate (based on the national moderate poverty line) fell from 30.5 percent in 1989 to 19.7 percent in 2002. However, based on an international poverty line of US$1 day, the poverty rate fell from 41.2 percent in 1990 to only 33.3 percent (Gasparini et al. (2007)); and since 2002, progress has been limited.

---

169. There are some limitations to this study, which suggest treating the results with caution.

Table A62. OECS Countries: Poverty Estimates

Country	Year	Poverty Line EC$ Annual	Population Below Poverty Line (%)	Households Below Poverty Line (%)	Poverty Gap
Antigua/Barbuda	2005/6	6318	18.5	n.a.	6.63
Dominica	2002/3	3400	39.0	29	10.2
Grenada	1998/9	3262	32.1	24	15.3
St Kitts (Nevis)	1999/2000	3361 (3941)	30.4 (32.0)	16 (16)	2.5 (2.8)
St Lucia	1995	1876	25.1	18.7	8.6
	2005/6	5086	28.8	21.4	9.0
St Vincent/Grenadines	1996	1558	37.5	30.6	12.6

Source: Downes and Lewis (2008), p. 82.

In the Dominican Republic, after hovering for years in the 8–9 percent range, poverty increased significantly following the financial crisis of 2002–03. Between 2000 and 2004, absolute poverty increased from 2 percent to 3.4 percent, whereas relative poverty (based on an international poverty line of US$2 a day) increased by 7.6 percent, from 8.8 percent to 16.4 percent (see Figure A1 and Gasparini et al. (2007)). The data shown in Figure 1 for the Dominican Republic suggest also that the crisis had an asymmetric effect on poverty: during the contraction in output (during which real GDP growth dropped by about 2 percent) poverty increased sharply (with a jump of almost 6 percentage points in 2003), whereas during the subsequent recovery—with real GDP growth of 2 percent in 2004, 9.3 percent in 2005, and 10.7 percent in 2006—it fell by much less: by the end of 2006 poverty rates had fallen by less than half of the amount by which it had previously increased.[170]

In addition to slow growth in some countries, the lack of progress in reducing poverty or deterioration of poverty indicators has been the consequence of severe external economic shocks (such as the removal of European preferences for ACP banana exports, in the case of St. Lucia and Dominica) and natural hazard occurrences (such as Hurricane Ivan, in the case of Grenada in 2004). In some cases (such as in the Dominican Republic, following the 2002–03 financial crisis), increases in poverty and unemployment have been positively correlated—although, as noted in previous sections, this correlation could go in the opposite direction.

The foregoing discussion suggests several policy lessons for Caribbean countries and the way forward in designing their trade reform agenda.

■ While there are good reasons to believe that trade liberalization will stimulate growth, increase employment, and reduce poverty in the long run, the ultimate outcome depends on many factors in addition to the precise nature of the reform measures undertaken, including initial conditions, the structure of the labor market, and the scope for complementary policy reforms.

---

170. See Agénor (2002, 2004*b*) for a more detailed discussion of the asymmetric response of poverty to business cycles and crises.

Table A63. Jamaica: Poverty Trends, 1989–2002

Indicator	'89	'90	'91	'92	'93	'94	'95	'96	'97	'98	'99	'00	'01	'02
Incidence	30.5	28.4	44.6	33.9	24.4	22.8	27.5	26.1	19.9	15.9	17.0	18.7	16.9	19.7
Poverty Gap		7.9	15.7	10.7	7.5	6.0	7.2	6.9	4.9	4.2	4.4	4.6	4.6	n.d.
Gini Coefficient		0.38	0.40	0.38	0.37	0.38	0.36	0.36	0.42	0.37	0.38	0.38	0.38	0.40
% persons food poor		8.3	n.d.	14.5	9.9	8.0	9.0	8.6	4.1	3.7	5.1	5.0	5.5	n.d.
Q1 + Q2 share of nat'l cons.		17.0	16.3	17.3	17.4	17.2	18.3	18.3	15.4	17.8	17.2	17.3	16.8.	16.6
Q5 share		45.9	47.1	45.2	44.8	45.9	44.7	44.5	49.1	45.3	45.9	46.0	45.9	47.6

Source: World Bank, *Jamaica: Public Expenditure Review* (December 2005).

- The way the labor market operates conditions the employment and wage outcomes of trade reforms; labor market distortions may actually prevent timely adjustment in response to these reforms, constraining job creation and creating persistent unemployment.
- In countries where the poor generate a significant share of their income from selling labor services, the labor market is also a crucial element in understanding the poverty effects of trade reforms. Trade liberalization should not be thought of as a policy to reduce poverty directly; its benefits for the poor stem essentially from being able to foster economic growth and creating high-paying jobs. However, it is important to take into account the structure of the labor market in designing trade liberalization strategies so as to implement complementary policy reforms aimed at removing the most pervasive distortions in the labor market and minimize

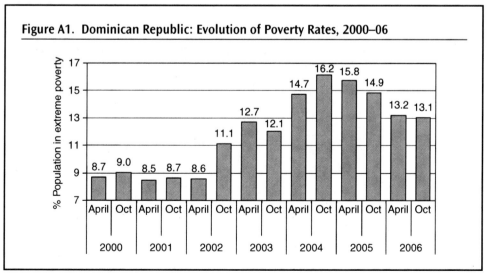

Figure A1. Dominican Republic: Evolution of Poverty Rates, 2000–06

Source: World Bank/DR Authorities.

adjustment costs, in terms of short-run reductions in employment and increase in poverty.

■ Minimizing short-run adjustment costs is also important because these costs (if deemed excessive) may have an adverse effect on the sustainability of the reform process, leading possibly to policy reversals or the complete abandonment of the reform effort. Doing so may involve the provision of short-term financial support (through increased aid, as discussed in Technical Appendix B) to give governments time to implement complementary reforms aimed at increasing tax revenues or improve the efficiency of public spending.

■ These considerations are particularly important for the Caribbean region, where the initial situation in one of high unemployment and high poverty in many countries. In such an environment, it is especially important to design policies aimed at reducing any adverse impact of trade liberalization on employment and poverty. The reason is that even a *transitory* increase in unemployment could exacerbate the already high propensity to migrate to industrial countries, with adverse effects on the long-run potential benefits of trade reform. Skill shortages may constrain the ability of Caribbean countries to expand production and promote growth in response to new trade opportunities—even though remittance flows associated with migrated labor may generate positive effects. This may be a particularly significant problem for OECS countries (Downes and Lewis (2008)). Thus, trade liberalization should not be seen in isolation and additional policies (and possibly substantial financial support) may be needed to enhance its impact.

■ Regarding poverty specifically, there is substantial evidence that poorer households (both as consumers and producers) are less able than richer ones to protect themselves against adverse shocks or to take advantage of new opportunities generated by trade reforms. In such circumstances there is an important role for complementary policies to accompany these reforms in the Caribbean, both to strengthen social protection for losers and to enhance the ability of poorer households to exploit potentially beneficial changes.

■ To enhance the impact of trade liberalization on poverty reduction, trade reform in the Caribbean must also be accompanied by a strategy aimed at identifying and removing obstacles to the poor participating in economic activities. In addition to reducing the scope of labor market distortions, this may also involve enhancing access to key production inputs, markets, or infrastructure. A proper sequencing of these various policies may be critical for the success of trade reforms in the region.

Key Characteristics of the CGE Models—GLOBE and Jamaican Models

Key Features of the GLOBE Model

The CGE models used in to assess the impact of the EPA on Caribbean region as a whole and on Jamaica are "static" in that they do not incorporate time explicitly and are used to generate comparative static scenarios, comparing model solutions "before" and "after" some shock. The time required to move from one equilibrium to another depends on assumptions about the speed of adjustment mechanisms in different markets. Differentiating between the "short run" (covering 1–3 years), "medium run" (3–5 years) or "long run" (more than 5 years) depends on the degree of flexibility in factor and product markets specified in the model. For example, a short-run model would specify fixed capital stocks in every sector and might limit labor mobility. The implementation of the CARIFORUM EPA is over a 25 year period from 2008 and the GLOBE and Jamaica models are used for the comparative static impact analysis of the phasing in of the EPA to 2033 in four steps in "long run" mode.

In assessing trade policy integration and liberalisation, policies and trends affecting both "shallow" and "deep" integration are important. Shallow integration involves the lowering or elimination of barriers to the movement of goods and services across national borders within the region. Deep integration involves establishing or expanding the institutional environment in order to facilitate trade and relocate production without regard to national borders. CGE models are designed to consider shallow integration within a neoclassical general equilibrium framework, and are well suited for the analysis of the market access aspects of the CARIFORUM EPA. Our analysis of the impacts on services through changes in tariff equivalents and productivity touch on deep integration issues, which are not as well grounded theoretically or empirically as the market access scenarios, and are therefore more illustrative in character. There are potential links between trade liberalization, expanded intra industry trade, and FDI that can induce technical change and

291

productivity growth. While multi-country cross-sectional and time-series empirical studies identify a positive correlation between increased openness and TFP growth, the causal channels are not well understood (Winters 2004). In addition sectoral, industry and firm level studies often throw up mixed results, indicating that liberalization affects different parts of the economy in different ways. Thus while there is general agreement that productivity in sectors which use a large variety of intermediate goods could potentially benefit from the EPA, quantifying the effect has proved difficult.[171]

Both the GLOBE regional and the Jamaica single country models have a similar set of indicators for assessing the impact of the CARIFORUM EPA. These include the levels of demand for skilled and unskilled labor and capital, for each national or regional economy, together with the estimated changes in the functional distribution of income for any particular scenario. Both models use changes in absorption (imports plus domestically produced consumption, government and investment commodities) as the overall welfare indicator. Absorption measures the aggregate supply of goods and services, both domestic and imported, available for use by demanders in a country.

The GLOBE multi-country CGE (Computable General Equilibrium) model was developed by Scott McDonald, Sherman Robinson and Karen Thierfelder.[172] The model has the following key characteristics. GLOBE models agents' micro economic behavior in consumption and production in the economy, treating tradable goods as imperfect substitutes for domestic production. GLOBE allows for a choice of how key markets operate (closure rules), allowing for different assumptions about the behavior of markets and actors to be examined. Given base data, key parameters, policy variables such as tariffs, GLOBE solves for real values of production, consumption, economic welfare, real exchange rates.

The GLOBE model is a member of the class of multi-country, computable general equilibrium (CGE) models that are descendants of the approach to CGE modeling described by Dervis and others (1982). The model is a SAM-based CGE model, wherein the SAM serves to identify the agents in the economy and provides the database with which the model is calibrated. The SAM also serves an important organizational role since the groups of agents identified in the SAM structure are also used to define sub-matrices of the SAM for which behavioral relationships need to be defined (Pyatt, 1987). The implementation of this model, using the GAMS (General Algebraic Modeling System) software, is a direct descendant and extension of the single-country and multi-country CGE models developed in the late 1980s and early 1990s (See McDonald and others 2007 for a more detailed description of the GLOBE model).

International Trade

Trade is modeled using a treatment derived from the Armington "insight"; namely domestically produced commodities are assumed to be imperfect substitutes for traded goods, both imports and exports. Import demand is modeled via a series of nested constant elasticity of substitution (CES) functions; imported commodities from different source regions to a destination region are assumed to be imperfect substitutes for each other and are aggregated to form composite import commodities that are assumed to be imperfect

---

171. See Evans, Gasiorek, McDonald and Robinson (2006) based on Evans, Gasiorek, Ghoneim, Haynes-Prempeh, Holmes, Iacovone, Jackson, Iwanow, Robinson and Rollo (2006).

172. The description below is based on McDonald, Thierfelder, and Robinson (2007).

substitutes for their counterpart domestic commodities. The composite imported commodities and their counterpart domestic commodities are then combined to produce composite consumption commodities, which are the commodities demanded by domestic agents as intermediate inputs and final demand (private consumption, government, and investment).[173]

Export supply is modeled via a series of nested constant elasticity of transformation (CET) functions; the composite export commodities are assumed to be imperfect substitutes for domestically consumed commodities, while the exported commodities from a source region to different destination regions are assumed to be imperfect substitutes for each other. The composite exported commodities and their counterpart domestic commodities are then combined as composite production commodities; properties of models using the Armington insight are well known (de Melo and Robinson 1989; Devarajan and others 1990). The use of nested CET functions for export supply implies that domestic producers adjust their export supply decisions in response to changes in the relative prices of exports and domestic commodities. This specification is desirable in a global model with a mix of developing and developed countries that produce different kinds of traded goods with the same aggregate commodity classification, and yields more realistic behavior of international prices than models assuming perfect substitution on the export side.

Agents are assumed to determine their optimal demand for and supply of commodities as functions of relative prices, and the model simulates the operation of national commodity and factor markets and international commodity markets. Each source region exports commodities to destination regions at prices that are valued free on board (*fob*). Fixed quantities of trade services are incurred for each unit of a commodity exported between each and every source and destination, yielding import prices at each destination that include carriage, insurance and freight charges (*cif*). The *cif* prices are the 'landed' prices expressed in global currency units. To these are added any import duties and other taxes, and the resultant price converted into domestic currency units using the exchange rate to get the source region specific import price. The price of the composite import commodity is a weighted aggregate of the region-specific import prices, while the domestic supply price of the composite commodity is a weighted aggregate of the import commodity price and the price of domestically produced commodities sold on the domestic market.

The prices received by domestic producers for their output are weighted aggregates of the domestic price and the aggregate export prices, which are weighted aggregates of the prices received for exports to each region in domestic currency units. The fob export prices are then determined by the subtraction of any export taxes and converted into global currency units using the regional exchange rate.

There are two important features of the price system in this model that deserve special mention. First, each region has its own numéraire such that all prices within a region are defined relative to the region's numéraire. We specify a fixed aggregate consumer price index to define the regional numéraire. For each region, the real exchange rate variable ensures that the regional trade-balance constraint is satisfied when the regional trade balances are fixed. Second, in addition, there is a global numéraire such that all exchange rates

---

173. The presumption of imperfect substitutability between imports from different sources is relaxed where the imports of a commodity from a source region account for a 'small' (0.0001) share of imports of that commodity by the destination region. In such cases the destination region is assumed to import the commodity from the source region in fixed shares.

are expressed relative to this numéraire. The global numéraire is defined as a weighted average of the exchange rates for a user defined region or group of regions. In this implementation of GLOBE the basket of regions approximates the OECD economies.

Fixed country trade balances are specified in "real" terms defined by the global numéraire. If the global numéraire is the U.S. exchange rate and it is fixed to one, then the trade balances are "real" variables defined in terms of the value of U.S. exports. If global numéraire is a weighted exchange rate for a group of regions, as in this case, and it is fixed to one, then the trade balances are "claims" against the weighted average of exports by the group of regions in the numéraire.

Production and Demand

The production structure is a two stage nest. Intermediate inputs are used in fixed proportions per unit of output—Leontief technology. Primary inputs are combined as imperfect substitutes, according to a CES function, to produce value added. Producers are assumed to maximize profits, which determines product supply and factor demand. Product markets are assumed to be competitive, and the model solves for equilibrium prices that clear the markets. Factor markets in developed countries are also assume to have fixed labor supplies, and the model solves for equilibrium wages that clear the markets. In developing countries, however, we assume that the real wage of unskilled labor is fixed and that the supply of unskilled labor is infinitely elastic at that wage. So, labor supply clears the market, and aggregate unskilled employment is endogenous rather than the real wage. In this specification, any shock that would otherwise increase the equilibrium wage will instead lead to increased employment.

Final demand by the government and for investment is modeled under the assumption that the relative quantities of each commodity demand by these two institutions is fixed—this treatment reflects the absence of a clear theory that defines an appropriate behavioral response by these agents to changes in relative prices. For the household there is a well developed behavioral theory; and the model contains the assumption that households are utility maximisers who respond to changes in relative prices and incomes. In this version of the model, the utility functions for private households are assumed to be Stone Geary functions; for the OECD countries they are parameterized as Cobb Douglas functions, that is, there are no subsistence expenditures.

Key Features of the Jamaican Model

The Jamaica single country CGE model is a member of the same class CGE models as the GLOBE model, a descendant of the approach to CGE modeling described by Dervis and others (1982). The model is also a SAM-based CGE model, wherein the SAM serves to identify the agents in the economy and provides the database with which the model is calibrated. The SAM also serves an important organizational role since the groups of agents identified in the SAM structure are also used to define sub-matrices of the SAM for which behavioral relationships need to be defined (Pyatt 1987). The implementation of this model uses the GAMS (General Algebraic Modeling System) software. The GLOBE model described above is a direct descendant and extension of the single-country and multi-country CGE models developed in the 1980s and early 1990s. Each regional or country block in the GLOBE model can be seen as a single country CGE model. In the single-country models, world prices are exogenous. In the GLOBE model, the regional CGE models are connected by trade flows and world prices are endogenously determined to clear world commodity markets. This short description of the Jamaica country CGE model draws out the key differences between the GLOBE and Jamaica CGE model rather than repeating the common elements already spelt out for the GLOBE model.

International Trade in the Country CGE model

As in the GLOBE mode, trade is modeled in the Jamaica country CGE model using the same Armington "insight"; namely domestically produced commodities are assumed to be imperfect substitutes for traded goods, both imports and exports. Import demand is modeled via a series of nested constant elasticity of substitution (CES) functions; imported commodities from different source regions to a destination region are assumed to be imperfect substitutes for each other and are aggregated to form composite import commodities that are assumed to be imperfect substitutes for their counterpart domestic commodities. The composite imported commodities and their counterpart domestic commodities are then combined to produce composite consumption commodities, which are the commodities demanded by domestic agents as intermediate inputs and final demand (private consumption, government, and investment). The difference between the GLOBE and single country CGE models is that, whereas in the GLOBE model, imports into one region are sourced from other regions identified in the GLOBE model, imports in the single country CGE model, imports are available either at a fixed world price, or are modeled with import supply functions for each commodity and region of destination.

In common with the GLOBE model, export supply is modeled via a series of nested constant elasticity of transformation (CET) functions. The composite export commodities are assumed to be imperfect substitutes for domestically sold commodities, while the exported commodities from a source region to different destination regions are assumed to be imperfect substitutes for each other. The composite exported commodities and their counterpart domestic commodities are then combined as composite production commodities; properties of models using the Armington insight are well known (de Melo and Robinson 1989; Devarajan and others 1990). The use of nested CET functions for export supply implies that domestic producers adjust their export supply decisions in response to changes in the relative prices of exports and domestic commodities.

The model distinguishes three regions with which Jamaica trades: the United States, the EU, and the rest of the world. Prices in these regions are assumed exogenous. The price of imported goods in Jamaica are prices from the region of origin plus any import duties or border taxes, converted to local currency by multiplying by the exchange rate. In Jamaica, the price of each composite import commodity is a weighted aggregate of the region-specific import prices, with the weights determined from the CES aggregation. Similarly, the price of a composite export commodity in Jamaica is the price of the CET aggregate of exports to the three regions of destination.

Common Elements in the Jamaica Country CGE Model and GLOBE Model

The treatment of production, demand, commodity markets, factor markets, factor market closure, macro closure, and fiscal closure is essentially the same as in the GLOBE model. The major differences in the Jamaica model from the regional CGE models in GLOBE arises from the size and structure of the SAM databases and the types of economic policy problems analyzed. Multiregional CGE models such as GLOBE use the GTAP database and focus on the analysis of international trade issues. The size of the regional models is limited by data restrictions imposed by the global character of the database—all regions have the same factors and commodities, and a very simple representation households, taxes, and government. In the case of Jamaica, the SAM reflects the structure of that economy, but has been aggregated to be as consistent as possible with GLOBE because we are using results on world prices from GLOBE in scenarios in the Jamaica model. The Jamaica SAM is for 2000, which is close to the 2001 base year of the GTAP data set used in GLOBE.

Regions, Sectors, Factors, and Households in the Jamaica Country CGE Model

For its base data the Jamaica country CGE model uses a SAM for 2000 details of which are shown in Table A64.

Table A64. Sectors, Factors and Regions in the Jamaica Country CGE Model

Activities	Commodities	Factors and Regions
Export Agriculture	Export Agriculture	**Factors**
Domestic Agriculture	Domestic Agriculture	Unskilled labor
Livestock	Livestock	Skilled labor
Forestry and Fishing	Forestry and Fishing	Capital
Mining	Mining	
Sugar Cane and Beet	Sugar Cane and Beet	**Regions**
Processed Sugar	Processed Sugar	United States of America
Beverages and Tobacco	Beverages and Tobacco	European Union
Textiles Clothing and Leather	Textiles Clothing and Leather	Rest if the World
Wood Products	Wood Products	
Paper and Printing	Paper and Printing	
Oil	Oil	
Chemical Products	Chemical Products	
Non Metal Products	Non Metal Products	
Domestic Machinery	Domestic machinery	
Machinery Export Processing	Exported machinery	
Electricity Water	Imported machinery	
Construction	Electricity Water	
Commerce	Construction	
Transport	Commerce	
Finance and Insurance	Transport	
Real estate and Business Services	Finance and Insurance	
Government Services	Real estate and Business Services	
Other Services	Government Services	
	Other Services	

Source: Jamaica SAM 2000, World Bank.

Structure of the Jamaican Economy

The structure of the Jamaican economy is presented in Tables 6.10–6.13 below, based on information from the 1990 SAM. As for other Caribbean economies, production is dominated by the service sectors (Table A65). Agriculture is a small share, representing only 5.8 percent of value added. Exports are dominated by tourism, included in the commodity "commerce" which represents 50.8 percent of total exports. Mining is also important, representing 4.3 percent of value added and 23.3 percent of total exports. Sugar cane and processed sugar together represent 3.5 percent of total exports, which is significant but smaller than other Caribbean countries.

Tables A21 and 22 show the regional composition of exports and imports. Jamaica's exports are diversified in the aggregate across the three regions, but there are significant variations across commodities (Table A66). The United States and the rest of the world, however, are much more important than the EU as sources of imports—43.0 percent and 45.3 percent, compared to 11.6 percent for the EU. An EPA with the EU thus has potential for diverting trade away from the United State and the rest of the world, which could lead to welfare losses for Jamaica. In terms of exports, the EU is the destination for all of Jamaica's processed sugar exports, so Jamaica potentially gains from any improved access for sugar in the EU market. The EU is also a significant market for Jamaican agricultural exports, although less than the rest of the world. In general, EU export markets are less important to Jamaica than the United States and the rest of the world, which would tend to lessen interest in Jamaica in an EPA unless it promised significant increased market access.

Table A68 shows factor shares in production in Jamaica. Agriculture and construction are intensive in unskilled labor, so any increase in market size for these sectors should favor unskilled labor. Assuming unemployment and a fixed real wage for unskilled labor, expansion

Table A65. Structural Shares by Commodity: Jamaica Base 2000

Commodities	VAshr	PRDshr	EMPshr	EXPshr	EXP-OUTshr	IMPshr	IMP-DEMshr
Export Agriculture	1.2	1.9	1.8	2.2	18.6	0.3	5.0
Domestic Agriculture	3.3	2.0	4.4	0.6	4.9	2.3	25.3
Livestock	0.9	1.6	1.4	0.0	0.0	0.1	1.4
Forestry and Fishing	0.4	0.6	0.5	0.2	5.3	2.0	51.6
Mining	4.3	5.2	1.5	23.3	74.7	0.4	7.6
Sugar Cane and Beet	2.6	9.3	1.9	1.7	3.0	6.2	17.1
Processed Sugar	0.2	0.7	0.4	1.8	40.4	0.7	35.0
Beverages and Tobacco	2.9	2.2	0.8	1.8	13.9	0.8	12.2
Textiles Clothing and Leather	0.1	1.1	0.3	0.0	0.6	1.1	22.5
Wood Products	0.2	0.6	0.4	0.0	1.0	0.5	19.0
Paper and Printing	0.3	0.6	0.4	0.0	0.9	2.0	48.5
Oil	0.8	2.7	0.3	1.0	5.8	12.8	56.5
Chemical Products	0.7	2.1	0.3	2.0	16.0	8.5	57.2
Non Metal Products	0.7	0.8	0.4	0.1	2.2	1.8	36.6
Domestic machinery	0.0	0.2	0.0			34.3	98.0
Exported machinery	0.1	0.2	0.1	1.2	100.0		
Imported machinery						0.7	100.0
Electricity Water	3.7	3.3	1.6	0.0	0.1		
Construction	10.5	12.0	11.9				
Commerce	20.1	19.6	12.9	50.8	42.8	1.7	3.7
Transport	12.8	12.1	12.1	9.2	12.6		
Finance and Insurance	6.0	3.8	3.2	1.3	5.5	3.7	20.9
Real estate and Business Services	6.5	4.7	6.8	2.4	8.5	19.8	54.3
Government Services	13.8	7.6	24.8				
Other Services	7.8	5.1	11.6	0.3	1.0	0.2	1.1
TOTAL-1	100.0	100.0	100.0	100.0	16.5	100.0	24.6
Total Agriculture	5.8	6.1	8.2	3.0	8.0	4.6	19.2
Total Rest	94.2	93.9	91.8	97.0	17.1	95.4	25.0
TOTAL-2	100.0	100.0	100.0	100.0	16.5	100.0	24.6

Source: Bank staff and IDS.

of sectors intensive in unskilled labor should lead to significant increases in employment. Mining and beverages and tobacco are highly capital intensive, as are many of the service sectors, including commerce (tourism). Given the wide variation in factor shares across sectors, one might expect trade agreements which change effective world prices facing Jamaica to have significant effects on the structure of employment and wages.

Table A66. Regional Export Shares by Commodity: Jamaica Base 2000

Commodities	United States	European Union	Rest of the World	TOTAL
Export Agriculture	14.9	35.9	49.2	3.2
Domestic Agriculture	62.7	13.9	23.4	0.9
Livestock	26.1		73.9	0.0
Forestry and Fishing	71.4	23.2	5.4	0.3
Mining	21.7	32.9	45.4	34.4
Sugar Cane and Beet	42.2	9.0	48.7	2.4
Processed Sugar	0.0	99.9	0.1	2.6
Beverages and Tobacco	36.9	22.2	40.9	2.7
Textiles Clothing and Leather	53.4	15.7	30.9	0.1
Wood Products	91.0	0.2	8.7	0.1
Paper and Printing	8.6	5.5	86.0	0.0
Oil	71.8		28.2	1.4
Chemical Products	62.8	1.4	35.8	3.0
Non Metal Products	47.0	0.3	52.7	0.2
Domestic machinery	65.9	6.9	27.2	1.8
Exported machinery	28.3	30.5	41.2	0.0
Imported machinery	28.3	30.5	41.2	75.0
Electricity Water	28.3	30.5	41.2	13.6
Construction	28.3	30.5	41.2	1.9
Commerce	28.3	30.5	41.2	3.6
Transport	28.3	30.5	41.2	0.5
TOTAL	28.3	30.5	41.2	147.6

Source: Bank staff and IDS.

Table A67. Regional Import Shares by Commodity: Jamaica Base 2000

Commodities	United States	European Union	Rest of the World	TOTAL
Export Agriculture	44.2	9.9	45.9	0.6
Domestic Agriculture	57.9	8.1	34.0	5.2
Livestock	30.2	0.2	69.6	0.2
Forestry and Fishing	22.3	4.4	73.2	4.7
Mining	9.2	11.4	79.4	0.9
Sugar Cane and Beet	48.9	9.2	41.9	14.3
Processed Sugar	22.8	3.4	73.8	1.6
Beverages and Tobacco	17.8	22.7	59.5	1.9
Textiles Clothing and Leather	57.4	4.3	38.3	2.5
Wood Products	31.8	2.6	65.7	1.2
Paper and Printing	43.1	5.1	51.8	4.6
Oil	27.5	4.8	67.8	29.5
Chemical Products	52.2	13.1	34.7	19.6
Non Metal Products	27.7	14.4	57.9	4.0
Domestic machinery	47.6	15.4	37.0	78.8
Exported machinery	47.6	15.4	37.0	1.6
Imported machinery	43.1	11.6	45.3	3.8
Electricity Water	43.1	11.6	45.3	8.5
Construction	43.1	11.6	45.3	45.6
Commerce	43.1	11.6	45.3	0.5
TOTAL	43.0	11.6	45.3	229.6

Source: Bank staff and IDS.

Table A68. Factor Shares within Sector: Jamaica Base 2000

Activities	Unskilled Labor	Skilled Labor	Capital	Total
Export Agriculture	57.9	24.4	17.7	100
Domestic Agriculture	54.4	19.9	25.7	100
Livestock	32.2	55.9	12	100
Forestry and Fishing	38.1	27.9	34.1	100
Mining	4.8	14.8	80.4	100
Sugar Cane and Beet	9.4	31.3	59.3	100
Processed Sugar	30.6	59.6	9.9	100
Beverages and Tobacco	3.0	12.7	84.3	100
Textiles Clothing and Leather	34.3	62.1	3.5	100
Wood Products	27.5	65.8	6.7	100
Paper and Printing	5.3	66.8	27.9	100
Oil	8.4	13.7	77.8	100
Chemical Products	2.5	25.3	72.1	100
Non Metal Products	7.9	24.9	67.1	100
Domestic Machinery	28.0	67.4	4.6	100
Machinery Export Processing	28	67.4	4.6	100
Electricity Water	3.5	20.4	76.1	100
Construction	33.9	29.0	37.1	100
Commerce	14.1	21.5	64.4	100
Transport	17.0	35.4	47.6	100
Finance and Insurance	3.7	26.2	70.1	100
Real estate and Business Services	18.5	39.8	41.7	100
Government Services	18.3	81.1	0.6	100
Other Services	29.2	53.4	17.5	100
TOTAL	18.8	36.7	44.5	100

Source: Bank staff and IDS.

SPAHD Models—Overall Structure and Links with Human Development Indicators

The model of the Dominican Republic used in this Report was developed by the country's Ministry of Economy, Planning, and Development, and is part of the SPAHD class of macroeconomic models first outlined by Agénor, Bayraktar and El Aynaoui (2008).[174]

SPAHD models were initially designed to capture the links between foreign aid, the level and composition of public investment, the supply-side effects of public capital, growth, and human development indicators. Public investment is disaggregated into education, core infrastructure (roads, electricity, telecommunications, and water and sanitation), and health. Because SPAHD models contain only one category of households, they are silent on distributional issues. However, this is very much by design; the fundamental premise of SPAHD models is that the ability to engage in substantial income or asset redistribution in many countries is limited for a variety of reasons (including the low level of income to begin with), and that the key to reducing poverty is a sustained increase in growth rates.

On the production side, the economy produces one composite good, which is imperfectly substitutable to an imported final good. Oil imports are assumed to be combined with value added to produce gross output through a constant elasticity of substitution (CES) function with a low degree of elasticity.

---

174. The acronym SPAHD stands for *Strategy PApers for Human Development,* a term proposed by Agénor (2006) as more encompassing than the "PRSP" concept used by the IMF and the World Bank. In addition to the original application to Ethiopia, SPAHD models have been applied to a number of other countries, including Burundi, Madagascar, and Niger (Pinto Moreira and Bayraktar 2008); a simplified version has also been developed for Haiti (see Haiti PEMFAR 2007).

Production of value added requires effective labor, private capital, and public capital in infrastructure and health. In addition to public capital in infrastructure improving the productivity of all private factors used in production, public capital in health improves the quality of labor employed in production. Effective labor is a composite input produced by the actual stock of educated labor and the flow of health services.

Stocks of capital are calculated by applying the standard perpetual inventory method.[175] In the case of public investment, however, the model accounts for the possibility that a fraction of the resources invested may not translate into an increase in the public capital stock—a point emphasized by Prichett (2000) in the context of developing countries in general. Domestic output is allocated between exports and domestic sales, based on relative prices (with the domestic-currency price of exports equal to the exchange rate times the world price of exports).

Population and "raw" labor grow at the same constant exogenous rate. The transformation of raw labor into educated labor takes place through the education system, which provides schooling services free of charge. A key input in this process is a composite public education input, which is a function of the number of teachers and the stock of public capital in education. But production of educated labor requires not only teachers and public capital in education, but also access to infrastructure capital.[176] A congestion effect is introduced by dividing the stock of public capital in education by the quantity of raw labor. Educated labor is employed either in the production of goods, or in government.

Income from production is entirely allocated to a single household. This household holds the domestic public debt and receives interest payments on it. It also receives government wages and salaries, unrequited transfers from abroad, and pays interest on its foreign debt. Disposable income is obtained by subtracting direct taxes from total income. Total private consumption (and thus private savings) is a constant fraction of disposable income.

Private investment is a function of the rate of growth in domestic output, private foreign capital inflows, and the stock of public capital in infrastructure. The latter variable captures the existence of a "complementarity" effect—by increasing the productivity of private inputs, or by reducing adjustment costs, a higher stock of public capital in infrastructure raises the rate of return on capital and leads to an increase in private investment.

Total demand for goods sold on the domestic market is the sum of private and public spending on final consumption and investment. Goods bought and sold on the domestic market are the combination of imported final goods and domestically-produced goods, in standard Armington fashion. The domestic good is imperfectly substitutable with the foreign good, and its relative price is endogenous.

The government collects taxes and spends on salaries, goods and services, interest payments, and accumulates public capital. Aid, defined only as grants, is accounted for "above the line." Taxes are defined as the sum of direct, domestic indirect, and import taxes. Total

---

175. It is thus assumed that it is the flow of services associated with a given capital stock that affects production, and that this flow is proportional to the prevailing stock.

176. As discussed by Brenneman and Kerf (2002), Agénor and Neanidis (2006), and Agénor and Moreno-Dodson (2007), a number of microeconomic studies have found a positive impact of infrastructure services on educational attainment, possibly through an indirect improvement in health indicators.

public investment, which is fixed as a share of GDP, is allocated (using fixed fractions) between health, education, and infrastructure. Maintenance expenditure is related to depreciation of all stocks of public capital, whereas other current non-interest expenditure on goods and services is assumed to be constant as a proportion of GDP. The deficit is financed through domestic borrowing and foreign borrowing.

The balance of payments is obtained by subtracting foreign interest payments and changes in net foreign assets of the central bank from the sum of net exports, private and public capital flows, aid, and private unrequited transfers from abroad. Stocks of private and public foreign debt are obtained by adding current period capital flows to debt levels of the previous period.

The price of the composite good is a function of the price of the domestically-produced good and the domestic-currency price of final imports (defined as the product of the nominal exchange rate and the world price of imports of final goods, inclusive of tariffs). Market equilibrium requires equality between total supply of goods on the domestic market and aggregate demand for these goods, which in turn determines the equilibrium (composite) price.

The SPAHD model of the Dominican Republic incorporates an additional feature, open unemployment. Nominal wage growth is related to excess demand for labor and changes in the cost of living. The model therefore generates open unemployment.

In SPAHD models, macroeconomic variables are typically linked with six human development (HD) indicators: poverty, literacy, infant mortality, malnutrition, life expectancy, and access to safe water. These indicators also interact with each other, in a way that is made precise through a series of cross-country regressions. The literacy rate, defined as the ratio of educated labor to total population, is a direct output of the model. The poverty rate is linked directly to consumption growth either through partial elasticities, or a household survey. The second method can be implemented through the "IMPPA approach" or the specification of an explicit distribution (for instance, log-normal). The IMMPA approach (which assumes implicitly that growth is distribution neutral) involves the following steps (see Agenor, Izquierdo, and Jensen (2006)):

a) From an existing household survey, extract the value of consumption for each household, and given the poverty line, calculate the initial poverty rate (for example, headcount index).

b) Following a policy or exogenous shock, generate the growth rate in per capita nominal consumption of the representative household in the macro component, up to the end of the simulation horizon (say, N periods).

c) Apply this growth rate to the consumption expenditure data for each household in the survey. This gives new consumption levels for each household in the survey, for periods $1, \ldots N$.

d) Update the poverty line in the survey by using the growth rate of the composite price index generated by the core macro component (implicit assumption: poverty line is constant in real terms).

e) Using new data on nominal consumption per household and poverty line, calculate "post-shock" poverty indicators. Compare with initial indicators to assess the poverty effect of the shock.

All other HD indicators (malnutrition, infant mortality, life expectancy, and access to safe water) are linked to the model through cross-country regressions, which alleviate the problem of lack of observations at the level of individual countries. In order to focus on long-run relationships, a cross-section estimation technique is used (for example, Agénor and others 2006).

Malnutrition prevalence is related positively to real consumption per capita and negatively to the poverty rate. Infant mortality is inversely related to poverty, and positively related to real income per capita and public spending on health. Thus, declining poverty may not be sufficient to decrease infant mortality if public investment in health is not increased sufficiently. Life expectancy depends positively on real income per capita and public spending on health, and negatively on the infant mortality rate. The share of population with access to safe water is positively related to population density, real income per capita, and public spending on infrastructure. The effect of population density on access to safe water is positive because the cost of building infrastructure capital tends to drop with higher density. Similarly, increasing real income per capita raises the share of population with access to safe water, possibly as a result of "demand" pressures.

To provide a synthetic view on progress toward improving HD indicators, SPAHD models also calculate a composite index by taking an unweighted geometric average of all the individual indicators defined earlier—the literacy rate, life expectancy, access to safe water, as well as the inverse of the poverty rate, malnutrition prevalence, and infant mortality. Thus, a rise in the index indicates an improvement in human development.

References

Agénor, Pierre-Richard. 2002. "Business Cycles, Economic Crises, and the Poor: Testing for Asymmetric Effects." *Journal of Policy Reform* 5(October):145–60.

———. 2004. *The Economics of Adjustment and Growth,* second edition. Boston: Harvard University Press.

———. 2004a. "Unemployment-Poverty Trade-offs." In Jorge Restrepo and Andrea Tokman, eds., *Labor Markets and Institutions.* Santiago: Central Bank of Chile.

———. 2004b. "Macroeconomic Adjustment and the Poor: Analytical Issues and Cross-Country Evidence." *Journal of Economic Surveys* 18(September):351–409.

———. 2006a. "The Analytics of Segmented Labor Markets." In P.-R. Agénor, A. Izquierdo, and H. T. Jensen, eds., *Adjustment Policies, Poverty, and Unemployment: The IMMPA Framework.* Oxford: Blackwell.

———. 2006b. "A Theory of Infrastructure-led Development." Working Paper No. 83, Centre for Growth and Business and Business Cycle Research.

Agénor, Pierre-Richard, and Blanca Moreno-Dodson. 2007. "Public Infrastructure and Growth: New Channels and Policy Implications." In Maura Francese, Daniele Franco, and Raffaela Giordano, eds., *Public Expenditure.* Rome: Banca d'Italia.

Agénor, Pierre-Richard, and Devrim Yilmaz. 2008. "Aid Allocation, Growth and Welfare with Productive Public Goods." Working Paper No. 95, Centre for Growth and Business Cycles, University of Manchester.

Agbeyegbe, Terence D., Janet Stotsky, and Asegedech WoldeMariam. 2006. "Trade Liberalization, Exchange Rate Changes, and Tax Revenue in Sub-Saharan Africa." *Journal of Asian Economics* 17(April):261–84.

Aghion, Philippe and Mark Schankerman. 1999. "Competition, Entry and the Social Returns to Infrastructure in Transition Economies." *Economics of Transition* 7(1):79–101.

Aizenman, Joshua, and Yothin Jinjarak. 2006. "Globalization and Developing Countries—A Shrinking Tax Base?" NBER Working Paper No. 11933, National Bureau of Economic Research, Cambridge, Mass.

Amiti, Mary, and Jozef Konings. 2007. "Trade Liberalization, Intermediate Inputs, and Productivity: Evidence from Indonesia." *American Economic Review* 97(December):1611.

Arnold, J., B.S. Javorcik, and A. Mattoo. 2007. "Does Service Liberalization Benefit Manufacturing Firms? Evidence from the Czech Republic." *World Bank Policy Research Working Paper* No. 4357, The World Bank, Washington, D.C.

Artuc, Erhan, Shubham Chaudhuri, and John McLaren. 2008. "Delay and Dynamics in Labor Market Adjustment: Simulation Results." *Journal of International Economics* (March).

Atolia, Manoj. 2007. "Public Investment, Tax Evasion, and Welfare Effects of a Tariff Reform." Florida State University. Processed.

Batra, Ravi, and Hamid Beladi, 1999. "Trade Policies and Equilibrium Unemployment." *Manchester School* 67(September):545–56.

Baunsgaard, Thomas, and Michael Keen. 2005. "Tax Revenue and Trade Liberalization." IMF Working Paper No. 05/112, International Monetary Fund, Washington, D.C.

Bose, Niloy, M. Emranul Haque, and Denise R. Osborn. 2007. "Public Expenditure and Economic Growth: A Disaggregated Analysis for Developing Countries." *Manchester School* 75(September):533–56.

Bundy, Donald, and others. 2005. "School Health and Nutrition Programs." In Dean Jamison and others, eds., *Disease Control Priorities in Developing Countries*, 2nd ed. New York: Oxford University Press.

Bussolo, M., and D. Medvedev. 2007. "Do Remittances Have a Flip Side? A General Equilibrium Analysis of Remittances, Labor Supply Responses, and Policy Options for Jamaica." *World Bank Policy Research Working Paper* No.4142, The World Bank, Washington, D.C.

Caribbean Community. Treaty of Chaguaramas.

Castalia and Associates. 2004. "Caribbean Infrastructure Review." Background paper for this report, Processed.

Chaitoo, Ramesh. 2008. "An Overview of Trade and Investment in Services in CARIFORUM States." Organization of American States. Processed.

Combes, Jean-Louis, and Tahsin Saadi-Sedik. 2006. "How does Trade Openness Influence Budget Deficits in Developing Countries?" *Journal of Development Studies* 42(November): 1401–16.

Cortázar, René. 2007. "Labor Market Institutions in the Caribbean." Working Paper No. RE3-07-005, Inter-American Development Bank.

de Melo, J., and S. Robinson. 1989. "Product Differentiation and the Treatment of Foreign Trade in Computable General Equilibrium Models of Small Economies." *Journal of International Economics* 27:47–67.

Dee, P. 2005. "A Compendium of Barriers to Services Trade." Report for the World Bank.

Dennis, Allen. 2006. "Trade Liberalization, Factor Market Flexibility, and Growth: The Case of Morocco and Tunisia." *World Bank Policy Research Working Paper* No. 3857, The World Bank, Washington, D.C.

Dervis, K., J. de Melo, and S. Robinson. 1982. *General Equilibrium Models for Development Policy*. Cambridge: Cambridge University Press.

Devarajan, S., J.D. Lewis, and S. Robinson. 1990. "Policy Lessons from Trade-Focused Two-Sector Models." *Journal of Policy Modeling* 12:625–57.

Dollar, David, Mary Hallward-Driemeier, and Taye Mengistae. "Investment Climate and International Integration." *World Development* 34(September):1498–516.

Downes, Andrew S. 2006. *Caribbean Labor Market: Challenges and Policies*. Santiago: CEPAL, United Nations.

Downes, Andrew S., and Lucilla Lewis. 2008. "Trade Policy Issues and Challenges facing the OECS." Organization of American States. Processed.

Downes, Andrew S., Nlandu Mamingi, and Rose-Marie Belle Antoine. 2003. "Labor Market Regulation and Employment in the Caribbean." Inter-American Development Bank. Processed.

Ebrill, Liam, Janet Stotsky, and Reint Gropp. 1999. *Revenue Implications of Trade Liberalization*. Occasional Paper No. 180, International Monetary Fund, Washington, D.C.

Edmonds, Eric V., Nina Pavcnik, and Petia Topalova. 2007. "Trade Adjustment and Human Capital Investments: Evidence from Indian Tariff Reform." IZA Working Paper No. 2611.

Emran, M. Shahe, and Joseph E. Stiglitz. 2005. "On Selective Indirect Tax Reform in Developing Countries." *Journal of Public Economics* 89:599–623.

Escobari, Marcela, Camila Rodriguez, and David Rabkin. 2005. *Improving Competitiveness and Increasing Economic Diversification in the Caribbean: The Role of ICT.*

Evans, H.D., M. Gasiorek, S. McDonald, and S. Robinson. 2006. "Trade Liberalization with Trade Induced Technical Change in Morocco and Egypt." *Topics in Middle Eastern and North African Economies* Vol.8. (http://www.luc.edu/orgs/meea/volume8/meea8.html)

Evans, H.D., M. Gasiorek, A. Ghoneim, M. Haynes-Prempeh, P. Holmes, L.Iacovone,K. Jackson, T. Iwanow, S. Robinson, and J. Rollo. 2006. "Assessing Regional Trade Agreements with Developing Countries: Shallow and Deep Integration, Trade, Productivity, and Economic Performance." Report prepared for DfID by the University of Sussex.

Fay, Marianne, and Mary Morrison. 2005. *Infrastructure in Latin America and the Caribbean: Recent Developments and Key Challenges,* two volumes. Washington, D.C.: The World Bank.

Fedderke, J.W., P. Perkins, and J.M. Lutz. 2006. "Infrastructural Investment in Long-Run Economic Growth: South Africa 1875–2001." *World Development* 34(June):1037–59.

Fernandes, A.M. 2007. "Structure and Performance of the Services Sector in Transition Economies." *World Bank Policy Research Working Paper* No. 4109, The World Bank, Washington, D.C.

Fosu, Augustin K., and Andrew Mold. 2008. "Gains from Trade: Implications for Labor Market Adjustment and Poverty Reduction in Africa." African Development Review 20(April):20–48.

Fujimura, Manabu. 2004. "Cross-Border transport Infrastructure, Regional Integration, and Development." Discussion Paper No. 16, ADB Institute.

Gasiorek, Michael, and J. Chwiejczak. 2007. "The Impact of the EPAs of the Cotonou Agreement on Trade, Production, and Poverty Alleviation in the Caribbean Region." DfID Report. Processed.

Gasparini, Leonardo, and Leopoldo Tornarolli. 2007. "Labor Informality in Latin America and the Caribbean: Patterns and Trends from Household Survey Microdata." CEDLAS. Processed.

Gasparini, Leonardo, Federico Gutierrez, and Leopoldo Tornarolli. 2007. "Growth and Income Poverty in Latin America and the Caribbean: Evidence from Household Surveys." *Review of Income and Health* 53(June):209–45.

Gyamfi, Peter, and Guillermo Ruan. 1996. "Road Maintenance by Contract: Dissemination of Good Practice in Latin America and the Caribbean Region." Latin America and the Caribbean Regional Studies Program Report 44, The World Bank, Washington, D.C.

Hall, Kenneth. 2001. *The Caribbean Community Beyond Survival.*

Hasan, Rana, Devashish Mitra, and K. V. Ramaswamy. 2007. "Trade Reforms, Labor Regulations, and Labor-Demand Elasticities: Empirical Evidence from India." *Review of Economics & Statistics* 89(August):466–81.

Hertel, Thomas W., and Jeffrey J. Reimer. 2004. "Predicting the Poverty Impacts of Trade Reform." Policy Research Working Paper No 3444, The World Bank, Washington, D.C.

Hoekman, Bernard, and Alan L. Winters. 2005. "Trade and Employment: Stylized Facts and Research Findings." Policy Research Working Paper No. 3676, The World Bank, Washington, D.C.

Inter-American Development Bank. 2003. *Good jobs wanted*. Washington, D.C.

———. 2005. *CARICOM Report No. 2*, INTAL.

Inter-American Development Bank and Caribbean Development Bank. 1996. *Infrastructure for Development: A Policy Agenda for the Caribbean*. Washington, D.C.

International Labor Office. 2006. *2006 Labor Overview: Latin American and the Caribbean*. Geneva.

Jha, Abhas K., ed. 2005. *Institutions, Performance, and the Financing of Infrastructure Services in the Caribbean*. World Bank Working Paper No. 58. Washington, D.C.: The World Bank.

Justino, Patricia, Julie Litchfield, and Hung Thai Pham. 2008. "Poverty Dynamics during Trade Reform: Evidence from Rural Vietnam." *Review of Income and Wealth* 54(June):166–92.

Kufa, P., A. Pellechio, and S. Rizavi. 2003. "Fiscal Sustainability and Policy Issues in the Eastern Caribbean Currency Union." IMF Working Paper No. WP/03/162, International Monetary Fund, Washington, D.C.

Lee, Ha Yan, Luca A. Ricci, and Roberto Rigobon. 2004. "Once Again, Is Openness Good for Growth?" *Journal of Development Economics* 75(December):451–72.

Li, Xiangming. 2004. "Trade Liberalization and Real Exchange Rate Movement." *IMF Staff Papers* 51:553–84.

Lloyd, Peter. 2000. "Generalizing the Stolper-Samuelson Theorem: A Tale of Two Matrices." *Review of International Economics* 8(December):597–613.

Matusz, Steven J., and David Tarr. 1999. "Adjusting to Trade Policy Reform." World Bank. Processed.

McDonald, S., S. Robinson, and K. Thierfelder. 2005. A SAM Based Global CGE Model using GTAP Data. *Sheffield Economics Research Paper* 2005:001. University of Sheffield.

———. 2008. "Asian Growth and Trade Poles: India, China, and East and Southeast Asia." *World Development* 36(2):210–34.

McGuire, James W. 2006. "Basic Health Care Provision and Under-5 Mortality: A Cross-National Study of Developing Countries." *World Development* (March):405–25.

McIntyre, Meredith. 2005. "Trade Integration in the East African Community: An Assessment of Kenya." Working Paper No. 05/143, International Monetary Fund.

Micco, Alejandro, and Natalia Pérez. 2002. "Determinants of Maritime Transport Costs." Working Paper No. 441, Inter-American Development Bank.

Naudé, Wim, and Marianne Matthee. 2007. "The Significance of Transport Costs in Africa." Policy Brief No. 5, United Nations University.

Nunes, Luis C., José Oscategui, and Juan Peschiera. 2006. "Determinants of FDI in Latin America." Working Paper No. 252, Pontificia Universidad Católica de Perú.

OECD. 2003. *The Sources of Economic Growth in the OECD Countries*. Paris.

Oslington, Paul. 2005. "Unemployment and Trade Liberalization." *World Economy* 28(August):1139–55.

Ozden, Caglar. 2008. "An Important Dimension of Caribbean Global Economic Integration—Migration and Remittances." The World Bank, Washington, D.C. Processed.

Peters, Amos. 2005. "The Fiscal Effects of Tariff Reduction in the Caribbean Community." Processed.

Pyatt, G. 1987. A SAM Approach to Modeling. *Journal of Policy Modeling* 10:327–52.

Rasmussen, Tobias N. 2004. *Macroeconomic Implications of Natural Disasters in the Caribbean*. IMF Working Paper, WP/04/224, International Monetary Fund, Washington, D.C.

Schott, Jeffrey J. 2001. *Prospects for Free Trade in the Americas*. Washington, D.C.: Peterson Institute for International Economics.

Sharma, Kishor, Sisira Jayasuriya, and Edward Oczkowski. 2000. "Liberalization and Productivity Growth: The Case of Manufacturing Industry in Nepal." *Oxford Development Studies* 28(June):205–22.

Stiglitz, Joseph E., and Andrew Charlton. 2006. "Aid for Trade." *International Journal of Development Issues* 5(December):1–41.

Taylor, Lance, and Rudiger von Arnim. 2006. "Modelling the Impact of Trade Liberalization: A Critique of Computable General Equilibrium Models." OXFAM International Research Report.

Vignoles, C. 2005. "An Assessment of Trade Performance and Competitiveness of OECS countries." Processed.

Wacziarg, Romain, and Jessica S. Wallack. 2004. "Trade Liberalization and Intersectoral Labor Movements." *Journal of International Economics* 64(December):411–39.

Wagstaff, Adam, and Mariam Claeson. 2005. *The Millennium Development Goals for Heath: Rising to the Challenges*. Washington, D.C.: The World Bank.

Winters, L. Alan. 2002. "Trade Liberalization and Poverty: What are the Links?" *World Economy* 25:1339–67.

———. 2004. "Trade Liberalisation and Economic Performance: An Overview." *Economic Journal* 114(February):F4–F21.

———. 2000. *Beautiful but Costly: Business Costs in Small Economies*.

Winters, L. Alan, Neil McCulloch, and Andrew McKay. 2004. "Trade Liberalization and Poverty: The Evidence so Far." *Journal of Economic Literature* 42(March):72–115.

World Bank. 1994. *World Development Report 1994*. Washington, D.C.

———. 2005a. "A Time to Choose: Caribbean Development in the 21st Century." Washington, D.C.

———. 2005b. "Organisation of Eastern Caribbean States: Towards a New Agenda for Growth." Report No. 31863-LAC, Washington, D.C.

———. 2006a. *Haiti: Options and Opportunities for Inclusive Growth*. Washington, D.C.

———. 2006b. "Jamaica Poverty Assessment: Breaking the Cycle of Unemployment, Vulnerability, and Crime." Washington, D.C.

———. 2006c. *Poverty Reduction and Growth: Virtuous and Vicious Circles*. Washington, D.C.

World Bank/Commonwealth Secretariat Joint Task Force on Small States. 2000. *Small States: Meeting the Challenges in the Global Economy*.

WTTC. 2004a. "The Caribbean: The Impact of Travel and Tourism on Jobs and the Economy." May 25.

———. 2004b. "Caribbean Travel and Tourism Navigating the Path Ahead." March 8, p. 24.

Yoshino, Yutaka. 2007. "Domestic Constraints, Firm Characteristics, and Geographical Diversification of Firm-level Manufacturing Exports in Africa." The World Bank, Washington, D.C. Processed.

Eco-Audit

Environmental Benefits Statement

The World Bank is committed to preserving Endangered Forests and natural resources. We print World Bank Working Papers and Country Studies on 100 percent postconsumer recycled paper, processed chlorine free. The World Bank has formally agreed to follow the recommended standards for paper usage set by Green Press Initiative—a nonprofit program supporting publishers in using fiber that is not sourced from Endangered Forests. For more information, visit www.greenpressinitiative.org.

In 2008, the printing of these books on recycled paper saved the following:

Trees*	Solid Waste	Water	Net Greenhouse Gases	Total Energy
355	16,663	129,550	31,256	247 mil.
'40' in height and 6–8" in diameter	Pounds	Gallons	Pounds CO_2 Equivalent	BTUs

green press
INITIATIVE